D0848848

This book explores the culture of conformity to the Church of England and its liturgy in the period after the Reformation and before the outbreak of the Civil War. It provides a necessary corrective to our view of religion in the period by a serious exploration of the laity who conformed, out of conviction, to the Book of Common Prayer.

Through the use of church court records and parliamentary petitions, the views of laypeople are examined – those who were neither 'puritan' nor 'Laudian', yet were committed to the reformed liturgy and episcopacy out of sincere belief, and not as a matter of political expediency. These 'prayer book protestants' form a significant part of the spectrum of society in Tudor and Stuart England, yet until now they have remained an almost completely uninvestigated group.

Cambridge Studies in Early Modern British History

PRAYER BOOK AND PEOPLE
IN ELIZABETHAN AND
EARLY STUART ENGLAND

Cambridge Studies in Early Modern British History

Series editors

ANTHONY FLETCHER
Professor of History, University of Essex

JOHN GUY
Professor of Modern History, University of St Andrews

and JOHN MORRILL
Reader in Early Modern History, University of Cambridge, and Vice-Master of Selwyn College

This is a series of monographs and studies covering many aspects of the history of the British Isles between the late fifteenth century and the early eighteenth century. It includes the work of established scholars and pioneering work by a new generation of scholars. It includes both reviews and revisions of major topics and books, which open up new historical terrain or which reveal startling new perspectives on familiar subjects. All the volumes set detailed research into our broader perspectives and the books are intended for the use of students as well as of their teachers.

For a list of titles in the series, see end of book.

PRAYER BOOK AND PEOPLE IN ELIZABETHAN AND EARLY STUART ENGLAND

JUDITH MALTBY

Corpus Christi College, Oxford

CAMBRIDGE
UNIVERSITY PRESS

PUBLISHED BY THE PRESS SYNDICATE OF THE UNIVERSITY OF CAMBRIDGE
The Pitt Building, Trumpington Street, Cambridge CB2 1RP, United Kingdom

CAMBRIDGE UNIVERSITY PRESS
The Edinburgh Building, Cambridge, CB2 2RU, United Kingdom
40 West 20th Street, New York, NY 10011–4211, USA
10 Stamford Road, Oakleigh, Melbourne 3166, Australia

© Cambridge University Press 1998

First published 1998

Printed in the United Kingdom at the University Press, Cambridge

Typeset in Sabon 10/12 pt   [CE]

A catalogue record for this book is available from the British Library

Library of Congress Cataloguing in Publication data

Maltby, Judith D.
Prayer book and people in Elizabethan and early Stuart England / Judith Maltby.
p.   cm. – (Cambridge studies in early modern British history)
Includes bibliographical references and index.
ISBN 0 521 45313 5 (hb)
1. Church of England – History – 16th century.   2. Church of
England – History – 17th century.   3. Church of England – Membership.
4. Church of England. Book of common prayer.   5. Church of England –
Liturgy – History and criticism.   6. Anglican Communion – England –
History – 16th century.   7. Anglican Communion – England –
History – 17th century.   8. England – Church history – 17th century.
9. England – Church history – 17th century.   I. Title.   II. Series.
BX5070.M35   1998
283′.42′09031 – dc21 97–15776 CIP

ISBN 0 521 45313 5 hardback

For
my parents

CONTENTS

ILLUSTRATIONS

TABLES

ACKNOWLEDGEMENTS

Writing the acknowledgements at the completion of a book, reminds one that what has so often felt a solitary occupation is, in fact, a highly corporate one.

This book, like many others, began life as a Ph.D. topic. My greatest academic debt in that regard is to three people. I began historical research under the scholarly and wise direction of Dorothy Owen and continued with Margaret Spufford, who offered guidance and insight in personal circumstances of extreme difficulty. John Morrill, as an almost countless number of graduate students know, whether his own or not, has never been anything less than generous with his time and careful criticism.

I was fortunate at Cambridge to find myself part of a generation of generous post-graduates, whose friendship and advice helped to create an atmosphere of co-operation rather than competition. Their influence on my work is real, if not always identifiable. Chief among them I wish to thank: Eric Carlson, Sarah Foot, Jamie Hart, Patrick Higgins, Anthony Milton, Kenneth Parker, Derek Plumb, Bill Tighe, and Tessa Watt. Over the years I have benefited much from the advice of Susan Amussen, Eamon Duffy, Ken Fincham, Andrew Foster, Jane Freeman, Andrew Pettegree, Bill Sheils, and David Underdown. Marjorie McIntosh has been particularly generous with her time, encouragement and constructive criticism over the years. The staffs of numerous record offices have provided good environments in which to work, especially the staffs of the Cheshire Record Office and the Lincolnshire Archives Office. My debt is great too to my undergraduate teacher, Caroline Hibbard. Her teaching first fostered my interest in the religious issues of the Tudor–Stuart period. At the same time Timothy and Mary Hallett taught me the importance of critically engaging with one's own religious tradition. The continued friendship of all three in the years since my first degree is greatly valued.

A significant aspect of my work on religious conformity would not have been possible without the kindness of Howard Talbot of Aston, Cheshire, who by allowing me access to the manuscripts relating to his ancestor Sir

Thomas Aston, provided the opportunity to explore this fascinating figure in greater depth. I am grateful to him and to his family, who always made me feel welcome when I worked on the papers at Aston Lodge.

My research found a home along with me in a number of welcoming institutions. First as a Research Fellow in History at Newnham College, Cambridge where I benefited from Gill Sutherland's wise counsel then and ever since. A home was also found at two theological colleges, first Wesley College, Bristol and later Salisbury and Wells Theological College, Salisbury. In Bristol and Salisbury my contemporary theological horizons were broadened by colleagues and students and I gained much from teaching church history in the context of those preparing to exercise ordained ministry. To the two principals, the late David Stacey and Philip Crowe, my debt is great and my respect constant. The final stages of completion have largely taken place in the congenial environment of Corpus Christi College, Oxford where I have received much encouragement from members of all three Common Rooms as well as from new colleagues in both the Theology and History Faculties in the University.

I must thank those whose comments have been particularly helpful: Michael Bentley, Lynn Botelho, Caroline Hibbard, Sean Hughes, Maija Jansson, Elisabeth Leedham-Green, Diarmaid MacCulloch, Jessica Martin, Michael Questier and Jane Shaw. Anthony Fletcher, who examined my Ph.D. thesis as well, deserves particular mention for carefully and patiently re-reading new drafts. All the imperfections, errors both of fact and judgement, remain my own.

Lastly, I must thank my parents for their support, and from whom I can remember nothing but encouragement for my interest in a subject so impractical as history.

In the text of the book dates are Old Style but the year is taken to begin on 1 January.

Advent Sunday, 1996

ABBREVIATIONS

AC	*Alumni Cantabrigienses*
Add. MS	Additional Manuscripts, British Library
AO	*Alumni Oxonienses*
Aston Lodge	Aston Lodge Manuscripts, Aston Lodge, Cheshire
BL	British Library
Bodl.	Bodleian Library, Oxford
BRO	Bedfordshire Record Office
Calamy Revised	*Calamy Revised*. A. G. Matthews, ed., 1934
CCRO	Chester City Record Office
CD 1628	*Commons Debates 1628*
CD 1629	*Commons Debates 1629*
CJ	*Commons Journals*
CRO	Cheshire Record Office
CROH	Cambridgeshire County Record Office, Huntingdon
CSPD	*Calendar of State Papers Domestic*
CUL	Cambridge University Library
DNB	*Dictionary of National Biography*
GRO	Gloucestershire Record Office
HLRO	House of Lords Record Office
JBS	*Journal of British Studies*
JEH	*Journal of Ecclesiastical History*
LAO	Lincolnshire Archives Office
LCRS	Lancashire and Cheshire Record Society
Leicestershire RO	Leicestershire Record Office
LJ	*Lords Journals*
'Loans 1620–1639'	'Loans, Contributions, Subsidies, and Ship Money, paid by clergy of the Diocese of Chester, in the years 1620, 1622, 1624, 1634, 1635, 1636, & 1639', ed. G. T. O Bridgeman, *Miscellanies Relating to Lancashire and Cheshire*. LCRS, xii, 1885
OED	*Oxford English Dictionary*

P&P	*Past and Present*
PRO	Public Record Office
Staffordshire RO	Staffordshire Record Office
THSLC	*Transactions of the Historical Society of Lancashire and Cheshire*
TRHS	*Transactions of the Royal Historical Society*
VCH Bedford	*Victoria County History of Bedford*
VCH Chester	*Victoria County History of Chester*
VCH Gloucester	*Victoria County History of Gloucester*
VCH Oxford	*Victoria County History of Oxford*
VCH Somerset	*Victoria County History of Somerset*
VCH Worcester	*Victoria County History of Worcester*
Walker Revised	*Walker Revised.* A. G. Matthews, ed., 1948
Walker, 1714	John Walker, *An attempt towards recovering an account of the numbers of and sufferings of the clergy of the Church of England.* London, 1714.

Introduction: the good, the bad, and the godly? The laity and the established church

Spending some of his money on prayers for the souls of relations, friends, and even benefactors and even more to make local churches fit for the worship of god, hardly makes him distinctive. It was for a fifteenth century gentleman conventional enough. That word conventional, however, has an air of condemnation about it; but we surely go far wrong in thinking a man who expresses his devotion under conventional forms necessarily shallow or complacent. His spiritual life might burn with a brilliance few even of his neighbours notice.[1]

I am, I confesse, naturally inclined to that which misguided zeale termes superstition; my common conversation I do acknowledge austere, my behaviour full of rigour, sometimes not without morosity; yet at my devotion I love to use the civility of my knee, my hat, and hands, with all those outward and sensible motions which may express or promote my invisible devotion.[2]

Moreover, by this book are priests to administer the sacramentes, by this book to church their women, by this book to visit and housle the sick, by this book to burie the dead, by this book to keep their rogation, to say certaine psalms and praiers over the corne and grasse, certayne gospels at crosswaies, etc. This book is good at all assaies [on every occasion]; it is the only book of the world.[3]

THE STUDY OF CONFORMITY AND ITS PROBLEMS

The protestant separatist Henry Barrow, cited above, assessing the religious state of English parishioners over a generation after the Reformation, noted with disapproval their overattachment to the rites and ceremonies of the reformed Church of England. Modern ecclesiastical historians, however, have largely ignored the suggestion of any enthusiasm for the liturgy and

[1] Colin Richmond, *John Hopton: a fifteenth century Suffolk Gentleman* (Cambridge, 1980), pp. 157–8.
[2] Sir Thomas Browne, *Selected Writings*, ed. Geoffrey Keynes (Chicago, 1968), p. 8.
[3] Henry Barrow, *A Briefe Discoverie of the False Church* in *The Writings of Henry Barrow 1587–1590*, ed. Leland Carlson (London, 1962), p. 362.

ceremonies of the established church. Yet among historians concerned with
the political and constitutional aspects of the period, the establishment of
the Church of England and its worship is often presented positively: 'when
Elizabeth died, the Church stood strong and, to all appearance, secure.
Founded as a political compromise – though never as purely a compromise
or as purely political as its attackers then and later pretended – it had
established itself in the faith and affections of the majority.'[4] By contrast,
historians of religion have concentrated on *dis*affection from the reformed
Church of England. The spotlighting of the spiritually disgruntled is
explained, if not justified, by the greater visibility of the non-conformist
over the conformist in the historical record as well as the confessional
needs which may at times influence the agenda of historical enquiry. The
result, however, has been to produce many and varied 'group portraits' of
Tudor and Stuart Christianity with some important figures never making it
on to the canvas. The women and men who did conform and whose
conformity grew beyond mere obedience to the prince (though we must
never lose sight of the *religious* significance of obedience) into an attachment, perhaps even love, for the Church of England surely deserve some
attention. As to whether they formed a majority – or even how to define 'a
majority' in this instance – is probably an unanswerable question.[5] This
study is an attempt to treat the religious concerns of conforming English
Christians with the same seriousness and respect that their godly neighbours have typically enjoyed from historians of the post-Reformation
church. To stay with the metaphor: the task set is not to 'paint over' any
existing faces from our group portrait but to expand the number of figures
in the painting to include conformists from conviction. It is hoped that this
book will be able to do this with more than just the rough brush strokes
required of background work, and bring those loyal to the Elizabethan
Settlement into the foreground with some greater clarity and detail.

The Book of Common Prayer will, for the most part, provide the
touchstone for this undertaking. Admirers of the literary power of the
Prayer Book, however, may be disappointed. Whether the Prayer Book
represents a magnificent and uplifting literary and spiritual achievement or
an oppressively sin-obsessed and wordy liturgical disaster is not an issue

---

[4] G. R. Elton, *England Under the Tudors* (London, 1974), pp. 428–9.

[5] Margaret Spufford, 'Can we count the "godly" and the "conformable" in the seventeenth
century?', *JEH* 36:3 (1985), pp. 429–30. We know that 75 per cent of those eligible made
their Easter Communion in 1603 in the diocese of Lincoln. Is this a 'majority'? The
interpretation of such a figure is highly problematic. Peter Burke, 'Religion and secularization', in *The New Cambridge Modern History: Companion Volume XII*, ed. P. Burke
(Cambridge, 1979), p. 309. Below, Chapter 5, explores subscription rates for five Cheshire
communities for a petition to uphold the Book of Common Prayer in 1641. Only one of the
five communities produced a subscription rate over 50 per cent.

that will be addressed here. It must be remembered that the Prayer Book is first and foremost 'liturgy'; that is 'work', intended not so much to be read in a passive sense, but to be used, performed, experienced. The Prayer Book is more than a text; it provided a framework of words and actions to address a wide range of human needs and was intended to involve its participants fully. To appreciate this is analogous to the transformation in understanding that can take place between reading a play and watching a particular production. But, like all analogies, it is an imperfect one, for worshippers are participants in the 'work' of liturgy, not observers. Despite their hostility, the authors of *A View of Popish Abuses* which accompanied the *Admonition to Parliament* in 1572, acknowledged the participatory nature of Prayer Book worship when they compared the antiphonal singing of the psalms to a tennis match.[6] To Richard Hooker, this very same exchange mirrored (imperfectly, of course) the glorious praises of the angelic choirs.[7] Whether we are experiencing a foretaste of paradise or are simply watching a tennis match is, of course, ultimately a matter of opinion. We would do well to remember T. S. Eliot's observation on the influence of the Authorized Version of the Bible on English literature. Its influence was profound, he maintained, not because the likes of John Donne or George Herbert were impressed by the magnificence of the prose, but because they believed it to be the word of God. To speak of the Authorized Version as 'a monument of English prose', Eliot believed, was to pronounce the epitaph on the influence of the Bible on English letters.

I could fulminate against the men of letters who have gone into ecstasies over 'the Bible as literature', the Bible as 'the noblest monument of English prose'. Those who talk of the Bible as a 'monument of English prose' are merely admiring it as a monument over the grave of Christianity . . . It is enough to suggest that just as the work of Clarendon, or Gibbon, or Buffon or Bradley would be of inferior literary value if it were insignificant as history, science and philosophy respectively, so the Bible has had a *literary* influence upon English literature *not* because it has been

---

[6] *A View of Popish Abuses* in *Puritan Manifestos*, ed. W. H. Frere and C. E. Douglas (London, 1954), p. 29.

[7] Richard Hooker, *The Lawes of Ecclesiastical Polity Book V*, ed. W. Speed Hill (Cambridge, Mass., 1977), v, 38. Psalms were sung, at least in parishes with musical resources, as described in a 1641 petition from the troubled St Wulfram's in Grantham, Lincolnshire.

We do further certify that we are still very willing to have the organ continued and used in our church as it has been, viz. to accompany the singing of the psalms after the common and plain tunes appointed to be used in the church. Finding by experience that by use of it hitherto practised in our church. First the Parish Clerk signifying which psalm is to be sung and the organist then distinctly playing the *tune*, all persons that can read have time to turn unto the psalms.

Quoted in Michael Pointer, *The Glory of Grantham* (Grantham, 1978), p. 30.

considered as literature, but because it has been considered as the report of the Word of God.[8]

English conformists did not believe that the Prayer Book was the 'word of God'. Their claims were more modest. In 1642 a group of Kentish petitioners for the Church of England decided 'upon debate' to omit from their draft text the phrase that the Book of Common Prayer was 'penned by the inspiration of the Holy Ghost'.[9] The belief among those who did conform was that when they worshipped according to the lawful liturgy, they were worshipping God.

Debates over the literary merits of the Prayer Book, therefore, need not detain us; rather, attention will be given to the role of liturgy as a means of persuasion no less important than the English Bible, the Book of Homilies, sermons, or Foxe's *Book of Martyrs*. The role of liturgy as propaganda has been in large part overlooked – yet there was probably no other single aspect of the Reformation in England which touched more directly and fundamentally the religious consciousness, or lack of it, of ordinary clergy and laity, than did the reform of rituals and liturgy. Doctrinal issues involved in the debate between predestinarians and 'Arminians', have received considerable attention in recent Tudor–Stuart historiography.[10] One could argue that more fundamental by far was the change from Latin to a 'tongue . . . understanded of the people'.[11] Liturgical reforms which embraced the vernacular, placed the altar centrally in the church and, initially at least, encouraged frequent reception of Communion, surely had far more widely felt repercussions than the soteriological debates. Furthermore, liturgy is an expression of a community's beliefs, as well as a shaper of them. The relationship is a dynamic and interdependent one; and one in which it is not always possible to distinguish between cause and effect.[12]

[8] T. S. Eliot, 'Religion and literature', in *Selected Prose*, ed. Frank Kermode (London, 1975), p. 98.
[9] Cited in Conrad Russell, *The Causes of the English Civil War* (Oxford, 1990), p. 124. See below, p. 115.
[10] R. T. Kendall, *Calvin and English Calvinism* (Oxford, 1979); Nicholas Tyacke, *Anti-Calvinists: the rise of English Arminianism c. 1590–1640* (Oxford, 1987); Peter White, 'The rise of Arminianism reconsidered', *P&P* 101 (1983); Kevin Sharpe, 'Archbishop Laud', *History Today* 33 (August, 1983). The recent debate on Arminianism has been lively. Peter Lake, 'Calvinism and the English church 1570–1635' *P&P* 114 (1987); Nicholas Tyacke and Peter White, 'Debate: the rise of Arminianism reconsidered', *P&P* 115 (1987). Andrew Foster discusses the competing historical factions in 'Church policies of the 1630s', in *Conflict in Early Stuart England: Studies in Religion and Politics 1603–1642*, ed. Richard Cust and Ann Hughes (London, 1989), pp. 193–6.
[11] Article 24 ('Of speaking in the Congregation in such a tongue as the people understandeth') of the 39 Articles of Religion, 1571.
[12] 'The Preface' of the *Alternative Service Book 1980* (Oxford, 1980), p. 10; Janet Morely, '"The faltering words of men": exclusive language in the liturgy', in *Feminine in the Church*, ed. Monica Furlong (London, 1984), pp. 56–70.

It is fair to say that though the traditional presentation of pre-Reformation popular religion as bankrupt and corrupt is undergoing revision, the understanding of the popular aspects of post-Reformation Christianity awaits as sympathetic and thorough a re-evaluation.[13] It is reasonable to question the assumption that English parishioners, whether pre- or post-Reformation, were incapable of holding critical opinions of the worship they experienced. Under Mary some humble parishioners in a poor urban living in York were able to demonstrate in the church courts their ability to understand and criticize their priest, who omitted phrases and used ungrammatical Latin at Mass and the daily offices.[14] Given a generation or two, it seems plausible to assert that the descendants of those Marian parishioners could exhibit a critical awareness of, and affection for, latter-day authorized services. Church-goers in the post-Reformation period may not have worried unduly about the freedom or bondage of the will but we can credit some of them – as we are starting to do with their fifteenth-century ancestors – with a critical appreciation of the worship conducted in their parish churches. That, as Eamon Duffy has noted, 'Cranmer's sombrely magnificent prose, read week by week, entered and possessed their minds, and became the fabric of their prayer, the utterance of their most solemn and vulnerable moments.'[15]

HISTORIOGRAPHICAL ISSUES

One of the problems which dogs the study of religious conformity is that its very legality obscures its existence. As John Morrill has rightly observed, 'religious commitment is best observed in conditions of persecution'; this is certainly true of Prayer Book conformity.[16] Evidence of loyalty to the reformed liturgy emerges at either end of the period under examination

---

[13] This point will be discussed more fully below, pp. 17–19. A. G. Dickens, *The English Reformation* (London, 1964, 2nd edn, 1989) presents the traditional view of late medieval English Christianity. It has been challenged by J. J. Scarisbrick, *The Reformation and the English People* (Oxford, 1984), especially ch. 1; from a European perspective by John Bossy, *Christianity in the West 1400–1700* (Oxford, 1985) and most recently by Eamon Duffy, *The Stripping of the Altars: traditional religion in England 1400–1580* (New Haven, 1992). The continuity of popular religion on both sides of the Reformation is stressed in a collection of excellent essays, *Parish, Church and People: local studies in lay religion 1350–1750*, ed. S. J. Wright (London, 1988). See Christopher Haigh's stimulating article 'The recent historiography of the English Reformation', in *The English Reformation Revised*, ed. C. Haigh (Cambridge, 1987).

[14] Claire Cross, 'Lay literacy and clerical misconduct in a York parish during the reign of Mary Tudor', *York Historian* 3 (1980), pp. 10, 12, 14.

[15] Duffy, *Stripping of the Altars*, p. 593. Margaret Spufford, *Contrasting Communities: English villagers in the sixteenth and seventeenth centuries* (Cambridge, 1974), p. 268.

[16] John Morrill, 'The Church in England 1642–9', in *Reactions to the English Civil War 1642–1649*, ed. J. Morrill (London, 1982), p. 91.

here due to official persecution: first by the regime of the Roman Catholic Mary and then by the puritan regime of the 1640s–50s. Use of the Edwardian Prayer Book in clandestine worship – presumably the 1552 book – became both a source of comfort and a means of self-definition *vis-à-vis* a popish state. The articles preferred against the London martyr Cuthbert Symson in March 1558 concluded:

That thou, contrary to the order of this realm of England, and contrary to the usage of the holy church of this realm of England, hath at sundry times and places within the city and diocese of London, been at assemblies and conventicles, where there was *a multitude of people* [my italics] gathered together to hear the English service said, which was set forth in the latter years of king Edward the Sixth, and also to hear and have the Communion Book read, and the communion ministered, both to the said multitude, and also to thyself; and thou hast thought, and so thinkest, and hast spoken, that the said English service and Communion Book, and all things contained in either of them were good and laudable, and for such didst and dost allow and approve either of them, at this present.[17]

The west country rebels of 1549 had grounds for comparing the new service to a 'Christmas game' as it enacted the fundamental shift in the language of worship from Latin to the vernacular. Nevertheless, even by Mary's reign the 'newe servye' had gained adherents.[18] It is after a century of familiarity, not surprisingly, that we find many more examples of constancy to Prayer Book worship in another period of persecution. The diarist John Evelyn succeeded in finding churches in the capital which used the banned Prayer Book or continued to observe the church year. On Christmas Day 1657, Evelyn and other devotees of the Prayer Book were attacked by parliamentary troopers.

I went with my wife &c: to Lond: to celebrate Christmas day. Mr. Gunning preaching in Excester Chapell on 7: Micha 2. Sermon Ended, as he was giving us the holy Sacrament, The Chapell was surrounded with Souldiers: All the Communicants and Assembly surpriz'd & kept Prisoners by them . . . [They] examined me, why contrarie to an Ordinance made that none should any longer observe the

---

[17] John Foxe, *The Acts and Monuments*, eds. G. Townsend and S. R. Cattley (8 vols., London, 1837–41), viii, p. 458. Two other persons arrested with Symson affirmed this article and added, 'that they have and will do so still while they live', Foxe, *Acts and Monuments*, viii, p. 461. Foxe's *Book of Martyrs* provided ammunition for conformists, especially with its portrayal of heroic bishops, as well as for the godly. See below, pp. 106–7, 115–16.

[18] Anthony Fletcher, *Tudor Rebellions* (London, 1968, 2nd edn 1973), pp. 135–6. Politically or piously (or perhaps a bit of both) the rebels gathered at Mousehold Heath in Norfolk signalled their brand of orthodoxy in 1549 by first procuring 'a priyst to mynister theyr morninge and euening prayer in the Inglish tonge then newly begon to bee frequentyd'. B. L. Beer, ed., 'The Commoyson in Norfolk, 1549', *The Journal of Medieval and Renaissance Studies* 6 (1976), p. 82. I am grateful to Diarmaid MacCulloch for this reference. See also Diarmaid MacCulloch, *Suffolk and the Tudors: politics and religion in an English county 1500–1600* (Oxford, 1986), pp. 167–8, 308–9 and Susan Brigden, *London and the Reformation* (Oxford, 1989), pp. 571, 602, 603, 616–18.

superstitious time of the Nativity (so esteem'd by them) I durst offend, &
particularly be at Common prayers, which they told me was but the Masse in
English . . . These were men of high flight and above Ordinances: & spake spiteful
things of our B: Lords nativity . . . These wretched miscreants, held their muskets
against us as we came up to receive the Sacred Elements, as if they would have shot
us at the Altar, but yet suffering us to finish the Office of Communion, as perhaps
not in their Instructions what they should do in case they found us in that Action.[19]

Clergy as well as laity could exhibit loyalty to the Book of Common Prayer,
though their calling often put them, quite literally, in the line of fire. To
priests like John Hacket, now remembered principally as a biographer of
his patron Archbishop John Williams, faithfulness to the liturgy even in
persecution was a keystone. According to his biographer, Hacket continued
coolly to read divine service even when a parliamentary soldier of the earl
of Essex had a pistol pointed at him. Shortly after the Restoration, Hacket
conducted the funeral of a notable puritan parishioner. Aware both of the
sensitivities of the godly and of his own, Hacket committed to memory the
whole burial office from the Prayer Book. At the funeral:

there being a great concourse of men of the same fanatical principles, when the
company heard all delivered by him [Hacket] without book, and, with free
readiness, and profound gravity, and unaffected composure of voice, looks, and
gestures, and a very powerful emphasis in every part (as indeed his talent was
excellent in this way), they were strangely surprised and affected, professing that
they had never heard a more suitable exhortation, or a more edifying exercise even
from the very best and most precious men of their own persuasion! But they were
afterwards much more surprised and confounded, when the same person who had
officiated assured the principal men among them, that not one period of all he had
spoken was his own; and convinced them by ocular demonstration how all was
taken word for word out of the very office ordained for that purpose in the poor
contemptible Book of Common Prayer.[20]

Examples of this type can be multiplied from around the country.[21] These

---

[19] *The Diary of John Evelyn*, ed. E. S. de Beer (6 vols., Oxford, 1955), iii, pp. 203–4. Evelyn
provides numerous examples of both the use of the Book of Common Prayer and
widespread observance of the holy days of the Anglican calendar. At certain times Evelyn
and his family had to make do with using the Prayer Book privately at home. See e.g.,
Diary, iii, pp. 97–8, 144, 225.

[20] Thomas Plume, *An Account of the Life and Death of the Right Reverend Father in God,
John Hacket, Late Lord Bishop of Lichfield and Coventry*, ed. Mackenzie M. C. Walcott
(London, 1865), pp. 64–6. Feats of memory such as Hacket's were necessitated by differing
circumstances. In 1655, Dr Bull, later bishop of Saint David's, committed the baptismal
service to memory for much the same reasons as Hacket. However, George Canner, a young
and blind protégé of the saintly Bishop Thomas Morton, committed large parts of the
Prayer Book to memory, as well as the portions of scripture appointed by the lectionary, so
that he could fulfil his duties as curate of Clifton Canvile in Staffordshire. The blind curate's
achievement reminds us how complex the notion of literacy and access to written culture is
in pre-industrial England. Plume, *Life of Hacket*, p. 66; Richard Baddeley and John Naylor,
The Life of Dr Thomas Morton, Late Bishop of Duresme (York, 1669), pp. 78–81.

[21] Morrill, 'Church in England', p. 104.

periods of persecution for Prayer Book conformists under Mary in the 1550s and by 'the godly' in the 1640s–50s, highlight the kind of religious commitment obscured by its very legality in the intervening decades. Despite the large body of work on religion in England before, during, and after the Reformation, we still lack any serious engagement with the tradition of commitment to the 'church of Elizabeth and James' as expressed in its public and corporate worship. This is particularly true of the vast majority of conformists, the laity. This study begins to address an important, but neglected, lay religious tradition, one which is revealed more starkly by times of persecution, and seeks a place for conformists in our group portrait of Tudor–Stuart Christianity.[22]

An important approach to the study of the Reformation in England has been provided over several decades by local studies inspired by Patrick Collinson's magisterial *The Elizabethan Puritan Movement* (1967). Such studies have pursued questions surrounding the impact of the national Reformation by a detailed study of a locality; a diocese, a county, or even a few parishes. The spotlight has largely been on those who failed to conform to the national church, including Roman Catholics and protestant separatists, but above all on non-conformist puritans who remained within the church but refused to conform to many of its lawful practices. This is partly a matter of sources: in the all too elusive world of the post-Reformation parish, individuals who failed to conform and were prosecuted for it leave a clearer trail to follow than those who did conform. As Patrick Collinson has noted, 'Practioners of commonplace prayer-book religion, unlike the more strident religious minorities, do not pluck at the historian's sleeve.'[23] A less satisfactory reason may also be suggested, however. Much of the work on religion at the local level rests on the assumption that non-conformists took their faith more 'seriously' than men and women who conformed to the lawful worship of the Church of England.[24] Collinson is surely right when he urges that the broadest possible meaning and applica-

---

[22] The strength Anglicanism exhibited after the Restoration is also worth noting here. In Restoration Wiltshire, Prayer Book worship appears to have commanded considerable loyalty, although less attachment to the ceremonial aspects has been noted. How 'changed' Anglican worship was by the experience of the Interregnum is an interesting question. Certainly the restored Church of England was not such a triumph for neo-Laudianism as is sometimes claimed. Donald A. Spaeth, 'Common Prayer? Popular observance of the Anglican liturgy in Restoration Wiltshire', *Parish, Church and People: local studies in lay religion 1350–1750*, ed. S. J. Wright (London, 1988), pp. 143–6 and *passim*.

[23] Patrick Collinson, *The Religion of Protestants: the church in English society 1559–1625* (Oxford, 1982), p. 192.

[24] This was never suggested – indeed the opposite is maintained – in Margaret Spufford's pioneering work on the world (economic, agricultural, religious) of early modern villagers. Nevertheless, Cambridgeshire protestant dissenters receive more attention than conformists due to the problems with sources already discussed in this chapter. Spufford, *Contrasting Communities*, chs. 10, 13.

tion of the term puritan be used. It is rightly understood as a movement *within* the Church of England, analogous to the Methodist movement in the eighteenth century before the crisis over the American ordinations and the formal separation which followed the death of Wesley.[25] This puritan tradition within the established church has been described as 'not alien to the properly "Anglican" character of the English church but . . . equivalent to the most vigorous and successful of religious tendencies contained within it'.[26] It is not the intention here to challenge the view that puritanism is best understood as an active and legitimate strand within pre-civil war 'Anglicanism' – on the contrary, that is a view this author strongly endorses.[27] It provides the necessary corrective to the 'Anglican versus Puritan' antithesis which has so distorted our understanding of early modern English Christianity.[28] Rather, the assumption challenged here is that puritanism had a monopoly on all that could be considered 'vigorous' or 'successful' in the Church of England. Under scrutiny is both the self-presentation of the godly and its acceptance by historians; that 'perception, realistic enough, that as sincere and genuine rather than merely conformable Protestants they were thin on the ground'.[29] Eamon Duffy has warned us to be wary of the accuracy of the godly's view of the multitude. If the parish church of the famous Ralph Josselin was empty, 'it may tell us more about the limitations of his ministry than the irreligion of his flock'.[30] Ecclesiastical historians, at the very least, need to apply greater scepticism

---

[25] The analogy is a helpful one, for equally present is the danger of hindsight which sees Methodism's evolution into an independent church as much of a foregone conclusion as the growth of puritanism into Dissent after the Restoration. Diarmaid MacCulloch, 'Was Methodism a mistake?', *The Epworth Review* 15:2 (1988).

[26] Patrick Collinson, 'A comment: concerning the name puritan', *JEH* 31:4 (1980), pp. 484, 488.

[27] See below, pp. 233–7.

[28] For example: J. H. New, *Anglican and Puritan, The Basis of Their Opposition 1558–1640* (Stanford, 1964); Horton Davies, *Worship and Theology in England* (Princeton, 1970, 1975), i, ii; Richard Greaves, *Religion and Society in Elizabethan England* (Minneapolis, 1981); J. Sears McGee, *The Godly Man in Stuart England: Anglicans, puritans, and the two tables, 1620–1670* (New Haven, 1976). John Booty's recent article 'Anglicanism' demonstrates that even in the late 1990s, puritans can still be marginalized out of the pre-Restoration Church of England. John Booty, 'Anglicanism', in *The Oxford Encyclopedia of the Reformation*, ed. Hans Hillerbrand (4 vols., Oxford, 1996), i, pp. 38–44. A helpful introduction to the historiography of the field can be found in Borden W. Painter, 'Anglican terminology in recent Tudor and Stuart historiography', *Anglican and Episcopal History* 56:3 (1987) and Kenneth Fincham, 'Introduction', in *The Early Stuart Church, 1603–1642*, ed. Kenneth Fincham (London, 1993).

[29] Patrick Collinson, *The Puritan Character: polemic and polarities in early seventeenth-century English culture* (Los Angeles, 1989), p. 27. However, such views contrast with his more favourable view of the Church of England elsewhere. See Collinson, *The Religion of Protestants, passim.*

[30] Eamon Duffy, 'The godly and the multitude in Stuart England', *The Seventeenth Century* 1:1 (1986), pp. 37–9.

10   *Prayer Book and people*

to the self-validating claims of the godly and their self-proclaimed spiritual superiority over their neighbours. We have, after all, only the godly's word for it.[31] Identification of 'sincere and genuine' movements either in contemporary Christianity or in the history of the church is a notoriously subjective exercise. Defining 'success' in spiritual matters is as fraught an exercise as defining it in educational matters.

In the complementary field of the social history of religion, the problems are different but the result has been the same neglect, even dismissal, of religious conformity. Keith Thomas redrew the map of popular religion in 1971 with his ground-breaking *Religion and the Decline of Magic* which opened a door on a hidden underworld of popular magic in popular culture. This portrait of the past presented the view that the type of conformity desired by the architects of the Elizabethan Settlement had little or no impact on the lives of ordinary people. For the mass of the population – especially the poor – any contest between the underworld of magic and folk religion and Christian orthodoxy led to the latter's quick retreat from the field.[32] Such socially determined views of religious identity have not gone unchallenged and one thinks chiefly of Margaret Spufford's work on Cambridgeshire, and her subsequent work.[33] Nevertheless, the view that England was a society of 'two cultures' – elite and popular, godly and ungodly – with few points of intersection, has been an influential one. As Keith Wrightson has remarked: 'the truly godly commonly found themselves in a minority. For many of their neighbours church attendance remained a gathering of neighbours rather than an intensely spiritual experience.'[34] We

[31] Diarmaid MacCulloch cuts 'the godly' down to size when he describes them as 'a spiritual freemasonry'. *The Later Reformation in England 1547–1603* (London, 1990), p. 82.
[32] Keith Thomas, *Religion and the Decline of Magic* (New York, 1971), ch. 6, esp. pp. 159–66.
[33] Spufford, *Contrasting Communities*, ch. 13. More recently, Spufford, 'Can we count'; Spufford, 'Puritanism and social control?', in *Order and Disorder in Early Modern England*, ed., Anthony Fletcher and John Stevenson (Cambridge, 1985); 'The importance of religion in the sixteenth and seventeenth centuries' in Margaret Spufford, ed., *The World of Rural Dissenters 1520–1725* (Cambridge, 1995). As its title suggests, this collection of essays concentrates on those drawn away from 'statute protestantism' to more exotic forms of Christianity. Nevertheless, Spufford argues strongly for the recognition of 'genuine conformists of conviction'. Spufford, 'The importance of religion', p. 7.
[34] Keith Wrightson, *English Society 1580–1680* (London, 1982), p. 213. However, see Wrightson's reflective postscript to his influential study of the village of Terling. There he states 'prior to the rise of Arminianism it is very hard to distinguish those characterized as "Puritans" from other English Protestants in terms of their theology . . . A Puritan was therefore not merely a godly person. A Puritan was a godly activist, an exponent of spiritual conflict in the public arena.' Keith Wrightson, 'Postscript: Terling revisited' in Keith Wrightson and David Lavine, *Poverty and Piety in an English Village: Terling, 1525–1700* (Oxford, 1995 edn), pp. 206–8. Prayer Book protestants could be forced by circumstances into activism, whether in the church courts or by petitioning parliament as the rest of this book demonstrates. One might offer a speculative generalization that conformists were, in contrast to puritans, more reactive than pro-active in their 'activism'.

encounter in much social history the same problem we noted in ecclesiastical history: too ready an acceptance of the verdict of the self-validating 'godly' on the quality of the religious experiences of those outside their fellowship, 'the multitude'.[35] Convinced conformists are caught between the rock of those interested only in the puritan agenda for the church and the hard place of those who assume that conventional Christianity had no place in the lives of ordinary men and women. Drawing clear boundaries between magic and orthodox belief, between 'superstition and the religion of sacrament and spirit' is a far more difficult matter than is often admitted, as Natalie Zemon Davies has noted.[36] The right of committed conformists, of Prayer Book protestants, to a place in our group portrait is only beginning to be raised.[37] This study is an attempt to put them in the picture.

An important voice of dissent can be heard in the work of Christopher Haigh. His contribution to the local studies approach to the period, *Reformation and Resistance in Tudor Lancashire* (1975), broke rank with the dominant interest in puritanism or separatism and attempted a more integrated view of English Christianity. He questioned the effectiveness of preaching as the best instrument for inculcating sophisticated protestant theology among the people and drew our attention to the role of liturgy as a means of importing, through repeated words and actions, the basic tenets of the reformers. As he has more recently quite rightly argued: 'In some parishes the opponents of the godly were clearly the profane, but those who defended ceremonies against the godly can hardly be called "the ungodly".'[38] Haigh's analysis of 'parish Anglicans' (the term he prefers) takes some far more controversial turns, however. He has suggested that

[35] Wrightson, *English Society*, p. 213, see also pp. 206–21. More recently, Collinson has challenged this view in *Religion of Protestants*, ch. 5, as has Spufford, 'Can we count?' and 'Puritanism and social control?' Martin Ingram has also offered a reassessment of early modern popular religion: 'The evidence from Wiltshire and elsewhere suggests that it is a mistake to overemphasise either the presence of "godly" groups or the existence of people largely indifferent to religion. Most people were located somewhere between these poles.' Ingram, *Church Courts, Sex and Marriage in England 1570–1640* (Cambridge, 1987), p. 94, see also ch. 3.

[36] She provides a thought-provoking critique of these issues in Natalie Zemon Davies, 'Some tasks and themes in the study of popular religion', in *The Pursuit of Holiness in late Medieval and Renaissance Religion*, ed. C. Trinkaus and H. Oberman, Studies in Medieval and Reformation Thought (Leiden, 10, 1974), pp. 307–12, and *passim*.

[37] For example in Spufford, 'Can we count?' which raises this very point.

[38] Christopher Haigh, 'The Church of England, the Catholics and the people', in *The Reign of Elizabeth I*, ed. C. Haigh (London, 1984), p. 218. Even Richard Baxter admitted that conformist clergy could be diligent and careful pastors and preachers: 'that excellent Man, Mr. William Fenner . . . who by defending Conformity, and honouring it by a wonderfully powerful and successful Preaching, Conference, and holy Living . . . stirred up the Nonconformists the more to a vehement pleading of their Cause'. *Reliquiae Baxterianea: or Mr. Richard Baxter's narrative of the most memorable passages of his life and times* (London, 1696), p. 13; Collinson, *Religion of Protestants*, p. 100n.

local support for the lawful liturgy and ceremonies directed by the rubrics of the Book of Common Prayer chiefly resided in a constituency abandoned to their fate by the failure of the Roman Catholic mission priests. These men and women are memorably, but rather unhappily, described by him as the 'spiritual leftovers of Elizabethan England'.[39]

In our search for difference, however, we must be careful not to turn Christianity in its protestant forms into an entirely different species from either medieval Christianity or the Roman Catholicism shaped by the Counter Reformation. When Sir Edward Hyde and Sir Simonds D'Ewes clashed in the Root and Branch debate over whether episcopacy was, as Hyde maintained, hundreds of years old in the church or as D'Ewes countered, 'that in *this* church it had continued rather less than one hundred', they were illustrating two competing ecclesiologies.[40] Disputes over the reformed Church of England's exact blend of continuity and discontinuity with the primitive *and* medieval church were at the centre of the theological tensions within it. The continued authorization and use of some pre-Reformation practices no more invalidates the label 'protestant' than it does for many areas of the Lutheran Reformation where by Genevan standards of reform an unjustified number of pre-Reformation ceremonies were retained as well. In a sermon preached in 1629 on the feast of the Conversion of Saint Paul (significantly, perhaps, on the feast day of a saint whose own life embodied issues of continuity and discontinuity with his religious tradition), John Donne placed the retention of some ceremonies in the Church of England in a European protestant context:

That in all such things [ceremonies], we always informe ourselves, of the right use of those things in their first institution, of their abuse with which they have been depraved in the Roman Church, and of the good use which is made of them in ours. That because pictures have been adored, we do not abhor a picture; Nor sit at the Sacrament, because Idolatry hath been committed in kneeling. That Church, which they call Lutheran, hath retained more of these Ceremonies than ours hath done; And ours more than that which they call Calvinist; But both Lutheran, and ours, [are] without danger, because, in both places, we are diligent to preach to the people the right use of these indifferent things.

Haigh, like many of the historians he is critical of, allows 'Geneva' to define the boundaries of protestantism more narrowly than need be.[41]

---

[39] Haigh, 'Church of England', p. 219.
[40] Russell, *English Civil War*, p. 72. See below for a fuller discussion, pp. 102–4.
[41] John Donne, *Sermons*, ed. Evelyn Simpson and George Potter (10 vols., Berkeley, 1956), viii, p. 331. R. W. Scribner, 'Politics and the institutionalisation of reform in Germany', p. 189 and Volker Press, 'Constitutional development and political thought in the Holy Roman Empire', p. 518, both in *The New Cambridge Modern History: the Reformation 1520–1559*, ed. G. R. Elton (2nd edn Cambridge, 1990). Even the vehemently anti-protestant Victorian designer A. W. N. Pugin acknowledged the preservation of medieval interiors and even medieval ceremonies in many Lutheran churches. See the fascinating

A further question presents itself: is the evidence for positive attachment to the liturgy of the Church of England really just church papistry or survivalist Catholicism in disguise as has been suggested by Haigh and supported further by Alexandra Walsham? The latter has rightly pointed out the amount of continuity the Prayer Book provided with the medieval past, though Andrew Pettegree's important new book on Marian protestantism reminds us that the Elizabethan Prayer Book and Settlement were less of a patched-up affair from the reformers' perspective than is often suggested.[42] It remains unclear by the end of Walsham's study of church papistry whether it was a point occupied on the religious spectrum by actual historical persons or whether church papists existed chiefly in the anxious minds of propagandists and polemicists. In other words, were 'church papists', or 'parish anglicans' the imaginary offspring of a bizarre set of bedfellows? Were they the products of the paranoia of some Roman Catholic clergy on one hand, for whom martyrdom, not collusion and compromise with a schismatic English church and its vernacular, reformed liturgy, was their preferred option for the laity; and, on the other, by puritan propagandists wishing to smear Prayer Book conformists with the charge of popery?

The identification of papist – and church papists – in early modern society was a correspondingly subjective process: less revealing, perhaps, of the phenomenon itself, than of the shape of the ideological prism through which the classifier viewed it. The use of such words illuminated more lucidly the attitudes of their utterers than the characteristics of the stigmatised. Religious insult and imputation in early modern England intrinsically involved self-definition.[43]

Nevertheless, when in 1590 parishioners of Flixton in Suffolk brought Prayer Books to church in an attempt to intimidate their vicar into conformity, he called them 'papists' and said 'that they which wolde have sarvice sayde according to the booke of common prayer are papists and atheists'.[44] This incident is described as 'telling' and revealing of a pocket of church popery.[45] However, as Walsham has herself argued, simply because those who objected to the Book of Common Prayer smeared its supporters with the label of 'papists' does not mean we should believe

account in Nigel Yates, *Buildings, Faith and Worship: the liturgical arrangements of Anglican churches 1600–1900* (Oxford, 1991), pp. 24–8, 41.

[42] Alexandra Walsham, *Church Papists: Catholicism, conformity and confessional polemic in early modern England* (Woodbridge, 1993), pp. 16–20; Andrew Pettegree, *Marian Protestantism: six studies* (Aldershot, 1996), pp. 135–6. I am grateful to Andrew Pettegree for letting me read chapters of his book before publication.

[43] Walsham, *Church Papists*, p. 108.

[44] This incident has been much cited, but we should note it was originally related in Nesta Evans, 'The community of South Elmham, Suffolk, 1550–1640' (University of East Anglia M.Phil., 1978), pp. 170–1. See below, pp. 44–5.

[45] Walsham, *Church Papists*, p. 111.

them.[46] The non-conforming vicar of Flixton also called the Prayer Book supporters 'atheists' as well. Were they 'atheists' as well as 'papists'? Clearly, the Flixton clergyman was on a rhetorical roll and this incident should be approached with caution. In the end, it was the vicar, not the parishioners, whom the diocesan authorities punished. He was deprived of his living; a severe penalty for an ecclesiastical court. What is clear is that some of his flock actually *owned* Common Prayer books. There was no legal requirement for the laity to own the reformed liturgy, simply to attend it. Individual ownership of the Prayer Book – presumably for its use in domestic and private prayers as well as in public worship[47] – is a step beyond the barest conformity which marked the church papist.[48] The attachment shown here to a liturgical *book*, as distinct from the liturgical *form* also marks a point of discontinuity with pre-Reformation Christianity; neither was it a feature of Counter Reformation Roman Catholicism.[49]

It would be unwise to hang a whole argument on one incident in a Suffolk village. Perhaps there were church papists as well as Prayer Book protestants in Flixton. No doubt the former found the latter more neighbourly and congenial than they found the abusive 'godly'. But Prayer Book protestantism cannot be dismissed as church papistry simply because the godly said so. As already noted, the Prayer Book was used in secret by protestants under Mary and again under the persecutions of Cromwell. The sophisticated level of theological reflection produced in 1641–2 when laypeople were forced, arguably for the first time, to defend the liturgy reveals the articulate end of a wider social spectrum of religious belief.[50] Even more convincingly, the subscription rates of five Cheshire communities for the Prayer Book petition top the 50 per cent mark in only one instance; strengthening the view that the men who signed or made their marks did so willingly.[51] It is argued here that committed conformists were nothing other than a minority, though a significant minority, on the religious spectrum. Further, the accumulated evidence presented here is about more than 'picking quarrels' over the surplice in order to pester a puritan cleric, however tempting such a thing might be:[52] we see laypeople

[46] From differing perspectives, the Jesuit Robert Southwell complained that anyone who owed money became a 'papist' and John Selden observed: 'We charge the prelatical clergy with Popery to make them odious though we know they are guilty of no such thing.' Cited in ibid., p. 114.
[47] See below, pp. 25–8.
[48] Hardline Roman Catholic polemicists railed against even that amount of collusion while others accepted an amount of accommodation. Walsham, *Church Papists*, esp. chs. 2 and 3.
[49] I am grateful to Natalie Zemon Davis for making this point to me.
[50] See below, Chapter 3.   [51] See below, Chapter 5.
[52] Walsham, *Church Papists*, pp. 111, 112–13.

actively demanding to receive the sacraments and to bury their dead according to a vernacular, reformed liturgy.[53] If such agitation was 'church papistry', then the Roman Catholic hierarchy had even greater grounds for anxiety about their free-wheeling laity than has been suggested.

The term 'church papist' began to appear in the early 1580s and may well indicate that 'religious rifts were widening and intensifying'.[54] Its appearance in polemic at that time may also indicate the penetration to the grass-roots of the Settlement of 1559. A generation into Elizabeth's reign, the Reformation 'from above' had reached 'down below': the Long Reformation was beginning to make headway. To the preciser sort, Prayer Book protestantism *looked* like 'popery'. To Roman Catholic hardliners, perhaps, there was the fear that the Prayer Book *was* offering a palatable replacement to medieval Christianity.[55] It is impossible, of course, to draw precise boundaries between mere passive conformity and conformists of conviction, just as it is often impossible to distinguish between non-conformity caused by indifference and laziness and that which arose out of theological principle.[56] Church papists probably did exist in fact as well as

---

[53] See below, Chapter 2 *passim*. Walsham is mistaken when she says that receiving the Eucharistic sacrament under Elizabeth was not required. Ibid., pp. 11–12. This was largely, but not exclusively, the case in statute law, though the 1559 Book of Common Prayer required the laity to receive a minimum of three times a year and was enforced by a parliamentary Act of Uniformity. In church law, however, from adolescence onwards, receiving the sacrament as well as simply attending church was required, as numerous visitation articles and injunctions as well as presentations for non-reception make clear. See, for example W. H. Frere and W. Kennedy, eds., *Visitation Articles and Injunctions of the Period of the Reformation* (3 vols., London, 1910), iii, pp. 167, 275, 287, 307, 337. For Elizabethan articles enquiring specifically after those who have failed to communicate, ibid., iii, pp. 93, 106–7, 156–7, 204, 212, 226, 344, 380. For the latter part of Elizabeth's reign, see W. P. M. Kennedy, *Elizabethan Episcopal Administration* (3 vols., London, 1924), ii, pp. 14, 70, 71, 95, 120, 130, iii, pp. 140, 148, 164, 179, 229, 248, 260, 289, 307, 320. If regular reception of the sacrament had not been required, as has been argued, it would make the demand for the sacraments to be administered according to the Book of Common Prayer all the more telling.

For the early Stuart period, note canon 21 of the 1603/4 Canons: '*volumus, ut parochiani singuli quotannis ter ad minimum (nominatim vero in festo Pasachatis) sicut in Libro Publicae Liturgiae iubentur, possint sacramentum illud percipere*'. An opt-out route was closed to recusants who had conformed by a 1606 act which required them to receive Communion in the Church of England. 3 Jac I c. 4. Michael C. Questier, *Conversion, Politics and Religion in England, 1580–1625* (Cambridge, 1996), pp. 102–12. I am grateful to Gerald Bray and Michael Questier for the Jacobean references. Many visitation articles of the early seventeenth century enquired whether Communion was available with enough frequency so that the laity could receive at least three times a year as directed by the Book of Common Prayer. Kenneth Fincham, ed., *Visitation Articles and Injunctions of the Early Stuart Church*, Church of England Record Society 1 (1994). It is correct to say, however, that explicit parliamentary 'test acts' belong to the period after the Restoration.

[54] Walsham, *Church Papists*, p. 114.

[55] Duffy, *Stripping of the Altars*, pp. 588–91.

[56] Was the defence of godliness sometimes a cover for simple idleness? See below, pp. 71–2, 75–6 and Chapter 2 *passim*.

in the mind. The seats they occupy in our group portrait of Tudor–Stuart Christianity, however, are not the same ones as those occupied by Prayer Book protestants; although no doubt church papists found it more congenial to sit next to them than next to the godly.

We must also question Haigh's assertion that these 'spiritual leftovers' formed the natural constituency for the controversial Laudian innovations of the 1630s. It does seem reasonable to conclude that such Prayer Book protestants did provide local backing for drives for liturgical conformity under Archbishop Whitgift and Archbishop Bancroft, for example. After all, often the only reason we know about the presence of non-conformity is because of the diligence of the supporters of the Prayer Book through the presentations they made in ecclesiastical courts. But it will be argued here that rather than forming a natural constituency for Laudianism, the descendants of these 'spiritual leftovers' helped to provide opposition to Laudian reforms which were perceived as an attack on parochial Prayer Book conformity.[57]

More recently Christopher Haigh has given us an impressive new map to the English Reformation*s* – now to be discussed in the plural. His point is important and not merely semantic. The people of mid-Tudor England experienced reform as an episodic, rather than as a smooth process. Eager to put 'clear blue water' between England and Europe, Haigh is keen to stress the differences between the Reformation in England and on the continent, where one can still apparently speak of '*the* Reformation' and where theologians as diverse as Luther and Calvin may be described as 'Luther, Calvin, and Co. Ltd.'[58] In a shift from his earlier work, the political elements are brought to the fore: obedience, not liturgy or preaching, is key. Most people 'experienced Reformation as obedience rather than conversion; they obeyed the monarch's new laws rather than swallowed a preacher's new message'.[59] In contrast, Andrew Pettegree, one of the few historians of his generation to research protestantism on both sides of the channel, reminds us that protestants resisted and survived in countries where the regime was committed, officially at least, to their conversion or

---

[57] Christopher Haigh, *Reformation and Resistance in Tudor Lancashire* (Cambridge, 1975), pp. 306–7; 'The Church of England', pp. 206–9, 211, 217–19; *English Reformations: religion, politics, and society under the Tudors* (Oxford, 1993), pp. 285–95. See also his stimulating article 'The recent historiography of the English Reformation'. See esp. below, Chapters 3 and 4.

[58] Haigh, *English Reformations*, pp. 12–13. For a concise but perceptive appreciation of the divergences within 'protestant' spirituality, see Rowan Williams, 'Religious experience in the era of reform', in *The Companion Encyclopedia of Theology*, ed. Peter Byrne and Leslie Houlden (London, 1995), pp. 576–84.

[59] Haigh, *English Reformations*, p. 21. One might suggest that a perusal of Eusebius or Bede would lead to the same conclusion about Christianity in general, rather than of sixteenth-century reform movements in particular.

extermination. That combined with his case for the strength of Marian protestantism should give us pause before accepting that the success of the English Reformation rested entirely on Mary's 'only serious' mistake: her death in 1558.[60]

Nonetheless, Haigh's most important contribution to the current historiographical strife is that the process of the Reformation took a long time. Yet as Felicity Heal has observed, we are left with the problem that a Reformation agenda, however quirky its English manifestations, *did* succeed, and current revisionism leaves the reader with more questions than answers about *how* that could be so.[61] What is clear is that the days are gone when anyone could write a textbook on the English Reformation which ends in 1559. While acknowledging the vigour of Marian protestantism, Elizabeth's reign can rightly be seen as the crucial period of consolidation. Backed by the laws of parliament and the protection of the 'godly prince', the most pervasive agent of change, the Book of Common Prayer, gained a place in the religious consciousness and even affections of the English laity. Its success may be explained in part by the element of continuity it gave its users along with innovation.[62] That it succeeded as an agent of change as well as of continuity from the middle of Elizabeth's reign onwards, is the chief argument of this study. A goodly proportion of the English people became 'people of the book' – but as much of the Prayer Book as of the Bible. For conformists that association represented no conflict, but rather a happy alliance at best, a manageable partnership at worst.

Although this book is concerned with a period often called 'post-Reformation', a discussion of the historiographical problems, however brief, would be remiss without reference to recent revisionary work on the state of the English church before and after the break with Rome. Under review is the bleak view that the late medieval church was composed of a superstitious laity, an ignorant clergy, and a corrupt hierarchy: in short a church ripe for Reformation. It is a view, for all its sophistication, which

---

[60] Pettegree, *Marian Protestantism, passim*, esp. pp. 152–6, 163–7; Haigh, *English Reformations*, p. 236.

[61] Felicity Heal, 'The English Reformation revisited', *Ecclesiastical Law Journal* 18:4 (1996); Susan Wabuda, 'Revising the Reformation', *JBS* 35:2 (1996), pp. 257–62.

[62] The service of Evensong, for example, was innovatory in the use of vernacular, yet is also a skilful merger of the ancient offices of Vespers and Compline. No longer only for the professionally religious or the wealthy lay owners of books of hours, Cranmer intended a popularization of the idea of daily worship for all the people of God. As historians and theologians argue endlessly about what Cranmer did or did not mean in his Eucharistic services, we ignore perhaps his greatest liturgical achievement, Evensong. It is unlikely, however, that the archbishop would have approved of the rich musical tradition it has inspired over the last 400 years. Diarmaid MacCulloch, *Thomas Cranmer: a life* (New Haven, 1996), pp. 629–30.

still owes a great deal to John Foxe and the *Book of Martyrs*. Historians like J. J. Scarisbrick, Peter Marshall and most significantly Eamon Duffy, however, have presented a picture of a church far from on its last legs at the beginning of the sixteenth century.[63] It is surely as right to challenge the dismissal of customs, indeed of a whole culture, as simply superstitious, as it is right to challenge the puritan contempt for Prayer Book conformity as shallow or simply post-Reformation 'popery'. Duffy's greatest contribution is to offer a window into a world of popular devotions and practices that are about as foreign to an English-speaking post-Vatican II generation as to other Christians, people of other faiths, agnostics and atheists. For this considerable achievement *The Stripping of the Altars* deserves high praise.

However, problems remain, especially in accounting for how the Reformation succeeded. The world of late medieval English Christianity is, in Duffy's view, almost an Eden. It is hard not to be moved by the emotive language of an impoverished form of Christianity slowly, but steadily, extinguishing these medieval fires of piety. The serpent takes the form of a hand full of religious zealots, and 'the Fall' is the Reformation, although it is a more protracted affair than its counterpart in Genesis and encounters greater resistance than was offered by our first parents. The Reformation stripped away the 'familiar and beloved observances, [it caused] the destruction of a vast and resonant world of symbols which, despite the denials of the proponents of the "new Gospel", [were] both understood and controlled'.[64] Rather like the great gothic designer A. W. N. Pugin in the last century, Duffy's late medieval England is a place of community and harmony, a 'merrie England' in which the War of the Roses is not even mentioned.[65] It is hard to reconcile the view that the complex symbolic structures of English Christianity in the early sixteenth century were so 'understood and controlled', with the anxieties, not of proponents of a 'new Gospel', but of Christian Humanists, many of whom remained loyal to the Church of Rome when religious polarization forced confessional allegiances to be made.[66] Silent in the world of *The Stripping of the Altars* are the voices of contemporary analysis provided by the loose federation of Christian Humanists, who were as forward as the protestant Reformers in delivering judgements on the quality of other people's religious experiences. Before Luther's revolt, the dean of Saint Paul's John Colet called his fellow clergy to a personal reformation which, he believed, would lead to a moral

---

[63] Scarisbrick, *The Reformation*; Peter Marshall, *The Catholic Priesthood and the English Reformation* (Oxford, 1994); Duffy, *Stripping of the Altars*.
[64] Duffy, *Stripping of the Altars*, p. 591.
[65] Margaret Belcher, 'Pugin writing', in *Pugin: A Gothic Passion*, ed. Paul Atterbury and Clive Wainwright (New Haven, 1994), pp. 108–11, but see also pp. 114–15.
[66] See Williams, 'Religious experience', pp. 576–8.

and spiritual renewal of the laity. Later, Cardinal Pole, no dove on heresy at home, transfixed an early session at Trent when he maintained that renewal would be possible only after Christian pastors accepted the judgement that it was their own corruption and sin that had brought the western church to its terrible present state. His remarks were greeted by stunned silence eventually broken by the president of the Council rising to his feet and leading his brothers in the hymn *Veni Creator Spiritus*.[67] It is hard to see Erasmus, Cardinal Pole, or John Colet, as proponents of a 'new Gospel', yet their concerns for the spiritual state of England and Europe sound, ironically, closer to A. G. Dickens than Eamon Duffy.[68]

What is most important for the task in hand about the contribution made by these historians, is the rescuing of pre-Reformation Christianity from the slur of 'superstition' and the genuine respect accorded to an important range of popular religious observances. To make the parallel explicit: we should no more accept uncritically the assessment of the Reformers on the religious health of the early Tudor laity than we should swallow the grim assessment of 'the godly' on the spiritual state of their post-Reformation conforming neighbours.[69] It should be clearly understood, however, that no claims are being made here for the spiritual superiority of Prayer Book conformity over any other religious tradition. Such claims, it could be argued, are outside the historian's remit.

CHURCH COURTS AND PETITIONS FOR THE CHURCH

The church courts

The difficulties involved in finding evidence of sincere conformists, by definition, dictate that a wide variety of sources must be used. Over the past several decades, numerous studies of puritanism at the local level have made extensive use of the ecclesiastical courts: the bodies which carried the major burden of enforcement in the locality of the religious changes authorized by the centre. Evidence of puritanism, recusancy or religious

---

[67] Dermont Fenlon, *Heresy and Obedience in Tridentine Italy: Cardinal Pole and the Counter Reformation* (Cambridge, 1972), pp. 119–20. I am grateful to Caroline Hibbard for this reference.

[68] John Colet, 'Convocation sermon' in J. H. Lupton, *A Life of John Colet, D.D.* (London, 1887), pp. 297, 299 and *passim*. This could even be said of the younger Sir Thomas More. What is not yet clear, however, is how this revisionism will affect views of the European Counter-Reformation, which has come to be seen not simply as a reaction to a protestant agenda, but as an authentic reforming movement in its own right – more fully understood as a 'Catholic' rather than a 'Counter' Reformation. Issues of continuity and discontinuity between the Christianity of the late middle ages and its Tridentine forms need also to be considered.

[69] Duffy, 'The godly and the multitude', p. 38.

indifference may be found in the non-conformity of individuals: for example, the clergy and laity who failed to conform to lawful ceremonies and were presented for it. It is suggested here, however, that just as this type of case reveals the failure to conform of some (for motives that often remain ambiguous) it also brings to light men and women who supported and approved of the religious settlement.[70] Such conformists are revealed by the fact that they used the church courts to protest against the non-conformity of their neighbours and clergy. The records of the ecclesiastical courts document clearly the existence of puritan or negligent ministers – a distinction that is sometimes difficult to make based solely on the information given in the sources – by drawing attention to their failure to use, or to use correctly, the Book of Common Prayer. Historians have made abundant use of such material. Documented as well, though made much less of, is the desire of at least some parishioners to bring the worship of their parish church into conformity with the Prayer Book.[71] For example, there were obviously members of the congregation at Tarporley in Cheshire in the late 1630s and early 1640s who disagreed with the assessment of the rector and curate when they said that the Book of Common Prayer was composed by the 'imps of hell and stank in the nostrails of god' and was no better than 'mass mumbled on beads'. Parishioners in Manchester, in a petition to the bishop of Chester in 1604, obviously took issue as well with their curate Ralph Kirk when he said that the Prayer Book 'was no scripture'. We know they objected because some church-goers felt strongly enough to prefer articles against their clergy through legal channels. In other words, it was the conformists' very dislike of non-conformity which led to the presentments in the first place.[72]

Historians making use of the ecclesiastical courts might well be compared to the blind philosophers in the famous fable examining different parts of an elephant and each producing in turn a different description of the animal; each one valid in terms of his or her own information. The problem is perhaps best illustrated by a particular example. As is clear from

---

[70] Examples of this approach are A. G. Dickens, *Lollards and Protestants in the Diocese of York 1509–1558* (Oxford, 1959); R. C. Richardson, *Puritanism in North-west England: a regional study of the diocese of Chester to 1642* (Manchester, 1972); Ronald A. Marchant, *The Puritans and the Church Courts in the Diocese of York 1560–1642* (London, 1960); W. J. Sheils, *The Puritans in the Diocese of Peterborough 1558–1610*, Northamptonshire Record Society (1979); Patrick Collinson, *The Elizabethan Puritan Movement* (London, 1967). The conformist dimension in this type of case has been emphasized by Haigh, *Reformation and Resistance*, p. 306.

[71] This point is well made by Ian Green, 'Career prospects and clerical conformity in the early Stuart Church', *P&P* 90 (1981), pp. 111–12.

[72] BL, Add. MS 36919, fol. 139v; CRO, QJF 71/4/24; QJB 1/6/87v; CRO, EDC.5/1604 misc. (Manchester). The difficulties in using evidence from the church courts are discussed in further detail below, pp. 31–6.

the title of his book, *Puritanism in North-west England*, R. C. Richardson was looking for puritans and found one in the person of a brewer, Thomas Benson of Chester. In 1612, Benson visited a fellow parishioner of Saint Bridget's, Thomas Marsland, who had been house-bound through illness for some months. But this was not an act of simple charity, as the 'godly' Benson took the opportunity to upbraid Marsland for his evil living, and accused the convalescent of keeping his wife from attending the local conventicle. Benson went on at length to accuse Marsland of being a drunkard, and of loving neither God nor his Word, and of claiming to be too 'ill' to go to church, but not being too 'ill' to frequent the ale house. 'Benson upon these speeches turned a book and did read to this deponent [Marsland] that though the children of Israel were as the sands of the sea, yet shall but a remnant be saved.' Benson was relentless. He said: 'our time was but short and there was but a remnant should be saved, and showed him in the text in his own testament [i.e. Marsland's own copy of the Bible] and [said] it behoves you and I to look about us and to serve God that we may be of that remnant'. There is little doubt that in Thomas Benson, a religious enthusiast of a particular kind was found. And this is where the story is finished in Richardson's account: as an example of a local godly man evangelizing one of his ungodly neighbours.[73]

Closer examination, however, reveals that the case may allow for a wider reading. This essentially domestic incident has left its mark on the historical record because Thomas Marsland brought an action against his 'godly' neighbour. In his deposition, Marsland relates that he had been ill for some months and began to recover towards the end of December. At that time, Saint Bridget's parson, a Mr Evans, sent the parish clerk to inform him that there was a celebration of Holy Communion the next day, being Sunday, and if he was able, Marsland should come to church to receive 'the hollie Sacrament'. Otherwise, the clerk assured Marsland that Evans would visit and celebrate the Eucharist in his house. Marsland, 'sente the said Mr Evans word that hee was not absolutely resolved [to receive Communion] for there was some thinge [that] troubled him in [his] mynd'. Both priest and layperson acted precisely as the Prayer Book directs: the minister giving notice of Holy Communion so that preparation can be made by the communicants, as well as showing a willingness to visit the sick and celebrate the sacrament. Marsland too, responded in a way thought proper for a layperson by the Prayer Book, that those too troubled in their conscience to receive Holy Communion should seek out a 'discreet and learned minister of God's Word' for pastoral advice.[74]

---

[73] CRO, EDC.5/1612 misc. (St Bridget's, Chester); Richardson, *Puritanism*, pp. 103–4, see also pp. 90, 132.
[74] *The Book of Common Prayer 1559*, ed. John Booty (Washington, DC, 1976), p. 257. All

Benson appeared shortly after this incident, according to Marsland, ostensibly to enquire about hiring a servant. Once in the house, he took the opportunity 'to speake of the Scriptures' and accused Marsland of keeping his wife from the local conventicle – a 'charge' which Marsland saw no need to refute. Benson continued calling Marsland a drunkard,

and saide this deponent [Marsland] was as ill as anie drunkard, and would gett custom thereby yea, and the devill and all, and saide to this deponent (in regard of this deponent's sickness and weaknes) that hee this deponent had one foote in the grave and that hee feared neither god nor his word, and therefore the Judgment of god hunge over this deponent.

Benson then followed with a reference to the remnant. The brewer, using a long established evangelistic practice, took advantage of a serious illness to press his case to the weakened Marsland. He succeeded in causing his neighbour who, after all, was just recovering from a long illness, considerable anxiety over the 'state of his salvacon'. It is clear, however, that though troubled by him, Marsland did not consider Benson a fit person to consult on the matter:

but what Benison could inferre whether this deponent was one the Number of the Remnant hee this deponent doth referre him selfe to the Judge of this Courte. Butt in regard that Benison did charge this deponent with drunkedness and other Crymes [and that] . . . this deponent was none of the remnant that should be saved yet this deponent saith Benison still protested that hee came to this deponent for love and courtesy's sake.

Marsland's version of events is supported by two other witnesses, a neighbouring husband and wife, who verified that the time of his illness had been spent in bed, not in the ale house. They concluded that Benson had defamed him. A further interesting point is that Marsland, his wife, and neighbour (a woman) could not sign their names to their depositions – they all made marks. Nonetheless, all three in their depositions exhibited concern and interest in religious matters and an ability to express themselves in theological terms.[75]

So the 'godly' brewer is only part of what this case reveals. It certainly does *not* reveal an 'ungodly' Thomas Marsland. Rather, what we have is a member of the laity whose long illness and accompanying spiritual crisis was exploited by a long-standing evangelistic technique: striking at a moment of vulnerability. In the end, Marsland found the resources within a Prayer Book discipline to assert his own place among the elect with some measure of humility and to present his preciser neighbour in court.

---

references from the 1559 Prayer Book come from this edition. See Plate 2.2. See also below for a fuller discussion of sick Communion, pp. 49–50.

[75] CRO, EDC.5/1612 misc. (St Bridget's, Chester).

Petitioning for the church

Church court records provide one source for understanding Prayer Book conformity; a second source are the petitions, nearly thirty in number, produced in support of the liturgy and episcopacy between 1640 and 1642. The growing perception that the Church of England was 'in danger' is a marked feature of conformist thought on the eve of the civil war. The Short and Long Parliaments provided a two-fold opportunity for the airing of grievances on religious and civil matters, as well as the means to seek their redress. Surprising in retrospect, perhaps, but the early months of the Long Parliament witnessed a degree of unity on religious matters. A shared hostility to Thorough provided a sense of unity of purpose; once the destruction of the Laudian ascendency over the English Church was under way, cracks began to appear quickly in the anti-Laudian coalition. The series of Root and Branch petitions against episcopacy, and proposals in the Commons for radical change in the government and worship of the Church of England, rallied conformists to defend the lawful liturgy and episcopal government – though not individual bishops.[76] These petitions provide little support for Haigh's view that 'parish Anglicans' had welcomed the ceremonial innovations of Archbishop Laud in the 1630s.[77] Huntingdon-shire conformists, for example, agreed that recent corruptions had been allowed in the church but suspected that many of the petitions calling for reform 'under [the] colour of removing some Innovation, lately crept into the Church and Worship of God' intended rather the destruction of the reformed Church of England.

[These petitions] which we conceiving and fearing not so much to aim at the taking away of the said Innovations, and Reformation of Abuses, as tending to an absolute innovation of Church Government and Subversion of that Order and Form of Divine Service, which hath happily continued among us, ever since the Reformation of Religion.

Petitioners from Somerset agreed and called for the 'condign punishment' of those responsible for introducing recent corruptions into the government

---

[76] J. Maltby, ed., *The Short Parliament (1640) Diary of Sir Thomas Aston*, Camden Fourth Series, xxxv (1988); William Abbott, 'The issue of episcopacy in the Long Parliament: the reasons for abolition' (University of Oxford D.Phil., 1981); John Morrill, 'The attack on the Church of England in the Long Parliament, 1640–42', in *History, Society and the Churches: essays in honour of Owen Chadwick*, ed. Derek Beales and Geoffrey Best (Cambridge, 1985), pp. 105–8 and *passim*. In contrast with the Root and Branch petitions against episcopacy, the petitions for the church were surprisingly neglected in studies of the period. Anthony Fletcher, however, has offered a perceptive study on the country's slide to civil war, and placed the petitions in their larger political context. Anthony Fletcher, *The Outbreak of the English Civil War* (London, 1981), esp. chs. 3, 9. See below, Chapter 3.

[77] See above, pp. 16–17; Walsham, *Church Papists*, p. 98n.

and worship of the established church.[78] In contrast both to the Laudians and to the Rooters, the conformist petitioners looked back favourably to the 'church of Elizabeth and James', rejecting the innovations of the 1630s and the proposals for radical reform in 1640–42, alike.[79]

After consideration of conformist petitions from a national perspective, this study will provide a detailed look at how one county organized petitions for the church and the sections of society from which such ventures drew support. Chapter 4 will address the former question and in addition will explore the theology and piety of the chief activist for the Church of England in Cheshire, Sir Thomas Aston. His activities on behalf of episcopacy and the Book of Common Prayer in the county transformed him briefly into a figure of national standing. Aston's form of 'Anglicanism' represents a desire to return to a Church of England free of Laudianism, but one in which the place of the Prayer Book, episcopal government, and the Reformation inheritance were secure.[80] The discussion of church court material in Chapter 2 will provide some evidence that conformity drew support from a cross-section of society. Such a view will be further strengthened by examination of the 9,000 subscribers for the Cheshire petition for the Prayer Book. The detailed economic and social analysis of five Cheshire communities in Chapter 5 provides a starting point for addressing this important question.

HOW 'COMMON' WAS COMMON PRAYER?

Given its many admirers, it is odd to think that a serious study of the publishing history of the Prayer Book has yet to be written. Even the revised *Short Title Catalogue* offers little immediate help, as so many of the dates of editions are uncertain. Ian Green has made a rough estimate of 290 editions of the Book of Common Prayer produced between 1549 and 1642. Given that the print run allowed for the Prayer Book was double the usual permitted maximum, he argues for over half a million Prayer Books in

---

[78] John Nalson, *An Impartial Collection of the Great Affairs of State* (2 vols., London, 1682), ii, pp. 720–2, 726.

[79] See below, Chapter 3, *passim*. I offer here and below a sharply contrasting interpretation of the petitions for the Prayer Book and episcopacy than that presented elsewhere: 'The petitions in defence of episcopacy and the Prayer Book in 1641 betray little sign that petitioners thought themselves to be defending any church other than that of the 1630s.' G. W. Bernard, 'The Church of England c.1529–c.1642', *History* 75 (1990), pp. 199, 200.

[80] In so far as there is continuity with the views that Aston represented, it may be found in the 'classical high churchmen' of the early nineteenth century whose dislike of evangelicalism was matched by their hostility to the excesses and anti-protestantism of the Oxford Movement. Reginald H. Fuller, 'The classical High Church reaction to the Tractarians', in *Tradition Renewed: the Oxford Movement Conference Papers*, ed. Geoffrey Rowell (London, 1986), pp. 51–62 *passim*.

circulation before the civil war. Furthermore, the size of print used was sometimes quite small, suggesting such books were intended for personal use in church or at home, rather than for liturgical use.[81] But we await a major study.[82] In the meantime the evidence for the availability of the Prayer Book for the laity remains largely of an indirect nature. The absence of Prayer Books in probate inventories, even clerical inventories, has been commented upon and it is true such appearances are rare.[83] Prayer Books, however, do occasionally appear in wills. John Downing of Saint Giles, Cambridge left his son Thomas, besides numerous articles of clothing, 'a Communion booke . . . [and] a psalme booke'. John's preamble reflects the theology and spirituality of the Prayer Book burial service:

First I will give, and bequeath, my soule unto the hands of Allmightie God whoe gave yt me, of whome I crave free pardon for all my sinns, and that for Jesus Christ his sake my saviour, and redeemer, throughe whome, and by whom, I am certeinelie perswaded and doe steedfastlie beleeve, that I shalbe saved, my bodie likewise to be buried in the churcheyarde of St Giles there to rest untill the second Comminge of my lord and Saviour Jesus Christe, at which tyme I am fullie assured that it shall rise againe; and soe my soule and bodie then beinge united together appeare before the judement seat of god there to receive the weede which Christe hathe purchased for me, In whom I do present and yeald myself to his mercie.

The phrase 'the weede which Christe hathe purchased for me' may be a reference to being clothed with a supernatural, or spiritual body, at the Last Day as described in 1 Corinthians 15, which is the appointed passage of scripture to be read at funerals in the 1559 Prayer Book. It is worth noting as well that Downing made his mark on his will rather than signing his name, yet appears not to have been cut off from written culture. He may well have been able to read, but not write.[84] Further, an exhaustive study of books in Tudor and Stuart Cambridge probate inventories found very few Prayer Books but Elisabeth Leedham-Green warns that appraisers for probate tended to lump all small books together.[85] Books of Common

---

[81] From correspondence with Ian Green.

[82] *STC*, ii, pp. 87–90. I am grateful to David McKitterick, Librarian of Trinity College, Cambridge for his help.

[83] Jane Freeman, 'The parish ministry in the diocese of Durham, c.1570–1640' (University of Durham Ph.D., 1979), p. 55; Patrick Collinson, 'Shepherds, sheepdogs, and hirelings: the pastoral ministry in post-Reformation England', in *The Ministry: clerical and lay*, ed. W. J. Sheils and Diana Woods, Studies in Church History, xxvi (1989), p. 209.

[84] Though due to their death-bed nature making a mark may be a sign of physical weakness rather than illiteracy. Cambridgeshire RO, Ely Archdeaconry Court, Will of John Downing, St Giles, Cambridge, 1598; *BCP 1559*, pp. 309–13. I am grateful to Eric Carlson for this reference. The separation of reading and writings skills is argued for by Margaret Spufford in 'First steps in literacy: the reading and writing experiences of the humblest seventeenth-century spiritual autobiographers', *Social History* 4:3 (1979).

[85] E. S. Leedham-Green, *Books in Cambridge Inventories: book-lists from vice-chancellor's court probate inventories in the Tudor and Stuart periods* (2 vols., Cambridge, 1986), ii,

Prayer of the rather grander sort intended for the leading of public worship do appear with regularity in churchwardens' accounts, of course, as do entries regarding their repair and maintenance – expenditure which indicates that they were receiving wear and tear.[86]

Another explanation, though not necessarily a conflicting one, may be offered for the lack of mention of Prayer Books in inventories. It concerns the practices involved in buying Bibles in the sixteenth and seventeenth centuries. According to the annotated catalogue of the Bible Society, the largest collection of Bibles in English, numerous copies of the Bible survive from throughout our period which have the Book of Common Prayer bound with them. The society has 677 English Bibles in its collection published between 1550 and 1680. Of that number, 105 of the Bibles have bound with them: tables for finding the lessons according to the Book of Common Prayer (20); an order for morning and evening prayer (7); Prayer Book psalters (4); and/or the Common Prayer Book itself (74). This constitutes 16 per cent of the total number of Bibles in the collection. From 1550 to the 1570s, binding the tables for finding the appointed lessons, epistles, and gospels was a more popular option than purchasing the entire Prayer Book. The practice of binding up the whole Prayer Book with the Bible increases dramatically in the second half of the 1570s. Perhaps the public, after the swings in liturgical order of the mid-Tudor period, wanted to be assured that the new liturgy was here to stay before investing in it.[87] It may also suggest that the Elizabethan Settlement was gaining acceptance a decade or two into the new regime.

It seems reasonable, therefore, to conclude that many of the Bibles that appear regularly in inventories include some with the Book of Common Prayer bound with them. Furthermore, these combined Bibles and Prayer Books may be said to truly reflect consumer demand. The point has been made elsewhere that publishers and booksellers were in business to make money and certainly would not back a bad business venture over so many years.[88] The practice with more expensive books seems to have been to buy

---

p. 640. The point about small books being lumped together was made to me by Elisabeth Leedham-Green and I am grateful for her help with these questions. Margaret Spufford, *Small Books and Pleasant Histories: popular fiction and its readership in seventeenth-century England* (London, 1981), p. 48, ch. 4, *passim*.

[86] For example, see below for the parish of Tilston in Cheshire, p. 200.

[87] Bible Society annotated catalogue in the Cambridge University Library. I am very grateful to Alan Jesson of the Bible Society for his advice in this area.

[88] Spufford, *Small Books*, ch. 4. There was a market for translations of the Book of Common Prayer as well, though such works were produced for a variety of reasons from evangelistic tools to linguistic exercises. D. N. Griffiths, 'The early translations of the Book of Common Prayer', *The Library*, 6th ser., 3:1 (1981) and Griffiths 'Prayer Book translations in the nineteenth century', *The Library*, 6th ser., 6:1 (1984), esp. pp. 20–4, a list which includes translations prior to the nineteenth century.

loose sheets that were later bound. The customer decided what other items to have bound up with his or her Bible. Metrical psalms, Common Prayer, genealogies and maps of the Holy Land were all popular choices. So the Bibles in the Bible Society collection which were bound with copies of the Prayer Book undoubtedly reflect the preferences of the purchasers.[89] This practice is delightfully illustrated by an incident in the journal of the New England patriarch John Winthrop. Mice had eaten an entire Book of Common Prayer and, though it was bound with a Greek New Testament and a psalter, the rodents had left the portions of scripture without even a tooth mark. Winthrop related that the 'common prayer [had been] eaten with mice, every leaf of it, and not any of the two other [books] touched, nor any of his other books, though these were above a thousand'. In a providential interpretation of events, even the mice of New England were instruments of the divine will.[90]

Further tantalizing evidence for the domestic use and private ownership of the Prayer Book does exist, but finding it is a matter of gleaning from widely differing sources. The result is anecdotal but suggestive. The Cheshire petitioners to parliament in 1641 for upholding the lawful liturgy maintained:

that scarce any Family or Person that can read, but are furnished with the Books of Common Prayer; in the conscionable Use whereof, many Christian Hearts have found unspeakable joy and Comfort; wherein the famous Church of England our dear Mother hath just Cause to Glory: and may she long flourish in the Practice of so blessed a liturgy.[91]

The widow Marjory Price of Chester testified in 1641 that a minor canon, William Clarke, had said in the cathedral that 'Puritans were about to take away the booke of Common Prayer' and added her own words 'whereby Ignorant people [have] found comfort as well in Church as at home'.[92] Despite being called a 'puritan' by his neighbours, Richard Baxter's (1615–91) father used the Prayer Book for family prayers.

[My] father never scrupled Common-Prayer or Ceremonies, nor spake against Bishops, nor ever so much prayed but by a Book or Form, being not ever acquainted then with any as did otherwise: But only for reading Scripture when the rest were

---

[89] This was called buying books 'in quires', in other words, 'in sheets' which were later bound. See *The Diary of Samuel Pepys*, ed. Robert Latham and William Matthews (11 vols., London, 1974), viii, pp. 237–8.

[90] John Winthrop, *History of New England*, ed. James Savage (Boston, 1853), ii, p. 24. I am grateful to Susan Hardman-Moore for this reference.

[91] Nalson, *Impartial Collection*, ii, p. 758.

[92] Marjory made her mark, not her signature, on her deposition. Bodl., Dep. C. MS 165, fol. 68. The comments about the use of Common Prayer at home, as well as in church, appear to be her own as they do not appear in any of the other depositions or in William Clarke's own copy of his speech. Bodl., Dep. C. MS 165, fols. 66–7, 69–72.

Dancing on the Lord's Day, and for praying (by a Form out of the end of the Common-Prayer Book) in his House, for reproving Drunkards and Swearers, and for talking sometimes a few words of Scripture and the Life to come, he was reviled commonly by the Name of Puritan.[93]

As already mentioned, in 1590, a group of Suffolk parishioners brought their own copies of the Prayer Book to divine service in order to note more accurately their non-conformist minister's deviations from the prescribed liturgy.[94] Reading out or repeating the matrimonial vows in the Prayer Book became a way of contracting a betrothal and ensuring a binding form of words was used that would stand up in a breach of promise suit. People appear to have had copies of Common Prayer available for this use.[95] Bishop Thomas Morton of Durham (1632–59) arranged to have thousands of Prayer Books and catechisms given to children and servants who were able to read. He paid for the books out of his own pocket.[96] More surprisingly, as late as 1647, 3,000 soldiers in the parliamentary army were reported to be using the Prayer Book.[97] That there must have been a market for Prayer Books is further strengthened by the case in 1634–35 against a customs officer called Egerton, and Thomas Cowper, a London stationer. Cowper admitted that he had received copies of the Bible and the Book of Common Prayer printed abroad and smuggled illegally into England, thus breaking the monopoly of the king's printer. This one episode alone revealed that the bookseller had received and sold, aided by the complicity of a corrupt customs officer, 50 contraband Genevan Bibles with notes, 500 small Bibles in duodecimo, 'and soe manye Bookes of Comon Prayer in twelve and not above vt credit, And of Bookes of Comon Prayer in 8° and 24° a thowsand of eache'.[98] The profit to be made from the public demand for copies of the Book of Common Prayer was enough to justify the risk of smuggling.

Evidence for the domestic and private use of the Prayer Book suggests that there were cheaper versions available than the expensive sort intended for public liturgical use itemized in churchwardens' accounts. Happily book prices remained steady from 1560 to 1635, at a time when other consumables doubled in price and wages rose by a half to two-thirds. So

[93] Baxter, *Reliquiae Baxterianae*, p. 3.
[94] Evans, 'Community of South Elmham', pp. 170–1. See below, pp. 44–5.
[95] Eric Josef Carlson, *Marriage and the English Reformation* (Oxford, 1994), pp. 124, 237. Despite some objection to the use of the ring in marriage, Carlson makes the interesting point that the Prayer Book marriage service enjoyed the support of many puritans. It helped, after all, to regularize the rite, ibid., pp. 47–9.
[96] Freeman, 'Parish ministry', p. 294.
[97] Bodl., Clarendon MS 29, fol. 235. I am grateful to John Adamson for this reference.
[98] *A Companion to Arber: being a calendar of documents in Edward Arber's transcript of the Registers of the Company of Stationers of London 1554–1640 with text and calendar of supplementary documents*, ed. W. W. Greg (Oxford, 1967), pp. 305–9, see also pp. 91, 92.

books were more, not less, affordable in real terms in the period under consideration.[99] In 1590–91 one inventory priced Common Prayer Books between 10d and 1s.[100] The appraisers of the London bookseller Charles Tias were untypically thorough and valued the Books of Common Prayer in his stock at $8\frac{1}{2}$d to 9d in 1664.[101] How 'affordable' were these books? They would still represent a considerable expense for labourers in our period, for whom it is estimated that the annual cost of living regularly fell below their earnings. Prayer Books were, however, cheaper than many Bibles.[102] Another major trend of the period works in our favour as well. Books were not only becoming more affordable, but more people were able to read them. The sixteenth and seventeenth centuries witnessed England's trans-formation from 'an oral society ruled by an educated elite to a semi-literate society in which some members, even of the humblest social groups . . . women and . . . agricultural labourers, could read'.[103] Economic and literacy figures cannot alone give the answer, of course. Then as now, how women and men chose to spend what surplus resources they possessed reflected an individual's own values and priorities. Watt rightly reminds us that, although an early seventeenth-century husbandman on a 30 acre arable holding had a 'surplus' of 14d to 18d per week, and therefore the purchase of a twopenny pamphlet every fortnight looks possible, it would nevertheless probably require the sacrifice of two quarts of strong beer.[104] A Common Prayer Book represented a lot more beer, making the indirect evidence for their private ownership in non-elite households all the more striking.

In one very real sense, however, none of this matters. Evidence for the private ownership of the Prayer Book – although it can only strengthen the case for the influence of, and attachment to, the lawful liturgy – is the less important part of the story. As has already been argued, a liturgical text exists principally to be *used*, not *read*. Repeated exposure to Common Prayer certainly meant that many must have had portions of it committed to memory, evidenced by their knowledge of the liturgical responses or

---

[99] Tessa Watt, 'Cheap print and religion c. 1550 to 1640' (University of Cambridge Ph.D., 1988), pp. 313–14. I am grateful to Tessa Watt for much assistance on this section. See also Watt, *Cheap Print and Popular Piety 1550–1640* (Cambridge, 1991).

[100] Leedham-Green, *Books*, ii, p. 640.

[101] Spufford, *Small Books*, pp. 92–3, 108n.

[102] T. H. Darlow and H. F. Moule, *Historical Catalogues of Printed Editions of the English Bible 1525–1961*, revised and expanded by A. S. Herbert (London, 1968), pp. 183–5.

[103] Spufford, *Small Books*, p. 19; David Cressy, *Literacy and the Social Order: reading and writing in Tudor and Stuart England* (Cambridge, 1980), pp. 168–71, 177. Spufford argues for a wider spread of literacy in our period than Cressy, and one in which very few would have been cut off from the written word, either by virtue of their own ability to read or that of a member of their household, *Small Books*, pp. 19–37.

[104] Watt, 'Cheap print', p. 315.

noting when their minister omitted prescribed passages. Attendance at church to participate in the liturgy was full of contradictions: a hierarchial and patriarchal society was reflected and reinforced by pew plans and the gender of the clergy and clerks. Yet at the same time, and in the same place, all were to participate. Liturgy was also a great 'leveller'; the Book of Common Prayer provided some common culture; a shared experience across the divides of class, sex, and age. In this way the Prayer Book (or indeed any liturgical text) cuts across the divide that exists between literate and illiterate, popular and elite, culture.[105] The well-intentioned, if less gifted, imitator of George Herbert, the poet Christopher Harvey, saw this when he wrote:

> 'What! Pray'r by th' book? and Common?'
>   'Yes. Why not?'
>   'The Spirit of grace
>   And supplication
>   Is not left free alone
>   For time and place;
>   But manner too.' 'To read or speake by rote
>   Is all alike to him that praies
>   With's heart what with his mouth he saies.'

To some of the godly, the use of set forms was a shallow exercise, as George Gifford's cartoon conformist 'Atheos' protests: 'shall we say God regardeth not his prayer, because he doth not understand what he prayeth?'[106] Laity and clergy were capable of praying together with the heart what the outward form directed. To the poet Harvey, that very 'commonness' of the Prayer Book was a positive strength, not a weakness, of the spirituality it offered the English people.

>   Devotion will adde life unto the letter;
>   And why should not
>   That which Authority
>   Prescribes esteemed be
>   Advantage got?
>   If the pray'r be good, the commoner the better;
>   Pray'r in the Church's words, as well
>   As sense, of all pray'rs bears the bell.[107]

---

[105] Duffy, *Stripping of the Altars*, pp. 121–3, 295–8.

[106] George Gifford, *Countrie Divinitie* (1581) cited in Walsham, *Church Papists*, p. 104.

[107] 'The Book of Common Prayer' from Harvey's collection of poems written in imitation of Herbert's *The Temple* called *The Synagogue* and first published in 1640. The poem on the Prayer Book did not appear until the 1647 edition. *The Complete Poems of Christopher Harvey*, ed. A. B. Grosart (privately printed, 1874), pp. 17–18.

2

Conformity and the church courts
c. 1570–1642

Among the manifold exercises of God's people, dear Christians, there is none more necessary for all estates, and at all times, than is public prayer and the due use of sacraments.[1]

Ceremony keeps up all things: it's like a penny glasse to a rich spirit or some excellent water; without it the water were spilt; the spirit lost.[2]

[Ceremonies] may be good in their Institution, and grow ill in their practise . . . To those ceremonies, which were received as *signa commonefacientia*, helps to excite and awaken devotion, was attributed an operation, and an effectual power, even to the ceremony itself . . . But what then? Because things good in their institution, may be depraved in their practise . . . shall therefore the people be denied all ceremonies, for the assistance of their weaknesses? . . . Wee must not . . . be hasty in condemning particular ceremonies: For, in so doing . . . we may condemn the Primitive Church, that did use them, and wee condemn a great and Noble part of the reformed Church, which doth use them at this day.[3]

CHURCH COURTS

The strengths and weaknesses of the records of the ecclesiastical courts for the study of religious attitudes of any complexion are well known. There remains the inescapable fact that the bulk of the business of the courts, and therefore the paperwork they generated which eventually becomes 'evidence' for the historian, was largely occupied with the worldly affairs of the proving of wills, issuing licences, and the sinful activities of slander, and sexual and moral offences.[4] 'Religion' was, in the narrow sense of religious

---

[1] 'Of Common Prayer and Sacraments', *Certain Sermons or Homilies Appointed to be Read in Churches in the Time of Queen Elizabeth* (London, 1938), p. 373.
[2] John Selden, *Table Talk*, ed. Frederick Pollock (London, 1927), p. 24.
[3] John Donne, from a sermon for Candlemas, in *Sermons*, ed. Evelyn Simpson and George Potter (10 vols., Berkeley, 1962), x, pp. 90–1.
[4] Ralph Houlbrooke, *Church Courts and the People during the English Reformation 1520–1570* (Oxford, 1979), p. 8; Ronald A. Marchant, *The Church Under the Law: justice*

31

belief and formal practice, a minor concern of the ecclesiastical authorities. It is therefore correspondingly time-consuming to search for religious cases, and sometimes, it has to be declared from the outset, the results are disappointingly thin. The cases discussed here in detail, taken from the largest diocese in post-Reformation England, the diocese of Lincoln, and the Cheshire part of the diocese of Chester, are not sufficient in quantity to form any kind of statistical basis for comparing active conformity to mere passive conformity. They do not, for instance, permit us to judge what proportion of the 75 per cent of those eligible who went to Easter Communion in the diocese of Lincoln in 1603 did so from conviction rather than unwillingness to pay a fine.[5] But these cases do make a starting place for balancing our historical impressions of post-Reformation popular religion as discussed in Chapter 1.[6]

Another limitation of the evidence for conformity from the ecclesiastical courts is its negative quality. What is one to do, for example, with the countless returns made by churchwardens to metropolitan, episcopal or archdiaconal visitations of *omnia bene* – 'all is well'? A superficial reading of the returns for the episcopal visitation of 1597 in the archdeaconry of Buckingham, for example, makes the hold of the Church of England on the population sound thoroughly integrated and complete. Public prayers were all done 'accordinge to the booke of commone prayers', not only on Sundays but on the frequently neglected days of Wednesday and Friday as well. Flesh was universally abstained from on appointed fasting days and the fortunate poor were provided for according to the Queen's Injunctions. Not only was the state of conformity good, but in the parishes of Buckingham it had never been better: 'we have publique prayers observed in our churche and [they are] better frequented than they have bene heretofore'.[7] The 1604 returns from parishes in all six archdeaconries of the diocese reported that the use of Common Prayer and the surplice was almost universal: in terms of the worship of the established church, 'all was well'.[8]

It is the very sameness of these returns, however, which makes one

administration and discipline in the Diocese of York 1560–1640 (Cambridge, 1969), p. 219; J. A. Sharpe, *Defamation and Sexual Slander in Early Modern England: the church courts at York*, Borthwick Papers, no. 58 (1980), pp. 3–4. More recently, Martin Ingram, *Church Courts, Sex and Marriage in England, 1570–1640* (Cambridge, 1987); John Addy, *Sin and Society in the Seventeenth Century* (London, 1989).
[5] Discussed by Peter Burke in 'Religion and secularization', in *The New Cambridge Modern History, Companion Volume XII*, ed. Peter Burke (Cambridge, 1979, 1980), p. 309. Jeremy Boulton argues for high attendance at Holy Communion in Southwark. Jeremy Boulton, *Neighbourhood and Society: a London suburb in the seventeenth century* (Cambridge, 1987), pp. 279–84.
[6] See above, pp. 5–19.
[7] LAO, Ch. P/2, fols. 5, 1.   [8] LAO, Ch. P/7 binders 1–5.

uneasy about their reliability as evidence for the true state of parochial religion. In the diocese of Ely, for example, the 1639 visitation of the particularly zealous Laudian Bishop Matthew Wren failed to reveal strong pockets of non-conformity. A year later, nine parishes with an *omnia bene* stamp in the visitation, contributed a significant number of subscribers to a petition demanding the abolition of episcopal government. The failure of the visitation procedure to produce even hints of strong puritan feeling in these particular communities – especially when carried out under the auspices of a vigorous and exacting diocesan like Wren – is striking. It may be explained by the predominance of committed protestant extremists amongst parochial officials in these particular Cambridgeshire villages.[9] The complaints, however, of some Northamptonshire churchwardens in 1607, that their minister had kept them from church during Holy Communion in order to obstruct them in making a return of non-conformists (one assumes, including recusants), serves to remind us that such conspiracies of silence organized by clergy and parish officers were not always, perhaps not usually, at work hampering the enforcement of diocesan discipline.[10] Clergy and churchwardens were as much, if not more often, agents of diocesan discipline than perpetrators of cover-ups.[11]

It would be over-hasty, therefore, to declare the church's machinery of enforcing discipline as redundant for our purposes. By comparing presentments examined in this chapter with extant visitation articles, a good case can be made for the visitation as a means of filtering the 'Reformation from above' down to the localities.[12] Otherwise, how did laypeople at the grassroots, when they made presentments in visitations or promoted causes against their clergy in consistory court, actually *know* which actions and omissions of their minister violated the boundaries of conformity? The cases also reveal parishioners' extensive familiarity with both the words and the rubrics of the Prayer Book. The inhabitants of Risely in Bedfordshire complained in the consistory court of the diocese of Lincoln in 1603 that their vicar had not read the Queen's Injunctions concerning ecclesiastical discipline, as he was directed to do in the canons: 'Item, he hath not read the Injunctions given by the lat Quenes majestie but hath

---

[9] Margaret Spufford, *Contrasting Communities: English villagers in the sixteenth and seventeenth centuries* (London, 1974), pp. 267–9, 232–4.

[10] W. J. Sheils, *The Puritans in the Diocese of Peterborough 1558–1610*, Northamptonshire Record Society (1979), p. 82.

[11] See below, pp. 192–7, 225–6, for a detailed analysis of the role of churchwardens as local leaders.

[12] Visitation articles consulted for the dioceses of Chester and Lincoln are as follows. For Chester: 1604, 1605, 1617, 1634, 1637. For Lincoln: 1571, 1574, 1577, 1585, 1591, 1601, 1604, 1607, 1613 (metropolitan visitation), 1614, 1618, 1625, 1630–31, 1635, 1641. Christopher Haigh, 'The recent historiography of the English Reformation', in *The English Reformation Revised*, ed. C. Haigh (Cambridge, 1987), pp. 26–7.

kept them from us to the extent [that] we should not knowe his dutie, *nor we perform ours.*'[13] The laity's view expressed here of *their* obligations and responsibilities within the established system of church discipline is also striking. Both clergy and people may at times speak of the laity as 'sheep' – but they were 'sheep' who exercised considerable responsibility in the maintenance of the discipline and harmony of the local Christian community. The Wiltshire rector George Herbert (1593–1633), endorsed this view of the responsibility of the laity and the necessity of communication between the churchwardens and the parish priest:

The countrey parson doth often, both publicly and privately, instruct his church-wardens what a great charge lyes upon them, and that, indeed, the whole order and discipline of the parish is put into their hands. If . . . [the parson] reform anything, it is out of the overflowing of his conscience; whereas . . . [the churchwardens] are to do so . . . by command and oath . . . Now the canons being the church-wardens' rule, the parson adviseth them to read or hear them read often, as also the visitation articles, which are grounded upon the canons, that so they may know their duty and keep their oath the better.[14]

Not even illiteracy was an excuse in Herbert's mind for ignorance of the canons or neglect by churchwardens of their duties.

It should not be thought axiomatic that members of the clergy and laity always lived in enmity, or held divergent and hostile views on such matters. It may be true that in post-Reformation England 'virulent anti-clericalism was [more] an "automatic reflex" of the landowning' rather than of ordinary parishioners.[15] The attitudes of the inhabitants of Risley and of the country parson described above, do not reflect 'clericalism' or 'anti-clericalism', but rather the existence of a 'working relationship'[16] between parish priests and their people, diocesan authorities and the larger flock. Those who desired the orderly and decent observance of the national protestant religion as laid down in the Book of Common Prayer, including members of the ordinary laity it would appear, were as capable of seeing themselves as part of the church as the 'visible saints' of radical dissent, or as those 'hotter sort of protestant' whom Patrick Collinson has described 'as not alien to the properly "Anglican" character of the English Church

---

[13] My italics. LAO, 58/2/66. Enquiries as to whether the Injunctions have been read is a common question in visitation articles of the period.

[14] George Herbert, *A Priest to the Temple, or the Countrey Parson his Character, and Rule of Holy Life* (London, 1908, 1927), pp. 269–70.

[15] Patrick Collinson, *The Religion of Protestants: the church in English cociety 1599–1625* (Oxford, 1982), pp. 40–1; Felicity Heal, *Of Prelates and Princes: a study of the economic and social position of the Tudor episcopate* (Cambridge, 1980), p. 215.

[16] Ian Green, 'Career prospects and clerical conformity in the early Stuart Church', *P&P* 90 (1981), p. 110.

but as equivalent to the most vigorous and successful of religious tendencies contained within it'.[17]

Given the elusiveness of popular religion as a subject, let alone popular conformity, churchwardens' presentments and certificates can nevertheless reveal evidence of conformist sentiments. In the same way as the preambles of wills have been used as a source for religious conviction, presentments and certificates are used in this chapter only when they depart from standard formulae and convey an element of individuality.[18]

An appropriate sense of caution aroused by the uniformity of most returns may also be applied to letters testimonial and dismissory, which were written references for eager would-be clerics for ordination to the diaconate and priesthood, or for a curacy or first benefice. In the case of an already ordained and beneficed minister, letters testimonial were required to certify his conformity and good behaviour when he was presented to a new living. They could be produced by neighbouring clergy, parishioners, or a combination of both. The diocesan archives at Lincoln have a particularly good collection of them.[19] The same litmus test of departure from standard forms has been applied to the letters testimonial and I have cited only those possessing unusual terminology.

The bulk of the material for exploring features of conformity in this chapter comes from the records of the consistory courts. It was in the consistory that disgruntled parishioners brought suits against non-conforming clergy who failed to provide the authorized services. A shortcoming of this evidence, it could be argued, is its 'reactionary' quality. In other words, the majority of cases cited here were episodes of lay reaction *against* clerical non-conformity. Given the nature of religious conformity, not least its legality, this is hardly surprising. Equally, however, the Cheshire and Lincoln evidence calls into question the historian's traditional touchstones of godly puritanism in the localities; such as refusal to use the Prayer Book, to make the sign of the cross in Baptism, and the frequently used equation that a preaching minister is a 'puritan' minister. As will be illustrated in detail, many of the clergymen proceeded against for refusal to use the Book of Common Prayer were also frequently complained of by their flocks for a failure to preach and for such things as railing, drunkenness and adultery – hardly what one thinks of as traditional 'puritan'

---

[17] Geoffrey E. Nuttall, *Visible Saints: the congregational way 1640–1660* (Oxford, 1957), pp. 43–69; Patrick Collinson, 'A comment: concerning the name puritan', *JEH* 31:4 (1980), p. 484; 'Puritans', *Oxford Encyclopedia of the Reformation*, ed. Hans Hillerbrand (4 vols., Oxford, 1996), iii, pp. 364–70.

[18] Spufford, *Contrasting Communities*, pp. 320–34.

[19] Dorothy M. Owen, *The Records of the Established Church of England*, British Records Association (1970), pp. 17–18; Kathleen Major, *A Handlist of the Records of the Bishop of Lincoln and the Archdeaconries of Lincoln and Stow* (London, 1953), p. 32.

activities. And if, as Ian Green has stated, complicity between parsons and churchwardens has hidden yet more non-conformity from our eyes, he also reminds us that in some cases it was the people's very dislike of puritan practices that led to the presentments of other ministers in the first place.[20] It could also be argued that cases of the second type are in themselves neutral, and it is the agenda of the individual historian which decides whether he or she chooses to lay the emphasis on the non-conformity of the minister, or on the conformist desires of the parishioners.

GOING TO CHURCH

Sundays, week days, and holy days

If one accepts the predominant historical assessment of the spiritual state of the post-Reformation Church of England, it should surprise us to find many people wanting to go to church at all. A puritan source noted in the 1570s:

In all their order of service there is no edification according to the rule of the Apostle, but confusion. They tosse the Psalms in most places like tennice balles. The people, some standing, some walking, some talking, some reading, some praying by themselves, attend not to the minister . . . When the Old Testament is read, or the lessons, they make no reverence; but when the Gospel cometh, then they al stand up . . . When Jesus is named, then of[f] goeth the cappe, and downe goeth the knees, with suche a scraping on the ground, that they cannot hear a good while after, so that the Word is hindered, but when other names of God are mentioned they make no courtesie at all.[21]

In fact, the assessment by the godly of the religious behaviour of their neighbours is most noteworthy, not for the indifference towards lawful ceremonies described, but for the enthusiasm ordinary layfolk brought to Prayer Book worship.

A presentation of case studies for the evidence of conformity from Cheshire and the diocese of Lincoln should begin at the most basic level: some laypeople wanted services on Sundays. Around 1609, four parishioners claiming to represent the townsmen and parishioners of Fenstanton and Hilton in Huntingdonshire presented their vicar Francis Smith for failure to read prayers on the sabbath at the usual time. They expressed

---

[20] Green, 'Career prospects', p. 112. Helena Hajzyk found that the majority of cases presented to the Lincoln consistory before 1604 were promoted by local individuals, rather than by diocesan officials. Helena Hajzyk, 'The church in Lincolnshire c.1595–1640' (University of Cambridge Ph.D., 1980), p. 53.

[21] *A View of Popish Abuses yet Remaining in the Englishe Church* in *Puritan Manifestos: a study of the origin of the puritan revolt with a reprint of the Admonition to Parliament and kindred documents, 1572*, ed. W. H. Frere and C. E. Douglas (London, 1907), p. 29.

their desire for Sunday services almost in terms of a 'contract' with their minister: 'we doe obiect that the said Mr Smith vicar of Fenstanton & Hilton hath received our tithes [and] since [then] he hath not preached ther neither have we praiers on the Saboth days in due time as we ought to have'.[22] At Fenstanton they paid their tithes and so expected services and sermons at 'due time'. In September 1606, the churchwardens and sidesmen of Thurleigh, Bedfordshire complained that their vicar held a Welsh living in addition to that of their own parish without dispensation to do so from the ecclesiastical authorities. As a result, since the last visitation of the diocese in 1604, they endured one sabbath entirely without divine service and the following week there was Morning but not Evening Prayer, 'thoroughe the defaulte of Mr William Ford our vicar'.[23] Depositions from 1628 by the inhabitants of Bruera, a dependent chapelry of Saint Oswald's, Chester, also reveal a desire to have divine service. They stated that previous incumbents of Saint Oswald's had always ensured that the chapel was ministered to by either the incumbent himself or a 'sufficient' curate or substitute. The present minister was failing to provide any of these options. One Elizabeth Williamson related that, as far as she could remember, the two previous incumbents had always cared for the spiritual needs of the chapelry.

When Mr Thirkus was vicar of St Oswalds, he serveth the Cure of Bruera . . . and this deponent hath divers times heard him read divine service and preache the sacred word of god . . . in the said Chapell and this deponent hath received the holie Communion att his hands therein . . . and [in] the said Mr Thirkus absence one Edward Pickett, mr Thirkus procurred a Toleration [for him] to read divine service in the chapell.

The deposition of Elizabeth Williamson (who could not sign it but made her mark) is substantiated by two others: all three witnesses expressed feelings of pastoral neglect.[24]

Conforming parishioners could be defrauded of their intent to have divine service, and to have it in a reverent manner, not only by negligent clergy, but also by troublesome neighbours. In 1592, Robert Shurlocke of Saint Michael's, Chester was accused of various forms of behaviour disruptive to the worshipping life of Saint Michael's parishioners. He

---

[22] LAO, 58/2/80. Undated, but it has been bundled with other manuscripts endorsed 1609. Francis Smith was vicar at Fenstanton and Hilton, Huntingdonshire from at least 1597 and he appears again in the *Liber Cleri* for 1603. See C. W. Foster, *The State of the Church in the Reigns of Elizabeth and James I as Illustrated by Documents Relating to the Diocese of Lincoln*, Lincoln Record Society, xxiii, (1926), pp. 210, 284.

[23] LAO, Ch.P/10, fol. 10. Bishop William Chaderton's articles of 1604 enquired specifically on the point of residence. Diocese of Lincoln, *Visitation Articles* (Cambridge, 1604), no. 3; see also articles for 1601, nos. 4, 5.

[24] CRO, EDC.5/1628, misc. (Bruera Chapel, St Oswald's, Chester).

acquired rights over the churchyard and transformed it into a cattle yard that was offensive apparently even by seventeenth-century standards. '[He] made it a hyghway for the beast and cattell before the chancell windowe eastward whereby it is putrified by the cattell and donge . . . that it is very noysome . . . to all the parishe.' Under Shurlocke's guidance, the church-yard became a gathering place for all sorts of evil livers (including apprentices) who played lewd and unlawful games in front of the chancel window. All in all, the distractions to public worship were such as to cause the parishioners to seek redress both through the local magistrate and the church courts.[25]

Perhaps more surprisingly, some parishioners expressed a frequent desire to have services on weekdays. So great was the dedication of the parson of Manton in Lincolnshire to the game of bowls, that he frequently failed to supply his flock with Evening Prayer on Wednesdays and Fridays, as he was required to do by the canons, and as members of his flock themselves pointed out.[26] The parishioners of Francis Smith reported that he failed to 'read praiers' on Wednesdays and Fridays 'as he ought to do'.[27] This too was a complaint against John Swan the minister at Bunbury in Cheshire in 1631.[28] The patron of the living of Whaplode in Lincolnshire, William Welby, proceeded against his vicar William Holden for failure to read prayers on weekdays in 1638.[29]

In addition to the proper observance of the sabbath and weekday prayers, there are numerous examples from the Lincoln records showing that some parishioners, at least, also wanted saints' days and holy days to be properly observed. In the mid-1590s, William Hieron claimed that the parish clerk not only failed to hold divine service on weekdays and holy days but went riding forth on such days and sent his servants deliberately to work in order to 'better . . . manifest his contempt upon holy days'.[30] Anger at irreverent behaviour on holy days could be directed at laypeople as well as clergy. The sensibilities of the neighbours of Edmund Day of Thurleigh were offended when he sent one of his men to work on Saint Luke's day during divine service.[31] In 1598, the parish clerk of Houghton cum Wyton in Huntingdonshire promoted a case against a parishioner Thomas Thompson for performing 'bodilye labor' on several Sundays *and* holy days.[32]

[25] CRO, EDC.5/1591/2, misc. (St Michael's, Chester).
[26] In 1577. LAO, 69/1/7.   [27] LAO, 58/2/80.
[28] CRO, EDC.5/1631/27 (Bunbury).
[29] LAO, 62/2/16.   [30] LAO, 58/1/5 (1595–7).
[31] LAO, Ch.P/10, fol. 10.
[32] CROH, Archdeaconry 4 No. 254, Houghton.

While it is true that the feast days of the Christian year had been considerably reduced in the Reformation, the Book of Common Prayer still directed the observance of about thirty-five days in addition to Sundays to celebrate various New Testament saints or events in the life of Christ and his mother. Despite the biblical basis of the people and events commemorated, it is fair to say that among apologists for the Church of England there was a large degree of ambivalence about holy days. The observance of feast days was lawful and helpful but must not be confused with the overriding command to observe the sabbath.[33] One critic of conformist spirituality, the separatist Henry Barrow, noted with sarcasm the enthusiasm of ordinary parishioners, as well as the clergy, for holy days:

The Sunday is a governing day, and is written in their Calendar with red letters, and ruleth all the dayes of the week, save certain unruly days and their eves, which will not be governed by it, but challenge to themselves a peculiar worship also: they having their days in the same Calendar written with red letters. And because they [i.e. holy days] are but strangers and come but once in the year, they look for the more solemn entertainment, that the priest should diligently watch, and the people wait for their coming accordingly. If they come in a cluster or at some solemn double feast, then to entertain them with new clothes, clean houses, garnished with green boughs or holly and ivy, with good cheer and much passtime, all work on these their idol [*sic*] days, laid aside. Yet though they come but one alone, and that on the week-day, yet that week is not St Sunday lord of the ascendent; it is part of his [the priest's] service to give warning unto the people of the others coming, that they keep his or her eve with fasting and prayer: that upon their day they keep an holy feast, abstain from labour, etc.[34]

In more sensitive hands, such traditional enthusiasms could be harnessed and redirected. The noted Elizabethan preacher Bernard Gilpen found he could attract a bigger congregation to his sermons on holy days than on ordinary week days.[35] Two of the Jacobean church's most respected

---

[33] Kenneth Parker, *The English Sabbath: a study of doctrine and discipline from the Reformation to the Civil War* (Cambridge, 1988), pp. 50–5, 112–14; David Cressy, *Bonfires and Bells: national memory and the protestant calendar in Elizabethan and Stuart England* (London, 1989), pp. 6–7. The six days of Holy Week are omitted from the figures. There were also the days of Rogationtide to bless the fields in early summer not authorized in the 1559 Prayer Book but required by the Royal Injunctions of the same year. The Book of Homilies contained sermons for Rogationtide. Ronald Hutton, *The Rise and Fall of Merry England: the ritual year 1400–1700* (Oxford, 1994), p. 123.

[34] Henry Barrow, *A Brief Discoverie* in *The Writings of Henry Barrow 1587–90*, ed. Leland Carlson (London, 1962), p. 362. See also *Hierurgia Anglicana*, ed. Vernon Staley (3 vols., London, 1902–4), iii, pp. 245–66; P. More and F. Cross, *Anglicanism: the thought and practice of the Church of England illustrated from the religious literature of the seventeenth century* (London, 1962), pp. 572–4.

[35] Jane Freeman, 'Parish ministry in the diocese of Durham c. 1570–1640' (University of Durham Ph.D., 1979), p. 274. Sermons and exercises were successfully linked to the observance of Saint Luke's day which had striking overtones to pilgrimages in some north Devon communities. Cressy, *Bonfires*, p. 9.

bishops, William Chaderton of Lincoln and Thomas Morton of Chester enquired in their dioceses whether any feast days were observed which were not authorized in the Prayer Book – a clear attempt to distinguish between 'reformed' and 'popish' holy days.[36] One William Beale added figures from Foxe's *Book of Martyrs* including Cranmer, Latimer, and Ridley to the Prayer Book calender in an almanac he produced in 1631 and was strongly attacked by the Laudian polemicist John Pocklington for his trouble.[37] The incident serves to remind us that the question of *who* to commemorate was as much a charged issue as the practice of commemoration itself.

It was often difficult for parishioners to know if there was a holy day appointed during the coming week, as Henry Barrow noted, 'they are but strangers and come but once in the year'. It was not uncommon, therefore, to find them desiring that the minister announce any holy days in the coming week on Sunday. John Pickering, a parishioner of Ellington in Huntingdonshire complained in 1602 that the vicar Anthony Armitage would never announce on the sabbath if there were holy days to be observed in the coming week in order that he and his fellow parishioners would know to keep them and not 'incure the penalties of the lawe'.[38] At the end of March 1605, twenty-one parishioners of King's Sutton in Northamptonshire certified their minister's current conformity and described his previous non-conformity which included his failure to announce holy days 'as we the Inhabitants of the said parishe have expected'.[39]

Worship according to the Book of Common Prayer

From the perspective of the Reformers, the worship of late medieval Christianity was, like the interior of the churches themselves, too compartmentalized. The medieval Mass involved a set of parallel liturgical activities, with the clergy involved in one set of devotions and the laity in another: the great moment of union of priest and people coming at the elevation of the consecrated host.[40] Cranmer and others promoted a

---

[36] See Chaderton's articles for 1604, no. 18; Morton's articles for 1617, no. 20. See n. 10. Both Chaderton and Morton promoted sabbath observances in their sees. Parker, *English Sabbath*, pp. 141–2, 148–52; Cressy, *Bonfires*, pp. 4–12.

[37] Anthony Milton, *Catholic and Reformed: the Roman and Protestant churches in English protestant thought, 1600–1640* (Cambridge, 1995), p. 314.

[38] LAO, 69/1/23.

[39] LAO, L.T.& D. 1605 (James Smith).

[40] Theodor Klauser, *A Short History of the Western Liturgy: an account and some reflections* (Oxford, 1979), pp. 148–9. The Constitution on the Sacred Liturgy (*Sacrosantum Concilium*, 14) of Vatican II promotes the ideal of active lay participation in the liturgy. See *Vatican Council II: the Conciliar and Post Conciliar Documents*, ed. Austin Flannery

different understanding of corporate prayer. It was to be 'common', not only in the sense of a uniform rite for the nation, but also in the sense that the priest and people attended to the same aspects of the liturgy together. Hence the repeated emphasis not only on the vernacular but on clerical audibility, as the opening rubrics for Morning Prayer direct that: 'the minister shall read with a loud voice'.[41] This Reformation ideal appears not to have fallen on stony ground as the records of the church courts reveal laity who desired not only that their worship conform to the Book of Common Prayer but also that they themselves participate actively in it. A generation past the Settlement of 1559, attachment had been formed to the Prayer Book's vernacular and antiphonal dialogue between priest and people, which 'the godly' so derisively compared to a tennis match.[42] When

---

(Leominster, 1981 edn), pp. 7–8. But cf. Eamon Duffy, 'Lay appropriation of the sacraments in the later Middle Ages', *New Blackfriars* 77 (January 1996). The Elizabethan apologist John Jewel, on the attack of course, commented:

> What one amongst the whole number of old [patristic era] bishops and fathers ever taught you either to say private Mass while the people stared on or to lift up the sacrament over your head (in which point consisteth now all your religion); or else to mangle Christ's sacraments and to bereave the people of the one part, contrary to Christ's institution and plain expressed words?

John Jewel, *An Apology of the Church of England*, ed. John Booty (Washington, DC, 1963), p. 92. This is part of an extended argument by Jewel in which he attempts to demonstrate that bishops were guardians of sound doctrine in the early church and therefore the office could be, as in England's case, on the side of the sixteenth-century Reformation. See also Virginia Reinburg, 'Liturgy and the laity in late medieval and Reformation France', *Sixteenth Century Journal* 23:3 (1992). The overwhelming majority of prayers provided in devotional books for the laity at Mass in the late medieval church were elevation prayers. Eamon Duffy, *The Stripping of the Altars: traditional religion in England 1400–1580* (New Haven, 1992), pp. 110–13, 118–30.

[41] *The Book of Common Prayer 1559*, ed. John Booty (Washington, DC, 1976), p. 49. The official *Homilies* argued for the superiority of corporate, or common, vernacular prayer over private prayer. Individuals, however, were allowed to pray privately in a tongue other than English if versed in the language. Corporate worship in Latin in Oxford and Cambridge colleges was allowed based on the same reasoning. 'An Homily or sermon concerning prayer', in *Certain Sermons or Homilies Appointed to be Read in Churches in the Time of Queen Elizabeth of Famous Memory*, ed. John Griffith (London, 1938), pp. 375, 378–88. Episcopal visitation articles from the period abound in queries as to whether 'the common prayer [is] said or sung by your minister both morning and evening, distinctly and reverently', from Bishop Chaderton's 1607 articles for Lincoln Diocese – just one of many examples. See Kenneth Fincham, ed., *Visitation Articles and Injunctions of the Early Stuart Church, Vol. I* (Church of England Record Society, i, 1994), p. 71 and *passim*; W. H. Frere and William Kennedy, eds., *Visitation Articles and Injunctions of the Period of the Reformation*, Alcuin Club (3 vols., 1910); W. P. M. Kennedy, *Elizabethan Episcopal Administration*, Alcuin Club (3 vols., 1924). John Merbecke produced a highly successful version of the Book of Common Prayer for singing which set one note for each syllable of Prayer Book texts so that the service could be sung yet the meaning of the words was not obscured. John Merbecke, *The Book of Common Prayer Noted* (n.p., 1550).

[42] See above, p. 3. To the godly, 'the solemnities of reform' had not done enough to 'slow and darken parochial worship'. Duffy, *Stripping of the Altars*, p. 129.

the inhabitants of Macclesfield petitioned the bishop of Chester in 1604 against the dismissal of Thomas Shert, who had been their curate for thirty years, and his replacement by the 'insufficient' Francis Jackson, they were concerned with, among other things, the latter's use of unlawful rites. '[Jackson] hath taken upon himself publiquely to read divine service [and] also to read publiquely the Book of resolutions or some other booke not allowed for publique service'.[43] Much later in 1643, parishioners from Tarporley petitioned the JPs at Quarter Sessions and complained that their rector, Nathaniel Lancaster, and curate, Mr Jones, 'doe utterly refuse to reade the booke of Common prayer'.[44] In 1604, articles were addressed to Bishop Richard Vaughan of Chester by parishioners at Manchester against the curate Ralph Kirk. Among the fifteen articles preferred against him, the longest and most detailed concerned his attempts to discontinue lay participation at Morning Prayer as directed in the Prayer Book. 'For the manner of morninge prayer whereas divers of the parishe, who have been used to helpe the parishe clarke, to readd verse for verse [i.e. to make the responses] with the Curate for fourtye yeares laste past and more . . . The sayde Ralph Kirke hath of late tymes not permitted them so to doe.' The parishioners claimed that Kirk had received a special monition from the chancellor of the diocese, ordering him to allow the people to make the accustomed and set responses of the Prayer Book service. It appears that conflict over this very point was what sparked the presentment of the set of articles against Kirk's non-conformity to the worship set down by law.

Notwithstanding [the chancellor's monition] he wolde not permitt nor suffer them so to doe . . . And spectaylle this morning July 27, 1604 having knowledge of mr Chancellor his directions, he beginninge to Reade [the people made the accustomed responses] . . . thereupon [he] stayed & commanded the people to hold their peace.[45]

The collegiate church at Manchester is characterized as a conservative community; its fellows in particular were slow to adapt to the religious changes of the mid-Tudor period. In 1571, one fellow of the college was reported as attempting to make the Prayer Book Eucharist as much like the pre-Reformation Mass as he could. Yet for all that, it is worth noting that

---

[43] CRO, EDC.5/1604, misc. (Macclesfield).

[44] CRO, QJF 71/4/24 (Tarporley). See also CRO, QJB 1/6/87v; BL, Add. MS 36913, fol. 139v.

[45] Kirk said the Prayer Book was 'noe Scripture' and also called the surplice the 'Ragg of the Poope [*sic*] and a mightye heresye in the Churche, and that he that doth mantayne yt cannot be saved'. CRO, EDC.5/1604, misc. (Manchester).

for 'fourtye yeares laste past and more' the people were accustomed to read in English with the parish clerk 'verse for verse'.[46]

The people of Hemingby in Lincolnshire complained in 1595 and 1597 not only of the minister's reading of the service in a hasty and irreverent manner, but also of his obstruction of their active participation in the service. Thomas Johnson, the parish clerk of Hemingby, complained that since he and others in the parish had persuaded the vicar William Hieron to say services according to the Prayer Book, it was: 'even against his owne hart, as appeared by his first beginning, he posted and hasteth over these prescribed prayers in [an] unreverent manner that he will not suffer the people either in the Letanye or in the Comandements to answer'. Johnson and his supporters, however, suspected that there was more at work in the parson's sloppy liturgics than a bruised and tender conscience: 'Thereby [he] maketh a confusion in the service, he himselfe pronouncinge one thing and the people another all at one instant which he doth [do] to fortifie his position that one prescript forme of prayer ought to be in the churche but such as the minister immediately conseaveth.'[47] The patron of Whaplode, William Welby, expressed the desire to hear the Prayer Book service clearly and complained that the vicar often failed to 'saye or singe' Common Prayer 'distinctlie and reverentlie'.[48]

Similarly, the parishioners of Ellington suspected their vicar Anthony Armitage of attempting to sabotage Prayer Book services. The minister's ingenuity in this regard included placing obstacles in the path of punctual attendance. Articles subscribed by five parishioners describe how Armitage would not let the clerk ring the last peal of the bells until 'he be in the church & then he doth make such haste that the prayers be half done before anie bodie can get to the church'.[49] Another parishioner, Christopher Gates, a 'husbandman', supported the charge that on numerous occasions Armitage had been approached and requested to allow time for his flock to gather: '[that] sondry tymes the said Mr Throckmorton [a parishioner] being in the church told the said Mr Armitage that he made such hast of service that a great parte of prayers was always done before he could get to the church although he made as much hast as he could.'[50]

[46] CRO, EDC.5/1604, misc. (Manchester); C. A. Haigh, *Reformation and Resistance in Tudor Lancashire* (Cambridge, 1975), pp. 209, 214, 217, 218–19, 220; F. R. Raines, *The Rectors of Manchester and Wardens of the Collegiate Church*, Chetham Society, v, vi (1885); *The Fellows of the Collegiate Church of Manchester*, Chetham Society, xxi (1891); R. C. Richardson, 'Puritanism in the diocese of Chester to 1642' (University of Manchester Ph.D., 1969), pp. 55–61. For more of Ralph Kirk's adventures, see this chapter, *passim* and R. C. Richardson, *Puritanism in North-west England: a regional study of the diocese of Chester to 1642* (Manchester, 1972), pp. 23, 27, 29, 40, 41, 81, 185.
[47] LAO, 58/1/5 (1595–7).   [48] LAO, 62/2/16.
[49] LAO, 69/1/24.   [50] LAO, 69/2/15.

Armitage reportedly responded 'that he would stay for no mans pleasure'.[51] The countermeasures of some parishioners to foil Armitage's ploy also failed: 'yf they come to the church before the last peals be ronge, then he will make them stay till he list . . . of purpose to wearie his parishioners thereby'.[52] Other parishioners confirmed this too in their depositions: 'that he hath knowne the parishioners (being assembled together to heare divine service) staie divers tymes in the church halfe an howre before Mr Armitage came dureing which tyme the clarke would not ringe'. Margaret Gates, 'laborer', endorsed this: 'that the said Mr Armitage will not suffer the Clarke to ringe the last peale till such tyme as he be there himselfe which is a causeth [sic] at his parishioners staie many tymes som things longe by reason of his absence.'[53] The minister's critics came from a broad cross-section of village society, from a 'Mr' Throckmorton to the labourer Margaret Gates. Getting to church on time was a problem, for the patron of Whaplode, William Welby, complained not only that William Holden failed 'to say or singe' the Common Prayer 'distinctlie and reverentlie' but failed to give 'warning of service' by ringing the bells.[54]

Parishioners also demanded that their ministers not tamper with the set order of the Prayer Book. William Hieron omitted set prayers and even rejected the idea of them, 'being as he [sees] . . . them a fewe dead lynes', the deponents complained in the articles against him.[55] In 1602 the churchwardens of Kimcoate, Leicestershire presented their minister for not reading the whole of the Common Prayer: 'in manie things he breaketh the order of the church and the booke of Common prayer'.[56] Parishioners at Husband's Bosworth wanted the entire Prayer Book service and complained that the curate Mr Hall was not reading the whole service, which indicates that some of the laity there knew what the order of the service should be. In Tarporley parishioners could tell that their curate John Jones was omitting the Ten Commandments from the Communion service 'and other parts of divine service contrary to Law and to the Contentment of your Ordinary and scandall of well affected people'.[57] In fact, not only did some laity know what the order of service should be, but some of them brought their own books to follow it in. This striking case comes from the diocese of Norwich. In 1590 Thomas Daynes, vicar of Flixton in Suffolk, was deprived of his living in the consistory court in a case in which all the witnesses against him were parishioners. In addition to his predictable failure to use the sign of the cross in Baptism, allow godparents, wear the

---

[51] LAO, 69/1/24.   [52] LAO, 69/1/24.
[53] LAO, 69/2/15.   [54] LAO, 62/2/16.
[55] LAO, 58/1/5.   [56] LAO, Ch. P/6, fol. 27.
[57] LAO, 58/2/67; Foster, *The State of the Church*, pp. 217, 290; CRO, EDC.5/1639/129; *1559 BCP*, pp. 248–9.

surplice, church women, or pray for the queen as supreme governor of the Church of England, he rebuked his flock and called them 'papists' for bringing their Prayer Books in order to see if he was observing the lawful service. He preached that:

'his parishioners were papists and that they would rather. . . heare masse . . . than to heare the worde of god trulie preached' . . . He reproved his congregation 'for lookinge in their books' and said 'that they which wolde have sarvice sayde according to the booke of common prayer are papists and atheists'.[58]

This knowledge of the liturgy and concern for its proper performance exhibited by post-Reformation parishioners is less surprising in the light of Claire Cross' evidence for similar ability and concern among Marian laity.[59] It would appear, then, that some parishioners supported the Book of Common Prayer with sufficient commitment to ensure that its services were reverently conducted by their minister. If he failed to do so, they would resort to the church courts – a time consuming process – in order to bring him to conformity with the ceremonies of the Prayer Book.

The failure or refusal to wear the white ecclesiastical overgarment, known as a surplice, could be a source of controversy as well. It was a particular point of grievance to the parishioners of Tarporley when they first began proceedings against their curate John Jones in the consistory court in 1639. Rather than simply stating his omission of the surplice, the articles against Jones gave detailed examples. Not only did he fail to wear it at non-sacramental services, but he failed to wear it 'in the ministration of the Sacraments of Baptisme and of the Lords Supper'. Furthermore, some lay people felt sufficiently indignant to mention by name the funerals of two of their neighbours which Jones had conducted improperly attired. One of the churchwardens approached Jones about the matter and 'there advised and willed you [Jones] to weare the surplice and you preemptorily answered him that you would not, or that or the like effect, nor indeed did you weare it'. The warden, John Venion was, of course, fulfilling his role as an instrument of discipline in the parish, which included confronting one of its ministers for non-conformity.[60]

---

[58] Nesta Evans, 'The community of South Elmham, Suffolk, 1550–1640' (University of East Anglia M.Phil., 1978), pp. 170–1. See above, pp. 13–14.

[59] Claire Cross, 'Lay literacy and clerical misconduct in a York parish during the reign of Mary Tudor', *York Historian* 3 (1980), pp. 10, 12, 14. That ordinary villagers were willing and able to use both the ecclesiastical and secular courts to present their grievances in the early modern period has been demonstrated for an Essex community. See Keith Wrightson and David Levine, *Poverty and Piety in an English Village: Terling 1525–1700* (New York, 1979), pp. 113–14.

[60] CRO, EDC.5/1639/129 (Tarporley). After he left Tarporley, Jones became a household chaplain and then was called to Marple in Cheshire as the minister during the Commonwealth. His ministry continued in a confrontational style, as Calamy reports that 'after

The ministry of word and sacrament: the Eucharist

Equating evidence of parishioners' desire to receive Holy Communion with sincere conformity would be to collude with the view that the more 'protestant' someone was, the less interest he or she had in the 'externals' of religion. Puritans, as well as conformists, took the Eucharist seriously – so seriously that the number of people deemed worthy of inclusion by the godly in so sacred an act could be quite small.[61] Rather, what is stressed here is the desire to receive Communion according to the lawful ceremonies and liturgy of the church. Examples from several different parishes indicate that there was sufficient popular demand for Holy Communion to necessitate the use of church courts to obtain it. The bowling parson of Manton, John Robotham, was hard at his game on Easter Eve 1577, so that his flock went without making their Communion which many were desirous to do:

upon Easter Eve laste the sayd parson was bowling at Kyrtone from ix of the clock in the morning tyll ii of the clocke in the afternoone the same daye so that manye of his parishioners that was [sic] determined to have receyved the Communion the sayd daye was defrauded of their intent.[62]

Non-residence, not sportsmanship, was the complaint of the churchwardens and a swornman of the parish of Folkingham, Lincolnshire concerning their rector in December 1597. They claimed that John Hoskins had been resident in the parish only forty days in the last twelve months. The churchwardens, endorsed by several additional witnesses, complained that he had hardly administered Communion at all in the past two years.[63] The churchwardens of Thurleigh, showing their acquaintance with the canons and visitation articles, reported in 1608 that their vicar had failed to administer the sacrament at least three times a year in the last two years, which was the minimum requirement. George Herbert, writing in the early 1630s, felt that Communion once a month was the ideal, but that six times a year was the best that could be reasonably hoped for.[64]

People resented interruptions in services when they 'wold fayne apply

some years thus spent he was forced to desist from preaching there even before the Restoration of 1660'. Cited in J. P. Earwaker, *East Cheshire*, (2 vols., London, 1877), ii, p. 57. Complaints about failing to wear the surplice were also made against John Swan of Bunbury. There was a long history of trouble over the surplice at Bunbury dating back to at least 1601. CRO, EDC.5/1631/27 (Bunbury); Richardson, 'Puritanism', p. 40. See the layman Francis Quarles' poem highly critical of clergy who, in his view, forsake their primary responsibility of caring for the flock because of their misplaced scruples over the surplice and ceremonies. 'On those that deserve it', in *The Metaphysical Poets*, ed. Helen Gardner, pp. 115–16. See below, pp. 231–2.
[61] Eamon Duffy, 'The godly and the multitude in Stuart England', *The Seventeenth Century* 1:1 (1986), pp. 37–9.
[62] LAO, 69/1/7.   [63] LAO, 69/1/9.
[64] Herbert, *A Priest to the Temple*, pp. 257–8.

themselves to devotion' – especially at celebrations of the Eucharist. At Saint Michael's, Chester, the general chaos of the 'noysome' churchyard, made it impossible to receive the Communion sacrament reverently. A chancel window had become a

spyinge hole for Rascalls, vagabonds, prentices & other lewed persons who as well upon the sundaies and holly daies and namelie at Easter at Communion time when the people wold fayne apply themselves to devotion, they cannot be ferverent nor earnest in theyr prayers, but are withdrawn from zealous intents by such gazers.[65]

At Saint Michael's, the state of, and misbehaviour in, the churchyard made it difficult for parishioners to give as much attention to their Eucharistic devotions as they felt they should. Care over the proper reception of Communion was not completely unknown among the laity in early modern protestant England.[66]

Neglect, rather than non-conformity, may have been a more familiar problem for inhabitants of dependent chapelries. The people of the chapelry of Lobthorpe in Lincolnshire proceeded against the rector of the parish of North Witham, John Sands, in 1608. Sands, the Lobthorpe promoters claimed, was obliged by custom and by law 'to minister & say & celebrate Sacraments & sacramental rights or other divine offices & services [at Lobthorpe Chapel]'. However, Sands claimed that he had no such obligation to the chapelry, although the Lobthorpe people stated that they had won a decision to that effect in the consistory court the previous year. Apparently there had been a long history of litigation in the church courts over this case and Sands may have been simply expressing his feeling that he was not legally bound to serve at Lobthorpe. The parishioners of the chapelry, however, were expressing a positive desire to have sacraments, divine service and pastoral care readily available.[67] Equally, when the inhabitants of the chapelry of Bruera complained in 1628 of the neglect of the present vicar, they were concerned not only with the failure to have divine service but also with being deprived of the sacramental life of the church. One Anthony Cotton deposed: 'duringe mr Case . . . his incumbancy in the vicarage, the Cure and Celebration of divine service and the sacraments have for the most parte bene much neglected'. The sincerity of the chapelry inhabitants about their desire to receive the Communion was verified by one Edward Haydocke. He deposed that he had served the people there for many years for an annual stipend of £5. He read divine service and arranged yearly at Easter for another minister in priest's orders

[65] CRO, EDC.1592, misc. (St Michael's, Chester).
[66] John Booty, 'Preparation for the Lord's Supper in Elizabethan England', *Anglican Theological Review* 49 (1967).
[67] LAO, 59/1/50.

Plate 2.1   Receiving Communion in the 1570s (Richard Day, *A Booke of Christian Prayers*, London, 1578)

to celebrate the Eucharist, 'this deponent being butt a deacon'. The inhabitants of Bruera Chapelry, according to their deacon of many years, did repair to receive the sacrament. So their feeling of being deprived seems to be genuine: it was not simply a peg upon which to hang dislike of a local clergyman.[68]

Not only did parishioners want Communion services but they often wanted to communicate themselves and in a certain manner. Historians have placed so much emphasis on either the priest who withheld the sacrament from parishioners who knelt, or members of the laity who refused to kneel at all, that the existence of parishioners who insisted on kneeling in the face of clerical criticism has been essentially ignored.[69] William Hieron, for example, had such retrograde persons in his flock, who complained that 'he hath refused to minister the Communion to such as kneele untill he hath lifted them up with his hands & then delivered them the sacrament'. He also railed against those who knelt at the Lord's Prayer.[70] Ralph Kirk's parishioners in Manchester objected to his failure to communicate them with the appointed words and were quite specific about his omissions: 'in the ministeringe of the Sacrament he doth not observe the

[68] CRO, EDC.5/1628, misc. (Bruera Chapel, St Oswald's, Chester). This is one of the very few examples I have found in the period of a 'permanent deacon', outside of institutions such as Oxford and Cambridge colleges.

[69] The rubric directs: 'Then shall the minister receive the communion in both kinds himself . . . and after to the people in their hands kneeling.' *1559 BCP*, pp. 263–4.

[70] LAO, 58/1/5. For a moderate non-Laudian defence of kneeling to receive Communion, see Ephraim Udall, *Communion Comlinesse* (London, 1641), pp. 2–4.

words sett downe in the booke of Common prayer but doth omitt these words, viz. "the body of our lorde Jesus Christ etc.", until he come past "preserve your bodye and soules unto everlastinge lyffe" '.[71] It was the first article in a long list of charges. In the early 1640s the parishioners of Tarporley challenged their rector Nathaniel Lancaster and his curate John Jones, in the church courts, in Quarter Sessions, and by petitioning the king and the House of Lords. In their petition to the king, forty-five subscribers complained that Lancaster and Jones:

Called your petitioners doggs . . . in the pulpit whoe will not be Conformable to his orders, nor will hee suffer any of the parishioners to receave the Communion at the feast of Easter, nether will they according to the Antient order of our Church of England prescribed in the booke of Common prayer.[72]

Lancaster also used an unlawful catechism and refused to admit any (including adults and especially 'ould persons') to Communion who refused to be instructed by his unauthorized catechism. When John Walley petitioned against Lancaster in Quarter Sessions, he lamented the passing of 'many orders and Customs which we have had in former tymes . . . [and are] nowe taken from us'. One of these customs was receiving at the Communion rails: 'the reales before our Communion table are Cast aside'. It would be mistaken, however, to see this as an expression of 'popular Laudianism' as described by Christopher Haigh. A plan for Tarporley church dating from perhaps 1613 shows that the holy table stood behind rails even then, but was free standing in the chancel. The distinction between 'reformed' rails that had existed before the onset of Laudian innovations and 'popish' rails imposed during the Personal Rule was one made by contemporaries in the early 1640s.[73]

There is evidence that administering Communion to the sick at home was still desired after the Reformation and the Prayer Book provided for

---

[71] My quotation marks. CRO, EDC.5/1604, misc. (Manchester).

[72] BL, Add. MS 36913, fol. 140. Unfortunately I have been unable to identify a schedule of subscribers from Tarporley for the Cheshire petition for the Book of Common Prayer. See below, pp. 182–71. However, the presence of a copy of this petition in the Aston Papers indicates some contact between the subscribers and the prime mover of the Cheshire petitions for episcopacy and liturgy. See below, pp. 143–56. See also CRO, QJB 1/6/ 87v–88; CRO, QJF 71/4/23–24; CRO, EDC.5/1639/129. A manuscript copy of Lancaster's sermons survives. CCRO, CR63/2/132. I am grateful to Peter Lake for this reference.

[73] BL, Add. MS 36913, fol. 140; CRO, QJF 71/4/23; Christopher Haigh, 'The Church of England, the Catholics and the people', in *The Reign of Elizabeth I*, ed. Christopher Haigh (London, 1984), p. 219; CRO, EDP.263/5 (Tarporley pew plan); James Hart, 'The House of Lords and the reformation of justice 1640–1643' (University of Cambridge Ph.D., 1985), pp. 99–105, 121, 225–6, 231; see below, pp. 137–41. See also Plate 2.1 for an Elizabethan illustration of receiving communion according to the rubrics of the Book of Common Prayer.

it.[74] On one occasion a number of parishioners at Hemingby sent for Hieron on behalf of a bedridden man who desired 'to reseave the Sacrament for the strengthening of his fayth'. The vicar responded to this request by saying 'let him live by the strength of the laste [Communion], I do not meane to make a popishe matter of it'.[75] The layman John Walley complained that one of the 'many orders and Customs which we have in former tymes' but which were taken away by Nathaniel Lancaster at Tarporley was that there was now 'noe visiting of the sicke, nor any Communion to them'.[76] This was a far cry from what Herbert advised in ministering to the sick or distressed. The country parson 'fails not to afford his best comforts, and rather goes to them than sends for the afflicted, though they can, and otherwise ought to come to him'. In ministering to the sick, Herbert urged the use of auricular confession, admonitions to charitable works, and the administration of the Eucharistic sacrament, stressing how 'comfortable and sovereigne a medicine it is to all sin-sick souls, what strength and joy and peace it administers against all temptations, even to death itself'. In short, Herbert advised nothing not contained within the rubrics themselves.[77] Poor Thomas Marsland's pastor in Chester may have accidentally brought about the abusive visit of Benson, by sending his clerk to enquire whether he needed Communion at home.[78] The behaviour of Hieron and Lancaster was a far cry from the high ideals of George Herbert or their practical workings out in the ministry of Thomas Marsland's parish priest in Chester.

In 1602 the churchwardens of Kimcoate complained that their minister Mr Baily had kept John Paine and several others unjustly from Holy Communion.[79] In what must have been a particularly frustrating episode, John Swan of Bunbury, after exhorting people to prepare for Communion, sent many away without receiving the sacrament: causing 'sundry men

[74] The Order for the Visitation of the Sick also makes provision for confession of sins and spiritual counselling. *1559 BCP*, pp. 300–8. Communion from reserve sacrament was forbidden and the parish priest was expected to celebrate Holy Communion in the house of the sick person. The Prayer Book specifies that there should be others present as a safeguard against private Masses. Hieron's parishioners were aware of the requirements as the bedridden man secured 'a convenient number with him [and] did send to the said Mr hieron [and] asked him for his Counsell'. LAO, 58/1/5. I am grateful to Sean Hughes for keeping me from error on this point. See Charles Neil and J. M. Willoughby, *The Tutorial Prayer Book* (London, 1963), pp. 458–68. I owe this reference and further advice to Gerald Bray and Timothy Hallett.

[75] LAO, 58/1/5. For an Elizabethan illustration of ministering to the sick with Holy Communion, see Plate 2.2.

[76] CRO, QJF 71/4/23 (Tarporley).

[77] Herbert, *A Priest to the Temple*, p. 246; *1559 BCP*, pp. 300–8; Freeman, 'Parish ministry', pp. 246, 421–2.

[78] For a discussion of the Marsland case, see above, pp. 21–2.

[79] LAO, Ch.P/6, fols. 26–7.

Plate 2.2 Sick Communion in the 1570s (Richard Day, *A Booke of Christian Prayers*, London, 1578)

that come prepared to the Communion to depart thence without any at all'.[80] The simple exclusion of parishioners from the sacrament by the minister cannot be taken as an indication of 'puritan' sentiments, however. We must remember that the church courts, the chief arm of the ecclesiastical authorities, frequently imposed excommunication on unrepentant offenders. Exclusion from the sacrament was well within the sphere of conformist action, as the Prayer Book rubrics directed that the minister should admit no one to Communion who was either an 'open and notorious evil liver' or those 'betwixt whom he [the curate] perceiveth malice and hatred to reign, not suffering them to be partakers of the Lord's Table until he know them to be reconciled'. So the purpose of exclusion from Eucharistic fellowship as described in the Prayer Book, and as used by the church courts, was that excommunication would prompt people to amend their lives. Another reason for excommunication was that reception under such conditions as those described in the rubrics would be an occasion of yet more sin for the receiver. He or she would, as the Prayer Book paraphrased Saint Paul: 'eat and drink [their] own damnation, not considering the Lord's body'.[81] There was another side to exclusion, however. The often cited case of Ralph Josselin, the minister of Earls Colne in Essex, may be presented in a different light. Josselin did not celebrate Communion for almost nine years in the 1640s and early 1650s. Like the Lincolnshire minister, William Hieron, he considered the vast majority of his congregation to be unregenerate and therefore unworthy of receiving

---

[80] In 1628, cited in Richardson, *Puritanism*, p. 48.   [81] *1559 BCP*, p. 258.

the sacrament. But Josselin chose to avoid antagonizing his 'flock' by excluding the majority of them from the Lord's Supper (he also feared a tithe strike) by simply not celebrating the Eucharist for nine years. When a Communion service was finally held, he allowed only thirty-four persons to communicate. A similar situation may also have arisen in Wilmslow in Cheshire in the late 1640s. We would do well to be more critical in accepting the godly's assessment of the multitude, as exclusion from Communion apart from occasional individuals, could cause great resentment and anger. If there was indeed any difference between conformist attitudes and the attitudes of the 'hotter sort of protestant' on the reception of the sacrament, it may be found in the size of the franchise.[82] Simply put, to Prayer Book protestants, as in the parable, all were invited but a few disqualified themselves; to the godly, the Supper of the Lamb was a select dining club indeed.[83]

The ministry of word and sacrament: Baptism

The popularity of Baptism, as with all enduring rituals, is based on its ability to function at a variety of levels and to meet a variety of human needs. It is not the suggestion here that the cases discussed below were motivated by purely 'religious' reasons – even if such pure motives have ever been possessed by any group of human beings. Baptism, like the Eucharist, fulfilled important social functions, such as extending the kinship ties of the infant by the use of godparents. Conforming parishioners wanted Baptism, like Holy Communion, to be performed lawfully.[84] The

[82] Ralph Josselin, *The Diary of Ralph Josselin 1616–1683*, ed. Alan MacFarlane (London, 1976), pp. 77, 235–6; Spufford, 'Can we count?', p. 432; see below, pp. 211–12, 214–15. For the way Josselin's account has been used as evidence for the irreligion of the multitude, see Keith Wrightson, *English Society 1580–1680* (London, 1982), pp. 218, 220. But cf. Duffy, 'The godly and the multitude', pp. 37–8. On sacramental theology see E. Brooks Holifield, *The Covenant Sealed: the development of puritan sacramental theology in Old and New England 1570–1720* (New Haven, 1974), pp. 38–73; Nuttall, *Visible Saints*, pp. 134–6.

[83] It is worth noting that the Book of Common Prayer provided clergy with separate Exhortations to Communion to be read aloud in order to help their people prepare themselves to receive the sacrament. It was the clergyman's job to chose the one which reflected more closely the collective spiritual state of his parishioners. Both draw on the rich imagery of St Luke's banquet and St Matthew's wedding feast (Luke 14.15–24; Matthew 22.1–14). Yet the first is directed towards a congregation which is reluctant to receive the sacrament, either because they are over-awed by its sacred character or simply negligent. The second was to be used if the curate detected a far too casual attitude towards receiving Communion on the part of his flock. *1559 BCP*, pp. 254–9.

[84] John Bossy, *Christianity in the West 1400–1700* (Oxford, 1985), p. 115. Conformists tended to value godparents highly and conforming gentry often carefully recorded their names in their diaries. Ralph Houlbrooke, *English Family Life 1576–1716* (Oxford, 1988), p. 103. In the northern part of seventeenth century Gloucestershire, 16 per cent of wills

rector of Folkingham, complained the churchwardens, had by his pro-longed absences caused grief to some parents and exposed their children to danger. While Hoskins was away, parents were forced to walk two miles to the next parish in order to have their infants baptized, 'to their parents grief & danger & parill to their infants'.[85] This same charge was made against Lancaster and Jones in Tarporley: parents of young children complained that they were forced to travel several miles to a neighbouring parish in order to procure infant baptism or baptism with the Prayer Book ceremonies.[86] As 'sermon-gadding' is a well-accepted feature of early modern religion, it is tempting to call this 'font-gadding'.

Parental grief and anger could be great when a child died unbaptized. Conflict of this sort had a long history at Bunbury in Cheshire. In 1611 the vicar Richard Rowe was presented, not only for not making the sign of the cross in baptism, but that he 'refuses to baptise any but on the Sabboth or holy day although it be in danger of death'. In 1626, it was charged against John Swan:

that you have . . . divers times or at least once . . . refused to baptise one or more child or children being in danger of death although you had notice of the same, in so much that they have died without that holy sacrament of baptism from you.[87]

The long-suffering parishioners of Anthony Armitage of Ellington accused him of refusing to baptize a child on a weekday. The child later died unbaptized.

[Armitage] did refuse to baptyse the Child . . . in the weeke daye, being made privey by the said Morley [the father] and other Ancient women of the parishe that the child was very weeke and in perill of death, in so much the child died without Baptysme to the great grefe of the parents.[88]

The refusal to baptize on a weekday is often seen by historians as an indication of puritan sentiments in a minister, reflecting the desire to discourage any magical connotations that the ceremony might have left to their 'semi-pagan' or 'crypto-papist' congregations. The model conformist parson, George Herbert, supported the view that Baptism was ideally a 'public' not a 'private' sacrament.

At Baptism, [the parson] being himselfe in white [wearing a surplice], he requires the presence of all, and baptizeth not willingly, but on Sundayes or great dayes . . . Baptisme being a blessing that the world hath not the like.[89]

---

made before 1640 made some provision for godchildren. Dan Beaver, ' "Sown in dishonour, raised in glory": death, ritual and social organization in northern Gloucestershire, 1590–1690', *Social History* 17:3 (1992), p. 412.

[85] LAO, 69/1/23; 69/1/14; 69/2/15.   [86] CRO, QJF 71/4/24 (Tarporley).

[87] Cited in Richardson, *Puritanism*, p. 28.   [88] LAO, 69/1/23.

[89] Herbert, *A Priest to the Temple*, p. 256.

Indeed, this was the view expressed by the Prayer Book itself:

the people are to be admonished that it is most convenient that Baptism should not be ministered but upon Sundays and other holy days when the most number of people may come together, as well for that the congregation there present may testify the receiving of them that be newly baptized into the number of Christ's Church, as also because in the baptism of infants every man present may be put in remembrance of his own profession made to God in his baptism.[90]

Under such conditions as described concerning Francis Morely's child, Herbert, as a pastor, made exception – as did the Common Prayer Book:

The pastors and curates shall oft admonish the people that they defer not baptism of infants any longer than the Sunday or other holy day next after the child be born, unless upon a great and reasonable cause be declared to the curate, and by him approved. And also they shall warn them, that without great cause and necessity they baptize not children at home in their houses. And when great need shall compel them to do, that then they minister it on this fashion.[91]

Rowe and Swan may well have been acting from one sort of theological conviction. But was Anthony Armitage's action – or lack of it – the result of conviction or negligence? We do not know. According to R. C. Richardson, Baptism to puritan clergy did not convey grace but marked admission to the congregation of Christ. To such clergy, he says, the death of an unbaptized child 'was not a catastrophe'. Based on their depositions, it is clear that to some parents the death of their unbaptized child *was* 'a catastrophe'. Their own words give us reasonable assurance of the 'great grefe of the parents'.[92]

The second Edwardian Prayer Book considerably reduced the ceremonies associated with Baptism. One unsinkable survivor, however, was making the sign of the cross on the forehead of the baptized person: an action which was part of an exorcism before baptism in medieval rites and in the

---

[90] *1559 BCP*, p. 269. The Prayer Book also makes it clear that baptisms should take place as part of the main worship on Sunday: 'And then the godfathers, godmothers, and the people with the children must be ready at the font either immediately after the last Lesson at Morning Prayer, or else immediately after the last Lesson at Evening Prayer, as the curate by his discretion shall appoint.' *1559 BCP*, p. 270.

[91] The Prayer Book also stated that 'if the child which is after this sort baptized do afterward live' he or she should be publicly presented at church and that priest should enquire into the circumstances of the baptism to determine its legality, receive the child into Christ's flock, and examine the godparents and administer their vows to them. *1559 BCP*, pp. 277–81.

[92] LAO, 69/1/23; Richardson, *Puritanism*, p. 28. It has been argued that the combination of high infant mortality and particular views of providential theology meant that parents grieved less at the death of their children than in the modern period. Lawrence Stone, *The Family, Sex and Marriage in England 1500–1800* (London, 1977), pp. 206–15. Arguing against this view are Linda Pollock, *Forgotten Children: parent–child relations from 1500 to 1900* (Cambridge, 1983), pp. 124–8, 134–7, 140–2; Ralph Houlbrooke, *The English Family 1450–1700* (London, 1984), pp. 202–7, 215–22. See also Bossy, *Christianity in the West*, pp. 14–19, 26–34, on Baptism and death.

1549 Book of Common Prayer. The 1552 rite removed it to *after* Baptism, distancing its associations with exorcism but retaining the action.[93] Even so, the ceremony was too much for some protestants and cases where it was omitted are presented in many studies as evidence of puritan conviction.[94] But how are we to regard the fact that other individuals insisted on the rite and went to some lengths to obtain it for their children?[95] William Hieron refused to make the sign of the cross as directed by the Prayer Book and refused the sacrament altogether if the child's parents were not present.[96] The articles against Ralph Kirk indicated that he was 'pestered' repeatedly by his flock to include the sign of the cross in Baptism. Obviously irritated by such a difficult laity, he started to insult the parents: 'he asketh them whether they will have a blacke, a Redd, or blewe, or a headless crosse & such other contemptuous woordes'. He was clearly no wit.[97] The parishioners of Anthony Armitage complained that he omitted the sign of the cross as well as the set prayer that went with the action.

[He] hath not observed the book of Common prayer in baptysing of Children for that he would not sygne them with the signe of the Crosse and use the wordes unto the same appointed untill such tyme as Complaint was made to the ordenarie.[98]

All the deponents in this case, who had information to contribute on this

[93] Duffy, *Stripping of the Altars*, pp. 280–1, 473; F. E. Brightman, *The English Rite: being a synopsis of the sources and revisions of the Book of Common Prayer* (2 vols., London, 1921), ii, pp. 730–1; Diarmaid MacCulloch, *Thomas Cranmer: a life* (New Haven, 1996), pp. 415–16.

[94] Failure to perform, or objections to, the sign of the cross in baptism have been used as evidence of 'puritanism' in, for example, Richardson, *Puritanism*, pp. 26–8, 79–80; Ronald A. Marchant, *The Puritans and the Church Courts in the Diocese of York 1560–1642* (London, 1960), pp. 225–317 *passim*; Sheils, *Puritans*, pp. 68, 69, 78, 84; Patrick Collinson, *The Elizabethan Puritan Movement* (London, 1967), p. 367.

[95] The conformist element in disputes over the sign of the cross in Baptism has been highlighted. Haigh, *Reformation and Resistance*, p. 306. See below, Plate 2.3 for an Elizabethan depiction of Baptism administered according to the rubrics of the Book of Common Prayer.

[96] LAO, 58/1/5.

[97] CRO, EDC.5/1604, misc. (Manchester). But those at Manchester who drafted the articles against Kirk should not be mistaken for the 'ungodly'. For example, they objected to Kirk's practice of baptizing bastards without indicating in the register, and churching their mothers before they had confessed their fault, as well as performing weddings in a common ale house without parental consent and marrying people who were drunk. Curious offences for a 'puritan', as he has been described, though he may have been attempting through his actions to undermine the credibility of these ceremonies. However, whatever Kirk's motives were, some members of his congregation at least, found fault with his actions.

[98] LAO, 69/1/23. 'Then the priest shall make a cross upon the child's forehead, saying. We receive this child into the congregation of Christ's flock, and do sign him with the sign of the cross, in token that hereafter he shall not be ashamed to confess the faith of Christ crucified, and manfully to fight under his banner against sin, the world, and the devil, and to continue Christ's faithful soldier and servant unto his life's end. Amen.' *1559 BCP*, p. 275.

Figure 2.3   Baptism in the 1570s (Richard Day, *A Booke of Christian Prayers*, London, 1578)

particular, confirmed it. Five witnesses confirmed that he was presented for omitting the ceremony two years previously, and since then had used it. Tempers apparently ran hot on this question. A yeoman, Richard Price, related that his child had been one of those the vicar had refused to cross '& this deponent found falt with yt'. Francis Moreley, the father of the child who had died unbaptized, described the disagreement between Armitage and Price more strongly and said they were 'at controversie because Armitage . . . would not signe yt with the signe of the crosse'.[99] Moreley and Price seem to have felt the same as George Herbert, and thought 'the ceremony not only innocent, but reverend'.[100]

Last rites: burial

Attachment to the Prayer Book rites which marked the end, as well as the beginning, of an earthly life can also be discerned in the records of the church courts. Conformists wanted their dead buried properly, reverently and with the rites authorised by the established church. In the various sets of articles preferred by Tarporley parishioners on the eve of the civil war, there were several concerned with proper burial. The rector Nathaniel Lancaster, it was complained, would not 'execute the holy order of the church in Burial'. He would not meet the corpse at the churchyard gate, nor permit mourners to come into the church, nor 'prayer [*sic*] amonge the Congregation that come with the dead' – all ceremonies directed by the

---

[99] LAO, 69/1/14.   [100] Herbert, *A Priest to the Temple*, p. 256.

Prayer Book rubrics. Lancaster even struck a man 'in a most inhumane manner' as he tolled a bell for a passing soul, as had been directed in visitation articles for the diocese.[101] John Swan of Bunbury also refused to meet the corpse at the churchyard gate, or use the Prayer Book rite:

Nether did you meet the said Corps [and bring it] into the churchyard & Church, nor reade the usual prayers and service (appointed for the buriall of the dead) when you went to accompany the same to the grave, but only carried the service booke under your arme.[102]

At the neglected chapelry of Bruera (1628), it was complained that no provision for decent and reverent burial had been made by the vicar of Saint Oswald's.[103]

Improperly conducted funerals were a point of great contention between parishioners at Ellington and Anthony Armitage. They felt that the vicar did not 'performe his dutie in the buriall of the dead'. The Saturday before these articles were preferred, Armitage had gone to Huntingdon at the time arranged for the funeral of Mary Hale. He did not return until dusk, having kept the mourners and 'the whole parish also' apprehensively waiting for two hours inside the church, where they had moved to await their pastor's return. Having returned, Armitage refused to say the service until the people had moved the corpse outside – though by then it was so late 'that he could scarse see to read praiers', complained one parishioner. Once hustled out of the church (according to the Prayer Book the burial service should begin outside in the churchyard), the frustrated mourners apparently decided to bury their neighbour properly and carried her body all the way back to the churchyard gate where, again according to the Prayer

---

[101] CRO, QJF 71/4/24 (Tarporley). See the *Visitation Articles* for Chester diocese of Richard Vaughan (1604, no. 30) and Bishop Thomas Morton (1617, no. 40). In both cases – as Kenneth Parker has established with sabbath observances – the issues involved were not black and white but a matter of degree. Bishop Vaughan enquired whether bells were tolled for sick persons 'to move the people to pray for the sicke person, especially in the greater Townes, when the sick person dwelleth neere unto the Church'. But Vaughan specified that there should be only one short peal just before burial and just after. Concern about 'superstitious' as opposed to 'religious' ringing was also made by Bishop Morton. The 'passing bell' should be tolled when any Christian person is sick 'and like to die, as ought to be'. After death the bishop was concerned with what he called 'superfluous' ringing. Morton also prohibited the burning of candles over the corpse 'after daylight', praying for the dead at cross roads and 'superstitious' use of towels, psalms, 'metwands or memories of idolatry at burials'. Bishop Bridgeman's articles make no mention of bell ringing at funerals but of their use to summon people to divine service (1637, no. 10). There was obviously no clear policy on the use of bells. Parker, *English Sabbath, passim*. See also *Hierurgia Anglicana*, ii, pp. 195–6; Claire Gittings, *Death, Burial and the Individual in Early Modern England* (London, 1984), pp. 133–5; Fincham, *Visitation Articles*, i, pp. 17, 47, 76, 85, 104, 182, 207; Beaver, 'Sown in dishonour', p. 405.

[102] CRO, EDC.5/1630, misc. (Bunbury). There were sentences of scripture appointed to be read while the body was carried from the church yard gate to the grave. *1559 BCP*, p. 309.

[103] CRO, EDC.5/1628, misc. (Bruera Chapelry, St Oswald's, Chester).

Book's rubrics, the officiating priest was required to meet the corpse. But Armitage, the subscribers lamented, refused at any time to meet the body at the churchyard gate and the burial of their neighbour Mary Hale was no exception.[104]

The evidence for Armitage's shocking behaviour at the funeral of Mary Hale is largely supported in the depositions of witnesses made in this case. Several deponents claimed that once the vicar finally arrived, he refused to 'read praiers' before the actual interment; probably meaning that he left out the part of the service which was to be read by the priest as the body was moved from the churchyard gate to the grave.[105] The tailor John Tall responded '*nescit deponere*' to the incident of Mary Hale's burial, but he related a similar experience: '*nescit deponere*, saving that this deponent at a time goeing to the said Mr Armitage & desyring him to meete the corps of one Richard Gates his wife late of Ellington deceased, he the said Armitage refused to doe yt.'[106] Parishioners also saw the duty of presiding at holy burial as one most desirably exercised by someone in holy orders; indeed this is what the Prayer Book directed. John Tall had such additional cause for grievance with Armitage, besides the vicar's treatment of his neighbour's deceased wife. Tall's child and the child of a neighbour Christopher Brit were buried by the parish clerk, even though Armitage was resident in Ellington: '[Armitage] being at home his selfe, but [he] appointed the Clarke of the parishe to put them into the Earth very undecently and undutifully, contrarie to the order of the booke of Common praier.'[107] The curate who had served Macclesfield faithfully for thirty years was dismissed

---

[104] LAO, 69/1/24. 'The priest meeting the corpse at the church stile, shall say or else the priests and clerks shall sing, and so go either unto the church, or toward the grave "I am the resurrection and the life".' *1559 BCP*, p. 309.

[105] *1559 BCP*, p. 309. This is the 'I am the resurrection and the life' passage from John 11, I Timothy 6, and Job 1, 19. Scandalous clerical behaviour at funerals is not limited to the seventeenth century. In the 1980s an Anglican bishop received a report concerning the conduct of one of the priests in his diocese at the burial of a respected local figure.

A relative said: 'The Vicar was in a bad way. He failed to remember the deceased's name. He staggered down the road in front of the coffin. He forgot to sing the hymn. He had to cling to the graveside to keep himself upright. Finally, during his oration, the Vicar said that although the dead man had five strapping sons and one strapping great wench of a daughter, he had himself been a thin, ugly, old man.' Interviewed at his rectory [the vicar], an ex-boxer, said: 'The church has no room for perfect people.'

Private Eye (21 September 1984).

[106] LAO, 69/2/15.

[107] LAO, 69/1/23; see also LAO, 69/2/14. Several decades earlier, the churchwardens of Apethorpe, Northamptonshire complained that they had no curate to perform clerical offices, so that 'for want of a priest, they have been compelled to bury the dead bodies themselves', neither had they service read, nor sermons preached. Cited in Sheils, *Puritans*, p. 91. Recusants, on the other hand, sometimes tried to avoid burial for their deceased by the lawful minister. Richardson, *Puritanism*, p. 171.

without authority by the mayor, and for no apparent reason. To add insult to injury, he was replaced by one Francis Jackson who was not only a nonconformist but was not even, it was claimed, ordained. Jackson had taken upon himself to 'exercise the office of the minister or Curate there, wherein the said Francis Jackson being a meer layman, hath taken upon him publiquely to read divine service [and] to burie the dead'. Jackson was not thought a 'sufficient' (their word) minister by the inhabitants of Macclesfield, because he was not in holy orders.[108]

The intensity of feeling revealed by these cases invite some reflection on the impact of the Reformation on attitudes towards death and dying in our period. It is argued that by destroying the vast and resonant symbolic structures that accompanied dying and surrounded the departed, the Reformers broke the bond the living felt for the dead. The rejection of purgatory continued this process at an intellectual level. Ritually and theologically the living were cut adrift from the dead:

Whereas medieval Catholics had believed that God would let souls linger in Purgatory if no masses were said for them, the Protestant doctrine meant that each generation could be indifferent to the spiritual fate of its predecessor . . . This implied an altogether more atomistic conception of the relationship in which members of society stood to each other.[109]

Eamon Duffy has powerfully described both the 'culture' of medieval death and its destruction. For him the greatest moment of discontinuity with the past in the Prayer Book rite lay not in its use of the vernacular or the forsaking of many popular rituals but in the abandoning of any direct form of speech to the deceased in the liturgy. The conforming cleric was directed to address the mourners at the point where in the past he would have addressed the corpse:

Forasmuch as it hath pleased Almighty God of his great mercy to take unto himself the soul of our dear brother here departed: we therefore commit his body to the ground, earth to earth, ashes to ashes, dust to dust, in sure and certain hope of the resurrection to eternal life, through our Lord Jesus Christ, who shall change our vile body that it may be like to his glorious body, according to the mighty working, where he is able to subdue all things to himself.[110]

Immediately following, perhaps to drive the point home that there was nothing the living could 'do' for the dead, or further that any more 'works' were required of the dead – that they were indeed 'at rest' – these verses

[108] CRO, EDC.5/1604, misc. (Macclesfield).
[109] Keith Thomas, *Religion and the Decline of Magic* (New York, 1971), p. 603. See also Ralph Houlbrooke, 'Death, church and family in England between the late fifteenth and early eighteenth centuries', in *Death, Ritual and Bereavement*, ed. Ralph Houlbrooke (London, 1989), p. 36.
[110] *1559 BCP*, p. 310.

from Revelation were to be said or sung: 'I heard a voice from heaven saying unto me, Write, From henceforth blessed are the dead which die in the Lord. Even so saith the Spirit, that they rest from their labours' (Revelation 14.13).[111] Duffy observes: 'Here the dead person is spoken not to, but about, as one no longer here, but precisely as departed: the boundaries of human community have been redrawn.'[112] Cranmer's biographer agrees, though expresses it more positively: the 'Church had surrendered its power over death back to the Lord of life and death in heaven: a move of perfect theological consistency'.[113] One might argue that the process Archbishop Cranmer began reached its logical conclusion in the middle of the seventeenth century when parliament's *Directory of Public Worship* replaced the hated Prayer Book and banned *any* funeral ceremonies and prayers:

When any person departeth this life, let the dead body, upon the day of Buriall, be decently attended from the house to the place appointed for publique Buriall, and there immediately interred, without any Ceremony . . . [ceremonies] are in no way beneficiall to the dead . . . and have proved [in] many wayes hurtful to the living.[114]

It has been argued that this attitude was not only 'puritan' but was becoming standard among many 'orthodox Anglicans' as well in the first half of the seventeenth century.[115]

But believers, lay or ordained, are rarely theologically consistent. There is very little evidence in churchwardens' accounts from the 1640s, for example, that anyone ever bought the *Directory*. In fact, there is more evidence in the 1640s and 1650s for the continued clandestine use of Common Prayer than even for the purchase of its intended replacement in the parishes, at least in the West Country and East Anglia.[116]

While allowing for the discontinuities of the sixteenth-century Reformation, it is worth paying attention to what people did to prepare for death and how the living regarded the dead and public burial in the post-Reformation period. In seventeenth-century Gloucestershire, bequests in wills left money to pay for food and drink for friends and relatives at the testator's funeral. One such testator left 20s, 'which my will is shall be

---

[111] Ibid.   [112] Duffy, *Stripping of the Altars*, pp. 301–76, 475.

[113] MacCulloch, *Cranmer*, pp. 509, 614.

[114] Cited in David E. Stannard, *The Puritan Way of Death: a study in religion, culture, and social change* (New York, 1977), p. 101.

[115] Ibid., pp. 103–4.

[116] John Morrill, 'The church in England, 1642–9', in *Reactions to the English Civil War 1642–1649*, ed. John Morrill (London, 1982), pp. 93, 104–8. I am grateful to Tim Wales for first bringing this to my attention in reference to Norfolk. Support for the Prayer Book seems to have played a partial role in the Clubman rising in south-west England. David Underdown, 'The chalk and the cheese: contrasts among the English clubmen', *P&P 85* (1979), pp. 35–7. See above, pp. 6–8.

bestowed upon a supper and wine to make merry withal'.[117] Attendance at funerals appears to have been high: they were occasions of almsgiving, of eating and drinking, of community, as well as a time to grieve. Purgatory may have slipped out of the mind of the collective culture but the dead had not done so entirely. Wills echo the language of 1 Corinthians 15, the reading appointed by the Prayer Book, which speaks of those who have died as not so much departed as asleep and awaiting the resurrection of the dead. Spouses left instructions to be buried in the same grave as their partners and the occasional testator asserted his or her assurance of being 'raised up' on the last day when the community of the elect would be rejoined.[118] Towards the end of Elizabeth's reign, Richard Hooker observed:

The end of funeral duties is first to show that love toward the party deceased which nature requireth; then to do him that honour which is fit both generally for man and particularly for the quality of his person; last of all to testify the care which the Church hath to comfort the living and the hope which we all have concerning the resurrection of the dead.[119]

Questions of Hooker's place in the mainstream of late sixteenth-century protestant theology aside, he seems to articulate the spirituality behind the cases discussed above.[120]

Streamlined though the Prayer Book funeral rite was compared to its medieval predecessors, to the preciser sort of protestant it provided the laity with too much, not too little. Their objections worked at two levels. Theologically, the rite was offensive, because it implied that *any* deceased person might be 'asleep in the Lord'. The Prayer Book liturgy was simply too inclusive for the godly. At the level of practice as well, they noted with disapproval the enthusiasm of their neighbours for Prayer Book ceremonies and the survival of folk customs at funerals. The separatist Henry Barrow saw little evidence of indifference towards the dead among his neighbours in the late sixteenth century:

Likewise also, as these priests visit and housel [sic] their sick by this book [of Common Prayer], so do they in like manner bury their dead by the same book. The priest meeting the corpse at the church stile, in white array (his ministering vesture), with a solemn song, or else reading aloud certain of their fragments of Scripture, and so carry the corpse either to the grave, made in their holy cemetery and

[117] Cited in Beaver, 'Sown in dishonour', p. 402, see also pp. 401–4.
[118] Ibid., pp. 401–8. See p. 393 for seventeenth-century wills conveying a sense of death as part of a pilgrimage. See also above, p. 25.
[119] From Book V of Richard Hooker's *Lawes* in J. Robert Wright, ed., *Prayer Book Spirituality* (New York, 1989), p. 418.
[120] On the subject of Hooker's place within English theology, see Sean Hughes, 'Richard Hooker's theology of grace, the sacraments and tradition in context' (University of Cambridge Ph.D. in progress).

hallowed churchyard, or else (if he be a rich man) carry his body into the church, each where his dirge and trental [a series of thirty Masses for the dead and the payment made for them – a deliberately unflattering comparison] is read over him after they have taken off the holy covering cloth and the linen crosses wherewith the corpse is dressed, until it come unto the churchyard or church, into that holy ground (lest sprites in the meantime should carry it away). The priest there pronounceth, that Almighty God hath taken the soule of that their brother or sister unto him, be he heretick, witch, conjurer, and desiring to meet him with joy in the resurrection, etc., who after he hath cast on the first shovel full of earth in his due time, with his due words, committing earth to earth, ashes to ashes, etc. Then may they boldly proceed to cover him, whiles the priest also proceedeth to read over his holy gear and say his Pater-noster (which fitteth all assaies) and his other prayers over the corpse.[121]

Equally the authors of the earlier *A View of Popish Abuses* saw much about which to complain:

We say nothing of the threefold peale, bicause that is rather licensed by Injuction than commaunded in their booke [of Common Prayer]; nor of their straunge mourning by chaunging theyr garments, which, if it be not hipocritical, yet it is superstitious and heathenish, bicause it is used onely of custome, nor of buriall sermons, whiche are put in place of trentalles, wherout spring many abuses, and therfore in the best reformed churches, are removed. As for the superstitions used bothe in Countrey and Citie for the place of buryall, which way they must lie, how they must be fetched to churche, the minister meeting them at churche stile with surplesse, with a companye of greedie clarks, that a crosse, white or blacke, must be set upon the deade corpes, that breade muste be given to the poore, and offrings in buryall time used, and cakes sent abrode to frendes, bycause these are rather used for custome and superstition than by the authoritie of the boke . . . But great charge will hardly bring the least good thing to passe, and therfore all is let alone, and the people as blinde and as ignorante as ever they were.[122]

The *detailed* list of ritual transgressions which the parishioners of Tarporley complained of for burials of kin and neighbours by their minister; the dogged persistence with which the parishioners of Ellington carried about the body of their dead neighbour Mary Hale in an attempt to secure the lawful and conformable ceremonies due her; the anger and grief expressed by the fathers, John Tall and Christopher Brit, over the irreverent inter-ments of their children; or the concern at Macclesfield that Christian burial was an office best performed by a clerk in holy orders; suggests that they failed to hold what Keith Thomas has called an 'altogether more atomistic conception' of their relationships to each other in the family and the village community.[123] It also suggests that Collinson's assessment that Prayer Book services 'neither transcended or challenged rustic existence' was too

[121] Barrow, *A Brief Discoverie*, p. 458.
[122] *A View of Popish Abuses*, ed. Frere and Douglas, p. 9.
[123] Thomas, *Religion*, p. 603.

severe.[124] Rather, Richard Hooker's conviction that funerals were 'to show that love toward the party deceased which nature requireth' may be an articulate expression of a widely held belief.[125]

The churching of women

Surviving the dangerous work of childbirth was marked by an authorised service of the Church of England with its roots deep in medieval practice and the Jewish faith. Opposition to the 'Thanksgiving of Women after Childbirth', also known as the churching of women, became, according to Keith Thomas, one of the surest signs of puritanism, whether from clergy or laity, before the civil war.[126] More recently, David Cressy has argued persuasively for the popularity of the service – especially among women – even in the face of objections from the godly.[127] From the diocese of Lincoln comes a case which complicates this problem of historical interpretation even more.

The wife of Richard Ravens[128] of Elstow, Bedfordshire was presented in the archdeacon's court for having 'churched herself'. Upon the failure of the priest to appear at the time appointed for her thanksgiving, she read the first part of the service from the Book of Common Prayer (presumably Psalm 121) 'openlie' in the church and considered herself quite satisfactorily churched, for she went home and apparently did not seek out the incumbent in order to go through the service again with him.[129] W. J. Sheils has related how the minister Humphrey Wildblood in the diocese of Peterborough was confronted by a group of angry women who demanded to be churched after childbirth. The godly Wildblood refused to hold the service.[130] But what are we to do with Ravens' wife or her conformist

---

[124] Collinson, *Religion of Protestants*, p. 105.
[125] Cited in Wright, *Prayer Book Spirituality*, p. 418.
[126] Thomas, *Religion*, p. 61. Sheils, *Puritans*, p. 63 is inclined to agree with this view. Richardson's *Puritanism*, however, stresses that in the diocese of Chester, cases involving opposition to churching are both 'ambiguous and uncommon' and are not sure signs of non-conformist sentiments (pp. 113–14). The situation probably is ambiguous. The wife of the notable puritan Robert Woodford was churched at home by the curate of their parish church, All Saints, Northampton. She was churched again at home a year later by another curate. New College, Oxford MS 9502 (10 September 1639, 13 September 1640). I am grateful to John Fielding for this reference.
[127] David Cressy, 'Purification, thanksgiving and the churching of women in Post-Reformation England', *P&P* 141 (1993). It is worth noting that the ceremony continued in parts of Lutheran Europe. Susan C. Karant-Nunn, 'Churching', in *Oxford Encyclopedia of the Reformation*, ed. Hans Hillerbrand (4 vols., Oxford, 1996), i, pp. 331–2.
[128] Or possibly Rowens. I am grateful to Diarmaid MacCulloch for his palaeographic help.
[129] For the order of service of 'The thanksgiving of women after childbirth, commonly called the churching of women' see *1559 BCP*, pp. 314–15.
[130] Sheils, *Puritans*, p. 63.

sisters in Peterborough? Her minister Mr Bird was cited to appear in the archdeacon's court after she was dismissed with a monition. A fortnight later Bird was proceeded against for neglecting his cure and failing altogether to say divine service on a recent Sunday. It is impossible to tell whether Bird's failure to church Ravens' wife was a form of non-conformity or plain neglect. Either way, however, a lay woman who was able to read was determined after childbirth to have the comfort of the lawful liturgy.[131] The element of purification in the churching service was a concern to both the rite's supporters and detractors: '[the] Churching of women after childbirthe, smelleth of Jewishe purification' observed one critic. However, the high rate of mortality for women in childbirth – estimated as high as 18 per cent in Terling in Essex for example – perhaps made the 'thanksgiving' element of the rite more immediate for women than for the male clerics who both defended and degraded the ceremony.[132]

The ministry of word and sacrament: preaching

A striking feature of conformity to emerge from some of these cases is the strong desire expressed to have services according to the Prayer Book juxtaposed with the desire to have a preaching minister. The flock of the bowling parson, John Robotham, complained that he failed to provide quarterly sermons or read from the Book of Homilies.[133] The inhabitants of Risely in Bedfordshire exhibited articles against their vicar John Thompson to Bishop Chaderton in 1603. With patience almost certainly unrivalled in pastoral history, they complained of neglect over twenty-five years in Thompson's refusal to preach or to say divine service according to the Book of Common Prayer.

[Our] desire was & is to have the word of god preached amongst us trulie . . . according to the lawe for that Case made & provided . . . [and] he hath not

---

[131] BRO, ABC. 5, pp. 247, 254. The parishioners at Tarporley also complained that their rector Nathaniel Lancaster refused to church women: '[he refuses to] Church or consecrate any women: but absolutely and inhumanely refuses to performe that holly duty'. BL, Add. MS 36913, fol. 140. The custom of wearing a veil at churchings continued after the Reformation, but with disagreement as to whether it was required by law or was simply more seemly and a matter left to local custom or the ordinary. *Hierurgia Anglicana*, i, pp. 219–22. In Southwark, the ceremony was highly popular and 'acceptance . . . was widespread across the social structure'. Boulton, *Neighbourhood*, pp. 276–9.

[132] I owe this insight to Susan Amussen. *A View of Popish Abuses*, p. 28; see also Barrow, *A Brief Discoverie*, pp. 462–4 [128–29]. Wrightson and Levine, *Poverty and Piety*, pp. 58–9. See Hooker's defence of the ceremony in *Lawes*, V, lxxiv, 1–4. Churching continued in the disruptions of the civil war. Houlbrooke, *English Family Life*, pp. 110–11. For an overview of the issues, see Cressy, 'Purification'.

[133] LAO, 69/1/7.

observed the booke of Common prayer in doinge divine service on Sundaies and weekdayes.[134]

But perhaps even more impressive than their patience was the apparent survival of the desire for the Prayer Book and preaching after a quarter century of neglect – illustrating an alternative response to that of some Northamptonshire parishioners which led Sheils to conclude that 'frustration at the hands of a negligent or absentee pastor could direct the pious towards puritanism'.[135] The more worldly parishioners at Fenstanton contrasted their parson's failure to 'read prayers' and preach with their willingness to pay their tithes.[136] While it has been admitted that the godly did not have a monopoly in setting a high value on the pulpit, the implications have not always been taken seriously.[137]

A picture of a cowed and timid laity uncritically lapping up their minister's words, provided they came from the pulpit, does not seem to hold true any more than the antithesis often created between Prayer Book protestantism and preaching religion. The parishioners of Hemingby were doubtless little pleased by what they heard from the pulpit:

> In [William Hieron's] sermons he vaineth he maye speake at his pleasure and no man dare controwle him. And he liketh his parishioners to the theeves in geole saying that divers of them sit before him with continences then suche as are going to hanging . . . and in the Pulpitt [he] devideth his auditorie thus, havinge one or towe that he thinketh assent his novelties. He pointeth unto them, I speake to you regenerat, and then turning his Bodie conntenance and hand to the rest of the parishioners he sayeth, I speake to you also.

Hieron also used the pulpit to attack any critics in his congregation which, considering he reckoned only one or two amongst his flock regenerate, must have been considerable in number. Johnson, the clerk, and others suggested to him that the opinions of grave and learned divines be sought out over the points on which they differed, which argues for a temperate, critical, and theologically aware laity. Hieron responded from the pulpit: 'He raseth in the next sermon against all learned men, authorities and degrees . . . saing that there is not above I or besides himselfe that are godlye, zealous ministers in the countye of Lincoln.'[138] The minister Mr Baily of Kimcoate, Leicestershire, was far less subtle in the abuse he hurled at his flock. He did, however, become somewhat more 'theological' when he was in the pulpit. In everyday conversation he called parishioners 'dogg, Jade . . . Carrion, skurvey, paramanger, skurvy companion and such like'. When he mounted the pulpit, he still called individuals 'Swyne & dogge'

---

[134] LAO, 58/2/66.　　　[135] Shiels, *Puritans*, p. 133.　　　[136] LAO, 58/2/80.

[137] For example, Paul Seaver, *The Puritan Lectureships: the politics of religious dissent 1560–1662* (Stanford, 1970), pp. 4–5, 15–16.

[138] LAO, 58/1/5.

but added a little more theological sophistication with 'reprobate, bankroute, hyprocryte etc.'.[139] The churchwardens who presented him were obviously not uncritical of his behaviour in the pulpit. Equally the parishioners of Folkingham in Lincolnshire followed the article complaining of their rector's failure to celebrate Communion, with another concerning his failure to preach more than once in the past year. When Hoskins did preach, however, it was not very satisfactory, as he stood in the pulpit wearing a sword and dagger and holding a cudgel in his hand, 'to the great terror and offence of the said parishioners and Scandall of the mynistry'.[140]

But the sermon was not at the centre of everyone's spirituality, even when it was done more skilfully than at Folkingham. In Tudor Lancashire, for example, the ineffectiveness of sermons alone as instruments of protestant evangelism has been described.[141] By the early seventeenth century – several decades before Archbishop Laud's attempt to replace afternoon preaching with catechizing – criticism was voiced of preaching ministers who neglected to catechize. As Ian Green had noted, 'What is . . . interesting is that so many authors [of catechisms] took pains to stress that sermons had little value without proper preparation of the congregation beforehand.'[142] In the diocese of Lincoln a complaint was made in 1578 against the minister at Barton in Bedfordshire who never read the set *Homilies* but only preached sermons made up by himself.[143] In 1617, William Dennys of St John's parish in Bedford was presented for going out of church in service time. He responded by saying that his father lay ill in nearby Kempston and that he and his wife did not leave church to visit him until the liturgical part of Sunday observance had finished and the sermon had begun. It is notable that he considered this a perfectly reasonable line of defence. Dennys' preference for liturgy over preaching ought to be kept in mind as much as the more commonly referred to practice of sermon gadding.[144] The 1604 petitioners to the bishop of Chester on behalf of their dismissed curate Thomas Shert were unimpressed with their mayor's reason for his dismissal after thirty years of ministry in Macclesfield: 'the said maior wold not give his consent . . . but only because the said Thomas

---

[139] LAO, Ch. P/6, fol. 27.   [140] LAO, 69/1/19.
[141] Haigh, *Reformation and Resistance*, pp. 175, 307.
[142] Ian Green, '"For children in yeeres and children in understanding": the emergence of the English Catechism under Elizabeth and the early Stuarts', *JEH* 37:3 (1986), pp. 416–17.
[143] The preference for the printed Homilies in place of home-grown sermons raises interesting questions about *bad* preaching practice; that is, not clergy who failed to preach but ones who did not do it very well. BRO, ABC 3, p. 7.
[144] BRO, ABC 5. pp. 205, 221. An example in the Lincoln diocese was that of Richard Robins of Ampthill who was presented for not frequenting his own church and going to hear sermons at neighbouring parishes. BRO, ABC 5, p. 116.

Shert was not a preaching minister'. No one had complained before of lacking a preaching minister 'some few humorists late sprung up there only accepted'. Shert, they claimed, was 'a minister lawfully admitted, of sufficient learning & a mann of good lyffe & conversacon & hath approved him selfe by all the tyme afforesaid to the good lyking of all or most of the Inhabitants of this said chapellary'. To some clergy and laity, the hour or so spent in the pulpit was the crowning point of the week. To others, the more mundane daily tasks of parochial ministry were what earned credibility and respect in the long run. Given that dependent chapelries were more vulnerable to neglect, Shert's commitment to the people of Macclesfield, although he was no preacher, appears to have been valued and regarded.[145]

Too much, perhaps, has been made of Richard Baxter's complaint about the failure of conforming ministers to preach. The sermon and even 'lectureships' were held close to the bosom of the established Church of England, as Collinson has emphasized.[146] George Herbert, who was to conformity what Baxter has come to be to dissent, felt that preaching was one of the chief obligations of the country parson:

The countrey parson preacheth constantly; the pulpit is his joy and his throne . . . and with particularizing of his speech now to the younger sort then to the elder, now to the poor, and now to the rich – 'This is for you, and this is for you'; for particulars ever touch and awake more than generalls . . . Sometimes he tells them stories and sayings of others, according as his text invites him; for them also men head, and remember better then exhortations; which, though earnest, yet often dy with the sermon, especially with country people, which are thick and heavy, and hard to raise to a point of zeal and fervency, and need a mountaine of fire to kindle them; but stories and sayings they will well remember . . . but the character of his sermon is holiness; he is not witty, or learned, or eloquent, but holy.[147]

The puritan lecturer at Bunbury in Cheshire, Samuel Torshell, warned against losing perspective on the preaching ministry:

It is hypocrisy . . . that makes men all for hearing, which is to some the easy duty, while they know not how to frame their spirits to prayer, which requires the labour of the soul, the exercise of humiliation and brokeness of spirit.[148]

[145] CRO, EDC.5/1604, misc. (Macclesfield); Richardson, 'Puritanism', pp. 46–7.
[146] Richard Baxter, *Reliquiae Baxterianae: or Mr. Richard Baxter's narrative of the most memorable passages of his life and times* (London, 1696), pp. 1–3; Patrick Collinson, 'Lectures by combination: structures and characteristics of church life in 17th-century England' (first published in 1975) in Patrick Collinson, *Godly People: essays on English Protestantism and Puritanism* (London, 1982), pp. 473–4. And again in his 'The Birkbeck Lectures' delivered in the University of Cambridge, Michaelmas Term, 1981. 'Exercises' by definition did not only concern non-conformists – Bishop Chaderton of Lincoln was a promoter of them. Hajzyk, 'The church in Lincolnshire', pp. 51–2.
[147] Herbert, *A Priest to the Temple*, pp. 226–7.
[148] Samuel Torshell, *The Hypocrite Discovered and Cured* (1644), cited in Richardson, *Puritanism*, p. 45.

Nor, really, should the juxtaposition of sacraments and preaching surprise us too much. Herbert emphasized the 'great confusion' the country parson was in at the Eucharist, 'being not only to receive God, but to break and administer Him', as well as his duty to preach.[149] John Donne, preaching in the evening on Easter Day 1625, described the complementary nature of sacrament and sermon:

Before that, saies [Christ], that is, before the resurrection of the body, there shall be another resurrection, a spirituall resurrection of the soule from sin; but that shall be, by ordinary meanes, by Preaching and Sacraments, and it shall be accomplished every day; but fix not upon that, determin not your thoughts upon that, marvaile not at that, make that no cause of extraordinary wonder, but make it ordinary to you, feele it, and finde the effect thereof in your soules, as often as you heare, as often as you receive, and thereby provide for another resurrection.[150]

Donne too failed to see an antithesis between altar and pulpit. It may be that the antithesis exists more in the mind of the modern ecclesiastical historian than it did in the mind of the early modern parishioner or even divine.

Catechizing

As well as preaching and attendance at divine service, catechizing was felt by the authorities to have an important role in maintaining the people in true religion. This feeling seems to have been shared by clergy, lay patrons, and ordinary parishioners as well – although when young people failed to come to be catechized, the clergy almost always blamed their parents, and parents almost always blamed the clergy. Teenage servants appear to have been the most difficult group to persuade to attend.[151] When William Welby proceeded against the vicar of Whaplode in 1638, he included Holden's failure to catechize for half an hour on Sundays and holy days as well as such things as his failure to 'say or singe' the Common Prayer reverently.[152] Most of the deponents in the case of Anthony Armitage

---

[149] Herbert, *A Priest to the Temple*, p. 256.

[150] Donne, *Sermons*, vi, p. 264. Bishop Williams of Lincoln in his visitation articles of 1635, urged the people of his diocese not to make 'a schisme or division (as it were) between the use of public prayer and preaching'. Cited in Hajzyk, 'The church in Lincolnshire', p. 113.

[151] Susan Wright, 'Catechism, confirmation, and communion: the role of the young in the post-Reformation Church', *Parish, Church and People: local studies in lay religion 1350–1750*, ed. S. J. Wright (London, 1988), pp. 204–8. Jane Freeman has emphasized that catechizing can be seen as an aspect of pastoral care, rather than as a 'safe' alternative to preaching. Freeman, 'Parish ministry', pp. 211–14. For an Elizabethan illustration of catechizing, see Plate 2.4. Ian Green's important new study of this significant area appeared as I was completing this book: *The Christian's ABC: catechisms and catechizing in England c.1530–1740* (Oxford, 1996), see esp. ch. 3.

[152] LAO, 62/2/16.

Figure 2.4 Catechizing in the 1570s (Richard Day, *A Booke of Christian Prayers*, London, 1578)

confirmed that he had not catechized in the last two or three years. Two of the deponents, however, thought he had catechized some youths once in that space of time, probably on the evening before they received Holy Communion. John Pickering related how he sought out Armitage on Palm Sunday afternoon and found the clergyman occupied in the ale house: 'I then told him that yt was fitter for him to be about catechizing of the youth there rather than to be in the alehouse at that time.' The previous Sunday, Pickering continued, he had stopped Armitage after Evening Prayer and had asked him to take greater pains in catechizing, claiming that the request 'came from the most parte of the parishe.' Armitage replied that he had been forbidden to catechize by Mr Throckmorton, a parishioner. When asked why, Pickering related that Armitage claimed:

that whereas he had used at the Christening of their children to call the gossips [godparents] first and to examine them upon the articles of their believe [belief] and other points of religion, the said Mr Throckmorton found himselfe greeved therewith and did forbid him.[153]

Armitage's behaviour at this baptism sounds like the complaints over his bell ringing – when he did perform a ministerial duty, it was in such a way as to attempt to undermine the practice.[154]

In Tarporley, the rector did not neglect catechizing, but used an unauthorized text. Anyone, whether old or young, who refused to be instructed in this way, was refused Communion by Lancaster and Jones.[155] Elizabethan and early Stuart England saw a massive growth in the number

153 LAO, 69/2/15.   154 See above, pp. 43–4.
155 BL, Add. MS 36913, fol. 140; CRO, QJB 1/6/87v.

of catechisms available for use. Legally, however, the texts authorized for use remained the Prayer Book catechism – the most frequently produced based on its Edwardian predecessor – and a much expanded version written by the Elizabethan dean of Saint Paul's, Alexander Nowells. What is striking about the great flood of catechisms is that they were overwhelmingly orthodox and uncontroversial. They were produced largely because the Prayer Book catechism was considered too short and Dean Nowell's too long and complex for ordinary parishioners. Ian Green is surely right to emphasize that unauthorized catechisms were often produced by conforming clergy who wished to meet a need in the educational market.[156]

MIXED MOTIVES

Interpreting the cases brought against a clergyman by his parishioners is further complicated by the unstable element of the minister's personality. The type of evidence presented here would have been used more commonly in a study of puritanism, placing the emphasis on the minister's non-conformity rather than on the wishes of at least some of his neighbours to have lawful services. However, we need to note that many of the clergy involved were not model 'puritans'.

John Robotham, the bowling parson of Manton, apparently fought protracted law suits with his parishioners. To blur the line even more between sacred and profane, he served summonses on individuals he quarrelled with while they were receiving Holy Communion, 'to the great griefe of such communicants'. Robotham himself claimed that the conformist proceedings against him were actually pursued through the enmity of one of his tenants.[157] William Holden of Whaplode, who was presented for his non-conformity by the patron William Welby, not only altered the Welby family pew, but placed his own wife in it as well.[158] William Hieron made no secret of his view that the congregation at Hemingby was largely unregenerate, but he was also suspected of concealing alms from the poor.[159] The parishioners of John Thompson who complained of his failure to preach and say divine service according to the Prayer Book also complained that Thompson lived like 'eny man in his parishe' following markets and fairs looking for bargains in the horse trade.[160]

---

[156] Green, 'English catechism', pp. 398–400, 402–11. Richardson cites a number of examples from the diocese of Chester of complaints for failure to use the *authorized* catechism in the Prayer Book, yet he still concludes that, 'the catechism, then, was of central importance in the organisation and practice of puritanism'. Richardson, *Puritanism*, pp. 38–9. It does not logically follow that 'puritans' were the complainants, as my examples show. See also Haigh, 'Church of England', pp. 209–13.

[157] LAO, 69/1/7.   [158] LAO, 62/2/16.   [159] LAO, 58/1/5.   [160] LAO, 58/2/66.

There is much evidence for a long history of clerical non-conformity in Bunbury, Cheshire. Frequent charges of failing to wear the surplice go back to the lecturer Christopher Harvey in 1601.[161] But there appears to have been considerable personal animosity between one parishioner and the vicar John Swan, which came to a head in 1634. Swan had been vicar since 1616, and had been proceeded against in the consistory court for a range of offences, including failing to wear a surplice and hold weekday services, irreverent conduct of funerals, and administering Communion to people standing and sitting, as well as to non-parishioners. Conflict came to a head in 1634 when a local layman George Spurstowe, 'esquire', brought a case against Swan in the consistory court. Spurstowe 'a Constant Communicant of the blessed and holy sacrament' complained that Swan had given him Communion in an irreverent manner:

For you [Swan] serve Rich and poore, poore and Rich, one with another without Respect, the begger with the gentleman & all together . . . knowing it would discontent Mr Spurstowe aforesaid . . . [you] served him with beggers, and amongst beggers, and them before him at one and the same tyme, and being yet pleased with him have administered the Cup with little or no wyne in it, and after he hath received it you have frequently snatched it away from him againe, to the dislike and disgrace of the said Mr Spurstowe and the Disturbance of the Congregation then and there assembled.

Spurstowe also claimed he had been insulted from the pulpit. The personal difficulties between vicar and layman had become so great that the bishop had intervened earlier, ordering that Spurstowe should only receive Communion from the parish lecturer Samuel Torshell. This does appear to be a case of personal animosity wrapped up in a religious guise, for Torshell, the parish lecturer, was a noted puritan divine and the author of a number of theological tracts. The most comprehensive indictment against Swan – the one taken up by Spurstowe – seems to be based on a considerable history of mutual loathing.[162]

Anthony Armitage, of whom we have heard a good deal already, was a

---

[161] Richardson, 'Puritanism', p. 40. Harvey's son however, also Christopher, was a poet and devoted imitator of George Herbert. His collection of poems in praise of the Church of England, *The Synagogue* was frequently appended to editions of Herbert's *The Temple* after 1640. He shared Herbert's enthusiasms but not his skill: 'What! Prayer by th' book? and common?/ Yes; why not?' From 'The Book of Common Prayer' in Christopher Harvey, *Complete Poems*, ed. A. B. Grosart (printed privately, 1874); see above, p. 30; G. Ormerod, *History of Cheshire*, revised by G. Helsby (3 vols., London, 1882), ii, p. 260; Barbara Lewalski, *Protestant Poetics and the Seventeenth Century Religious Lyric* (Princeton, 1979), pp. 283, 427.

[162] CRO, EDC.5/1634/34; see also CRO, EDC.5/1630 misc. (Bunbury); CRO, EDC.5/1631/ 27; Richardson, 'Puritanism', p. 40; Ormerod, *Cheshire*, ii, p. 261; e.g. Richardson, *Puritanism*, p. 194; William Urwick, *Historical Sketches of Nonconformity in the County Palatine of Chester* (London, 1864), pp. 144–7.

railer and quarreller. Common fame reported that he had committed adultery with the wife of one of his parishioners. He spent far too much time in alehouses – including one Palm Sunday when he should have been catechizing the youth. It was said that he was often drunk; a report that is both confirmed and denied by two neighbouring vicars. Robert Clark, the vicar of Spaldwick, told how when he was accompanying Armitage home after a drinking session at the bishop's residence at Buckden, he 'seemed to be very merrie, using some unseemly speeches', Armitage fell into a dispute with some of the bishop's men, calling them knaves, at which point Clark decided that 'this deponent thinketh the said Mr Armitage had then taken too much drinke'. However, Henry Marret, the vicar of Doddington, admitted to being a frequent drinking companion of Armitage's, but claimed that he never knew him to be drunk 'but sometimes verie merrie & pleasant'.[163] Perhaps Marret was in no fit condition to judge.

In all these cases, the evidence against the clergymen is complicated by their openly secular, or socially offensive behaviour. We are on slightly surer ground in the case of Mr Hall, the curate of Husbands Bosworth, who did not apparently commit adultery, play bowls, frequent alehouses, misappropriate alms, or even engage in the horse trade. His parishioners seem to have had more purely 'religious' reasons for their dislike.[164]

The verbal insults and abuses which the godly Mr Baily hurled from the pulpit at his Kimcoate parishioners in 1602 have already been discussed. He also removed the holy table from the church and converted it to his own use. Here, however, we have additional evidence for Baily's difficult personality and his churchwardens' conformity. At the direction of John Chippingdale, commissary and official in the archdeaconry of Leicester,[165] two other Leicestershire clergymen, John Higginson and Francis White, investigated the allegations against Baily. They largely confirmed both the charges against the cleric and the conformity of the parishioners. The people of Kimcoate were, they said, 'tractable and well affected to religion and have heretofore lived peaceable and in much kindness intreated other honest ministers that lived amongst them'. The only blame, therefore, that the investigating vicars could offer for the great strife at Kimcoate was laid squarely on the shoulders of the minister.

Therefore why Mr Bailie should growe to theis extremities with them, we cannot conceive but onlie that wee doubte he is to well conceited of himself and inclined to faction . . . wee thinke yt easyer for you to remove him [than] to reforme him in the rest.[166]

Higginson and White, with congregations of their own, were probably

[163] LAO, 69/1/24; LAO, 69/2/15.   [164] LAO, 58/2/67.
[165] Hajzyk, 'Church in Lincolnshire', p. 23.   [166] LAO, Ch.P/6, fol. 26.

painfully acquainted with the tensions and trials of parochial ministry. It is all the more striking, therefore, that Baily received such a thoroughly negative report from his fellow clergy on his treatment of his flock.[167]

Of the rector of Tarporley, Nathaniel Lancaster, and his curate, John Jones, we have heard a good deal already. Two things are particularly striking about this case. First, the sheer determination exhibited by some parishioners as they pursued the pair through a number of legal channels, both ecclesiastical and civil. Second, how little time it took after the rector's arrival in 1638 for conflict to erupt. There is, in fact, little evidence to support the assertion that clerical puritanism was present in Tarporley as early as 1578. Tarporley was one of a group of Cheshire churches that agreed to be 'beautified' by Bishop Lloyd's order in the early seventeenth century.[168] The picture of Tarporley as a reasonably conforming parish is strengthened by the speed with which conflict came to a head after Lancaster's arrival in 1638 (a consistory court case against Jones occurred the following year) and the vigorous and informed nature with which it was pursued.

In 1639, a parishioner, Stephen Fisher, brought a suit against John Jones for his non-conformity and offensive behaviour. The curate omitted many lawful ceremonies, such as reading services on Wednesdays and Fridays and eves of holy days, and the Ten Commandments in the Communion service. Further, despite having been specifically asked by the churchwardens to wear the surplice, he refused to conform.[169] Jones spread his offensive practices to neighbouring parishes, as about this time he also preached at nearby Harthill:

I am perswaded that the reading of Common prayer hath beene the meanes of sending many souls into hell. That the booke of Common prayer doth stinke in the nostraills of god. That reading of Common prayers is as bad or worse than the mumbling of the masse upon beades.[170]

Such strong opinions were obviously offensive to some, as the churchwarden and parson at Harthill reported Jones' remarks. It also indicates that Jones was not a man likely to compromise.

---

[167] For a discussion of the idea of an *esprit de corps* among the clergy see Rosemary O'Day, *The English Clergy: the emergence and consolidation of a profession* (Leicester, 1979), pp. 160–1. It is a profession given to considerable rivalry as well.

[168] This assertion of the antiquarian Ormerod, repeated by Richardson, seems to be based on two Elizabethan clerics calling themselves a 'minister of god's word' in the register and a refusal by one couple in 1611 to respect the sacramental ministry of the curate because he was 'a reading minister' – that is, not a preaching minister. Ormerod, *Cheshire*, ii, p. 236; Richardson, 'Puritanism', pp. 22–3; Richardson, *Puritanism*, pp. 99–100; *VCH Chester*, iii, p. 28.

[169] CRO, EDC.5/1639/129. See above, p. 45.

[170] BL, Add. MS 36913, fol. 137.

In 1640, the year following the consistory case, parishioners brought their quarrel with their clergy to the secular courts. They may have felt that the Quarter Sessions had greater influence particularly in the months between the Short and Long Parliaments. Lancaster and Jones were accused not only of failing to use the Prayer Book, but the rector was charged with committing an assault in the church.[171] Even the civil war did not interrupt the legal proceedings at Tarporley – indeed it may have heightened them and given them a new urgency – as concern for the survival of the Church of England had been growing since the early days of the Long Parliament. Two petitions went forward to the JPs in 1643, listing a comprehensive catalogue of the clerical pair's non-conformity: no sign of the cross in Baptism; no observance of holy days, fasting days, passion week or Christmas; no visiting of the sick and providing Communion; improperly conducted funerals; rails and crosses broken down. As already noted, Lancaster actually struck a parishioner who was tolling for the dead. Lancaster and Jones were also accused of dabbling in politics and stirring up trouble between the king and the people. In a petition to the king, possibly from this time, forty-five parishioners again catalogued a long record of non-conformity, but also described Lancaster's co-operation with the parliamentarian leader Sir William Brereton and his refusal to read any royalist declarations. In 1643, Lancaster's parsonage was plundered by troops loyal to the king. We might think, however, that national issues were secondary to the Tarporley parishioners, as they came quite far down on their lists. Their grievances were heightened by the fact the living was worth about £200 a year and they felt they could do much better for the money. In fact, they threatened to withhold their tithes.[172] In the end, Lancaster held on to his living until his death, which came conveniently in January 1661, shortly after the restoration of the monarchy. He was followed by Rowland Sherrad, who may have been more to the liking of the conformist parishioners at Tarporley. Sherrad was a favourite of Robert Sanderson and had received episcopal ordination during the Commonwealth.[173] Jones, not surprisingly given his weakness for offensive outbursts from the pulpit, was in trouble with the classis in the 1650s while he was curate at Marple. After the Restoration he became a dissenter.[174]

---

[171] The articles of indictment appear to be lost but this information comes from the order book and in fact concerns some misconduct among two jurors in the case (14 July 1640). CRO, QJB 1/6/87v–88.

[172] CRO, QJF 71/4/23–24; BL, Add. MS 36913, fols. 139v–40; BL, Thomason Tracts E.84(37), *The Unfaithfullness of Cavaliers* (London, 1643).

[173] AC; Ormerod, *Cheshire*, ii, p. 236.

[174] *Calamy Revised*; Urwick, *Historical Sketches*, pp. 54–8, 319–20, 484–5.

The Tarporley case is noteworthy in a number of ways. Although Jones could be theologically offensive in the pulpit and Lancaster struck a man while he tried to toll for the dead, and they both supported the parliamentary cause in the 1640s, there is no hint of any of the usual accusations of evil living against the two clerics. In fact, the political offences, judging from the fact they are listed after liturgical and pastoral offences of various sorts, would appear not to have been uppermost in the minds of the promoters of the actions against them. Also, the parishioners pursued Lancaster and Jones through almost every available legal channel open to them: the ecclesiastical courts, Quarter Sessions, and petitioning the king. They were determined, and their determination was motivated primarily by concern to have the lawful ceremonies and ministry of the Church of England.

An additional question raised by consideration of the minister's personality is, which straw of misbehaviour broke the laity's back? Was non-conformity more likely to be winked at by churchwardens if it was practised by someone of relatively upright life? Certainly, when the ruling orthodoxy changed, conforming ministers in Lincolnshire, who were proceeded against in the 1640s by the Committee for Scandalous Ministers for their support of episcopacy and the Common Prayer Book, were also frequently described as quarrellers, adulterers, and drunkards. One could argue, therefore, that 'Anglicanism' was also likely to be winked at in the 1640s and 1650s if the practitioner was an upright man, and that 'puritanism' gave offence in the period under discussion in the case of a negligent minister or scandalous liver. On the other hand, both sets of objections could simply reflect a standard 'conceit' of the age: that is, one threw in a list of moral misdeeds simply to strengthen the case against a particular clergyman.[175] It is also impossible to tell in many of the cases cited in this chapter, whether the priest's non-conformity was the result of conviction or of negligence and laziness. In other words, the evidence for clerical 'puritanism' is very often the *failure* to act, not what an individual actually *did*. Green is surely right to lament the 'slender or

---

[175] Conformist activist John Werden, writing on Good Friday 1641 to Sir Thomas Aston concerning the actions of a Cheshire clergyman, put the man's non-conformity into a moral framework:

One Borden a Notoryous, infamous Adultrer beinge the Curate there [Wybunbury] would not reade the absolution, nor the letany, he did not nor ever doth reade either proper lessons or psalmes for the day & the psalmes he does reade [*sic*] he would not reade them out of the service booke but the bible. And in the Creede (which is most observable) when he should have said I beleeve in the holy Ghost, the holy Catholick Church, he read [*sic*] I beleeve there is a Catholique Church.

BL, Add. MS 36914, fols. 214v–15.

incomplete' evidence often used as proof of the presence of 'puritan sentiments'.[176]

EVIDENCE OF SUPPORT FOR CONFORMING CLERGY

Conformity was obviously felt by some parishioners to be congenial. The absence of it was also grounds for appeal against a difficult minister or neighbour, who was possibly also personally disliked. But it would be wrong to push the evidence to demonstrate more than a general feeling that the lawful worship as laid down in the Book of Common Prayer was desirable, without other supporting evidence of real conviction. Such evidence can be inferred in a number of cases. The support shown by the inhabitants of Macclesfield for the man who had been their conforming curate for over thirty years and his replacement by a non-conformist has already been discussed. They petitioned the bishop of Chester in 1604 and it appears that Shert was reinstated, for he died listed as 'curate at Macclesfield' in the parish register in 1610.[177] The cases of the happily named Benedict Grace, curate of Brill in Buckinghamshire, and Thomas Adams, curate of Northill in Bedfordshire, demonstrate the point. They were very different men from Robotham, Holden, Thompson, Armitage, and Baily. In these cases, the only personal feelings the parishioners exhibited were in their favour. All we lack is conclusive evidence that the desire for conformity was the only motive lying behind the public support given by their parishes.

Benedict Grace had fallen foul of his patron, Sir John Dynham,[178] and this struggle caused a testimonial to be written to Bishop John Williams of Lincoln. Grace's troubles, in the opinion of the forty signatories, were caused 'only out of malice and ill will'. He had apparently taken the part of his flock in a legal dispute with Sir John involving common rights in the forest of Bernwood. There would, of course, probably be no quicker way to win popular affection. When the testimonial letter dated 25 January 1629 was written, the curate was paying the price for defending the interests of his humbler parishioners. The letter written by his parishioners to plead his cause described Grace as 'our neighboure and minister' and chose to praise him for his godly living, pastoral diligence and conformity. '[A] man well devoted and of Civell and honest carriage in life and conversacon and

---

[176] Green, 'Career prospects', pp. 112, 112n. 168; J. W. F. Hill, 'Royalist clergy of Lincoln-shire', *Lincolnshire Architectural and Archaeological Society, Reports and Papers*, new ser., 2 (1940), pp. 34–127 *passim*. The problem of negligent clergy is discussed in Haigh, *Reformation and Resistance*, pp. 237, 241, 243–4.

[177] Earwaker, *East Cheshire*, ii, p. 503; Ormerod, *Cheshire*, iii, p. 752.

[178] Foster, *The State of the Church*, p. 272.

conformable to the Church haveing a good and provident care in the discharging of his ministerial funcion.' So far from being 'anti-clerical', the signatories at Brill were so inclined towards support (at least of this particular clergyman) that they included a striking clause concerning Grace's small stipend and desired that it be increased to a 'reasonable competente Spirituall mayntenance'. At any rate, the Brill parishioners had strong views on this matter, basing their request for a reasonable stipend for their minister in order that 'his sole and chiefe care and studdie may be to breake unto us the breade of spiritual foode'.[179] Economically depressed clergy were often forced to augment their meagre incomes by seeking additional sources of funds which, not surprisingly, led to the neglect of some ministerial duties. In 1603, the curate's stipend at Brill was only £10 per annum.[180] However, it is only reasonable to admit that in Benedict Grace's case the very desirable objective put to the bishop, that his 'sole and chiefe care . . . may be to breake unto us the breade of spiritual foode', may have been tinctured, in their minds, with support for a priest who, in turn, had upheld their rights of common.

The affection and esteem which the inhabitants of Northill held for Thomas Adams was similar to that which the people of Brill had for Grace.[181] In their case there is no hint of any 'secular' motivation lying behind their support. Yet, if we are using extreme caution, we cannot be absolutely sure that genuine conviction lies behind their words on his behalf, even though these words are not the conventional ones of a letter testimonial. The parishioners of Northill had plenty of experience with non-conformity before fifty-four of them subscribed their names to a letter to Bishop William Barlow in February 1611. In the 1585 episcopal visitation of the diocese, the then curate Anthony Hodget was presented for not wearing a surplice or reading the litany. He was cited to appear again before Bishop Chaderton in October 1604, again for not wearing the

---

[179] LAO, L.T.& D., 1628/9 (Benedict Grace).

[180] Foster, *The State of the Church*, p. 264.

[181] It is possible that this is the same Thomas Adams (d. 1653) who later became a noted preacher. Nothing is known of the more noted Thomas Adams before he was mentioned as 'a preacher of the Gospel' at Willington, Bedfordshire in 1612. *DNB*. If this is the same man, the Northill letter may have been produced in 1611 to ease the sacked curate's path to the post of preacher at Willington. The sermons of the noted preacher Thomas Adams, place him in that elastic middle ground of early Stuart religion. A defender of both episcopacy and the Book of Common Prayer, Adams sermons are also full of the conventional anti-popery of his day. Sears McGee suggests that his silence in print from the 1620s onwards may reflect, despite his articulate apologetics for conformity, how out of step he was with the new Laudian orthodoxies. I am grateful to Sears McGee for suggesting to me this possible connection and for a copy of his unpublished paper on which these comments are based. Sears McGee, 'Puritanism in Jacobean London?': The case of Thomas Adams' which was read at the Pacific Coast Conference on British Studies, 23–24 March 1984.

surplice, and then in the following December when he refused to subscribe *ex anima* to the Three Articles. Less than a fortnight later, Chaderton suspended Hodget from the execution of his office and a new minister, Thomas Adams, was licensed to the curacy at the end of March 1605.[182]

Over the next six years Thomas Adams apparently spared little as he laboured in the vineyard. When the patronage of the living of Northill changed from one Richard Browne (who had presented both Adams and Hodget) to a Mr Osbourne, Adams was discharged from his curacy, 'without any . . . iust desert procuring the same to our knowledge'. At this point Adams reaped the personal fruits of his years of pastoral dedication among the people at Northill – and the flock rallied around its shepherd. The parishioners wrote their letter testimonial to the bishop at Adams' request, but they seem to have needed little prodding:

We therefore the Inhabitants of Norrell [*sic*] do humbly beseech your Lordship to accept this our testimony, whereby we doe assure your Lordship that during the space of foure yeares and upwards (which time he hath continued with us) he hath behaved himselfe soberly in his conversation, painfully in his calling, lovingly amongst his neighbours, conformable to the orders of the Church, and in all respects befittingly to his vocation.

The people of Northill were not going to let the patron remove a man they liked without a fight, especially one who fulfilled his priestly duties more than adequately.[183]

Even if extreme caution suggests that unknown motives and personal affection could have influenced the parishioners of Northill on Thomas Adams' behalf, in the case of John Maltby, of Grainthorpe in Lincolnshire, such caution seems too far-fetched. Unlike the testimonials for Grace and Adams, there was no stain of conflict between a patron and the minister in the letters written on behalf of Maltby. We first encounter him as parish clerk at Grainthorpe in the late 1580s. Five ministers of nearby parishes wrote to Bishop Wickam to commend his 'honest lyffe and Conversation'. The parish of Grainthorpe was populous: it had 340 communicants in 1603,[184] and yet had no 'allowed preacher to feed the lords Flocke'. They commended Maltby, who was himself bearing the letter to Lincoln, to be appointed curate there. Maltby was not a graduate at a time when the proportion of university educated men in the ministry was on the increase.[185] According to his referees he overcame this handicap, even on a tiny income, by buying many improving books 'the better to further him in

[182] Foster, *The State of the Church*, pp. xxx, cxviii, 364, 366; Stuart Barton Babbage, *Puritanism and Richard Bancroft* (London, 1962), pp. 220–32.
[183] LAO, L.T.& D., 1611 (Thomas Adams).
[184] Foster, *The State of the Church*, p. 323.
[185] Hajzyk, 'The church in Lincolnshire', p. 47; O'Day, *The English Clergy*, pp. 135–6.

his vocation [and] he is not inferier [in learning] to many of his bretheren'. Taking a familiar, but still powerful metaphor, Maltby's referees pushed home their point:

Knowing that nothing is so deare to youre Lordship as to see the lords vineyard plenished with good woorkmen and his harvest reaped with faithfull and painfull labours, we are more embolden to desyre youre good lordship to send out him [*sic*] amongst others. Whereby we hope that both his Floocke shalbe better Feed and him selfe better. . . [able] to proceed in his studie and godly exercise.

Apparently Bishop Wickham found Maltby and his testimonial letter satisfactory, for he was appointed curate at Grainthorpe around 1588.[186]

John Maltby received such accolades not only from his clerical peers, but from members of the laity as well. In 1605, after over twenty-five years in a curacy, he was presented to the benefice of Aby, Lincolnshire by the patron, Lord Willoughby. His parishioners at Grainthorpe wrote to the bishop (now William Chaderton) to certify his conformity and good behaviour, which was the usual procedure when a minister was presented to a new living. What was not usual was the enthusiasm, warmth, and distinct stamp of Maltby's testimonial.

In pastoral care, John Maltby was not only dedicated but successful as a promoter of harmony among his flock and in ministering to the poor. 'A greate freinde to the poore, & very charitable to all: A painfull peace maker amongst all men . . . In comforting the sick both poore & Riche [he is] very paynfull: doinge alwaies what good he can to all: hurting none, worthy to be beloved, and is in our Towne & countrye very well beloved.' In his personal life, he was a model to imitate: 'Cyvill & sober in his conversation, wyse in government, of very honest lyfe & carriage'. Like the ministers who over a quarter of a century before had commended Maltby for the curacy of Grainthorpe, the parishioners were impressed by his learning – all the more so for having been accumulated on a tiny budget.

[And] of his small stypend [he] hath even from his necessary manteynance mayd such husbandly sparinge for provyding good bookes the better to further him in his vocation, that he therein is not inferiour to many of his callinge, and dothe soe well bestow himselfe in his studye with greate laboure & painfull Industrie in & amongst his books, whereby wee receyve greate comforte daylie from him.

The people at Grainthorpe also soundly praised their curate for his conformity to the Book of Common Prayer and to the authorized worship of the established church. 'A very diligent observer of the booke of Common prayer, and all other decent, reverent & comelie ceremonies

---

[186] LAO, L.T.& D., 1591–6 (John Maltby). Undated but possibly misdated by the Lincoln-shire Archives Office. Maltby is first mentioned as curate at Grainthorpe in 1588. Foster, *The State of the Church*, pp. 12–13.

continued, ordeyned & appoynted in our Church of England by Anthenti-
call [sic] Authoritye.' It is noteworthy that although they referred to
Maltby as a 'fruitfull mynister & preacher', they made no other specific
reference to his role as preacher – a role which his clerical referees had
made such a point of twenty-five years before – and which we have often
seen juxtaposed with an emphasis on a minister's liturgical conformity.[187]
Both his pastoral commitment and his liturgical conformity seem to have
been what mattered to his Grainthorpe supporters. Maltby enjoyed approbation from a cross-section of the community, as over a third of his
supporters could not sign their names, but made their marks.[188]

THE SOCIAL SPREAD OF CONFORMITY

Any assertions at this stage concerning the social spread of religious
conformity are necessarily very impressionistic and incomplete.[189] From
the cases cited here, however, there emerge hints that conformity had a
fairly wide appeal socially and drew supporters from both the humble and
the substantial.[190] The Whaplode minister William Holden was proceeded
against by the local squire, Sir William Welby.[191] Twenty-one parishioners
of James Smith of King's Sutton certified his current conformity in 1605;
two described themselves as 'gentlemen' and three others as churchwardens
or sidesmen; a total of twelve, or over half, made marks rather than
signed.[192] Of the four promoters of the action against Francis Smith of
Fenstanton (the minister who took their tithes but provided nothing in
return) all four made their marks.[193] There are no marks among the forty-
five subscribers to the petition to the king against Lancaster and Jones but
this is probably because the surviving manuscript is a copy.[194] Thirteen of
the deponents against Anthony Armitage of Ellington were spread widely
across the social spectrum. They included one gentleman, one yeoman, two
labourers (one of whom was a woman), three tailors, one draper, three
husbandmen, one 'sheerman', and one whose occupation was unstated.
Seven or eight of them, again over half, made their marks.[195]

---

[187] Clive Holmes, *Seventeenth Century Lincolnshire* (Lincoln, 1980), p. 61. Clive Holmes is
right to describe Maltby as a 'paragon', yet he cites only his pastoral dedication and
learning and makes no mention of him as a 'diligent observer of the booke of Common
Prayer'.

[188] LAO, L.T.& D., 1605 (John Maltby).

[189] The question will be taken up again in greater depth in Chapter 5.

[190] That dissent was capable of crossing economic and social boundaries and drew men and
women from both the humble and the wealthy, at least in Cambridgeshire, has been
shown. Spufford, *Contrasting Communities*, pp. 299–315.

[191] LAO, 62/2/1; Foster, *The State of the Church*, p. 312.

[192] LAO, L.T.& D., 1605 (James Smith).   [193] LAO, 58/2/80.

[194] BL, Add. MS 36913, fol. 141.   [195] LAO, 69/2/15.

In the cases in which there were no personal or moral charges against the priest by his parishioners, and either personal liking or positive desire for conformity was involved, the social status of the deponents was not given. However, the inability of large numbers of them to sign their names indicates that support was drawn from a wide social spectrum.[196] Of the fifty-four signatories to the letter on behalf of Thomas Adams in 1611, twenty-nine, again over half, made marks. Of John Maltby's thirty-one supporters in 1605, eleven, or over a third, could not sign their names.[197] I am placing emphasis here on the number of marks to signatures for two reasons. The first is that the presence of marks is a good sign of authenticity. Second, that the presence of marks is evidence of a reasonable social spread. This is not to suggest that those who could not sign their names were easy targets for 'social control' by their betters. The inability to sign one's name in the seventeenth century was by no means a sure indication of the inability to read. There is a strong likelihood that many individuals who put their marks to a letter testimonial could, in fact, read and approve of it.[198]

CONCLUSION: CONFORMITY AND THE CHURCH COURTS

The conclusions arrived at in this chapter about conformity as a legitimate – albeit neglected – dimension of English early modern religion are necessarily impressionistic. For all the richness of the ecclesiastical courts as an historical source, it is impossible to be 'scientific' about the conclusions drawn from them. They always provide a distorted picture of the relationship between priests and parishioners, as cases arise only when co-operation and consensus have broken down. In that way they are a source always tinged with pastoral failure. This is as true for using the church courts as evidence for 'puritanism' and the activities of the 'godly', as for conformity and Prayer Book protestantism.

A different type of evidence for conformist sentiments, however, comes not from the courts but from the petitions produced by counties in support of episcopacy and the Book of Common Prayer on the eve of the civil war. The Cheshire petitions for the established church, in fact, are among five of the thirty-odd petitions of this nature to survive with the names of the thousands of signatories still attached.[199] These petitions and the people

---

[196] David Cressy, *Literacy and the Social Order: reading and writing in Tudor and Stuart England* (Cambridge, 1980), ch. 6, *passim*.

[197] LAO, L.T.& D., 1611 (Thomas Adams); LAO, L.T.& D., 1605 (John Maltby).

[198] Margaret Spufford, *Small Books and Pleasant Histories: popular fiction and its readership in seventeenth-century England* (London, 1981), pp. 19–44.

[199] HLRO, Main Papers, HL [27] February 1640/1 and 20 December 1641.

behind them will now be analyzed in depth. First they will be analyzed from a national perspective, discussing their theological and ideological concerns. Second, the process by which two such petitions were organized in one particular county community, Cheshire will be discussed. The views of the leading lay protagonist, Sir Thomas Aston, will be explored. Lastly, the vexed issue of the social spread of conformity will be re-examined by a socio-economic and religious profile of five Cheshire communities which subscribed for the Book of Common Prayer and lawful ceremonies of the church. With evidence taken from these widely varied sources, we will be somewhat closer to filling the historiographical black hole caused by the overemphasis on puritan studies. We will be closer also to understanding the feeling of one conforming Elizabethan when he said, 'thus do we spend the sabeoth daie in good and godlie exercises, all doone in the vulgar tong, that each one present may heare and understand the same'.[200]

[200] William Harrison, *The Description of England*, ed. Georges Edelen (Washington, DC, 1968, 1994), p. 34.

The rhetoric of conformity, c. 1640–1642

Though for no other cause, yet for this; that posterity may know we have not loosely through silence permitted things to pass away as in a dream, there shall be for men's information extant thus much concerning the present state of the Church of God established amongst us, and their careful endeavour which would have upheld the same.[1]

Episcopacy and Lyturgie are both legally planted, [and] at this time both violently assaulted: The question is, whether the battery, or the defense, be stronger, the one side charges furiously, the other suffers silently.[2]

> But not a Reformation so
> As to reform were to o'erthrow;
> Like watches by unskillful men
> Disjointed, and set ill again.[3]

PROVINCIAL PETITIONS FOR THE NATIONAL CHURCH

Sir Thomas Aston of Cheshire reflected a few months before the outbreak of the civil war that episcopacy and the Book of Common Prayer were being undermined, not simply by those who were actively hostile to them, but by the very silence of those who most valued these two distinctive features of the reformed Church of England. The rise of Laudianism in the 1630s on one hand,[4] and the open hostility to the religious settlement expressed by many in the Long Parliament on the other, combined to force conformists to speak out in defence of the lawful liturgy and episcopal

---

[1] Richard Hooker, _Of the Lawes of Ecclesiastical Polity_, ed. John Keble (3 vols., Oxford, 1874) (Preface, i.1), i, p. 125.

[2] Sir Thomas Aston, 'The Collector to the Reader', _A Collection of Sundry Petitions Presented to the King's Most Excellent Majestie_ (London, 1642).

[3] Richard Lovelace, 'To Lucasta, from Prison', in _Ben Jonson and the Cavalier Poets_, ed. Hugh Maclean (New York, 1974), p. 313.

[4] For a working and workable definition of 'Laudianism' see Peter Lake, 'The Laudian style: order, uniformity and the pursuit of the beauty of holiness', in _The Early Stuart Church 1603–1642_, ed. Kenneth Fincham (London, 1993).

polity. Conformists by their nature made reluctant activists, as Aston was only too aware, and he hoped by the publication of his tract *A Collection of Sundry Petitions* (1642) to show the strength of the 'silent majority' and to encourage other convinced conformists who had not spoken out, to do so. The increasingly polarized nature of the country in the critical years of 1641–42 and the growing perception that the church was 'in danger' forced – arguably for the first time – diverse members of the laity to construct coherent and public defences of the Church of England. It is not unjust to say that in the vast industry of early Stuart historiography, the convictions represented by these petitions have not been given their due place.[5]

Equally problematic in achieving an understanding of religious views represented in these petitions has been the error of equating any criticism of Thorough with 'puritanism' or presbyterianism – or indeed any expressions of anti-puritanism for 'Laudianism'.[6] The petitions considered in detail in this chapter present a more nuanced picture. They reveal a collection of interests from most parts of the country eager to construct a spirited defence of the established church. Delighted to see the practitioners of Thorough punished for a decade of liturgical innovation and 'prelacy' inflicted on the 'pure Church of Elizabeth and James', the petitioners sought to reclaim and defend the two main bulwarks of the church, episcopacy and the Book of Common Prayer, from the taint of Laudianism. In their view these two great treasures of the English settlement had lost credibility due to the policies of the Personal Rule and now stood in danger from fellow protestants who could not distinguish the abuses of Laudianism from the essential soundness of the lawful liturgy and episcopal government. The petitions represent the views of those who sought to

[5] Important exceptions include Anthony Fletcher, *The Outbreak of the English Civil War* (London, 1981) and a series of important articles by John Morrill, 'The attack on the Church of England in the Long Parliament, 1640–42', in *History, Society and the Churches: essays in honour of Owen Chadwick*, ed. Derek Beales and Geoffrey Best (Cambridge, 1985); 'The church in England 1642–9', in *Reactions to the English Civil War 1642–1649*, ed. John Morrill (London, 1982); 'The religious context of the English Civil War', *TRHS*, 5th ser., 34 (1984). This chapter examines the common and contrasting themes of these 1641–42 petitions for the established church. Readers who would like more detailed information, with each petition and its context discussed in turn, should see my 'Approaches to the study of religious conformity in late Elizabethan and early Stuart England: with special reference to Cheshire and the diocese of Lincoln' (University of Cambridge Ph.D., 1991), pp. 99–196.

[6] For example G. W. Bernard, 'The Church of England, c. 1529–c. 1642', *History* 75 (1990), pp. 199, 200, where he suggests that these petitions 'betray little sign that petitioners thought themselves to be defending any church other than that of the 1630s'. See also Kevin Sharpe, *The Personal Rule of Charles I* (New Haven, 1992), esp. ch. 6; Christopher Haigh, 'The Church of England, the Catholics, and the people', in *The Reign of Elizabeth I*, ed. C. Haigh (London, 1984), pp. 206–9.

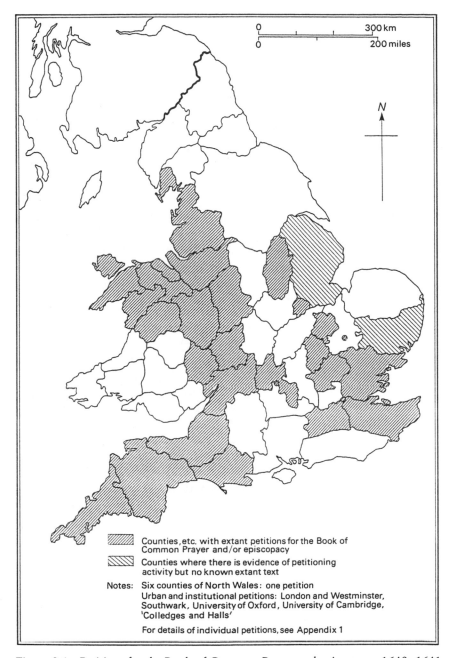

Figure 3.1   Petitions for the Book of Common Prayer and episcopacy, 1640–1641

distinguish between the purge and punishment of corrupt individuals within the church and the wholesale deconstruction of the English religious settlement. By treating the content of these provincial petitions seriously, an important dimension is added to the lively debate about the degree of innovation represented by the Laudians. Anthony Milton persuasively modifies the view of the Laudians as innovators in doctrinal matters, showing that they differed from 'Jacobean' conformists at times more in degree than in substance. But one can push the envelope too far, however, even in the Church of England. It is sobering to bear in mind in the midst of the heady debates over soteriological matters (Arminianism, sacerdotalism and so on), that issues of liturgical innovation and the 'style' of *episkopé* exercised, were among the areas of chief concern articulated in the provinces.[7] This chapter is a detailed analysis of nearly thirty petitions produced in defence of the established church in 1641–42.[8] It forms the first of three chapters which will explore religious conformity by concentrating on the petitions produced in support of the Book of Common Prayer and episcopacy in the early 1640s. The focus will move from a concern with broader themes, as presented in the rhetoric of conformist petitions from around the country, to an examination of active conformity in one county, Cheshire (Chapter 4), and conclude with a detailed analysis of the social distribution of subscribers for the Prayer Book in Cheshire and the factors which may have influenced the rate of subscription (Chapter 5).

Obviously these petitions share a great deal of common ground and concerns. Nevertheless one of their most striking features is their individuality. Sir Thomas Aston aptly named his *Collection of Sundry Petitions*: 'sundry' they are, yet bound by a set of common concerns. Their textual individuality suggests strongly that they were products of the localities – in sharp contrast to many Root and Branch petitions which were often formulaic and followed a lead set by powerful interests in Westminster.[9] The royalist poet Abraham Cowley remarked ironically on the textual similarities of many petitions against the church.

---

[7] Anthony Milton, *Catholic and Reformed: the Roman and Protestant churches in English Protestant thought, 1600–1640* (Cambridge, 1995). See also Nicholas Tyacke, *Anti-Calvinists: the rise of English Arminianism c. 1590–1640* (Oxford, 1987); Peter White *Predestination, Policy and Polemic: conflict and consensus in the English church from the Reformation to the Civil War* (Cambridge, 1992); N. Tyacke and P. White, 'Debate: the rise of Arminianism reconsidered', *P&P* 115 (1987). These are tricky waters indeed. For help see Kenneth Fincham, 'Introduction', in *The Early Stuart Church 1603–1642*, ed. K. Fincham (London, 1993), *passim* and Peter Lake, 'The Laudian style', also in *The Early Stuart Church*, pp. 161–3.

[8] See Figure 3.1; Appendix 1.

[9] Fletcher, *Outbreak*, p. 92. However, though not centrally organized, activists for the established church did not work entirely in isolation. See below, pp. 175–7.

Petitions next for every *Towne* they frame,
To be restor'd to those from whom they came.
The same stile all and the same sense does pen,
Alas, they'allow set *formes* of *Prayer* to *men*.[10]

Shared themes and concerns will be explored in this chapter but never-theless the textual individuality and the importance of the local context will emerge. There appears to have been no 'party line', which again argues against the initiative originating from the centre and places it in the localities.[11] Most importantly, this chapter complements the preceeding one in which church courts were used as a way to explore the nature of post-Reformation religious conformity: of adherence to, and even affection for, the rites and ceremonies of the Church of England in a period, which, though not free from controversy, nevertheless enjoyed a degree of con-sensus.[12] The 'consensus' of the Elizabethan and Jacobean church did not mean a lack of pluralism, but is perhaps better understood as a common understanding about where the boundaries of religious discourse lay. The breakdown of consensus meant a changed context for conformists in 1641–42 compared to the earlier period explored in Chapter 2. This chapter attempts to treat the ideas presented in these petitions, not uncritically, but seriously. They have a political and social context which shaped their rhetoric but they also represent a significant strand within the pluralism of the established church forced (and indeed freed) to articulate itself after the end of the Personal Rule and at a time when the consensus over the boundaries of religious discourse lay fatally wounded.[13] Milton

---

[10] Abraham Cowley, *The Civil War*, ed. Alan Pritchard (Toronto, 1973), p. 77, see also p. 131. Cornish petitioners also remarked on the textual similarity of the their opponents 'having seene and heard the many (*though scarce divers*) Petitions to this Honourable Assembly'. Aston, *Collection*, p. 65 (my italics). Notable exceptions are the similarity of the Herefordshire and Staffordshire petitions and repeated phrases in Shropshire's petition from Worcestershire's pro-church petition and Cheshire's petition for the Book of Common Prayer. See below, Appendix 1. This feature is all the more notable because of its rarity. Petitioners in different counties, were no doubt aware of each others activities, however. A copy of 'A petition Delivered to the Lords Spirituall and Temporall by Sir Thomas Aston, Baronet, from the County Palatine of Chester concerning Episcopacie' (1641) appears in the papers of the Gloucestershire gentry, Richard Berkeley and Sir Maurice Berkeley who are sponsors of a Gloucestershire petition for the liturgy and episcopacy. GRO, D2510/13. I am grateful to Sears McGee for this reference. See below, pp. 94–5.

[11] These are features which have often not been appreciated or explored. See M. J. Mendle, 'Politics and political thought 1640–42', in *The Origins of the English Civil War*, ed. Conrad Russell (London, 1973, repr. 1981), p. 240.

[12] As Patrick Collinson has so brilliantly shown in *The Religion of Protestants: the church and English society 1559–1625* (Oxford, 1982).

[13] The strong sense of grievance after eleven years without parliament is strongly conveyed in Judith Maltby, ed., *The Short Parliament (1640) Diary of Sir Thomas Aston*, Camden Fourth series, 35 (1988).

has recently given us a brilliant 'top down' study of competing ecclesiologies within the reformed Church of England and shows how the English church related to the churches of Europe.[14] The view presented here is more 'bottom up' and it is my contention that these petitioners could indeed think theologically – though often lacking formal theological training or clerical status. Further, it is the very fact that these petitions were penned largely by laypeople in the provinces that makes the theology of the church presented in them all the more revealing and valuable. We hear in these petitions (as in the church court records discussed in Chapter 2) the voices of the 'consumers' of the spirituality offered by conformity to Book of Common Prayer and of the people on the receiving end of government by bishops. The petitions give us insight into their reasons for supporting, perhaps even loving, episcopacy and Common Prayer. They reveal critical consumers, attached to what had become in 1641 the 'old religion', but as with the laity traumatized by the Reformation which Eamon Duffy has so vividly described, able to provide theological reasons to defend the Christian tradition they were about to lose.[15]

CAMPAIGNING IN THE PROVINCES

The petitions under examination came from all around the country and were produced in the intense brief period between the end of the Personal Rule and the outbreak of the civil war. They reveal the fact that conformists constructed an apologetic for the established church by drawing on a set of complex and varied resources: from the doctrinal, historical, biblical, and ecumenical, to the always emotive witness of martyrs. Before considering such a complex and not always consistent set of opinions, some contextual questions need to be addressed. What event or events galvanized conformists into petitioning; who authored them; how were subscribers acquired and what segments of society subscribed; was the leadership lay or clerical?

'Not in imitation, but rather by provocation'

The immediate causes which sparked a local petition vary but some common features emerge. Many, but not all, of the pro-church petitioners said they were driven into action by a Root and Branch type petition, in the name of their county or community, being presented to parliament or by the general volume of Root and Branch activity in the

---

[14] Milton, *Catholic and Reformed.*
[15] See Eamon Duffy, *The Stripping of the Altars: traditional religion in England 1400–1580* (New Haven, 1992).

country.[16] Conformists, true to form, needed to perceive the status quo as under serious threat in order to be prodded into action. Lord Falkland made this very point when he described petitioners for the established church as 'people who, because men petition for what they do not have rather than for what they have, had not been as vociferous and as noticeable as the root-and-branchers'.[17] The second of three Cornish petitions for the church illustrates Lord Falkland's point precisely:

> Wee therefore the Gentlemen, and other Inhabitants of *Cornwall*, with as many good willes, though not persons, not in imitation, but rather by provocation, and necessity, in these times . . . Having seene and heard the many (*though scarce divers*) [my italics] Petitions to this Honourable Assembly, by the Inhabitants of divers Counties and Cities of this Land . . . against Bishops, some against the Common Prayer, and all against such things Super-elementary to the region of the their capacity of judging.[18]

This petition was followed by a third Cornish petition which was prompted directly by a Root and Branch petition from the county.[19]

The Protestation Oath, which all adult males were required to take in an attempt to create religious solidarity in the country and 'flush out' the enemy all could agree on, that is, Roman Catholics, had differing effects on petitioners. In Oxfordshire, a pro-church petition was produced at a gathering to subscribe to the Protestation.[20] The Oxfordshire pro-church petition is perhaps the most lukewarm of all those examined but it is among one of the earliest petitions drafted, probably in the late spring of 1641. They did claim, however, that an earlier petition from the county against the lawful religious settlement had 'not *received* Publique Examination *among us at any Generall meeting directed by* Authority *for the service*

---

[16] For example: Bedfordshire, Oxfordshire, Nottinghamshire, Gloucestershire, Herefordshire, North Wales, Kent, Cornwall and Lancashire, London and Westminster.

[17] Cited in William A. Abbott, 'The issue of episcopacy in the Long Parliament: the reasons for abolition' (University of Oxford D.Phil., 1981), pp. 187–8.

[18] Aston, *Collection*, pp. 66, 65.

[19] BL, Thomason Tracts E.150(28). However, there appears to be no trace of an anti-episcopal petition from Cornwall. Fletcher, *Outbreak*, p. 93.

[20] Although the Protestation was not printed and dispersed to the country until January 1642, in many places it was circulated in manuscript and subscriptions gathered in advance of parliament's formal order. David Cressy, *Literacy and the Social Order: reading and writing in Tudor and Stuart England* (Cambridge, 1980), pp. 66–7; see also, pp. 71–8, 84 for further information on the Protestation. Cressy's use of Protestation returns to measure literacy by comparing signatures to marks has been challenged. Margaret Spufford, 'First steps in literacy: the reading and writing experiences of the humblest seventeenth century spiritual autobiographers', *Social History* 4:3 (1979) and Tessa Watt, *Cheap Print and Popular Piety, 1550–1640* (Cambridge, 1991), *passim*. See also David Underdown, *Revel, Riot and Rebellion: popular politics and culture in England 1603–1660* (Oxford, 1985), pp. 144–5, 158–9 on the Protestation Oath and see illu. 3 in Underdown, *Revel* for a contemporary woodcut of a clergyman and his parishioners taking the oath.

of the County'.[21] The Commons were thanked for their 'unwearied
labours, and happy effects thereof' and they humbly expressed their,
'unanimous desires that the *Government of this Church* may continue, as it
is by Law established: and that the *Liturgy* may be settled with such
alterations (if there be cause) as your Wisdomes shall approve'.[22] This mild
defence of the established church may have resulted from an absence of
awareness of danger or urgency. It required a good deal of imagination to
see the Protestation sent to the provinces by Westminster as a clarion call
for reform – radical or otherwise – of the English church. In the provinces,
in fact, taking the Protestation was seen by many as a unifying act.[23]

> I, A.B., do, in the presence of God, promise, vow and protest to maintain and
> defend, as fare as lawfully I may, with my life, power and estate, the true reformed
> religion, expressed in the doctrine of the Church of England, against all Popery and
> Popish Innovation within this realm, contrary to the said doctrine, and according
> to the duty of my allegiance to his Majesty's royal person, honour and estate; as
> also the power and privilege of Parliament, the lawful rights and liberties of the
> subjects.[24]

This hardly sounds like a radical agenda.[25] The very act of gathering to
hear and subscribe to the Protestation may have awakened in conformists
reflection on just *what* it was they were swearing to 'maintain and defend'.
To some, the tone of the Protestation was simply too innocuous as is best
demonstrated by parliament's attempt to clarify it. Less than a fortnight
later, the Commons issued an Explanation to the Protestation's phraseology
'the true reformed religion, expressed in the doctrine of the Church of
England'.

> This House doth declare, that by these words was and is meant only, the public
> doctrine professed in the said Church, so far as it is opposite to Popery, and Popish
> innovations; and that the said words are not to be extended to the maintaining of
> any form of worship, discipline, or government; nor of any rites or ceremonies of
> the said Church of England.[26]

The 'Explanation', not the Protestation, must have caused alarm bells to
ring in the minds of many supporters of the 'church of Elizabeth and
James'. Though ceremonies may have indeed been held to be indifferent to

---

[21] Aston, *Collection*, p. 63.   [22] Ibid.   [23] Underdown, *Revel*, pp. 144–5.

[24] 'Protestation of the House of Commons, 3 May 1641' in J. P. Kenyon, *The Stuart
Constitution* (Cambridge, 1966), p. 223.

[25] Some individuals did use the Protestation as a licence for attacking the Prayer Book
claiming, with some grounds due to the innovations of the Personal Rule, that it was no
longer the rite that had been authorized by the queen and parliament. Essex conformists
pleaded with Charles to confirm that the liturgy was the very same approved in the first
year of Elizabeth's reign. Leicestershire RO, Acc. No. DE221/13/2/26. I am grateful to John
Walter for this reference.

[26] 'An explanation of the Protestation, 12 May 1641' in Kenyon, *Stuart Constitution*, p. 258.

the substance of religion – where, if not in the worship, discipline, or government of the church, was the 'doctrine of the Church of England' to find expression?[27] The Southwark petitioners may well have been reacting in alarm to the Explanation. They stated clearly that *their* understanding of the phrase 'the true reformed Protestant religion, etc.' was incompatible with the Explanation:

That whereas we have of late received a Protestation from this most Honourable House, to maintain the Protestant Religion established, and in all godly submission have taken the same Protestation, to maintain the same Religion, which we understand to be the same, that was by King *Edw.* 6, of famous memory, refined and reformed from Popery, and established by his[?], and Parliament in his time. Then afterwards persecuted by the Papists in the Raigne of Queen *Mary*, and againe by the great mercy and goodness of God re-established by Queen *Elizabeth* of blessed memory, and by Parliament in her time, as appeareth in the Acts and Monuments of the Church, and Acts and Statutes of the Realme, and since continued by King *Iames* of most worthy memory for his great learning and Piety, as also by our now most gracious Soveraign Lord King Charles, and the whole state for ought we know to the contrary.[28]

Southwark petitioners, demonstrating that Foxe's *Book of Martyrs* could be read in a conservative way, were in clear conflict with the drafters of the Explanation concerning what was negotiable in the English church settlement.

The view that local petitions for the church could be sparked by events in Westminster is further demonstrated by Herefordshire conformists. The catalyst there, according to Jacqueline Eales, was the impeachment of Bishop Coke of Hereford and eleven other bishops by the Commons in December 1641 – a ploy to reduce the number of votes for the king in the Lords.[29] The 'parochial' interests of many of the petitioners – concern with issues affecting the daily life of the church – did not mean they were untouched or untroubled by national events.

The support or hostility of individual Members of Parliament could influence the relationship between conformists in the localities and Westminster. In MPs like Sir Ralph Hopton and Sir Edward Dering, conformists in Somerset and Kent respectively had a representative voice in the Commons. Both Hopton and Dering illustrate how opposition to the policies of the Personal Rule in the Long Parliament could turn to alarm as

---

[27] Another explanation for the lukewarm nature of the Oxfordshire petition is the lack of any active puritanism in the county. *VCH Oxford*, ii, p. 42; Fletcher, *Outbreak*, p. 290.

[28] BL, Thomason Tracts E.151(11), p. 6. The Southwark petition is dated 12 June 1642 in the Thomason Tracts list.

[29] Jacqueline Eales, *Puritans and Roundheads: the Harleys of Brampton Bryan and the outbreak of the English Civil War* (Cambridge, 1990), pp. 130–1; *CJ*, ii, pp. 333–4. Coke was a 'Calvinist bishop'. Conrad Russell, *The Causes of the English Civil War* (Oxford, 1990), p. 59.

the radical nature of Pym's agenda became apparent.[30] Cornish conformists complained that they had intended 'to rest upon the abilities, and care of our knights and Burgesses, our hands and mouths, for matter of our particular concernment' but now felt that:

since their abse[n]ce from us, and attendance in Parliament, finding and feeling our owne grievances, giving us just grounds and feare of sudden misery, by disobedience and Contempt of Lawes; thus provoked with bleeding hearts, we beg the helpe of your Wisdomes.[31]

Relations were already polarized between the puritan Harleys and other gentry families in Herefordshire, prompting conformists, frustrated by Sir Robert's obstruction of their original petition in the Commons to produce a further *Declaration or Resolution of the Countie of Hereford*, which was presented on 8 July 1642.[32] The Commons reacted aggressively towards those responsible, though no one in the Commons denied that the *Declaration* 'embodied the opinion of the County'.[33] It has been suggested that as the country moved closer to civil war, there was a growing sense in the provinces that normal access to the legislature was becoming restricted. Other felt that their own MPs were either too unsympathetic or too timid in the face of a House of Commons increasingly under the sway of radicals.

There was, of course, interplay between national and local events – the national and local 'communities'. Supporters of the lawful liturgy in Essex claimed they were galvanized into action by the failure of local magistrates to punish one William Harvie who came from that Jerusalem of godliness, Earls Colne. Acting out a bizarre ritual of his own invention, Harvie confessed that he had, 'taken the Common prayer Booke out of his parish Church on a Sunday morning and throwne the same into a pond of water & the next day finding it swimming took the same & tearing it in pieces threw parte of it into the fire & burnt it'. The parallels to the treatment of witches is striking. Harvie showed no repentance for his action 'since he had taken the protestacon [he] could not sleep quietly till he had done the same . . . that it [the Prayer Book] was a popish Booke & against the word

---

[30] David Underdown, *Somerset in the Civil War and Interregnum* (Newton Abbot, 1973), pp. 25–8; cf. T. G. Barnes, *Somerset 1625–1640: a country's government during the 'Personal Rule'* (Oxford, 1961), ch. 10 for the view that the county was much more divided than Underdown claims. *DNB*; *VCH Somerset*, ii, p. 204. For Dering, see Maltby, 'Approaches', pp. 152–62, 165–8.

[31] BL, Thomason Tracts E.150(28) [p. 41].

[32] Eales, *Puritans and Roundheads*, pp. 100–35.

[33] John Webb, *Memorials of the Civil War between King Charles I and the Parliament of England as it affected Herefordshire and the Adjacent Counties*, ed. T. W. Webb (2 vols., London, 1879), i, pp. 84–90, ii, pp. 343–4; Maltby, 'Approaches', pp. 144–8; Eales, *Puritans and Roundheads*, ch. 6.

of God'.[34] A growing trend of violence and unrest in parish churches against the liturgy, sometimes in the context of the divine service itself, also prompted the Essex petitions to protest as did conformists in Southwark.[35]

Authorship and opportunity

It is difficult to determine, apart from a few exceptional cases, the exact authorship of the pro-church petitions. It seems certain, for example, that Sir Thomas Aston was the chief composer of the Cheshire petitions and Sir Edward Dering and Sir George Strode were the authors of a draft petition put before a committee of the Kentish Grand Bench and Jury organized by Sir Roger Twysden. It is thought that Dering's published *Speeches* influenced the content of the Kentish petition and Sir Roger, a former election rival of Dering's, had a hand in reworking the earlier draft.[36] Two clergymen, a Mr Mason, vicar of Yazor, and a Mr Sherburn, rector of Pembridge, were the chief authors of the Herefordshire petition.[37] The mention of two clergymen at this point is an anomaly – for it is the *absence* of clerical influence and leadership which is striking about the organization and composition of these petitions. It is clear that the composers of the petitions were overwhelmingly members of the laity. The campaign to defend episcopacy and the liturgy by petition against attack in 1641–42 – though not one enjoying any central co-ordination – was a lay led and lay supported campaign. The clergy were not altogether absent in the process and often took key roles in acquiring the marks and signatures of adult males. Strikingly absent, it must be said, is any evidence that bishops were taking a lead in their localities. It may be that they were too embroiled in affairs at Westminster – though that could be said of any Member of Parliament. Or it could anticipate what John Morrill has noted for the 1645–60 period, that the outlawed practices of the 'old church' were kept alive largely by members of the laity and the priesthood – bishops proving remarkably quiet in a time of persecution.[38]

---

[34] Leicestershire RO, Acc. No. DE221/13/2/26.

[35] For a further discussion of this point, see below, pp. 117–24.

[36] See below, pp. 143–4. Sir Edward Dering, *Collection of Speeches* (London, 1642); Frank W. Jessup, *Sir Roger Twysden 1597–1672* (London, 1965), pp. 47–8, 133–44; *DNB*; Maltby, 'Approaches', pp. 160–1. The events surrounding the Kent petitions for the liturgy and episcopacy are the best documented and the most complex. For a detailed discussion, see Maltby, 'Approaches', pp. 151–73.

[37] Eales, *Puritans and Roundheads*, pp. 128–9.

[38] Morrill, 'Church in England', pp. 98–100. Sir Thomas Aston made excuses for episcopal silence, see below, pp. 156–7. However, Kenneth Fincham argues convincingly that the Jacobean episcopate had regained a respected place in local society not enjoyed by their Tudor predecessors. Kenneth Fincham, *Prelate as Pastor: the episcopate of James I* (Oxford, 1990), ch. 3. Perhaps this helps to account for the level of support in the localities.

Once conditions were right – the threat perceived – how were conformist petitions organized and subscriptions acquired?[39] As defenders of the lawful settlement it is hardly surprising that they were confident enough to use existing structures. The use of meetings to take the Protestation Oath has already been mentioned, but perhaps a more common method was to use the regular occasions for a county's elites to gather: quarter sessions and assizes.[40] Worcestershire conformists, by their own account, their concerns already heightened by the Irish Rebellion and a letter from the Lord Keeper to the shire's officers to be vigilant against recusants, met at the Christmas quarter sessions and drew up their petition for the church, addressed to parliament and the king.[41] After the failure of a Root and Branch type petition to gain support at the January quarter sessions in Hereford, a pro-church petition was presented to JPs.[42]

In Gloucestershire, we know for certain what might well be true for other petitions, that conformists organized themselves in anticipation of quarter sessions and assizes. In December 1641, a group of ten Gloucestershire JPs and others met at Cirencester and drafted a petition in support of the established church. They appear to have written a 'cover letter' to be sent to the county's gentry to solicit more support:

Sir, Our present meeting at Cirencester whereat your selfe was desired, hath produced a unanimous consent of all then present unto this inclosed peticon, Such gentlemen promising his best furtherance by giving out Coppies & Collecting of subscriptions in their severall neighborhoods.

The gentlemen suggested that the correct response to make if the enclosed petition met with the reader's approbation, was to become actively involved in the mechanics of 'getting hands' for it:

of this our determinacon we thought good to acquaint you, commending it likewise to your approbacon, that if you ioyne with us in opinion, you will also in your subscripcon, & care to promote it in your partes desiring that the severall papers . . . subscribed may by you be delivered in upon Tuesday the 11th of January (being the first day of the Quarter Sessions) unto the Will Master at Cirencester, At which

---

[39] For a detailed discussion of this topic for one county, see below, pp. 151–6.

[40] Huntingdonshire conformists accused puritan petitioners of meeting at 'all publick Conventions of Assizes, Sessions, Fairs, Markets, and other publick Assemblies' in order to solicit signatures and marks. Such comments reveal a great deal about conformists' own methods of acquiring hands. John Nalson, *An Impartial Collection of the Great Affairs of State* (2 vols., London, 1682), ii, p. 722.

[41] Henry Townshend, *Diary of Henry Townshend of Elmley Lovett 1640–1663*, ed. J. W. Willis Bund, Worcestershire Historical Society (3 vols., London, 1917–20), ii, pp. 44–8, i, pp. xiii–xiv. *VCH Worcester*, ii, p. 67; Maltby, 'Approaches', pp. 121–2.

[42] Eales, *Puritans and Roundheads*, pp. 113–14, 129–30; Maltby, 'Approaches', pp. 141–2. For evidence of the use of Suffolk quarter sessions, though no text survives, see BL, Tanner MS 66, fol. 181. See also Maltby, 'Approaches', pp. 116–17, 141, 160, 165–7 for examples of the use of sessions and assizes in petitioning campaigns.

time & place we have appointed our next meeting, in expectacon whereof we remaine Your very Loving friends.[43]

The Gloucestershire conformists were at least initially better organized than their counterparts in Kent. The Kentish pro-church petitioners met at an inn just before the start of the March 1642 assizes at Maidstone, whereas the Gloucestershiremen planned well in advance – making careful preparations in order to make a bigger impact at the January 1642 sessions at Cirencester. Moreover, whereas in Kent subscriptions were solicited *after* the petition was presented at the Maidstone assizes, the Gloucestershire conformists sought to make a greater impression on the gathered worthies by revealing their petition appended with what they hoped would be schedules of many subscribers.[44]

'Getting hands'

Once drafted and vetted by at least part of a county's elites, how were subscriptions obtained? It is at this point in the process that clergy, along with the gentry, became critical players.[45] Soliciting hands after, or even during divine service was an obvious point of contact. At Pluckley in Kent, Sir Edward Dering 'addressed parishioners in church after evensong and solicited their support'.[46] Appealing to worshippers was a method used in cathedrals as well as parish churches. At Chester Cathedral, worshippers were encouraged to come up to the Communion table after the blessing and subscribe.[47] In Lincolnshire, the Committee for Scandalous Ministers reported retrospectively the activities of a Mr Barcrofte of Welborn who was, according to one witness: 'very active and stirringe in gettinge hands to the peticion for the holding upp of Bishopps in theire former glory & hee urged many persons to sett theire hands to the said peticion telling such as scrupled att itt that hee would open the meaninge of itt to them'.[48]

---

[43] GRO, D2510/13.

[44] GRO, D2510/13. A manuscript copy of the petition survives with the signatures of the same ten gentlemen whose names appeared at the bottom of the letter soliciting support. Perhaps the copy was one that had been enclosed with one of the form letters. If that is the case, the recipient failed to perform his end of the bargain. The petition claimed to have 'severall schedules hereunto annexed' but whether the petition ever gained more subscribers is unknown. BL, Add. MS 11055, fol. 130v.

[45] Anthony Fletcher has observed the role of the parochial clergy (and parish constables) at this important point in the process of petitioning both for and against episcopacy and the liturgy. Fletcher, *Outbreak*, pp. 195–6; Maltby, 'Approaches', pp. 116–17, 192–6. See below, pp. 153–4.

[46] T. P. S. Woods, *Prelude to Civil War 1642: Mr Justice Malet and the Kentish petitions* (Salisbury, 1980), p. 45; see also *CJ*, ii, pp. 513, 510; *LJ*, iv, p. 721.

[47] For West Kirby in the Wirral and Chester Cathedral, see below, pp. 153–4.

[48] J. W. F. Hill, 'The royalist clergy of Lincolnshire', Lincolnshire Architectural and Archae-

Barcrofte was apparently skilled at putting scruples to rest. Another Lincolnshire clergyman, Thomas Holt of All Saints, Stamford not only attempted to 'get hands' for the petition but with the help of an alderman, to hinder the success of a local Root and Branch type petition. The town cleric also had the use of underlings. One witness reported, 'that Mr Holt at that time sent his Clerke about the towne of Stamford to get hands to a peticion for the continucon of Bps And with those they could not prevaile for their hands of themselves they brought before the Alderman to see if they could that way prevaile with them'.[49] One gentry opponent of pro-church petitions described with almost grudging admiration the zeal of Thomas Dove, vicar of Islington in Devon:

Hee hath bestirred him selfe to gett hands, to uphold Episcopacy and the govmt of bishops, theis 7 or 8 dayes, that he solicited hedgers at the hedg, plowmen at the plow, threshers in the barnes. And some of them being asked what they had done sd that now they should have peace evermore, for thes nots [?] were to conclude peace: and had been sent by the governors of the church.[50]

There can be little doubt that at this point in the petitioning process, the clergy played a crucial role.[51]

In such an environment of growing polarization, it is hardly surprising that each side accused the other of foul play in the acquisition of hands. It has already been observed that Root and Branch petitions often originated in Westminster and were sent down to the localities whereas pro-church petitions originated from the locality and came up to the centre. In Devon, clergy were accused of using trickery to gain subscriptions for the church:

A petition is forwarded in favour of the hierarchy, diverse ministers as I heere have papers to wch they gett handes of diverse men who never see the petition, the papers having only two lines at the toppe & when meane men have putt theire hands to it they adde [a] gent for the credit thereof. This is done by the parsons of each parish where there is one that will serve the turne.[52]

---

ological Society, Reports and Papers, new ser. (1940), pp. 49, 47; Barcrofte was ejected from his living by the earl of Manchester on 20 September 1644, pp. 44–57.

[49] Ibid., p. 85, see also pp. 78–89; Maltby, 'Approaches', pp. 194–6.

[50] 'W. Howell to Thos. Wise, Knt for the Co. of Devon at his lodgings at Savoy' (20 February 1641) in *Buller Papers*, Buller Family (n.p., privately printed, 1895), pp. 33–4.

[51] However, it is not my intention to argue that the views of parish clergy were critical in the subscription rates of the laity in individual parishes, but rather to argue for a good deal of lay independence of mind. See below, pp. 224–7. Margaret Stieg has broken down the clerical subscribers for the Somerset petition. Of the 221 divines listed, 131 were beneficed; 45 were later 'sufferers' for their commitment to the Church of England, while 68 continued in their cures after the abolition of the established church. Margaret Stieg, *Laud's Laboratory: the diocese of Bath and Wells in the early seventeenth century* (London, 1982), p. 78. In Bedfordshire it is estimated that a fifth of clergy were ejected either for royalism or refusal to conform to parliamentary church services. *VCH Bedford*, i, pp. 337–8.

[52] 'Sr S. Rolle to T. Wyse' (undated, but the author mentions his daughter's forthcoming wedding in Easter Week) in *Buller Papers*, p. 81.

Obviously both Devon reports in the *Buller Papers* were unsympathetic to the cause of the preservation of the Church of England, so some scepticism must be applied. One may take issue, however, with Anthony Fletcher's observation that these parishioners were 'certainly infinitely gullible'.[53] An intriguing question as well is whether the greatest disapproval in the minds of these Devonshire gentlemen concerned the methods used in obtaining hands, or rather the low status ('plowmen at the plow') of the subscribers.

Bedfordshire and Huntingdonshire conformists accused their opponents of masking their true aim with arguments too subtle for ordinary folk: the destruction, rather than the reform, of the Church of England. In Bedfordshire they complained that most subscribers against the church were 'persons of inferior quality, either wanting true information, or [the] capacitie to apprehende the Contents of [the] sayd petitions, the same beinge full of subtilities and dangerous insinnuations not obvious to the discovery of vulgare apprehension'.[54] In Huntingdonshire too, they perceived that petitions against the liturgy and bishops were 'framed and Penned in a close and subtile Manner, to import more then is at first descernable by any ordinary Eye' hiding their true purpose:

under [the] colour of removing some Innovations lately crept into the Church and Worship of God . . . which we conceiving and fearing not so much to aim at the taking away of the said Innovations, and Reformation of Abuses, as tending to an absolute innovation of Church Government and Subversion of that Order and Form of Divine Service, which have happily continued among us, ever since the Reformation of Religion.[55]

Few examples of corrupt petitioning practices in this period can match for lack of imagination that of Sir William Brereton, MP for Cheshire. Not only did Sir William neglect to circulate his petition against bishops in the shire, he compounded his offence by simply doubling the number of subscribers in each social category claimed by his rival Sir Thomas Aston.[56] In the interest of balance, however, few examples can match the heavy-handedness and melodrama of Sir Richard Lovelace's disruption of a meeting to draft a petition to counter Kent's pro-church text. On 19 April 1642, Sir Richard with other young 'cavaliers', filling a vacuum created by the imprisonment and disgrace of older and wiser heads, burst into the planning session and 'in a furious manner cried No, No, No; and then, with great contempt of the court, clapped on their hats and said . . . that

---

[53] Fletcher, *Outbreak*, p. 289. For an incident which demonstrates that rural people were not always 'gullible' but capable of 'critical literacy', see Margaret Spufford, *Contrasting Communities: English villagers in the sixteenth and seventeenth centuries* (Cambridge, 1974), p. 209.

[54] PRO, SP16 476. [55] Nalson, *Impartial Collection*, ii, pp. 721.

[56] This produced the result that Brereton's petition claimed more subscribers from the nobility and gentry than there were in the entire county. See below, p. 148.

... [there were] many falsities therein [the draft petition] and ... they were ashamed of it'. Lovelace, prefiguring his career as a 'cavalier poet', skewered the new draft on his sword and melodramatically sliced it in pieces.[57] The point for reasoned debate, at least in Kent, had passed.[58]

SOCIAL SPREAD

What can be said at this point about the social distribution of support for these petitions is necessarily anecdotal and impressionistic, as has already been discussed in reference to the ecclesiastical courts.[59] The Cheshire petition for the Book of Common Prayer, due to the survival of its schedule of subscribers, provides a rare opportunity to examine in detail the social range of support within a parochial community for the established church.[60] Here the evidence can only be suggestive, and probably tells us more about the worn rhetorical devices employed in early Stuart religious disputes than any hard facts on social distribution.[61] It stretches credulity, for example, to accept the statement from North Wales that their pro-church petition was unopposed: 'we finde it to bee [the] unanimous and undivided request and vote of this whole Countrey'.[62] Other conformists, more plausibly, claimed simply to enjoy the support of the 'better part' of their community – usually intended to be understood in both numerical and social terms.[63] So claimed Herefordshire petitioners, only to be accused of drawing on the lowest levels of society: 'much pains hath been taken to get hands, no matter how foul or mean'.[64] In Gloucestershire, subscribers for the church were denounced by puritan clergy 'by the name of papists, common drunkards, base and lewed livers' and lists were being kept of subscribers for future retribution.[65] Though no text survives, Clive

---

[57] Cited in Alan Everitt, *The Community of Kent and the Great Rebellion 1640–60* (Leicester, 1966), p. 102. Despite the sword play, Thomas Blount did organize his counter-petition to Dering's which was presented to parliament on 5 May 1642. *LJ*, v, p. 44. For more detail, see Maltby, 'Approaches', pp. 168–70.

[58] The seventeenth-century biographer and gossip John Aubrey said of Sir Richard Lovelace '[he was] one of the handsomest men in England. He was [an] extraordinarily handsome Man, but proud.' John Aubrey, *Brief Lives*, ed. Oliver Lawson Dick (Harmondsworth, 1978), p. 353.

[59] See above, pp. 80–1.   [60] See below, Chapter 5.

[61] For the numbers of subscribers claimed by the petitions, where stated, see Appendix 1.

[62] Aston, *Collection*, p. 49.

[63] Like those representing the cities of London and Westminster who claimed the support of 'many, and those of the better sort'. CUL, Syn. 7.59.30(10).

[64] Cited in Fletcher, *Outbreak*, pp. 289, 302–6. It is not clear whether this is an assessment of the methods or the social status of the subscribers.

[65] So records John Smyth of Nibley, an 'enthusiastic supporter' of the pro-church petition in his area. Cited in Fletcher, *Outbreak*, pp. 289–90. See also David Rollinson's excellent article 'The bourgeois soul of John Smyth of Nibley', *Social History* 12:3 (1987), pp. 309–30 and below, pp. 172–4.

Holmes maintains that a Suffolk petition for the church probably enjoyed the support of the majority of the gentry, freeholders, and ministers.[66] Pro-church petitioners themselves were concerned to display on the text of the petition itself the different groups of society from which they drew support. Sir William LeNeve Clarencieux wrote to one Martin Calthorpe in September 1641:

In my passages through Suffolke, I observe[d] peticions to the parliament in Agitacon on the behalfe of Episcopacy, botommied with foure Columnes[;] first Baronetts & Knts, second Esqrs: & Gent, 3dly Clergie, 4th freeholders, the wch (as said) is affectionately & ready signers by all, Not yett is knowne [a] Gent refusing, & but one Clergie man, wch refuseth to Christen & bury e[t]c.[67]

In Somerset, David Underdown has concluded that the lower orders 'appear from what evidence exists on the subject to have favoured the Established Church'.[68]

EPISCOPALIANISM AND ANTI-LAUDIANISM

Crucial to conformist rhetoric on the eve of the civil war was the distinction between an individual and the public office that he (far less often she) held. The fate of an office or a whole system of distributing power and authority did not hang, in the minds of many early Stuart men and women, on the slender and vulnerable thread of individual competence. An incompetent or even wicked parish schoolmaster, for example, should be replaced, not the office abolished.[69] Put like that, the contention seems far from controversial. Yet when we turn to attitudes towards episcopacy, there has been until recently a widespread failure among historians to recognize that many contemporaries *were* making such a distinction about bishops. The pro-church petitions from around the country reveal a clear ability among conformists to distinguish between the system of episcopacy and the occupants of individual sees. There has been a tendency to equate opposition to Laud's policy of Thorough with presbyterianism or expressions of anti-puritanism with Laudianism and as a result the history of non-Laudian

---

[66] Clive Holmes, *The Eastern Association in the English Civil War* (London, 1974), p. 27.

[67] BL, Tanner MS 66, fol. 181.

[68] Underdown, *Somerset*, p. 22; *DNB*; *VCH Somerset*, ii, p. 204. See also Underdown, *Revel* for a fuller discussion of political allegiance below the rank of gentry. William Coates in his edition of D'Ewes' diary comments that among the subscribers to the pro-church petition from Somerset and Huntingdonshire were many 'that could not sign their names . . . [and] it is unlikely that all whose names [were] attached to these petitions understood the contents'. While this is no doubt true, it is an observation that should be applied to *all* petitioning activity in this period. Sir Simons D'Ewes, *The Journal of Simons D'Ewes*, ed. W. H. Coates (New Haven, 1942), pp. 290–2, n.3.

[69] It may be helpful to compare religion with education. Agreeing the criteria by which to measure 'success' is a difficult task.

episcopalianism has barely been written. These conformist petitions reveal a third position between support for radical Root and Branch views and Laudianism.

The theological case for episcopal polity

First of all, on what grounds did pro-church petitioners defend the *im*parity of ministers in the face of the 'levelling' claims of the presbyterian party? Not surprisingly, many petitions emphasized the antiquity of the order. What might surprise some modern readers more is that some conformists claimed episcopal polity was apostolic, that is, carrying the authority of Christ's apostles based as much on their understanding of the practice of the primitive church as on their reading of the Christian scriptures. The petitioners from Rutland made a lengthy and impassioned case (the smallest county produced the longest petition) for episcopal government from apostolic, patristic, and English constitutional sources:

We therefore humbly beg of you, to leave us in that state the Apostles left the Church in; That, the Three Ages of Martyrs were governed by; That, the 13 Ages since them have always gloried in, by their Succession of Bishops from the Apostles, proving themselves members of the Catholique and Apostolick Church; That, our Laws have Established, so many Kings and Parliaments have protected, into which we were baptized; as certainly Apostolical as the Observation of the Lords Day; as the distinction of Books Apocryphal from Canonical; as that such Books were written by such Evangelists and Apostles; as the Consecration of the Eucharist by Presbyters; as any thing; which you will do by upholding the Government of the Church by Bishops, which we again and again beg of you to do, having Pity on our Consciences, and not forcing us to seek Communion as yet we know not where.[70]

Clearly for the Rutland petitioners, the assertion that bishops could claim descent directly from the apostles was their strongest card. In their minds, furthermore, the consequences of the abolition of episcopacy would undermine features of Christianity as fundamental as baptism, the sanctity of Sunday, the canonical scriptures, and the exclusive role of priests as presiding celebrants at the Eucharist.[71] Kent demanded the continuation of episcopal government, as it was as, 'ancient in this Island as Christianity

---

[70] Nalson, *Impartial Collection*, ii, p. 656. The Rutland petition also appears in Aston's *Collection*. The petition was produced in November 1641 and claimed the subscriptions of 800 laymen and 40 ministers. This is a small number compared to other pro-church petitions but as the Restoration apologist John Nalson commented: 'Though the number seem but small, yet the County is so too', see p. 660.

[71] It has been demonstrated how 'cross party' sabbath observance was in the pre-Laudian church. Kenneth Parker, *The English Sabbath: a study of doctrine and discipline from the Reformation to the Civil War* (Cambridge, 1988). Sir Thomas Aston was concerned too that laymen would usurp what he saw as functions exclusive to the presbyterate or priesthood. See below, pp. 168–9.

itself, deduced and dispersed throughout the Christian World even from Apostolical Times [that it may be preserved as] the most pious, most prudent, and most safe Government for the Peace of the Church'.[72] Other petitions too stressed the antiquity of the order, such as Herefordshire, North Wales, London and Westminster, Surrey and Oxford University.[73] Welsh conformists combined the antiquity argument with a concern for 'Britishness' of the church, asserting that episcopacy 'is as wee beleeve, that forme which came into this *Island*, with the first Plantation of Religion heere, and God so blest this *Island*, that Religion came earely in with the first dawning of the day, very neere or in the time of Apostles themselves'.[74] Gloucestershire conformists went so far as to give thanks to God for episcopacy 'believinge it to be the best [government] instituted that anie Kingdome hath bine blest withall since the Appostles tymes'.[75] The petitioners from London and Westminster not only asserted that the polity was lawful by its 'immediate, universall and constant practise of all [the] Christian World' but more significantly maintained that 'the most learned Protestants, even in those very Churches which are now not governed by Bishops, doe not only hold the Government by Episcopacy to be lawfull, but wish that they themselves might injoy it'.[76]

Provocative or unexpected though it might sound to modern ears, was the insistence on antiquity and apostolicity merely a rhetorical device to avoid entering the theological and political minefield of the debate over whether episcopal polity was *iure humano* or *iure divino*? Was it safer ground in an immediately post-Laudian church, in 1641–42 – to insist on the apostolic origins, rather than the *iure divino* status of episcopacy? At least two county petitions drew specific attention to the controversy by refusing to comment and stating that the theological complexities of the debate were all quite beyond them. 'We will not presume to dispute the Right of Episcopacy, whether it be Divine or not; it sufficeth us to know, That the Church Government by Bishops is ancient, even near to the Apostles Days.'[77] The apostles were obviously not divine but it would be

---

[72] *LJ*, iv, p. 677.

[73] Webb, *Memorials of the Civil War*, ii, p. 337; Aston, *Collection*, p. 49; *The Humble Petition of the Cities of L. and W.*, CUL, Syn.7.59.30(10); BL, Thomson Tracts E. 151(11), p. 2; Nalson, *Impartial Collection*, ii, pp. 305–7. The Oxford petition is dated 22 June 1641 by Nalson. It is unclear whether these are the same petitions reported as presented to the Commons on 11 May 1641. See Fletcher, *Outbreak*, p. 107.

[74] Probably a reference to the myth that Joseph of Arimathea brought the Christian faith to Britain.

[75] BL, Add. MS 11055, fol. 130v.

[76] CUL, Syn. 7.59.30(10). See below, pp. 116–17, 159–60, 169–70 for other ways conformists placed their agenda within an European context.

[77] The Somerset petition. Nalson, *Impartial Collection*, ii, pp. 726. See Stieg, *Laud's Laboratory*, pp. 34–7. Herefordshire petitioners made the same point. Aston, *Collection*,

widely agreed that they had unique insight into the mind of Christ: therefore institutions perceived to be associated with them could only be altered or set aside with the greatest care. As we have seen, the episcopate was repeatedly described as apostolic and/or stemming from the first centuries of the church's history – an age widely held to have been theologically and liturgically the purest.[78] Perhaps *iure divino* arguments were simply too explosive in 1641–42. Or perhaps, very simply, they stressed apostolicity because that is what they meant. In his lengthy tract defending episcopacy, Sir Thomas Aston observed that it was the presbyterians, not the moderate episcopalians, who made *iure divino* claims for their polity. Such claims for divine sanction, Aston maintained, elevated the presbyterian minister above *any* earthly authority which might check his will: king, parliament, JPs, custom, or lay elders. In short, the rule of law was set aside by such claims.[79] The apostolic emphasis has a theological pedigree in the established church as the Ordinal makes clear:

It is evident unto all men, diligently reading Holy Scripture, and ancient authors, that from the Apostles' time there hath been these orders of ministers in Christ's church: Bishops, Priests, and Deacons . . . therefore to the intent these orders should be continued, and reverently used and esteemed in this Church of England.[80]

It would leave a false impression, however, if one concluded that the argument from apostolicity and antiquity was chosen as a path of least resistance. These petitions illustrate competing ecclesiologies in the Caroline church as regards issues of continuity and discontinuity with pre-Reformation Christianity. London and Westminster episcopalians asserted not only that the polity was the 'constant practise of all the Christian World', consistent with scripture, apostolic 'to this last Age, for above 1500 yeares together', they also saw themselves in continuity with the medieval church: 'It being utterly incredible, if not impossible, that the

pp. 69–70. See also BL, Add. MS 11055, fols. 130v–131 for Gloucestershire. It is striking to note that the petitions skirt the issue of apostolicity, not claiming it in precise terms but 'beleiveinge it to be the best constituted that anie Kingdome hath bin blest withall since the Apostles tymes'. BL, Add. MS 11055, fols. 130v–131. Also worth noting is the wording in the Somerset and Gloucestershire petitions on the *iure divino* question is almost exactly the same. This is all the more striking because of its rarity in the pro-church petitions. See above, pp. 86–7.

[78] See below, pp. 143, 157–8 for more discussion of this point.

[79] See below, pp. 166–9.

[80] Ordinal of 1550 in *The Two Liturgies A.D. 1549 and A.D. 1552: with other documents set forth by authority in the reign of King Edward VI*, Parker Society (1844), p. 331. The wording is the same in 1552 Ordinal and virtually untouched in the Restoration rite. However, considerable simplification of ceremonies was made between the 1550 and 1552 rites. F. E. Brightman, *The English Rite* (2 vols., London, 1921), ii, pp. 930–1. Paul Bradshaw, *The Anglican Ordinal: its history and development from the Reformation to the present day* (London, 1971), ch. 6. Diarmaid MacCulloch, *Thomas Cranmer: a life* (New Haven, 1996), pp. 460–1.

whole Church for so long a time, should not discover by God's word this Government to be unlawful, if it had been so.'[81] Ecclesiologically, the petitions reflect a tradition of thought which saw the Church of England as part of the ancient, but reformed, Christian Church of the British Isles. It was a debate about the contemporary church's relationship to the past and what implications for its present life might be drawn from that debate. This difference of opinion is nicely illustrated by an exchange between Sir Edward Hyde and Sir Simonds D'Ewes during the debate on the Root and Branch bill. Hyde, no admirer of Laud, maintained that episcopacy was hundreds of years old in the church. D'Ewes countered by saying 'that in *this* church it had continued rather less than one hundred'.[82] Conrad Russell has noted the similarity between Hyde's statement and the views of the archbishop, which is surely right. Here we see a point of agreement between moderate conformists and episcopalians on one hand and the Laudians on the other.[83] Though the former objected to a good deal of Thorough's agenda, the identification of the established church with the ancient British church was a point in common. However, it is vital to keep in mind that the Laudian agenda was objectionable precisely because it was seen as innovatory. To put it crudely, the pro-church petitioners were hardly proto-anglo-catholics as nineteenth and twentieth-century high Anglican myth makers have sometimes presented the 'Caroline divines'.[84] They were too at ease with the notion that the non-episcopal churches of Europe *were* actually Christian churches, after all, providing another important point of division between them and the Laudians.[85] It is worth noting that in this regard – the appeal to antiquity and apostolicity coupled with an acceptance of the non-episcopal churches of the continent – there are strong echoes of divines such as John Jewel and Richard Hooker. Hooker, of course, developed these ideas much more fully than his patron, Jewel. Could it be that Hooker was better known before the civil war than is often suggested and that we are seeing here the 'trickle down' effect of 'formal theology' on 'the laity'? Or rather, do Hooker's views represent not an original 'invention of Anglicanism' but his position within one developing tradition of a theologically pluralist English church? A famous passage of *The Lawes* expresses the tension:

---

[81] CUL, Syn.7.59.30(10).   [82] Russell, *English Civil War*, p. 72.

[83] Ibid. p. 72: Laud insisted 'we live in a church reformed, not made new'.

[84] Those anglo-catholic myths have been potent beyond confessional boundaries, as has been brilliantly shown. Diarmaid MacCulloch, 'The myth of the English Reformation', *JBS* 30 (1991).

[85] Laud, for example, attacked Bishop Joseph Hall for having too high an opinion of the continental protestant churches. Hall was also upbraid by Laud's henchman Peter Heylyn for saying that episcopacy was apostolic, not divine, in origin. Milton, *Catholic and Reformed*, pp. 489, 460.

As they [the Church of Rome] follow reason and truth, we fear not to tread the selfsame steps wherein they have gone, and to be their followers. Where Rome keepeth that which is ancienter and better [such as episcopacy], others whom we much more affect leaving it for newer and changing it for worse, we had rather follow the perfections of them who we like not, than in defects resemble them who we love.[86]

Conformists on the eve of the civil war, defended the Church *of* England as the reformed, but ancient, Church *in* England. Whether they were 'right' to do so moves beyond the historian's task and enters the world of apologetics, genuine ecumenical dialogue, and even polemic.[87]

It should be noted that affirmation of the apostolic nature of the episcopate did not mean, even to its supporters, that it was an institution beyond alteration. Schemes for a 'reformed' episcopate flowered during the early days of the Long Parliament; the intent was to restore the office to its 'primitive pattern'. But whether dioceses were multiplied and redrawn on county lines to make administration and discipline more effective, or bishops were to be banned from temporal office to prevent distraction from their spiritual duties; or, even more radically, if bishops were to be elected from among the presbyterial college of a diocese – nevertheless all these reforms maintain what could be argued to be the most distinctive feature of episcopacy *vis-à-vis* other forms of church polity in the mainstream Christian churches of the seventeenth century: the *im*parity of ministers.[88]

---

[86] Hooker, *Lawes*, V. xxviii. 1. Hooker also stressed the apostolicity of bishops, not their *iure divino* status. However, his writings on this subject were not published until the Restoration. I am grateful to Mark Perrott for making this point to me, see Perrott, 'Richard Hooker and the problem of authority in the context of Elizabethan church controversies' (University of Cambridge Ph.D., 1997). John Jewel, *An Apology of the Church of England*, ed. John Booty (Charlottesville, 1963, 1974), pp. xliv, 83–93. For a discussion of the antiquity argument, see, but to be used with caution, A. J. Mason, *The Church of England and Episcopacy* (Cambridge, 1914), ch. 1. See also Peter Lake, *Anglicans and Puritans? Presbyterian and English conformist thought from Whitgift to Hooker* (London, 1988), ch. 4; Milton, *Catholic and Reformed*, ch. 9. See Milton also for the debate over whether bishops differed in degree from presbyters or formed a distinct order, pp. 466–70. Under James VI and I, this question took on an immediacy that it perhaps lacked before as the relationship between the Scottish and English churches became yet another complicating factor for a ruler of 'multiple kingdoms'. For Archbishop Bancroft's not entirely gracious acceptance of Scottish polity, see Russell, *English Civil War*, pp. 48–9. Also note James' sensitivity in arranging the consecration of new Scottish bishops not by the archbishop and two others (avoiding any suggestion of the subjection of the Scottish church to the see of Canterbury), but by the theologically inclusive threesome of George Abbot, Lancelot Andrewes, and Richard Montaque, pp. 48–9.

[87] See Eamon Duffy, 'Prejudice unmasked: the Reformation revisited', *The Tablet* (4 March 1995) for his interpretation and application of the English Reformation to modern relations between the Anglican and Roman Catholic denominations.

[88] The Long Parliament saw such a multiplication of schemes for reorganizing the established church that the London and Westminster petitioners – those closest to the parliamentary action – maintained that those who wished to be rid of episcopacy had best first propose a concrete replacement. The burden, they argued, was on those who agitated for change.

Grace

If the rock-filled waters of *iure divino* or *iure humano* controversy about the nature of episcopacy were largely sailed around rather than through by the pro-church petitioners, even more striking is the complete refusal in any of the extant petitions to plunge into the shark-infested waters of the disputes over the nature of grace.[89] The doctrinal clash of titans between the assertion of God's absolute sovereignty over the eternal destiny of women and men versus the view that the free response of human persons to the work of Christ plays a part, albeit small, in their salvation, does not feature at all in these petitions. The question that posed itself about the origins of episcopacy poses itself again over the conflict between Calvinist and Arminian views of grace. After all, one might assume that Arminian-bashing could have provided a focus of unity between episcopalians and presbyterians – albeit the fragile type of unity created by the presence of a mutual enemy, rather than one springing from an underlying like-mindedness. Attacks on 'Arminianism' would have established the undisputed 'orthodoxy' of the pro-church petitioners in the face of Root and Branch detractors. Or could it be that the minority voice among early Stuart historians is correct: that the mainstream of the Church of England contained a spectrum of views not only *within* the parameters of predestinarian discourse, but clearly outside of its boundaries as well? Is the much vaunted 'Calvinist Consensus' of the Elizabethan and Jacobean church really just a creation of a numerically more successful historical school? Was the principle concern of petitioners for the Prayer Book and episcopacy to avoid the risk of division within their own ranks by raising an issue that

CUL, Syn. 7.59.30(10). Sir Edward Dering, for example, proposed plans for reform. Maltby, 'Approaches', pp. 153–61; Abbott, 'Issue of episcopacy', pp. 4, 11–13, 19–25, 136–40; Morrill, 'The attack on the Church of England', pp. 108, 113; Morrill, 'The church in England', pp. 92–4, 98–100.

[89] It might be significant, however, that in Lincolnshire, the only county for which any direct connection can be made between Arminianism and pro-church petitioning, there is no text of the petition extant and what evidence there is comes from the proceedings of the Committee for Scandalous Ministers, a hostile source. As with church court presentations before the war, clergy who were presented were often accused of wide-ranging offences, such as 'evil living', as well as promoting 'Arminian' doctrines. Though it must be said that presentations in ecclesiastical courts for Arminianism are rare. It was related, for example, that one Hugh Bancrofte the minister at Welborn, was 'a great extoller of the church Liturgye saine wee had cause to bless God for it', as well as a preacher of 'Arminian' doctrine. His message from the pulpit was: 'preached and delivered for a truth [that is] this popishe Arminion and false doctrine that noe man canne bee assured of his salvaccion in this life or much in effect'. Hill, 'Royalist clergy', p. 47. Even amongst the proceedings of Committees for Scandalous Ministers, accusations of Arminianism are not common. Clive Holmes, *The Suffolk Committee for Scandalous Ministers 1644–1646*, Suffolk Record Society (1970). See also Clive Holmes, *Seventeenth-Century Lincolnshire* (Lincoln, 1980), p. 145; Fletcher, *Outbreak*, pp. 312–13.

might divide and detract them from their chief aim: the preservation of the two most distinctive features of the Elizabethan Settlement – the Book of Common Prayer and the historic episcopate?[90]

A way through this sea of speculation may well be the view that such debates remained largely the preoccupation of certain university divines, MPs, and the court. The provincial silence might indicate not ignorance, nor indifference either, but a different theological agenda about what matters in the life of the church. In the localities such abstract theological disputes may have seemed remote and irrelevant whereas the familiar words of the liturgy which gave shape to the day, the week, and the year, and which accompanied the rites of passage of birth, coupling, and death were anything but abstract. This is surely not less 'sophisticated' than arguing over whether people were predestined before, during, or after the Fall, but reflects a different set of theological and pastoral priorities about the role and purpose of the church in the lives of both individuals and human communities.[91] It is important to note, however, that pro-church petitioners did not eschew more abstract theology. Bishops and theories about episcopacy were not seen as remote. Perhaps, like the liturgy, they helped to give structure to the life of the church, authenticating the ministry of the parish priest by giving him a reference outside the congregation and symbolizing the union of the parish with the larger Christian community. Here too we may be seeing, for all the damage done by the Laudians, that the prelate could still indeed be a pastor.[92]

'By their fruits ye shall know them'

Given the largely lay leadership which produced the pro-church petitions, it is perhaps not surprising that they defended the office of bishop even more forcefully on the basis of the results it produced, than on theoretical grounds. After all, it is usually the members of any profession who are most drawn to theoretical discussions of its nature. Saint Paul's aphorism 'by their fruits ye shall know them', on the other hand, is a testing one. It is

---

[90] It is an understatement to say that the bibliography on this debate is extensive and complex. R.T. Kendall, *Calvin and English Calvinism* (Oxford, 1979); Tyacke, *Anti-Calvinists*; Peter White, 'The rise of Arminianism reconsidered', *P&P* 101 (1983) and his *Predestination*; Tyacke and White, 'Debate'. Help through this minefield is provided by Andrew Foster, 'Church policies of the 1630s', in *Conflict in Early Stuart England: studies in religion and politics 1603–1642*, ed. Richard Cust and Ann Hughes (London, 1989), pp. 193–6 and Fincham, 'Introduction'. Theologically, one observes a shift in the debate which might be described as a move away from competing soteriologies to competing ecclesiologies – a broader questioning of what constituted 'the church' in early modern English theology. See Milton, *Catholic and Reformed*.

[91] See above, pp. 2–5.

[92] As Fincham has so ably shown for the Jacobean church. Fincham, *Prelate, passim.*

even more striking, given the credibility gap for bishops created by the ascendency of Thorough during the years of the Personal Rule, that conformist petitioners were so ready to emphasize the 'fruits' of episcopal government rather than stressing the theoretical claims for its authority. One might have thought that 1641–42 was *precisely* the time to make a case for the authenticity of episcopacy from the safety of ministerial theory as opposed to practice.

One of the chief 'good works' of episcopacy in the minds of conformists was the English liturgy and is discussed more fully below.[93] It was a circular argument that only worked if one considered Prayer Book worship to have validity and integrity as opposed to the view that it was 'no better than mass mumbled upon beads'.[94] Bishops could also be honoured not for their leadership, but for their stewardship of the protestant tradition – a tradition which Shropshire petitioners said they had 'bin bredd up in' thanks to numerous acts of parliament. Authenticated by parliament, Salopian conformists saw the chief role of the episcopate as one of protecting, or 'policing' the reformation by statute.[95] In the same way as the liturgy gained status from association with martyrs, so the standing of the office of bishop benefited from the deaths – as well as the lives – of Cranmer, Latimer, and Ridley. Herefordshire petitioners were not alone when they claimed episcopacy was 'Glorious for ancient and late Martyrdoms'.[96] Gloucestershire episcopalians argued that God had raised up the order as the 'most glorious instruments for propagatinge and preservacon of [the] Christian religion, which with their [the bishops'] blood they have sealed posteritie'.[97] Standing in a long tradition, and one hardly exclusive to Christianity, the testimony of martyrs was seen as the ultimate sign of authenticity.

Evil men in a good office

Conformists on the eve of the civil war argued in favour of episcopacy in both theoretical and practical terms. The institution was ancient, if not actually apostolic. Bishops had been at the forefront of the war of liberation from an imperial Roman church and had given the English

---

[93] See below, pp. 115–16.

[94] So said the puritan curate of Tarporley in Cheshire. BL, Add. MS 36913, fol. 137 and above, p. 73.

[95] Nottingham University Library PW2/HY/173. As did those from London and Westminster: bishops since the period of martyrdom under Mary were 'the best and ablest champions for the defense of it'. CUL, Syn. 7.59.30(10).

[96] Webb, *Memorials of the Civil War*, ii, p. 337.

[97] BL, Add. MS 11055, fols. 130v–131. Also Lancashire's petition: Aston, *Collection*, pp. 52–3.

people a godly order of service both to instruct them in sound doctrine and to enable the corporate worship of God true to primitive traditions but purged (it was perceived) from Romish error. Although relatively silent on some important issues already noted[98] conformist petitioners did not completely shun topicality or fail to articulate their differences with the anti-Prayer Book/anti-episcopacy party. Episcopalians and presbyterians, however, had enemies in common, namely particular members of the hierarchy and the set of policies they promoted. The opening lines of the Hertfordshire petition suggests that conformists there were hedging their bets as to whether puritans or Laudians are responsible for the current turmoil in religion. There were, they maintained:

indiscreete cleargy men, who in many Towns of this County under pretense of authority have boldy violated and audaciously attempted many things contrary to the Canons of the Church, the Rubrick, and Book of Common Prayer, the Proclamations of our religious Kings and Princes, and our most gracious Soveraigne King Charles and to the acts of Parliament established, and in our Bibles imprinted.

Hertfordshire conformists went on to complain of exclusion from the sacrament.

They daring to deny even the holy sacrament, even for a yeare together, to hundreds in our Congregations, and *where they have found no opposition* to reject great numbers which wee well know to be conformable persons and to give no offence in ther live[s] to the Congregation.

However, it soon becomes clear that the Laudian ascendancy is what troubled them, as 'the course hath beene to cite great nombers of the poorer sort of people to the Ecclesiasticall Courts (wherein themselves are for the most part the Judges)'.[99] Sir Thomas Aston perceived the fellowship created by shared opposition to Laudianism when he observed 'wee have had our swarme of flies to destroy our fruits; wee have felt the storme of a distempered fate, as well as they'.[100]

In common with Rooters, presbyterians, and radicals, pro-church petitioners were unhappy about the direction of the established church during the 1630s. Corruption and innovation were frequently and forcibly attacked in the texts; this challenges recent attempts to present Laudianism as 'popular'.[101] Bedfordshire petitions made it clear that their support for

---

[98] Such as whether episcopacy was *iure divino* or not or whether the human will plays any part in salvation. See above, pp. 101–2, 105–6.

[99] Esther Cope, ed., *Proceedings of the Short Parliament of 1640*, Camden Fourth Series, xix (1977), p. 277.

[100] Cited in John Morrill, *The Revolt of the Provinces: conservatives and radicals in the English Civil War 1630–1650* (London, 1976), p. 49. See below, p. 162; Russell, *English Civil War*, p. 123.

[101] Haigh, 'The Church of England', pp. 218–19; Sharpe, *Personal Rule*, ch. 6. Cf. the view that an anti-Laudian and anti-puritan stance in the period is 'a nexus . . . both tenuous and

the institution of episcopacy and of the lawful liturgy did not mean that they were content with the present administration: 'The exorbitances[?] of ecclesiastical jurisdiction, and the innovations lately obtruded upon our Church we apprehende as greate, and insupportable grievances.' The Long Parliament's attempts to curb the excesses of Thorough met with the approval of these petitioners: 'and with thankfulnesse, we acknowledge, and reioyce in the pious provision for the suppressing of Popery, the removing of innovations, and regulation of ecclesiastical proceedings'.[102] The nine Herefordshire JPs who wrote to the knights of the shire on 5 March 1642 in support of the Prayer Book and episcopacy, were pleased to report that the cathedral had been purged of:

'copes, candlesticks, basins, altars, with bowing and other reverances unto it' which had been introduced against the will of the cathedral clergy by a 'former Bishop' (probably Lindsell or Wren), and expressed their hope that 'the present government of the Church (abuses therein being reformed) and the uniformity of common prayer shall be so established as my preserve peace and unity amongst ourselves'.[103]

The petition itself was clear that its support of the Church of England did not include the recent innovations under Archbishop Laud:

[The petitioners] being most confident in your Honors Wisdom and Justice, that all Excesses Exorbitances and Encroachments that shall be found issuing, not from any poyson in the nature of the Discipline, but rather from the infirmity and corruption of the persons (unto which the very best Government is subject) shall be duly regulated and corrected.[104]

Appeal to an earlier *status quo* and opposition to innovation marked the conformist mind-set. The Welsh petitioners described themselves as persons 'who cannot without some trembling entertaine a thought of change'.[105] So strong was this feeling that in the autumn of 1641 Sir Edward Dering met with other Kentish friends and drew up a petition expressing their unease

difficult to establish with any exactitude'. Alexandra Walsham, *Church Papists: Catholicism, conformity and confessional polemic in early modern England* (Woodbridge, 1993), p. 98n. Underdown offers the most nuanced and convincing picture. While stressing that the Laudian support for popular customs such as maypoles and church ales, he notes that such a policy was pursued to gain support and that Laudian liturgical innovations such as placing the holy table 'altar-wise' show little sign of popularity. Underdown, *Revel*, pp. 129–31, 138–40. See also Maltby, '"By this Book": parishioners, the Prayer Book and the established church', in *The Early Stuart Church 1603–1642*, ed. K. Fincham (London, 1993), pp. 115–20.

[102] PRO, SP16 476.

[103] Cited in Eales, *Puritans and Roundheads*, p. 131; Webb, *Memorials of the Civil War*, ii, pp. 343–4.

[104] Webb, *Memorials of the Civil War*, ii, p. 338. In Gloucestershire they thought along similar lines: 'If of late tymes through the faultiness of men some things needelesse and some things of ill consequence are stolen and thrust into it [the church] wee desire they may be reformed and the church restored to its former puritie.' BL, Add. MS 11055, fol. 130v.

[105] Aston, *Collection*, p. 49.

at the course the Commons seemed to be charting in religion. These Kentish petitioners criticized the excesses of recent innovations but warned parliament against committing the same sin themselves in an attempt to dismantle Thorough:

> May it please this Honorable House, wee do earnestly and heartily concurre with the sayd Petitioners, for Reliefe and Ease against the many exorbitances and pressures generall suffered of late, both in Church and State. But wee, doe, withall, earnestly and heartily, as possibly as we can, beseech and pray this Honourable House, both in the Church Government and in our present Liturgie, to give us a severe Reformation, not an absolute Innovation.[106]

This sits well with one view of the religious complexion of Kent. Alan Everitt describes the Kentish gentry of the late 1630s and early 1640s as a county community whose puritan faction had been kept in check by moderate and conforming men until this latter group were antagonized by the reforms of Archbishop Laud.[107] The year 1640 saw the production in Kent of sixty or more local petitions but their tone is temperate. None complained of episcopacy as a system and only two of 'prelatical tyranny'. Eighteen objected to Laudian innovations such as east-ended altars and rails, but not to the ceremonies prescribed in the Prayer Book. This is especially striking in a county much of which lies in Laud's own diocese of Canterbury. Approximately 140 minor gentry were involved in these Kentish petitions, with only 45 becoming Committeemen and the rest royalist or neutral. This flurry of petitioning against Thorough in 1640, therefore, was not an explosion of 'puritanism'. Everitt has expressed it well: 'Countrymen did not believe, with orthodox puritanism, that the curate they drank with of an evening at the inn was an emissary of the pope.'[108] He argued that the puritan elements in the county, despite the assertions of Laud to the contrary, would not have been a cause of concern had the archbishop not succeeded in alienating the conformists of the county, and thereby weakening the position of the established church.[109]

One area of reform of the established order which was about structures rather than simply a matter of punishing corrupt individuals, concerned the system of ecclesiastical courts. One of the earliest petitions – if not the earliest – complained of the 'exorbitances [?] of ecclesiastical jurisdiction'

---

[106] L. B. Larking, ed., *Proceedings in Kent*, Camden Society, lxxx (1862), p. 61. Text also in BL, Stowe MS 744, fol. 13; BL, Add. MS 26785, fols. 49–50. This is not the major petition from Kent in support of the established church. See *LJ*, iv, pp. 677–8; Maltby, 'Approaches', pp. 159–60; Appendix 1.

[107] Everitt, *Kent*, p. 60.

[108] Ibid., p. 60; *Proceedings in Kent*, pp. 160–2, 168, 171, 173, 174, 175.

[109] Everitt, *Kent*, pp. 60, 84; C. H. Chalklin, *Seventeenth-Century Kent: a social and economic history* (London, 1965), pp. 212–13. For a further discussion of rails, see below, pp. 122–4.

and welcomed the plans 'regulating of ecclesiastical proceedings'.[110] Lancashire conformists were delighted to see two chief organs of Laudian
oppression, Star Chamber and High Commission, suppressed, but did not
refer directly to the diocesan courts.[111] More radically, Kentish conformists
called for the coercive power of the ecclesiastical courts by means of excommunication to be abolished and a new and presumably more effective
authority established, with a clear programme of reform worthy of any
godly reformation of manners. They called for:

> the suppressing of the heinous and now-so-much abounding Sins of Incest, Adultery,
> Fornication, and other Crimes, and for the recovering of Tithes, repairing of
> Churches, Probates of Wills, church Assesses, and Providing Bread and Wine for the
> Communion, and choice of Church-wardens and other Offices in the Church, and
> especially for Ministers who neglect the celebrating of Holy Communion, and for
> Parishioners not receiving.[112]

All this discontent had a focus in the individuals identified with innovation
in the established church during the Personal Rule. Conformists were clear,
however: punish the person, do not abolish the office. They were perfectly
capable, indeed their position would have been untenable otherwise, of
distinguishing the personnel from the polity. Sir Ralph Hopton, for
example, a leading figure in promoting the Somerset pro-church petition,
also voted for the attainder of Strafford and the abolition of the chief
instruments of Thorough, Star Chamber and High Commission. Sir Ralph
was not alone in Somerset in thinking thus, as the county's petition makes
clear:

> Though we may not deny, but through the frailty of Men and Corruption of Times,
> some things of ill Consequence, and other needless, are stolen or thrust into it [i.e.
> the episcopal office] which we heartily wish be reformed, and the Church restored
> to its former Purity: And to the End it may be the better preserved from present and
> future Innovations, we wish the wittingly and maliciously guilty of what Condition
> soever they be, whether Bishops or other inferior Clergy, may receive condign
> punishment. But, for the miscarriage of Governors, to destroy the Government, we
> trust it shall never enter into the hearts of this Wise and Honorable Assembly.[113]

---

[110] Bedfordshire. PRO, SP16 476.
[111] Aston, *Collection*, pp. 52–3. As did Huntingdonshire petitioners who were pleased by
the impeachment and imprisonment of particular bishops and the abolition of High
Commission and Star Chamber. HLRO, Parchment Coll., 8 December 1641. This had
been accomplished by the summer of 1641, though the Huntingdon petition was not
presented until December. Clive Holmes accounts for its tardy presentation by suggesting
it was due to uncertainty about the direction of the Long Parliament in religious matters.
Holmes, *Eastern Association*, p. 28; Conrad Russell, *The Crisis of Parliaments* (New
York, 1971), p. 330; *LJ*, iv, pp. 467, 469; *The Journal of Sir Simonds D'Ewes*, Coates
ed., pp. 290–1.
[112] *LJ*, iv, p. 677.
[113] Nalson, *Impartial Collection*, ii, p. 726; *DNB*; Underdown, *Somerset*, pp. 21–3.

In attempting to sway his MP, Sir Edward Dering, the Kentish clergyman Robert Abbot robustly criticized his archbishop but defended episcopacy, warning the socially conservative baronet that anti-episcopacy petitioning was masking a radical agenda.[114] Two different Cornish petitions made the same point. One called on parliament 'to continue the reverend Office . . . [but] punish the offending persons of Bishops'[115] and the other insisted on both the preservation of the episcopate and the punishment of the 'deliquences of any particular person' which they hoped would not allow 'that high and holy Office, or Calling, to suffer'.[116] The argument used by Rooters for the abolition of the entire office of episcopacy due to the wickedness of particular bishops was put into a larger context by Bedfordshire conformists who queried the Rooters' premise:

But (on the Contrarie) for the sayd petitioners [the Rooters], from personal abuses, to conclude the eradication of the function: we conceive it a dangerous inference in relation to any profession: neither can we assent unto it as agreeable to iustice, or charity.[117]

Clearly such a doctrine had disturbing implications for all professions.

Gloucestershire conformists certainly had first-hand experience of a bishop who abused his office in the person of Godfrey Goodman (d. 1656) – though for more traditional forms of wickedness, simple greed and corruption.[118] These petitioners knew what they were talking about when they described the 'wittinglie and malitiousely guilty' occupying episcopal office. They called for the 'condigne punishment' of such persons but expressed what would prove to be misplaced confidence that parliament would never fall victim to excessive zeal and destroy the system as well as punish particular offenders:

but for the miscarriage of governors[,] to destroy the government we truste it shall never enter into the hearte of this wise and honorable assemblie . . . [Parliament

---

[114] William Lamont, 'The Squire who changed sides', *History Today* (May 1966), p. 352; Maltby, 'Approaches', pp. 154–9.

[115] Aston, *Collection*, p. 67.

[116] BL, Thomason Tracts E.150(28) [p. 42]. This petition, one of three from Cornwall, is included in the copy of Aston's *Collection* in the Thomason Tracts.

[117] PRO, SP16 476.

[118] Goodman was far from a model of episcopal ministry. He was pastorally negligent of his flock and suspected of crypto-popery. In fact, he succeeded in alienating almost everyone. Laud had no more patience for a lax administrator or a suspected papist than most of his contemporaries. When Goodman bribed his way to the see of Hereford, while still attempting to hold Gloucester, Laud had the king revoke his translation. On several different occasions, Charles and Laud were compelled to order Goodman to be resident in his own diocese. In the end, Goodman's will revealed that he had converted to Roman Catholicism, though he never renounced his Anglican orders. *DNB*; *VCII Gloucester*, ii, p. 33. For Laud and Neile's treatment of another lax administrator, Bishop John Bridgeman of Chester, see below, pp. 139–41.

should resist those] who soe hastily conclude that a Bishopp and a good man or a good government are terms incompatible. Our hearts desire therefore is that the pretious may be separated from the vile[,] that the bad may be reiected and the good retained.[119]

Nottinghamshire petitioners made the same distinction as Gloucestershire: 'that the abuses and errours of some particular persons may not cause the alteration of the Ancient Government: but rather such persons should suffer according to their Demerits'.[120] It is striking to note of the over half dozen petitions which specifically make this distinction between office and person, that there is no obvious correlation with whether their bishop was an advocate of Thorough or not.

WORSHIP ACCORDING TO THE BOOK OF COMMON PRAYER

With a 'holy love embraced'

Support for the lawful liturgy in the pro-church petitions covered a spectrum of intensity and was justified for a variety of reasons. Some of the petitions convey a sense of surprise and shock that *any* dissatisfaction had been expressed about the Book of Common Prayer. Petitioners in Worcestershire presented themselves as true products of a reformed Christian tradition, stressing 'That we [have been] bred up in the true Protestant religion and doctrine of the Church of England.'[121] They had little within their own experience of Roman Catholicism either to react against or to cling to – but understandably they clung to what was familiar: 'And having been likewise blessed with an uniform Liturgy ratified by law and with general consent received and continued amongst us, Unto which doctrine and government your petitioners have hitherto with much satisfied consciences lived conformable.'[122] It was a cautious and conservative stance, but cannot be dismissed as simply 'reactionary'. Descriptions of their experience of lawful worship such as 'with much satisfied consciences lived conformable' do not need expression unless they are perceived to be under attack. The Kentish petitioners, working in politically more sensitive conditions nearer the outbreak of the civil war, stressed as well the popularity of Common Prayer: 'That the solemn Liturgy of the Church of England . . . [be] enjoyed, and [with a] . . . holy Love [is] embraced by the most and best of all the Laity.'[123] Cornish conformists, whose enthusiasm for the established church manifested itself by the production of at least three different pro-church petitions, spoke of 'the Divine and excellent

---

[119] BL, Add. MS 11055, fols. 130v–131.   [120] Aston, *Collection*, p. 13.
[121] Townshend, *Diary*, ii, p. 45.   [122] Ibid.   [123] *LJ*, iv, p. 677.

forme of Common Prayer'.[124] In Lancashire too, the Prayer Book was seen as a 'soleme Liturgy of this Church, of long continuance, and generall approbation of the most pious and learned of this Nation'.[125] Petitioners from North Wales made this point even more dramatically. They defended the 'publique Service of God' and warned of the dangerous consequences that might arise as a result of innovation in this area of 'nearest importance'. What 'scruples and jealousies', they argued, were likely to arise among the people if, after years of being persuaded by the authorities of the lawfulness and scriptural soundness of the Prayer Book and years of use ('so many yeares in the practice thereof'), it should now be called into doubt. In fact, they reported that the mere rumour of innovation in the established forms of worship had caused great anxiety:

> The meere report hereof [of innovation] hath already produced no good effect, breeding in the mindes of ill-disposed persons Insolence and contempt, in others perplexities and griefe, not knowing how to settle themselves, or forme their obedience in such distractions and sometimes repugnancy of commands.[126]

Not only were the unholy disruptions of opponents of the Prayer Book causing them distress, the lack of firm support from Westminster for the liturgy was causing even greater distress. These Welshmen were undivided churchmen, they said, 'who cannot without some trembling entertaine a thought of change'.[127]

The Book of Common Prayer: purged and refined

Caroline conformists saw the lawful liturgy of the English church not simply as an English invention. The Book of Common Prayer is presented not as an 'innovation' but as a text standing within an ancient tradition of Christian worship. Rejecting the view represented in Root and Branch petitions that the 'Liturgy for the most part is framed out of the Romish Breviary, Rituals, [and] Mass-book',[128] the Huntingdonshire petitioners

---

[124] Aston, *Collection*, p. 67. There were three Cornish pro-church petitions: two of which were printed in the Cambridge University Library edition of Aston; the third appeared along with the other two in the edition of Aston's *Collection* in the Thomason Tracts. BL, Thomason Tracts E.150(28). Apart from pagination, this is the only difference between the Thomason Tracts copy and the edition of Aston in the Cambridge University Library.

[125] Aston, *Collection*, pp. 52–3. On this theme see also the petition from Bedfordshire. PRO, SP16 476.

[126] Aston, *Collection*, p. 48. The counties of North Wales included: Flint, Denbigh, Montgomery, Caernarvon, Anglesey, Merioneth, see pp. 47–50. For further discussion of conformist ire at irreverent behaviour in church, see below, pp. 117–24.

[127] Ibid., p. 49.

[128] 'The Humble Petition of many of His Majesty's subjects in and about the City of London, and several Counties of the Kingdom' in S. R. Gardiner, *The Constitutional Documents of the Puritan Revolution 1625–1660* (3rd edn, Oxford, 1906), p. 141.

emphasized the Prayer Book was purged of 'all former Corruptions and Romish Superstitions,'[129] as did the Bedfordshire conformists.[130] In Herefordshire too, it was the Prayer Book's harmony with antiquity which gave it authority: 'That the present publique forme of Gods Worship, and the Administration of the Blessed Sacrament, with other Rites agreeable to Gods holy Word, and purest Antiquitie . . . be to God's glory, and [the] Churches Peace, re-established and confirmed.'[131] Lancashire conformists saw Common Prayer as 'compozed according to the Primitive Patterne by our blessed Martyrs, and other religious and learned men'.[132] On the theoretical plane, this was about as far as conformists would go in defending the Book of Common Prayer, and they had their own experience of Prayer Book worship to authenticate the liturgy as well.[133] In March 1642 attempts to include in the Kentish petition the phrase that the Book of Common Prayer was 'penned by the inspiration of the Holy Ghost' was 'upon debate omitted'.[134] While some puritans claimed that the Common Prayer Book was drafted by the 'imps of hell', defenders of the lawful liturgy declined to invoke supernatural authorship of either a demonic or heavenly kind.[135]

Written in the blood of martyrs

Given some of the exaggerated rhetoric of the pro-church petitions, the Common Prayer Book was nonetheless presented as a product of merely human, though inspired, creativity. Further, the Prayer Book shared in the limelight created by the sanctity of those who were responsible for the English liturgy. Not only did the Prayer Book, purged of Romish corruptions, have continuity with the worship of the early Christians, but the liturgy had been composed by individuals who had suffered the fate of martyrdom. The deaths of the Marian martyrs added stature to the Book of Common Prayer. The status of Cranmer as a martyr – and the kudos that imparted both to the office of bishop he occupied and to the liturgy he composed – is a recurring theme through these diverse petitions. The Kentish petitioners were keen to draw attention to the fact that the Prayer Book was a 'gift' to the nation by bishops who had been victims of Roman oppression. They spoke of 'the solemn Liturgy of the Church of England, celebrious of holy Bishops and Martyrs, who composed it'.[136] Defences of the liturgy and episcopacy became conflated. The Prayer Book stood on its

---

[129] Nalson, *Impartial Collection*, ii, p. 721.   [130] PRO, SP16 476.
[131] Webb, *Memorials of the Civil War*, ii, p. 337.   [132] Aston, *Collection*, p. 53.
[133] As, for example, Cheshire petitioners noted. See below, pp. 150–1.
[134] Cited in Russell, *English Civil War*, p. 124.
[135] See above, p. 20 and below, p. 151.   [136] *LJ*, iv, pp. 677.

own merits, but it was also evidence of the positive contribution made by bishops to the life of the whole church. In other words, since bishops were responsible for giving the church such a godly form of service, their important role in the creation and maintenance of true religion should be acknowledged, valued, and even honoured. Clearly there were many unimpressed by this line of argument; as they were hostile to the Prayer Book, so they were hostile to episcopacy – or vice versa. To some post-Reformation men and women, nonetheless, such an argument made sense and carried great weight. They saw the Church of England, purged and refined by the fires of the Marian persecutions, quite differently from its deriders: not as a church 'but halfly reformed' but as a church that was governed and worshipped 'according to the Primitive Patterne' and which had been preserved by martyrs.[137] The 'blood of Christians' was indeed 'the seed' of the church.[138] The corporate memory of the deaths by burning of Cranmer, Latimer, and Ridley so graphically described in John Foxe's *Book of Martyrs* (1563) (as well as the deaths of many very ordinary laypeople who were put to death under Mary also described in Foxe), seems to have been still deeply engrained on English protestant consciousness. Foxe's power to shape religious perceptions and myths appears to have been as potent for conformists as for those 'godly' folk who desired further reformation of the established church.[139] Diarmaid MacCulloch has recently shown how Cranmer's standing was quickly restored under Elizabeth and was used by both conformists and puritans. Indeed, by the early 1640s, the archbishop was invoked by all interest groups seeking to undo the works of the next archbishop of Canterbury to suffer public execution.[140]

Approved by foreign divines

In the rhetoric of the pro-church petitions the lawful liturgy was bought at the high price of martyrdom and enjoyed wide popular acceptance and affection. The Prayer Book had theological credibility, however, not only because of the approval of the best of England's divines. It was important to some petitioners to stress the approval of foreign divines of the

---

[137] Lancashire petition in Aston, *Collection*, p. 53. See also the Huntingdonshire petition in Nelson, *Impartial Collection*, ii, pp. 720–2.

[138] Tertullian, *Apology*, L.13 in *Apology, De Spectaculis*, ed. T. R. Glover (London, 1960), p. 227. See also *Apologetic and Practical Treatises*, ed. C. Dodgson (Oxford, 1854), pp. 105, 105n. I am grateful to my colleague Robin Osborne for his help with this reference. Literally the reference is: '*semen est sanguis Christianorum!*'

[139] William Lamont's assertion for Foxe's waning influence seems hard to sustain. *Godly Rule* (London, 1969), pp. 56–77.

[140] See MacCulloch, *Cranmer*, ch. 14. I am grateful to Diarmaid MacCulloch for sending me a copy of this chapter in advance of publication.

Settlement.[141] The Kentish petitioners maintained that 'the solemne Liturgy of the Church of England, celebrious of holy Bishops and Martyrs, who composed it, established by the supreme Law of this Land' was also 'approved by the best of Foreign Divines'.[142] The Worcestershire petitioners emphasized this point as well.[143] Sir Thomas Aston, in his lengthy defence of episcopacy published in 1641, was insistent that the English Settlement existed happily within the network of the mainline European reform movement.[144] In this way provincial conformists chimed nicely with the views of theologians like the moderate Calvinist, Bishop Joseph Hall, who insisted that there was no great conflict between the Book of Common Prayer and continental liturgies. In fact, there is a decidedly modern ring to Hall's style of 'Anglican' ecumenics when dealing with protestant, rather than Roman, Christianity: 'he insisted that the Church of England was more fit to lead than follow in such matters'.[145] Moderate conformists sought to convince hotter protestants that the Prayer Book was acceptable to continental churches by emphasizing foreign acceptance of its legality and the role played by prominent divines such as Bucer, Calvin, and Peter Martyr in its evolution. Also in their sights was the Euro-scepticism of the Laudians and the view that such foreign contact had 'tainted' the English liturgy.[146]

'Impiety not to be endured'

In the largely measured rhetoric of the pro-church petitions on the subject of the lawful liturgy, it would be surprising if they did not contain some expression of the irrational: for worship cannot properly be understood as a purely rational and intellectual experience or process. Worship is intended to engage the whole person: heart and mind, body and spirit. Indeed, not only is it the engagement of the whole person which is desired, but that

[141] This is illuminating to note in terms of the historiographical debate over English ecclesiology in this period. See Anthony Milton's magisterial contribution to the debate: *Catholic and Reformed*.

[142] *LJ*, iv, p. 677.

[143] Townshend, *Diary*, ii, p. 45; *VCH Worcester*, ii, p. 67. In the view of Shropshire conformists the Church of England's professed doctrine in the 39 Articles accorded 'with the confessions of all reformed churches' and both episcopacy and the Book of Common Prayer were 'approved by the reformed churches abroad'. Nottingham University Library, PW2/HY/173.

[144] See below, pp. 169–70.   [145] Milton, *Catholic and Reformed*, p. 497.

[146] Hall also noted that there was no imperative for all churches to have the same liturgy nor was he the only or the first bishop to say so. In the early years of the Elizabethan Settlement, Bishop John Jewel noted that among the reformed churches there was no need for uniformity, as the ecclesial communities of the New Testament varied in custom and practice – but not, of course, in 'essentials' of the faith. Milton, *Catholic and Reformed*, pp. 497–8; Jewel, *Apology*, pp. xxx–xxxi.

person as she or he is in relationship to a worshipping community. Private prayers are one thing – corporate worship quite another. To believers, corporate worship, whether in the form of the Prayer Book liturgy or not, brings an individual into relationship not only with the transcendent reality of God, but also with the all too material reality of one's neighbour. The potential for conflict which is not simply intellectual is even better understood if it is remembered that in worship diverse individuals come together at times and in places infused with significance out of the ordinary. It is not for nothing that both modern liturgists and anthropologists speak of worship as the 'sanctification of time and space' – the meeting point, however that is understood, of the ordinary and extraordinary.[147]

It is argued here – and in conflict with views put forward in recent works – that the Reformation in England did not bring to an end these less 'rational', more 'emotional', aspects of public worship. To state, as Christopher Haigh has done, that the 'comfortable old rituals were scrapped, and replaced by the sterilized services of the Book of Common Prayer' does not begin to do justice to the religious experience of post-Reformation conformists. I would also challenge Haigh's assertion (as I assume Duffy would too) that for 'unthinking Christians at least, the religion of works was not, and perhaps could not be, replaced by the religion of the Word'.[148] The 'godly' may have assessed attachment to Prayer Book ceremonies (though their roots were far older than the Reformation) as a sign of low intelligence or impiety, but historians should not. The lawful liturgy of the Church of England may have been protestant – perhaps even 'reformed' – but it was not vacuous or empty of meaning or of the sense of the sacred for many who participated in it.[149] Ironically, the reformed liturgy received both praise and blame for its emphasis on seeing, hearing, receiving, and understanding as communal activities. Yet while the worship of late medieval Christianity, and the Roman Catholicism shaped by the Counter-Reformation, are receiving a great deal of scholarly attention as regards their corporate nature, there has been little reflection on this aspect of lay experience of Prayer Book worship.[150] The conformist

---

[147] Marion J. Hatchett, *Sanctifying Life, Time and Space* (New York, 1976), ch. 1; Joseph Martos, *Doors to the Sacred* (London, 1981), ch. 1; George Guiver, CR, *Company of Voices: daily prayer and the people of God* (London, 1988), pp. 3–45.

[148] Christopher Haigh, *English Reformations: religion, politics, and society under the Tudors* (Oxford, 1993), pp. 288, 288–9; Duffy, *Stripping of the Altars*, esp. chs. 14, 17; see also his excellent article 'The godly and the multitude in Stuart England', *The Seventeenth Century* 1:1 (1986).

[149] Lake draws attention to the Laudian emphasis on the sacred character of the church building and of public prayer. However, in describing the distinctive positions of Laudians and puritans on these matters, one might conclude that the disciples of Thorough were the only proponents of such a view. Lake, 'Laudian style', pp. 164–6, 176–80.

[150] Virginia Reinburg, 'Liturgy and the laity in late medieval and Reformation France',

petitions prompt one to consider that it was not only the Mass which should be understood 'as social'.[151]

Nowhere is this point more clearly illustrated than by the recurring note of outrage expressed in the pro-church petitions against disruptions of Common Prayer services nearly a century after the first vernacular Prayer Book came into use. Whether these disturbers were 'the godly' or merely troublemakers looking for an excuse for destruction and violence, was a secondary question to petitioners as far flung as Bedfordshire, Worcestershire, Huntingdonshire, Somerset, Gloucestershire, Kent, Cornwall, and Southwark.[152] Bedfordshire conformists were distressed by the disturbances of a few 'infectious example of tumulteous spirits interuptinge the administration of divine service' as well as the 'generall annimations to distemper' caused by the great bulk of pamphlets and seditious sermons prepared for consumption 'amongst the vulgar'.[153] The Worcestershire petitioners felt that the pressure for further reformation of the liturgy and government of the Church of England was a slur on 'those religious princes of ever blessed memory Queen Elizabeth and King James [who are] traduced as Anti-Christian'. They also suggested that the desire for more 'reform' had led to such 'Insolences and extravagences' that they 'do much discomfort your petitioners'.[154] The Huntingdonshire petition contained a sharp attack on the dangers of congregationalism. The supporters of such a polity were stirring up trouble in London and the countryside with seditious pamphlets and sermons, 'dangerously exciting a Disobediance to the established Form of Government and Church Service', little regarding that the bulk of public affection rested behind these things:[155]

yea though the things in themselves be never so indifferent, of never so long continuance in Use and Practice, and never so much desired and affected by others, so that where three or four of them be in a Parish, though 500 others desire the use and continuance of things long used, all must be altered, or taken away as Schandals and Grievances for these three or four, though to the Offence of many others . . . whereby multitudes of Godly people well affected, are in some things deprived, or abridged of what they desire and take comfort in . . . what high Presumption is it? and how great a Tyranny may it prove over the Minds and Consciences of Men?

The petition gave another view of puritan disruptions of services:

Sixteenth Century Journal 23:3 (1992); John Bossy, 'Christian life in the later middle ages: prayers', *TRHS*, 6th ser., 1 (1991) (see also Reinburg's response in the same issue). I am grateful to Virginia Reinburg for our e-mail discussions on early modern worship. R. W. Scribner discusses this aspect of protestant worship in 'Ritual and Reformation' in R. W. Scribner, *Popular Culture and Popular Movements in Reformation Germany* (London, 1987), pp. 105–6, 120–2. For England, the most impressive study of late medieval lay piety is without doubt, Eamon Duffy's *Stripping of the Altars*.
[151] John Bossy, 'The mass as a social institution, 1200–1700', *P&P* 100 (1983).
[152] See below, Appendix 1.   [153] *CSPD*, 1640–1, p. 446.
[154] Townshend, *Diary*, ii, p. 45.   [155] See Fletcher, *Outbreak*, p. 287.

The great increase of late of Schismatics and Sectaries, and of Persons not only separating and sequestering themselves from Publick Assembly at Common prayers and Divine Service, but also opposing, and tumultuously interrupting others in the performance thereof, in the Publick Congregation.[156]

Kentish petitioners declared that this irreverent behaviour was leading to a complete breakdown of the church's sacramental system:

[That] the Liturgie and booke of Common Prayer [is] depraved, and neglected, That absolute modell of Praier, *The Lords Prayer*, vilified, The Sacrament of the Gospell in some places unduly Administered, in other places omitted, Solemne dayes of fasting observed appointed by private persons, Marriages illegally Solemnized, Burials uncharitably performed, And the very Fundamentall of our Religion subverted, by the publication of a newe Creed, and teaching the Abrogation of the Morrall Law.[157]

Not only was regular weekly worship seen as under attack, but the important 'occasional' offices as well, those central and emotionally charged rites of passage such as weddings and funerals.[158] We may well be seeing here the results of a process begun under James of perceiving the 'purist of the purifiers' as an 'alien force' within the Church of England.[159]

In Somerset, petitioners defended the liturgy, insisting that those who despised it had either misunderstood or had been misled:

Furthermore, having heard, that our Common Prayer hath been interrupted, and despised of some mis-understanding or mis-led People, to the Great Schandal of the Religion professed in our Church; We humbly beseech you to take into your Care the Redress thereof, as of an Impiety not to be endured; as also to take Order for the severe punishment of those Men, if they be discovered, who frequently publish Pamphlets, under a Veil of Confusion and Rebellion.[160]

Feelings ran high over disruptions of services by dissidents, and the accusation that conformists were attached to a defective, or even popish, form of worship was felt to be deeply offensive. One Somerset magistrate, the 'godly' John Harington, reacted against this view at the quarter sessions in January 1641. ' "Ungodly and pernicious attempts" to "innovate or alter anything in the service of God or the decent order lawfully used . . . in the

---

[156] Nalson, *Impartial Collection*, ii, pp. 721–2.

[157] Aston, *Collection*, p. 45. This petition is a different one than the major petition presented in March 1642. See Appendix 1.

[158] The text of this Kentish petition is in Aston's *Collection* and is much shorter than the one in the House of Lords Record Office. Unusually the petitioners identified themselves as all residing in the diocese of Canterbury. Expressions of diocesan identity, rather than of the county, are rare among the pro-church petitions. See also the Devon and Herefordshire petitions (see Appendix 1).

[159] Margaret Aston, 'Puritans and iconoclasm, 1560–1660', in *The Culture of English Puritanism 1560–1700*, ed. Christopher Durston and Jacqueline Eales (London, 1996), pp. 92, 106–7.

[160] Nalson, *Impartial Collection*, ii, p. 727. See Stieg, *Laud's Laboratory*, p. 35.

Church" ought, he declared, to be severely punished'.[161] The Gloucestershire petitioners described attacks on the Prayer Book as 'noe lesser
greivance' than attacks on the system of episcopacy. They complained of
services interrupted and despised, 'even whilst it [Common Prayer] stands
established by act of Parliament'. It would appear that the episcopate was
not the only source of authority under threat in the minds of conformists,
but violent disruptions of church services also threatened the authority of
parliament.[162] Scope for minor reform in occasional Prayer Book phrases
or particular ceremonies was conceded but this should be done 'warily'.
They asked if irreverent despising of so 'wholesome an ordinance' should
be suffered in 'a peaciable comonwealth'.[163] It is interesting that disruptions of services were seen as acts of impiety, suggesting that some who
conformed to the Church of England attached sacred value to their
corporate worship.

In the case of a rare urban pro-church petition, it is possible to put these
feelings of anger at 'defilers of Gods House' into some larger framework.
The Southwark petition complained of the offence caused by the 'insolent
carriage' of many clergy and laity during the time of divine service:

some [of them] calling the doctrine & discipline of our Church cursed, others
refusing to reade the Booke of Common prayer, enjoyned by Statutes, others calling
it Popish, others behaving themselves most unreverently at those prayers, or
standing without the Church till they be done, refusing to joyn with the Congregation, in those prayers.[164]

London had been the scene of church rioting in the two parishes of Saint
Saviour and Saint Olave on a scale sufficient to receive a fair amount of
attention from the House of Lords. In January 1641, the activities of a
group of 'anabaptists' in Saint Saviour's parish were brought to the
attention of the Lords. They rejected the Book of Common Prayer, claimed
that the church was only where the faithful were gathered, rejected the
king's authority in religious matters and even called into question whether
he was among the elect. The Lords reacted by reaffirming that the Prayer
Book had the full authority of law, that only ceremonies and rites
prescribed by it should be observed, and that all such disturbers of the

[161] Underdown, *Revel*, p. 140.
[162] BL, Add. MS 11055, fols. 130v–131. See below, pp. 126–8.
[163] BL, Add. MS 11055, fols. 130v–131. During the Interregnum there is evidence that the
    Prayer Book was not completely abandoned but continued in use in parts of Gloucester-
    shire. Bishop Juxon (archbishop of Canterbury after the Restoration), for example,
    continued to say divine service at his estate at Little Compton. Perhaps among his gathered
    congregation were some people responsible for the county's petition in support of the
    established church. *VCH Gloucester*, ii, p. 38.
[164] BL, Thomason Tracts E.151(11), pp. 6–7.

peace should be punished.[165] Later in the summer seven or eight men were complained against for 'pulling down the Rails about the Communion table in an insolent and tumultuous Manner' and were found guilty of the charges brought against them in a petition to the Lords. New rails were ordered to be put up 'in the same Manner as they were for the Space of Fifty Years last past, but not as they were for Four of Five Years last past' – an order which reflected the majority attitude concerning Laudian liturgical innovations. It was also ordered that the expense of the new rails would be charged to the delinquents, that they must make a public acknowledgement of their faults in church on the sabbath, and finally they were committed to the Fleet to await the pleasure of the House.[166] The Saint Saviour rioters pleaded poverty, expressed due humility and sorrow at their actions, and their release was ordered by the House on 20 July 1641.[167] This distinction between sound 'ancient' rails and unsound Laudian rails was made by others, as well as by members of the House of Lords. Ephraim Udall, rector of Saint Augustine's, Watling Street, maintained that rails, strictly speaking, were not:

an innovation. This is apparent enough in the Railes about the Table, for use of the Communion have been the custom in many churches, Towne and Countrey, beyond the memory of many people of 60 or 80 yeares old, who tell of Railes in Churches when they were borne.

Udall attacked the Laudian practice of east-ended altars, but defended rails and kneeling to receive the sacrament. He is describing the custom of railing a centrally placed holy table in the chancel or transept. He was adamantly against people receiving in their pews, claiming that there was a real danger of spilling wine on communicants' heads, as well as it being unseemly for clergy to scramble over women and maids while attempting to communicate them.[168]

The House of Lords received another London petition from the minister and parishioners of Saint Olave, which complained against four men:

for making, and causing to be made, a great Tumult and Disorder in the Church of the said Parish, in the Time of the Administration of the Blessed Sacrament and for the Hinderance of the performing of the same, and for the great abuse of the

---

[165] BL, Harl. MS 6424, fols. 6–6v (16, 18 January 1641).
[166] *LJ*, iv, pp. 270, 277 (17 June 1641). For the petition brought against the rioters, see *LJ*, iv, p. 270 (9 June 1641). See also James S. Hart, 'The House of Lords and reformation of justice, 1640–1643' (University of Cambridge Ph.D., 1984), pp. 99–105, 121, 225–6, 231 and his *Justice Upon Petition: the House of Lords and the reformation of justice 1621–1675* (London, 1991), pp. 71–5, 158–64; and below, pp. 137–40.
[167] *LJ*, iv, pp. 300, 318, 321 (20 July 1641).
[168] Ephraim Udall, *Communion Comelinesse* (1641), pp. 20, 4–5. Udall claimed he was often accused of being a puritan and was the son of the prominent puritan divine John Udall. *DNB*.

minister that administered the same, and for using unreverent Speeches when the said Duty was performing.[169]

All four Saint Olave rioters were found guilty. Two of the four, Robert Wainman and George Bonace, were committed without bail to six months imprisonment, fined £20 to the king, and required to stand upon 'high stools' in Cheapside and Southwark for two hours on two market days and acknowledge their faults. The other two, Hugh Evans and John More, were ordered to stand committed to the King's Bench until sureties were found, and at the next assizes held in the county of Surrey 'their Faults and Offences in disturbing and hindering the Administration of the Blessed Sacrament' were to be proceeded against according to the law. Eventually the former two Saint Olave men reappear in the *Lords Journal* as having acknowledged as just and honourable their punishment and expressed, according to the *Journal*, great sorrow at causing a 'tumult at the time when the sacrament was administered'. They were set free and pardoned with this admonition: 'That this shall be a Warning to them (all others) for offending hereafter in the like kind.'[170]

The strength of support for the established church in Southwark is further illustrated by the high number of parishioners who received Communion in the late Elizabethan and Jacobean period. Levels of Communion were perhaps as high as 80 per cent to 98 per cent in Saint Saviour's parish during that time.[171] The Southwark pro-church petition was produced, then, out of a context of strong conformity in which religious controversy had erupted into violence – violence which received considerable attention from Westminster:

And our Ministers who by the Statutes are bound to use the forme of the Booke of Common prayer, and no others, together with those Rites there enjoyned are, for making conscience to obey the Statutes, mocked and abused by base terms in the Church, and in the Streets, nay some have been threatened so that they dare not weare their Ministeriall garments, nor use the formes of Service by Law prescribed. And our ancient Vestry men, who were wont to keepe their Parishes in good order, are contemned and abused by a rude company of young, poore, and unworthy fellows; which disorders have bred great schandall and distractions among all true hearted Subjects and Protestants, and much griefe we verily beleeve to every one save Papists and Schismatickes, who make a sport at Gods dishonour, and this our Church of *Englands* troubles.[172]

The relatively non-vindictive but nevertheless firm way in which the

---

[169] *LJ*, iv, p. 277.
[170] *LJ*, iv, pp. 277–8 (17 July 1641), 323 (22 July 1641); Fletcher, *Outbreak*, pp. 111, 288.
[171] Jeremy Boulton, 'The limits of formal religion: the administration of Holy Communion in late Elizabethan and early Stuart London', *London Journal* 10:2 (1984), p. 148; *Neighbourhood and Society: a London suburb in the seventeenth century* (1987), pp. 14–15.
[172] BL, Thomason Tracts, E.151(11), p. 7.

Southwark church rioters were dealt with by the House of Lords in the pre-war days of the Long Parliament, certainly gives weight to the assertion that conformist petitioners were not entirely misguided in expecting some satisfaction from parliament. The conformists of Southwark had good reason to expect a sympathetic response from a parliament which had punished the rioters. The sentiments expressed in the Lords' order that at Saint Saviour the Communion rails should be repaired and put up 'in the same Manner as they have been for the Space of Fifty Years last past, but not as they were for Four or Five Years last past' was one that no doubt met with the approval of those responsible for the conformist petition.[173]

'THE COMMON ENEMY OF ROME'

There can be little doubt that the petitioners for the established church saw themselves aligned with the protestant churches of Europe. It is striking, therefore, that 'popery' is not a major obsession of conformist petitioners. They certainly did not like it, but the common coinage of so much religious rhetoric of the period – the refrain of the 'pope as anti-christ' – is largely, though not entirely, absent.[174] Petitions from Herefordshire and Staffordshire did stress that episcopacy was responsible for victories over 'Schismes and Heresies and especially of late yeares, against that *Hydra* of Heresies, the Roman Papacy'. To them it was an institution 'happy before the corruption of Popery'.[175] One might think that beating extensively on an anti-popery drum might provide a point of agreement with hotter protestants. However, as with anti-Arminianism – though not to that degree – the opportunity was not taken.[176] Perhaps their greater sense of belonging to the ancient, but reformed, Church *in* England, made this less of a pressing issue for conformists.[177] It is interesting to speculate (for that is all the evidence allows) that these petitioners may be closer to Milton's '*avant*

---

[173] See above, pp. 99–104 for a discussion of conformist anti-Laudianism. See below for more about rails, pp. 137–41. This picture of the Long Parliament and attitudes towards religious reform is more complex than saying that the Long Parliament 'caught up with Puritan objectives'. Aston, 'Puritans and iconoclasts', p. 117.

[174] Lake has convincingly established its importance in English protestant thought. Peter Lake, 'Anti-popery: the structure of a prejudice', in *Conflict in Early Stuart England: studies in religion and politics 1603–1625*, ed. Richard Cust and Ann Hughes (London, 1989); 'The significance of the Elizabethan identification of the pope as Antichrist', *JEH* 31:2 (1980).

[175] Aston, *Collection*, p. 69; see also pp. 42–3 for Staffordshire.

[176] The subject on which so much historians' ink has been spilt – the debate over grace – is almost completely absent from the pro-church petitions. See above, pp. 105–6.

[177] For example, note their emphasis on the 'purity' of the Prayer Book from Romish corruptions. See above, pp. 114–16.

garde conformists' in seeing the Church of Rome more as a corrupt and corrupting communion than as a completely false church.[178]

Allusions in the petitions to Roman Catholicism are largely limited to taking umbrage at accusations of popery by stressing that the Church of England was purged and refined from Romish corruptions, rather than engaging in fresh attacks on the errors of Rome.[179] Bedfordshire petitioners did stress how English bishops had shed their blood 'against the common enemy of Rome'.[180] Of greater contemporary significance to the petitioners about popery seemed to be concern that attacks from within the established church on its polity and liturgy were providing a great propaganda boost for the Church of Rome – even, it was ventured, playing into their hands. The eclectic group calling themselves the '*Colledges and Halls and others*' claimed that petitioning against the Church of England caused 'great disheartening of all Learning (if such designes find favour), the grievous schandall of the Reformed Religion as unstable, and the unspeakable advantage of our Enemies of *Rome*'.[181] Surrey petitioners pragmatically stressed that abolishing bishops and the liturgy after nearly a century of apologetics for the Elizabethan Settlement, would strengthen the 'Roman party':

What apparent cause of insultation and triumph would be given our Adversaries of the Roman party . . . that both our Doctrine and Government, [which] have been first and principally authorized by the divine and heavenly Sentence of holy Scripture, and have had the full approbation and testimony of the most pure and incorrupt times of the Primitive Church. With what face of countenance shall we now look upon them, if we shall at once cast off, as altogether polluted and Antichristian, that *Hierarchie*, that Sacred and Apostolicall Government?[182]

Sir Edward Dering was expressing such views on the floor of the Commons as well when he complained in November 1641:

If I would deale with a Papist, to reduce him, he answers (I have been answered so already) To what Religion would you perswade me? What is the Religion you professe? Your nine and thirty *Articles* they are contested against: your publique solemne Liturgy, that is detested: And which is more than both of these, the three essentiall, proper, and onely Markes of a true Church [Lord's Prayer, Apostles' and Nicene creeds], they are protested against: what Religion would you perswade me

---

[178] See Milton, *Catholic and Reformed*, part i, *passim*, esp. pp. 146–72. For a briefer discussion of many of the same ideas see his 'The Church of England, Rome and the true church: the demise of a Jacobean consensus', in *The Early Stuart Church, 1603–1642*, ed. Kenneth Fincham (London, 1993).

[179] As in the petitions for Bedfordshire, Southwark and Huntingdonshire. PRO, SP16 476; BL, Thomason Tracts E.151(11); Nalson, *Impartial Collection*, ii, pp. 720–2. There were also calls for the enforcement of laws against papists and sectaries as in the Oxfordshire petition. Aston, *Collection*, p. 63.

[180] PRO, SP16 476.   [181] Aston, *Collection*, p. 38.

[182] BL, Thomason Tracts E.151(11), p. 2.

to? where may I find, and know, and see and read the Religion you professe? I beseech you (*Sir*) help me an answer to the Papist.[183]

Loss of face seems to have been as much a concern to conformist petitioners as the battle with the anti-christ itself.

ISSUES OF AUTHORITY AND POWER

To stop the discussion of the rhetoric of the petitions at this point might leave the reader with a false impression of the ecclesiology contained in them. On one hand, the stock is high both of the episcopal ministry and the Book of Common Prayer: the former clearly apostolic with heroic martyrs in its ranks; the latter a liturgy composed by martyrs, in harmony with the primitive church and the protestant churches of Europe and which clearly nourished the spiritual hunger of a not insignificant part of the population. To stop here, however, would be to avoid the whole issue of power and authority in the life of the church. In the minds of conformist petitioners, how was the divine will for the church authenticated for English Christians? What was the process as opposed to the content?

The petitions present a complex picture of the roles of the crown and parliament in authenticating and preserving the religious settlement. On one hand emphasis is given to the roles of Elizabeth and James as establishers and protectors of the Church of England. Lancashire petitioners defended the pre-Laudian church as conforming 'to the modell of Queene *Elizabeths* dayes, (of ever blessed memory)'.[184] Worcestershire conformists suggested that attacks on the polity and liturgy of the established church were affronts to 'those Religious princes of ever blessed memory Queen Elizabeth and King James' and that those two sovereigns were 'traduced as Anti-Christian'.[185] As Margaret Aston has observed, the debate within the immediately post-Laudian Church of England was a debate over whether a pure church had once existed and was being restored or whether it was only now being brought into existence.[186] On the other hand, petitioners also stressed that the Book of Common Prayer and episcopacy benefited from the backing of both crown *and* parliament. Gloucestershire conformists emphasized their point by remarking that disruptions of Prayer Book services 'even whilst it [the Prayer Book] stands established by act of Parliament'[187] were an affront to the authority of the

---

[183] Dering, *Speeches*, p. 100; see also pp. 93–4.
[184] Aston, *Collection*, p. 53. As did Southwark, Dorset and Shropshire. Dorset: BL, Add. MS 29975, fol. 130. Southwark: BL, Thomason Tracts E.151(11); Shropshire: Nottingham University Library, PW2/HY/173.
[185] Townshend, *Diary*, ii, p. 45.   [186] Aston, 'Puritans and iconoclasm', pp. 120–1.
[187] BL, Add. MS 11055, fols. 130v–131.

very body which had passed the Act of Uniformity. Cornish petitioners called on parliament to take a stand firmly behind the lawful liturgy and enforce conformity with enthusiasm.

[That parliament should] have in high account, and externize (as farre as in you lies) the Divine and excellent forme of Common Prayer, to correct braine-forged doctrine, [and] by your exemplary precepts strike a Reverence of Gods House into every Mans breast.

These petitioners made a link between the failure to achieve a consensus on church reform, the resulting uncertainty, and the declining spiritual welfare of the nation: 'That you will be pleased to intimate to the people, your Honourable and wise intentions concerning Divine Service, lest while you hold your peace, some rejecting it in part, others altogether, they vainly conceive you continance them.'[188] The Cornish petitioners clearly had hopes that the Long Parliament would be on the side of the church 'of Elizabeth and James'. Significantly too, it was to parliament that they appealed for remedy in a time of religious uncertainty. At an ideological level, this may represent how engrained the Tudor policy of using the legislature to validate religious policy had become. At the level of *Realpolitik*, it may show yet again how deep was the mistrust of Charles I, even among religious conservatives.

It is striking that almost none of the petitions under discussion are addressed exclusively to the king.[189] Dorset petitioners certainly expressed a sense of religious decline during Charles' reign from earlier, purer times, when they called for the protection of the 'antient church government by Bishopps and this holy forme of divine service established by the Lawe of this Kingdome & used in the *purest times* of Queen Elizabeth and King James of Blessed memory'.[190] If the stock of the safely dead Elizabeth and James was high, the standing of the all too alive Charles I was in decline. There was, in fact, serious mistrust of Charles among supporters of the established church. Sir Edward Dering and other activists for the Kentish pro-church petition consciously decided not to forward a copy of their petition directly to the king.[191] Sir Thomas Aston's *A Collection of Sundry Petitions*, in which many of these texts appear, did receive royal approval but Aston's own preface is addressed to 'the Reader' and makes no direct reference to the role of the present monarch in church matters.[192] In fact,

---

[188] Second Cornish petition in Aston, *Collection*, p. 67. See also the third Cornish petition on this same theme: BL, Thomason Tracts E.150(28) [p. 41].

[189] See below, Appendix 1.　　[190] My italics. BL, Add. MS 29975, fol. 130.

[191] *LJ*, iv, pp. 677–8; Everitt, *Kent*, p. 96.

[192] Aston, 'The collector to the reader', in *Collection*. This mistrust of Charles and desire to undermine his power (not only in religious matters) helps to explain why some members of the Lords supported the exclusion of bishops from the upper house but were also in favour

there is a 'real absence' in the pro-church petitions of calls for Charles to involve himself in saving the church from the Rooters or the promoters of Thorough, or indeed to personally rescue the church of which he was the supreme governor.[193] If there was to be any substantive reform of the church as opposed to correction of abuses and punishment of their perpetrators – though petitioners professed they saw little need for the former – it was to be authorized by parliament under the guidance of a synod of divines.[194] Oxfordshire conformists doubted the need for substantive change but if the discussion was to be opened up, desired the creation of a synod of divines to be called by parliament:

[We urge] that the *Government* of this *Church*, may continue, as is now by Law established: and that the *Liturgy* may be settled with such alterations (if there be cause) as your Wisdomes shall approve . . . That a free *synod* of *Orthodox* and peacable *divines* may be convened, according to the forme of the *Primitive*, and Purest times of *Christianity* for the composing of all differences in Doctrine, and *Ceremonies* of *Religion*.[195]

Sir Edward Dering in a speech in November 1641 called for a national synod of divines to settle religious matters, stressing that MPs were not trained theologians and had no great expertise in divinity.[196] The sentiments found here no doubt reflect the deep mistrust Charles had created in the provinces – even amongst those like Sir Thomas Aston, who would be drawn to royalism in the summer of 1642. In fact, as is gaining wide acceptance, concern for the future of the liturgy and episcopal government was a significant factor in drawing many to overcome their particular unease about Charles I and to take up arms in the royalist cause.[197]

of the Book of Common Prayer. Conrad Russell, *The Fall of British Monarchies 1637–1642* (Oxford, 1991), p. 337.

[193] Exception to this generalization includes the petitions from Essex and Lancashire. Leicestershire RO, Acc. No. DE221/13/2/26; Aston, *Collection*, pp. 51–4.

[194] So said petitions from Dorset, Nottinghamshire, Gloucestershire, Cornwall, and Oxfordshire.

[195] Aston, *Collection*, p. 63.

[196] Dering, ever consistent in his inconsistency, formulated his own plans for a 'primitive episcopate' which he put forward in a speech in June 1641. He suggested that dioceses should be coterminous with county boundaries, thus making them administratively more manageable and that bishops should be chosen from among the clergy in each shire. Under his scheme bishops would also be forbidden secular office. Dering, *Speeches*, pp. 66–78.

[197] Fletcher, *Outbreak*, p. 283; Peter King, 'The reasons for abolition of the Book of Common Prayer in 1645' *JEH* 21:4 (1970), pp. 335–6. David Smith, *Constitutional Royalism and the Search for Settlement, c.1640–1649* (Cambridge, 1994), ch. 4, pp. 143–56. Smith plays down religious zeal among the small group of future royalists he highlights in his important study and emphasized that they 'wished to make the Caroline Church acceptable not to God, but to "Jacobethan" values'. These petitions suggest that other future royalists were convinced that the church of Elizabeth and James was clearly already acceptable to God. Smith, *Constitutional Royalism*, p. 62.

There can be little doubt that the sentiments expressed in these petitions between 1641 and the summer of 1642 help to account for the creation of a royalist party. Attachment to the Prayer Book was genuine and respect for the episcopal office was made of sterner stuff than even the policies of Archbishop Laud could corrupt. Episcopacy had an advantage in 1642, but not by 1645, which monarchy had not: individuals could be replaced while the office was maintained. This was an attitude towards monarchy, despite medieval precedent, which would require civil war and an English republic to alter. The fortunes of the later Stuarts show that, as with bishops, the distinction between office and person could be applied even to the monarchy. Subsequent events show that concern for the safety of the established church would continue to shape the political loyalties of many well into the nineteenth century.

═══════════════ ⤛ *4* ⤜ ═══════════════

Sir Thomas Aston and the campaign for the established church, c. 1640–1642

> Aston, thou ventur'st faire, that dost not greet
> That Church, as others, with a winding sheet.
> That cryest not Downe with order, nor wilt say
> The miter's Aaron's calfe, the vestments gay
> Are the whore's robe, The Liturgie is naught
> With magicke, and Amens (god blesse us) fraught.[1]

Perhaps I had better explain why we are so firmly Church.[2]

THE WORLDLY CONCERNS OF A CHESHIRE CONFORMIST

In 1642, as a result of Sir Thomas Aston's activities on behalf of the Book of Common Prayer and episcopacy, an obscure Oxford undergraduate was moved to praise him in verse form. By that time, Aston had achieved prominence not only in his county of Cheshire, but nationally, as a recognized leader in the cause to preserve the reformed Church of England from destruction. His reputation was based exclusively on his activities between his failure to be reselected for the Long Parliament in the autumn of 1640 and the outbreak of the civil war in August 1642. In less than two years, a relatively obscure – though relatively learned – Cheshire gentleman became an important player in a doomed cause. Aston's role in the campaign to defend the lawful ceremonies and liturgy of the Church of England and a non-Laudian theology of the episcopate will now be explored in detail.

The larger set of concerns for the future of the Church of England, of which Aston can be seen as representative, have been the subject of some

---

[1] Aston Lodge, MS Poem by T. Tarne. *Alumni Oxonienses* (Oxford, 1891–92); A. G. Matthews, ed., *Walker Revised* (Oxford, 1948), p. 32. The manuscripts at Aston Lodge were unlisted when I began work on them. Part of the collection was photocopied for my own use and this is indicated by 'JM' followed by a number. The owner of the Aston papers has been developing his own reference system subsequently.

[2] Rose Macaulay, *The Towers of Trebizond* (London, 1981), p. 7.

scholarly attention.[3] These supporters of the church described themselves as 'Church of England Men' or as 'conformable men'. They shared with 'hotter' protestants (or 'puritans') an intense dislike of the innovations associated with the religious policies of the Personal Rule. This body of opinion, anti-Laudian, but pro-episcopalian, is found best expressed in the nearly thirty petitions produced for the Long Parliament (see chapter 3). These petitions, while decrying the damage done to the institution of episcopacy and to the Prayer Book by Laudian policy, nevertheless maintained their fundamental soundness. The key to understanding the main preoccupations of the petitioners was their dread of innovation in the church's worship rather than obsession with its doctrinal purity. The petitions made almost no reference to the soteriological question of whether the reception of saving grace by an individual is predetermined by God or requires, however minutely, a degree of human response and co-operation. Rather, it was liturgical novelty that caused this constituency distress, evident in the way conformists from North Wales described themselves as people 'who cannot without trembling entertain the thought of change'.[4] They constantly referred back to the 'church of Elizabeth and James', a preoccupation which, as Patrick Collinson has shown, cannot simply be dismissed as nostalgia or rhetoric.[5]

Aston's own biography and ancestry do little to support any anticipation of his remarkable, if brief, mid-life career as an apologist and activist for the Church of England. Sir Thomas Aston of Aston near Runcorn in Cheshire, was the first baronet of an ancient and notable Cheshire family. It was his achievement to raise his family to the level of major gentry in the county. The family had settled at Aston near Runcorn many generations before the seventeenth century, and several of Aston's medieval ancestors were knighted. Sir Thomas' father John (d. 1615), was sewer to Queen Anne and married Maude, daughter of Robert Needham of Sherton in Shropshire. Maude remarried twice after John's death. However, it was

---

[3] John Morrill, 'The church in England, 1642–9', in *Reactions to the English Civil War 1642–1649*, ed. John Morrill (London, 1982); 'The religious context of the English Civil War', *TRHS*, 5th ser., 34 (1984); 'The attack on the Church of England in the Long Parliament, 1640–1642', in *History, Society and the Churches: essays in honour of Owen Chadwick*, ed. Derek Beales and Geoffrey Best (Cambridge, 1985); Anthony Fletcher, *The Outbreak of the English Civil War* (London, 1981), esp. chs. 3 and 9; Anthony Milton, *Catholic and Reformed: the Roman and Protestant churches in English Protestant thought, 1600–1640* (Cambridge, 1995).

[4] 'Petition of North Wales', in Thomas Aston, *A Collection of Sundry Petitions* (London, 1642), p. 49.

[5] Patrick Collinson has given us a revised look at the Elizabethan and Jacobean church and stressed the vigour of its 'mainstream' in *The Religion of Protestants: the church in English society 1559–1625* (Oxford, 1982); see also, Kenneth Fincham, *Prelate as Pastor: the episcopate of James I* (Oxford, 1990); see above, pp. 126–7.

Thomas who improved both the social and financial position of his family in the county.[6]

Aston was born in 1600 and educated at Macclesfield Grammar School and Brasenose College, Oxford. He matriculated in 1617. It seems likely that he proceeded to the B.A. degree in 1619 and afterwards spent some time at Lincoln's Inn.[7] He married twice and, in both cases, to his advantage. His first marriage in 1627, was to Magdalene, daughter of Sir John Poultney and sister and co-heir to John Poultney of Misterton in Leicestershire. They had four children, none of whom survived to adulthood. Magdalene herself died in 1635.[8] Four years later Aston married Anne, sole heir of the future parliamentarian Sir Henry Willoughby of Risley in Derbyshire. Aston and Anne had a son, Willoughby, and two daughters, Magdalene and Mary, all of whom were still living in the 1660s. Willoughby survived the dangers of early modern childhood to become an important figure in Cheshire politics after the Restoration.[9]

Aston was created baronet in 1628 and his activities in the 1630s both in the 'county community' and in the court, resulted in his election to the Short Parliament in the spring of 1640.[10] Sir Thomas had connections at court. He was a gentleman of His Majesty's privy chamber by 1635 and his brother John was a courtier and later served on behalf of his elder brother in the Bishops' War.[11] However, it was his role in the controversy between

[6] J. P. Earwaker, *East Cheshire* (2 vols., London, 1877), ii, pp. 10, 160, 317, 448–9; G. Ormerod, *History of Cheshire*, revised by G. Helsby (3 vols., London, 1882), i, pp. 532–5; *DNB*; *VCH Chester*, ii, p. 42.

[7] *AO*; *VCH Chester*, iii, p. 237. Wood claims he entered as gentlemen commoner in 1626/7 but was soon called home by his relations. This, however, seems highly unlikely. Anthony Wood, *Athenae Oxonienses*, revised by Philip Bliss (5 vols., London, 1815), ii, pp. 184–5.

[8] Magdalene's death occasioned the commissioning of an extraordinary death-bed portrait of the Aston family by John Souch, which now hangs in the Manchester City Art Gallery. Aston's grief appears to have been profound; so argues Malcolm Rogers from an examination of the details of this highly complex painting. Malcolm Rogers, 'Acquisition in Focus: An English *Memento Mori*', *The Art Quarterly of the National Art Collections Fund* 11 (1993), pp. 39–41. I am grateful to Andrew Loukes of the Manchester City Art Galleries for this reference. See also Nigel Llewellyn, *The Art of Death* (London, 1991), pp. 47–9; C. H. Collins Baker, 'John Souch of Chester', *Connoisseur* 80 (1928), pp. 131–3. Aston also erected a memorial to Magdalene in Aston Chapel with the lines: 'Heere, reader, in this sad but glorious cell/ Of death lyes shrind a double miracle,/ Of woman and of wyfe, and each soe best,/ Shee may be fame's fayre coppy to the rest.' Ormerod, *Cheshire*, i, p. 727.

[9] Ormerod, *Cheshire*, i, p. 535; *VCH Chester*, ii, p. 119.

[10] *CSPD*, 1628–9, pp. 222, 225.

[11] I am grateful to Peter Salt for bringing to my attention a warrant in the Lord Chamberlain's warrant books describing Aston as 'a Gentleman Extraordinary of the Privy Chamber' (PRO, LC5/134, p. 170). John Aston (d. 1650) was active in royal service (e.g. *CSPD*, 1629–31, p. 161) and his adventures in the Bishops' War are described in his journal published in 'North counties diaries', *Surtees Society* 118 (1910). John appears to have been an able man in civil as well as military matters. Papers at Aston Lodge reveal the part he played in the running of the estate and the effort he expended after Sir Thomas' death in 1646 to defend successfully the family property from severe sequestration and fines on

Plate 4.1   Portrait of Sir Thomas Aston at the deathbed of his wife (probably by
John Souch ?c. 1635) (Manchester City Art Galleries)

the county and city of Chester over assessment for ship money that secured
Thomas' place among the leading gentry of the county.[12]

The Council in the 1630s increasingly by-passed traditional points of

---

behalf of his fatherless nephew Willoughby. Aston's second wife, Anne, also played an
important part in preserving the estate for her son. R. N. Dore, ed., *The Letter Books of Sir
William Brereton*, vol. II, LCRS, 123 (1983–4), pp. 37, 410.

[12] The following summary of Aston's activities in this sphere is indebted chiefly to an article
by Peter Lake, 'The collection of ship money in Cheshire during the Sixteen-thirties: a case
study of relations between central and local government', *Northern History* 17 (1981),
passim. See also Elaine Marcotte, 'Shrieval administration of ship money in Cheshire, 1637:
limitations of early Stuart governance', *Bulletin of the John Rylands University Library of
Manchester* 58 (1975), pp. 148–50.

contact in the localities through the development of the office of ship money sheriff as a direct agent of central government. Fortuitously for Sir Thomas, the conflict of interests over assessment between the city of Chester and the shire allowed him to appear both as a careful servant of the crown's rights and as a defender of the county's interests against the city. The city claimed exemption from the jurisdiction of the ship money sheriff and was attacked by Aston for attempting to set a precedent that would prove prejudicial to the king's interests. This, combined with Aston's record as a successful collector of the levy in 1634–35,[13] greatly increased his prestige with central government, while his zealous campaign on behalf of the county against the city improved his standing in the county establishment. It also meant that the larger question of the legality of ship money was not addressed, obscured as it was by the dust clouds of local controversy.

Aston's initial success against the city, however, soon proved to be a mixed blessing, and he found himself assessed by a vengeful city for his own French wine-importing business in Chester. This meant that he was facing a double assessment: for the city, where his business was located, and for the county, where he was resident. This was a jurisdictional dispute with possible implications for the interests of the county and Aston's new-found standing in it. He refused to contribute towards the city's assessments. This action was viewed with favour locally, but Aston's position with the Council began to show signs of strain. The Council, dangling the carrot of future preferment, urged Sir Thomas to pay the assessment, noting that the sum in question was only £5. But Aston was now waist deep in his role as defender of the county's interests – indeed his new-found standing in Cheshire depended on it – and he continued to resist payment. His tenacity on behalf of the county did not go unappreciated. When the dispute came to a head in late May 1638, no fewer than twenty-two Cheshire gentlemen journeyed up to London with Aston when he appeared

---

[13] However, the methods employed by Aston in his successful tenure as ship money sheriff left problems for his successors. He raised a third of the sum by assessing the personal wealth of the more substantial men in Cheshire, concerned that the tax burden was already too great and fearful of the social unrest that could be caused by the imposition of a tax which reached further down the social scale than usual. Not surprisingly, such a practice was greeted with mistrust and Aston undertook a series of meetings with constables and local gentlemen to assure them that this step would not set a precedent. Indeed, in the mid-1630s the view that ship money was an extraordinary measure was still credible and accounts for its success nationally as well as in Cheshire. This argument, however, was obviously becoming threadbare towards the end of the decade. Another significant factor in the falling collection rate of ship money sheriffs was the additional financial strain caused by the unpopular Scottish War. Lake, 'Collection of ship money', p. 58; John Morrill, *The Revolt of the Provinces: conservatives and radicals in the English Civil War 1630–1650* (London, 1976, 1980), pp. 25–7.

before the Council. By this time, however, both the king and the Lord Keeper were supporting the city's claim against him. The meeting was a stormy one and included the unedifying scene of Sir Thomas pleading on his hands and knees until the king ordered him from the room. Aston's continued resistance in the face of royal disapproval may appear to have gone beyond prudent self-interest.[14] However, by 1640 Sir Thomas was established among the leaders of the county community: he was perceived as a zealous critic of ship money and defender of the county's interests against the city, although not against central government. All this had come about despite his admirable record as a collector of the levy five years before, and the fact that his attack on ship money was essentially of a jurisdictional nature and did not touch fundamental questions of the levy's legality. All in all, the events of the 1630s reveal Aston as a capable and astute navigator in the treacherous currents of the Personal Rule.[15] His firmly established reputation in the county community was undoubtedly decisive in his election for the shire in the spring of 1640. The unfortunate brush with royal displeasure put in place the very sort of network with his peers that would become crucial in producing the Cheshire petitions for episcopacy and the Book of Common Prayer.

The spring elections in Cheshire were contentious and bitter. The shire was badly under-represented in the House of Commons, with only two seats for the city and two for the county. Too many gentlemen chasing too few seats no doubt inflated their value. The fact that the elections were fiercely contested, however, owed more to the existence of long-standing local rivalries among the gentry, than to the existence of ideological parties. Ironically, Aston was partnered with Sir William Brereton, his future military adversary, who had served in the parliament of 1628. They received the backing of the 'barons' (chief among them Lords Cholmondeley and Kilmorey), but were challenged by the 'patriots' (or 'baronets'), led by Sir George Booth and Sir Richard Wilbraham, who probably articulated a more blatantly 'anti-court platform'. John Werden, a minor Cheshire gentlemen, and later a staunch ally in Aston's pro-church activities,[16] observed in letters to Sir Thomas Smith, a candidate for one of the

---

[14] It is important to note, as Lake has done, that the Privy Council was not perceived as a monolithic institution and Aston's persistence beyond the point of apparent prudence may have been the result of having friends and supporters on the Council. He may have been playing for time, hoping for a meeting from which the king and Lord Keeper were absent.

[15] Morrill has noted that many MPs who became noted for opposition to ship money in the Long Parliament were diligent collectors of the levy, while others who eventually supported the king were ardent critics of the tax. Morrill, *Provinces*, p. 25.

[16] BL, Add. MS 36914, fols. 206–206v, 210–211v, 214–215v. 'John Werden' is mistranscribed as 'Thomas Murden' in the *CSPD*.

Chester seats, that the contest was more the result of personality and ambition than of ideology:

[These] lords have so bitter a distaste of the neglect given them by our two great patriots [Booth and Wilbraham], as for aught I see, the matter grows very high, and the contestation like to be the greatest that ever we heard in our country . . . Sir William Brereton and Sir Thos. Aston were both lately with me, and both of them are pretty confident and full of reproaches against the two popular patriots . . . neither of whom will appear at the election, it is said, or, if they do, they are sure to be boldly accused in the face of their country as adversaries to the peace of it . . . I sit down in silence to see what God will do in the ambition of these men, who all joined in their own profit where there was a bare pretence of a public good, and now rend the bowels of it to advance their own interest and popularity.[17]

It certainly was a bitter 'contestation', including accusations against Aston that he had overassessed as ship money sheriff and pocketed the difference.[18] When the lord lieutenant declared for Aston and Brereton, the 'patriots' finally withdrew from the contest.[19]

At the time, the combination of Aston and Brereton as representatives of the shire in the Commons must have seemed an appealing one. Brereton knew Westminster, having sat for the county in 1628. He was one of the most active of the JPs and popular with 'the godly'.[20] The full extent of his radicalism at this point was either well concealed, or latent, as John Morrill has suggested.[21] The fact that Aston was later to emerge as an ardent episcopalian and royalist, and Brereton as a religious radical and parliamentarian, demonstrates sharply the depth of the sense of grievance with royal policies which united these two representatives of the county establishment on the eve of the Short Parliament.

Given the strength of Aston's position, his failure to be reselected in the autumn is surprising. The sudden dissolution of the Short Parliament on 5 May revealed a stunning lack of achievement: the king still had no subsidies for the Scottish War, and the representatives of the political nation 'rode

---

[17] *CSPD*, 1639–40, pp. 564–5, 590–1. The elections for the city were also contentious, though not to the degree of those for the county.

[18] Aston denied the charges. Lake, 'Collection of ship money', pp. 67–8; *CSPD*, 1639–40, p. 564.

[19] *VCH Chester*, ii, p. 108.

[20] *CSPD*, 1639–40, p. 565; Lake, 'Collection of ship money', p. 62; John Morrill, *Cheshire 1630–1660* (London, 1974), pp. 25, 33.

[21] Brereton's exact position on ship money abounds in ambiguities. In the mid-1630s, the corporation of Chester undertook a series of legal actions against exempt jurisdictions within its bounds. The city claimed that the tenants of Brereton's former monastic property should be prepared to perform watch and ward. When the Privy Council found for Brereton in the dispute, they noted that he had promptly paid his ship money assessment. In 1638, however, the sheriff, Sir Thomas Cholmondeley, accused Sir William of personally encouraging his (Brereton's) tenants to default on their ship money payments. Brereton denied this accusation. John Morrill, 'Sir William Brereton and England's Wars of Religion', *JBS* 24:3 (1985). For the second point, see Marcotte, 'Shrieval administration', pp. 157–8.

home . . . yt day' with neither redress of grievances, or even the promise of it.[22] The Short Parliament revealed, despite its brevity, that although the Commons were united in identifying points of grievance in religious matters, property, and the liberties of parliament, there was no consensus over what form redress and reform should take. In this way, Brereton's radicalism began to manifest itself to the 'barons' and perhaps to Sir William himself. In the autumn elections, the 'barons' decided to drop their support for Brereton.[23] Peter Venables, Lord Cholmondeley's brother-in-law, was put in his place and paired with Aston. Significantly, Venables too enjoyed a reputation as 'an open instigator of resistance to ship money in 1639–40'.[24]

Abandoned by the 'barons', Brereton ran an independent and, as it turned out, highly successful campaign. Venables won the second seat and Aston was completely left out. As Morrill has noted, Brereton's victory in spite of the opposition of the county establishment 'exemplifies the case recently argued that the gentry sought to avert polls, not simply because of expense, but also because . . . the volatility of the electorate made the outcome unpredictable'.[25] While this goes some way to explaining Sir William's impressive *coup*, it does not clear up the riddle of Aston's defeat. It may have been, as Peter Lake has suggested, that the individuals responsible for the rumours concerning Aston's alleged misconduct as ship money sheriff were motivated by the realisation that his attitude to the court was at best ambiguous, and that his 'opposition' to the levy rested on technicalities over jurisdiction, rather than on constitutional principles. Venables, who was also a future royalist, had the joint advantage of a close Cholmondeley connection and a name as a hard-liner on ship money.[26] However, the autumn elections may also be seen not so much as a rejection of Aston, but rather as an impressive personal achievement for Sir William Brereton.

AN ACTIVIST FOR THE CHURCH OF ENGLAND

Sir Thomas Aston: a 'godly' gentleman?

We know little of Aston's religious views before 1640, except for what may be discerned from his patronage of Aston Chapel. In 1635, he oversaw the

---

[22] *Proceedings of the Short Parliament 1640*, ed. Esther Cope, Camden Fourth Series, xix (1977), p. 244; see also *The Short Parliament (1640) Diary of Sir Thomas Aston*, ed. Judith Maltby, Camden Fourth Series, xxxv (1988).

[23] *VCH Chester*, ii, p. 108. It should be noted, however, that Brereton appears never to have contributed to debate in the Short Parliament.

[24] Lake, 'Collection of ship money', p. 68.

[25] *VCH Chester*, ii, p. 108. A reference to Derek Hirst, *The Representative of the People?* (Cambridge, 1975).

[26] Lake, 'Collection of shipmoney', p. 68.

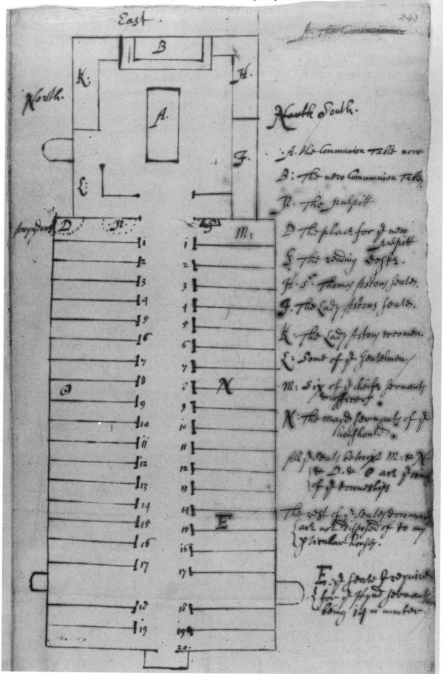

Plate 4.2 Plan of Aston Chapel, Cheshire, c. 1635 (British Library)

refurbishment of the chapel, following instructions of the bishop of Chester, John Bridgeman. A ley was imposed on the locality to cover the costs of the 'improvements' and Aston Chapel also had parochial rights and status conferred upon it at the same time by the bishop. A surviving floor plan of the building shows the way Aston, as patron, redistributed the pews, which inevitably led to some disagreement over their allocation – in this case with his cousin Elizabeth Warburton.[27] However, the plan also reveals that until the bishop's intervention, the Communion table had stood squarely in the chancel, in the so-called 'table-wise' position, in full accordance with the practice of the Elizabethan and Jacobean church.[28] Bridgeman, however, ordered compliance with the new Laudian orthodoxy concerning the location of the holy table:

At which day it is ordered by the said Reverend Father that with all convenient speed the Communion Table which stands undecently in the middle of the Chancell be removed and set North and South under the East window of the said Chancell, and be decentlye made about the same, and also that the vestry Chest be taken from the said East wall, and sit in the Bellfrey or some more convenient place.[29]

There can be little doubt that Bridgeman, who had been appointed to the diocese in 1619 in the more irenic days of James I, was buckling under pressure from Charles, and from Archbishop Neile and Archbishop Laud. His reputation before Laud's archepiscopate was one of winking at minor non-conformity among his own diocesan clergy. It should be understood that the bishop's latitude in matters of ceremony was not the result of

---

[27] BL, Add. MS 36914, fols. 187, 189, 193; BL, Add. MS 36919, fols. 217–217v, 219, 219v, 243–244v. The floor plan of Aston Chapel is BL, Add MS 36919, fol. 243. See Plate 4.2. The allocation of seating in a place of worship was a highly volatile issue, involving as it did ancient privileges and contemporary social status in the local community. Refurbishment of churches along Laudian lines often required reallocation of the pews, which not infrequently led to disputes in church courts about who had the right to occupy which pews. It is with such costly and protracted suits in mind that Neile in a letter dated 7 January 1635, advised Bridgeman against his plan to segregate the sexes:

Touching the reducing of the seats in the parish Churches and Chappells to an uniformity, the worke is such as I thinke no man will distaste or oppose. But for the rest of your intentions for the disposing of the seats, as to sitt the men on the one side of the Church and the woemen on the other side, otherwise then in times past hath been used, or to remoove any from the place where they and their ancesters have time out of mind accustomed to sitt, will begett more brabbles, suits in law, & prohibitions, then either you or I would be contented to be trouble with.

Staffordshire RO, D1287/P/399/123. For a further discussion of social dimension of church seating, see below, pp. 197–9.

[28] In other words, with the short sides of the holy table facing east–west, rather than north–south. Also the pulpit was moved further to the north side of the chapel. BL, Add. MS 36919, fol. 243. See Plate 4.2.

[29] 'Order prescribed by the lord Bishop of Chester for the Chapple of Aston in Runcorne parish, the xii[th] Day of April 1635'. BL, Add. MS 36919, fol. 217.

administrative ineptitude on his part. Bridgeman's zeal knew no bounds when it came to extracting every possible source of income, however obscure or long forgotten, due his impoverished see. It was the combined and relentless pressure from the crown and both primates over the course of the 1630s that eventually forced Bridgeman to bring his zeal in money matters to bear on matters of ceremony. The bishop was the target of a particularly rigorous and stinging investigation by the crown into his management of the diocese in 1633.[30] His surviving correspondence reveals systematic and persistent intervention into diocesan affairs by both primates. Neile used his metropolitical powers to bring Bridgeman to heel. Laud, often stating that he was acting at the king's direction, frequently frustrated the hapless bishop over appointments to livings.[31] Even the bishop's apparent strong distaste for rigour in ceremonial discipline would have had trouble resisting such a systematic campaign to enforce conformity from his superiors. Bridgeman gave way and, as one nineteenth-century historian of non-conformity in the north-west remarked, was 'a forced persecutor, [and] like a conscript soldier, soon [learned] to fight as fiercely as a volunteer'.[32]

The tangible results of this pressure can be seen by comparing Bridgeman's visitation articles of 1634 and 1637. The 1634 articles simply inquired whether the church or chapel possessed 'a Communion Table with a hansome Carpet or Covering of like stuffe [as the pulpit cover], with a faire linnen cloth to lay upon the same'.[33] By 1637, however, Bridgeman was using the formal machinery of diocesan discipline to enforce a Laudian pattern on his cure. The holy table was to be: 'incompased with a decent raile: And is your Communion table removed long waies to the Chancell wall and set close thereunto, and no forme or seat above the Communion

---

[30] Kenneth Parker, *The English Sabbath: a study of doctrine and discipline from the Reformation to the Civil War* (Cambridge, 1988), pp. 164–5; Fincham, *Prelate as Pastor*, pp. 76–7, 109, 152, 171–2. Bridgeman's laxness in dealing with non-conformity did not go completely uncriticized by James I either. Fincham, *Prelate*, pp. 227n., 302. B. W. Quintrell, 'Lancashire Ills, the King's Will and the Troubling of Bishop Bridgeman', *THSLC* 132 (1983), pp. 67–102.

[31] For example, Staffordshire RO, D1287/P/399/124–31, 149, 169, 171, 183.

[32] Robert Halley, *Lancashire: its puritanism and nonconformity* (2 vols., Manchester, 1869), i, p. 259. Considering the fact that the bishop was threatened with criminal charges in 1633, his obedience brought about a major transformation in the relationship between Bridgeman and Laud. Before the meeting of the Short Parliament in 1640 the archbishop wrote to Bridgeman thanking him for sending a horse and offered the bishop accommodation near Lambeth Palace, and to share his river barge across the Thames as a means of getting to and from the House of Lords. Staffordshire RO, D1287/P/339/198.

[33] In common with many other early Stuart articles. *The Articles of which the Church-wardens and Swornemen throughout the Diocese of Chester* (London, 1634), article no. 47. See Kenneth Fincham, ed., *Visitation Articles and Injunctions of the Early Stuart Church*, vol. i, Church of England Record Society, 1 (1994), *passim*.

Table or betwixt it and the upper most wall of your Chancell.'[34] Judging from the bishop's instructions concerning Aston Chapel made in April 1635, the king and his metropolitans had forced Bridgeman's 'conversion' to their view well before the visitation of 1637.[35]

Judging by the floor plan of Aston Chapel, Sir Thomas complied with the bishop's orders.[36] However, given Aston's hostility towards the Laudians in 1640–42, expressed both in petitions and in his published writings, it is not unreasonable to suggest that he conformed, as many did, without enthusiasm. Sir Thomas' open criticism of Laudianism in 1640–42 cannot simply be dismissed as trimming his sails to suit new winds. Some historians may think so, but there is much to suggest that contemporaries at least saw the issue differently. The House of Lords, in its role as a place of judicial review, recognized that in the 1630s many laypeople had been forced to comply with Thorough or face prosecution from Laudian authorities. The Lords in the early 1640s, therefore, both vindicated parish officers who had suffered for standing against Thorough, and also absolved those who had been forced to comply on the basis that they were acting out of obedience.[37] It is in this light that the refurbishment at Aston Chapel should be seen.

Sir Thomas and his brother John both were involved in supporting a preaching minister, Robert Martin, at Aston from 1620 until the clergyman's death in June 1645. Martin appears to have laboured tirelessly in this small vineyard, as his flock later testified: '[he] was a constant Preacher at the said Chappell for the space of Twentye five years before his death or thereabouts. And that duringe all the sayd time hee was verye laborious and diligent in his Callinge never failinge to preach twice everye Lords Daye.'[38] So zealous a preacher of God's Word was he that the clergyman dropped dead in the pulpit in 1645. John took a leading role in organizing

[34] *Articles to be considered on . . . [in] the Diocese of Chester* (London, 1637), article no. 51.

[35] For Neile's commitment to the innovation of celebrating Communion on altars placed at the east end of the church rather than in a more central place as the Prayer Book directed, see Andrew Foster, 'Church policies of the 1630s', in *Conflict in Early Stuart England: studies in religion and politics 1603–1642*, ed. Richard Cust and Ann Hughes (London, 1989), pp. 203–7.

[36] BL, Add. MS 36919, fols. 243–44v.

[37] James S. Hart, 'The House of Lords and the reformation of justice, 1640–1643' (University of Cambridge Ph.D., 1984), pp. 99–105, 121, 225–6, 231. See also *The Book of Common Prayer 1559*, ed. John Booty (Washington, DC, 1976), p. 248; Ephraim Udall, 'To the Reader', in *Communion Comlinesse* (London, 1641), pp. 17–22.

[38] BL, Add. MS 36919, fol. 226. It is worth noting that the practice of preaching twice a day was condemned by Charles' *Instructions* of 1633, which ordered that the afternoon sermon should be replaced by catechizing. Edward Cardwell, *Documentary Annals of the Reformed Church of England* (2 vols., Oxford, 1834), ii, p. 178. I am grateful to John Morrill for making this point to me.

a collection for his widow.[39] In *A Remonstrance Against Presbytery*, Sir Thomas argued for the necessity of a preaching ministry as exercised by lawfully ordained clergy against those who maintained that anyone under the guidance of the Holy Spirit possessed the authority to preach:

> God (they say) rebuked Moses, *for excusing himselfe to be a man of imperfect lips*, And though the Apostle saies, *I am ordained a Preacher* [I Timothy 2.7], which implyes the necessity of lawfull Calling, whereupon is grounded an Article of our Religion, *That no man ought to Preach or minister the Sacrament, before he be lawfully called or sent* [Article 23 of the 39 Articles]: (with which acord the Confessions of all the Reformed Churches). And St. Paul seemes to rebuke all intruders into the Ministry, asking, *Are all Teachers?* [I Corinthians 12.28] Yet they contrary to the example of the Apostle, in absolute opposition to the Article of our Religion, will answer St. Paul in the Affirmative, yes.[40]

Important though it is that Sir Thomas defended the value of the preaching ministry in his published and private writings, far better evidence of his beliefs was his encouragement and patronage of such a diligent preacher and pastor as Robert Martin from as early as 1620, when Thomas would have been only about twenty years of age. Taken together, it argues for his place in mainstream conformity.

The brief but eventful period between Aston's failure to be returned to the Long Parliament and his military service in the civil war will now be examined. During these two years, Sir Thomas was occupied with petitioning, writing, and publishing on behalf of the established church. As a result of his activities Aston emerged as a leading lay defender of both episcopacy and the Book of Common Prayer. The baronet, like many of his contemporaries, longed for a return to the 'Anglicanism' of a Church of England uncorrupted by the recent and peculiar innovations of the Laudians.[41] This longing was expressed in terms of a return to the purity of the 'Church of Elizabeth and James'.[42] Aston's activities on behalf of the Church of England in Cheshire eventually earned him a national reputation, and transported him from a local stage onto a national platform. His activities certainly repaired any breach with the king caused by the unfortunate affair over his assessment a few years before.

---

[39] BL, Add. MS 36914, fols. 226–227v; BL, Add. MS 36919, fols. 226–28. This may be the Robert Martin of Cheshire who matriculated a plebian at Brasenose in April 1599, aged 20, and proceeded to the B.A. in 1602. Brasenose was also Sir Thomas' college. *AO*.

[40] Sec. 7, 'Episcopacy', in Thomas Aston, *A Remonstrance Against Presbytery* (n.p., 1641). The *Remonstrance* is discussed in greater detail below, pp. 156–70.

[41] Contemporaries understood and used the word 'Anglican' to mean conformity to the canons and constitutions of the Church of England. See Morrill, 'The church in England, 1642–1649', pp. 89, 231n.2.

[42] See above, pp. 126–7.

Petitioning for episcopacy and liturgy

Episcopalians in the provinces were slow to react to the threat posed by the Root and Branch petition in December 1640.[43] Supported by many of the leading gentry, Aston produced one of the first petitions supporting episcopal government in the winter of 1640–41.[44] A petition with over 6,000 subscribers was produced and presented to the House of Lords in late February.[45] There is virtually no extant evidence to relate how this first Cheshire petition in support of the established church was organised.[46]

The petitioners began with a complaint against 'divers Petitions', presumably of the Root and Branch variety, which had circulated in the county. They stated it was their clear duty to disavow such petitions.[47] The Cheshire petition went on to defend the episcopal order in terms which were echoed in other petitions.[48] The apostolicity and the antiquity of the order were stressed, as well as the martyrdoms of many early bishops as evidence of their commitment to the gospel:

Yet when we consider, that Bishops were instituted in the time of the Apostles; that they were great Lights of the Church in all the first General Counsils; that so many of them sowed the Seeds of Religion in their Bloods, and rescued Christianity from utter Extirpation in the Primative 'Heathan' Persecutions: that to them we ow [*sic*] the Redemption of the purity of the Gospel, we now profess, from *Romish* corruption.[49]

Aston's marginal notes on a printed broadsheet copy of the petition reveal what sort of evidence he believed to support the case laid out in the petition. Scriptural passages such as Philippians 1:1 and I Timothy 3:1 are noted. A list of early councils also appears, giving the number of bishops reportedly in attendance with a reference to Eusebius.[50] Rather than

---

[43] See above, pp. 88–93.

[44] Fletcher, *Outbreak*, pp. 107–8; William A. Abbott, 'The issue of episcopacy in the Long Parliament: the reasons for abolition' (University of Oxford D.Phil, 1981), pp. 187–8.

[45] *LJ*, iv, p. 174; the petition with its schedules of subscribers: HLRO, Main Papers, HL, [27] February 1640/1. For other copies, see below Appendix 1.

[46] See below, pp. 151–6.

[47] This may have been the petition text which comes near the beginning of the Cheshire petition for episcopacy in the House of Lords Record Office. Unfortunately the folios of this lengthy manuscript have never been numbered. HLRO, Main Papers, HL, [27] February 1640/1.

[48] See above, Chapter 3, *passim*.

[49] John Nalson, *An Impartial Collection of the Great Affairs of State* (2 vols., London, 1868), ii, pp. 759–60.

[50] Aston Lodge, MS JM/27 'A Petition Delivered in to the Lords Spirituall and Temporall by Sir Thomas Aston'. 'Paul and Timotheus, the servants of Christ Jesus which are at Philippi, with the bishops and deacons' (Philippians 1.1). 'This is a true saying, if a man desire the office of a bishop, he desireth a good work' (I Timothy 3.1). This point is discussed more fully below, pp. 156–61.

describing episcopacy as a remnant of years of 'Romish Corruption' over the English church, bishops were portrayed as a defence and remedy against such corruption:

That to them we ow[e] the Redemption of the purity of the Gospel, we now profess, from Romish Corruption; that many of them for the propagation of the Truth, became such Glorious Martyrs, that divers of them, lately, and yet living with us, have been so great Asserters of our Religion, against the common Enemy of Rome.

Aston's notes make clear which particular bishops he had in mind when the petition spoke of those who had redeemed the 'purity of the Gospel . . . from Romish Corruption [and] . . . became such Glorious Martyrs'. He listed in the margins: Cranmer, Latimer, Hooper, Ridley, Parkhurst, Parker, Grindal, Whitgift, 'etc'. Contemporary and near-contemporary bishops who have been 'so great Asserters of our Religion, against the common Enemy of Rome', he listed as Jewel, Hooper (again), Andrewes, White, Usher, Morton, Davenant, and Hall.[51]

Aston's ability to distinguish between individual bishops, approving of some and being critical of others, hardly made him unique. Other petitioners from other parts of the country did so as well.[52] Furthermore, in the early days of the Long Parliament, the credibility of certain individual bishops was still high. Bishop John Williams of Lincoln received a hero's welcome 'by the greater part of both houses' when he was released from the Tower and took his place in the upper house on 16 November 1640. Williams, who had opposed Laud on a number of issues in the 1630s, including the archbishop's altar policy, certainly had the credentials of a 'sufferer'.[53] Due to the energetic animosity of Laud's henchman Peter Heylyn, Williams, the bishop of the largest and one of the wealthiest dioceses in England had spent a good part of the 1630s either under investigation, on trial, or in prison.[54] John Williams was not the only bishop viewed sympathetically by members in the early days of the Long Parliament. Morton of Durham, Hall of Exeter, Potter of Carlisle, and

---

[51] Aston Lodge, MS JM/27 'A petition Delivered in to the Lords Spirituall and Temporall, by Sir Thomas Aston'. In some ways the presence of Lancelot Andrewes and Francis White in Aston's list is surprising. Andrewes, however, had been safely dead since 1626 and White, who died in 1638, had a reputation as a writer against popery. Hugh Trevor-Roper emphasizes his 'moderation' compared to his other Arminian contemporaries. Hugh Trevor-Roper, *Catholics, Anglicans and Puritans* (London, 1987), pp. 65, 80. Milton, *Catholic and Reformed*, pp. 32, 86, 365. I am grateful to Anthony Milton for making this point to me. For a selection of White's writings, see P. More and F. Cross, *Anglicanism: the thought and practice of the Church of England illustrated from the religious literature of the seventeenth century* (London, 1962).

[52] See above, pp. 107–13.

[53] John Williams, *The Holy Table, Name and Thing*, Diocese of Lincoln (1635).

[54] Abbott, 'Issue of episcopacy', p. 128; B. Dew Roberts, *Mitre and Musket: John Williams, Lord Keeper, Archbishop of York 1582–1650* (London, 1938).

Curle of Winchester were the bishops most frequently appointed to committees in the Lords in the first eight months. James Usher, archbishop of Armagh was resident in London by this time and was also highly regarded. In fact, according to William Abbott, Usher's fame as a scholar and preacher and his deliberate distance from Strafford's policies in Ireland, meant his popularity was even greater than Williams' or Morton's.[55]

To the Cheshire defenders of episcopacy, arguments from scripture and from the early and reformed church were obviously considered to be of central importance. Nevertheless, the petition also mentioned that episcopal government had the approval of English law: 'And that their [bishops'] government hath been so long approved, so oft established by the common and statute-lawes of this Kingdome.' Again, Aston's marginalia listed references from Coke and statute law on his own printed copy of the petition.[56] There is a sense in the petition as well that whatever the sins of individual bishops, the attack on the institution of episcopacy by members of the House of Commons was unwarranted and inappropriate: 'And as yet [there is] nothing in their doctrine (generally taught) dissonant from the Word of God, or the Articles ratified by Law.' Aston added his marginal gloss: 'particular new errors cannot be taken from the tenets of the Church'. To attack the entire institution for the errors of some individuals was, to put it bluntly, over-kill:

In this case to call their government a perpetuall vassalage, an intolerable bondage; And (*prima facie & inaudita altera parte*) to pray the present removall of them, or (as in some of their Petitions) to seeke the utter dissolution and ruine of their offices (as Antichristian) wee cannot conceive to relish of justice or charitie, nor can wee joyne with them.[57]

The petition continued by drawing out the civil implications of the attack through preaching and pamphlets on the ecclesiastical rule of bishops:

all of them dangerously exciting a disobedience to the Established Form of Government, and their several intimations of the desire of the Power of the Keys . . . We cannot but express our just Fears, that their desire is to introduce an absolute Innovation of Presbyterial Government, whereby We who are now governed by the Canon and Civil Laws, dispensed by Twenty six Ordinaries

---

[55] Abbott, 'Issue of episcopacy', p. 129. Abbott describes how these 'godly' bishops failed to capitalize on the good will they enjoyed in late 1640. Given that Williams is often described as the archetypal politician-prelate, he became surprisingly rigid in his dealings with those who desired a reformed episcopate. Abbott, 'Issue of episcopacy', pp. 129–38.

[56] Aston Lodge, MS JM/27 'A Petition Delivered in to the Lords Spirituall and Temporall, by Sir Thomas Aston'.

[57] Nalson, *Impartial Collection*, ii, p. 760; Aston Lodge, MS JM/27 'A Petition Delivered in to the Lords Spirituall and Temporall, by Sir Thomas Aston'.

[diocesan bishops], easily responsible to Parliaments for any deviation from the Rule of Law, conceive we should become exposed to the meer Arbitrary Government of a numerous Presbytery.[58]

Aston's hand in the composition of this petition may be reasonably assumed, as these themes were expanded in his *A Remonstrance against Presbytery*.[59] The day after its submission, the Cheshire petition was referred to the newly formed Committee for Religion in the Commons, the chairman of which, Sir Edward Dering of Kent, would eventually play a leading role in the production of a pro-church petition from his own county.[60]

Cestrians sympathetic to the preservation of the Church of England, as they perceived it, did not rest after the production of their petition in support of episcopacy. If the juggernaut of campaigning conformity was hard to start rolling, once begun it assumed momentum. Aston's chief allies in the county concerned with the nuts and bolts of the campaign were his brother John and an obscure Cheshire gentleman called John Werden. Sir Thomas' brother appears to have travelled frequently between Cheshire and Westminster on behalf of the cause. A letter from Werden to Aston at his brother's lodgings in London, reveals that within a fortnight (13 March 1641) after the presentation of the petition for episcopacy, they were busy again on behalf of the Church of England. Werden relates that such Cheshire worthies as Lord Cholmondeley and the earl of Derby had been contacted concerning their cause.[61] A week later, Cholmondeley himself wrote to Sir Thomas to express his support: 'I pray most humblie to god for the churches saftie from innovation.'[62] Towards the end of the month (24 March), however, Werden was finding it difficult to arouse support for the cause: 'All . . . here [in Cheshire are] now in a midnight sleepe . . . [and] yet they have had noe Generall Meetinge,' he complained. However, Werden also wrote that he had contacted a number of clergymen, conveying Aston's 'noble respects' and related 'theire humble acceptacons'.[63] Werden was obviously laying the groundwork for obtaining signatories for the next petition.

Aston was not only taking steps to consolidate support in the county, but was playing on a larger stage as well. In a letter dated two days later than Werden's (26 March), Aston was informed by Lord Cholmondeley that the king 'by a letter hath been pleased to acknowledge his aceptance of our

[58] Nalson, *Impartial Collection*, ii, p. 760; also HLRO, Main Papers, HL, Feb. [27] 1640/1.
[59] See above, pp. 126–9; below, pp. 166–9.
[60] 1 March 1641, *LJ*, iv, p. 174. See above, pp. 91–2, 95, 109–10; T. P. S. Woods, *Prelude to Civil War 1642: Mr Justice Mallet and the Kentish petitions* (Salisbury, 1980).
[61] BL, Add. MS 36914, fols. 197–197v.   [62] BL Add. MS 36914, fol. 199.
[63] BL, Add. MS 36914, fols. 206–206v. None of these divines are listed in either *Walker Revised* or *Calamy Revised*.

petistione [*sic*]'.[64] Certain passages in Cholmondeley's letter suggest that Charles wished to ensure that fences were mended with the baronet after the humiliating incident with the king and Privy Council over ship money assessments.[65] The early stages of the Long Parliament witnessed a number of attempts by Charles to woo the moderates he had alienated by the policies of the Personal Rule.[66] What is clear is that Aston's earlier breach with the court, necessitated by his desire to champion the interests of the county against the city of Chester, was forgotten in the face of a national crisis.[67]

An undated letter from Lord Cholmondeley, almost certainly from about this time, indicates that Werden's earlier anxieties concerning the lack of organization by Cheshire conformists were finally being addressed. Perhaps alarmed by Werden's earlier report of the lack of progress in the county, Aston expressed these concerns to Lord Cholmondeley. The peer responded by endeavouring 'to satisfie your queries, of which all you understand by honest mr Worden'.[68] Cholmondeley enclosed a copy of the letter he had circulated among Cheshire worthies to rally their support:

Sir, I am confident you have long agone [sic] taken notice of a petition, preferred to the higher house which came from this County which was signed by all the Lords, which were not Popishly affected, and by most of the best Gentry with divers freeholders and inhabitants of good ranke. I understand that now lately there hath beene a petition, put into the house of Commons by one Calvin Briant [Bruen] with some few more of meane condition, which petition scandaliseth that which was preferred to the Lords and rather clamours uniustly, than is able to prove truely, those aspersions they cast upon it.[69]

Calvin Bruen's petition claimed that names had been affixed to the pro-church petition by agents of Lord Cholmondeley and Sir Henry Bunbury without their knowledge, and Werden admitted there were some grounds for the charge. However, Werden also observed that Bruen's petition had come largely from interests in the city rather than the county.[70] Both

---

[64] BL, Add. MS 36914, fol. 201.

[65] 'For the King will want servantes for to further his desires if they be thus opressed onely being forward for to serve that King, who believe never deserved ill of any, if he weare truly informed.' BL, Add. MS 36914, fol. 201.

[66] The translation of Williams to York and other appointments and promotions of moderate bishops (such as Hall's move from Exeter to Norwich) is a good example of royal back peddling and belated attempts at fence-mending. According to Russell, Williams was convinced that most of the objections to bishops would be removed if the king ceased to appoint them and episcopal elections were returned to deans and chapters of cathedrals. It seems a remarkably foolish stance for such an astute ecclesiastical and political operator. Conrad Russell, *The Fall of the British Monarchies 1637–1642* (Oxford, 1991), pp. 251–2, 437.

[67] See above, pp. 133–5.   [68] BL, Add. MS 36914, fol. 203.

[69] BL, Add. MS 36914, fol. 205.

[70] Morrill, *Cheshire*, p. 53; BL, Add. MS 36914, fols. 210v–211, 214–215. Bruen also

Werden and Aston surely remembered that Bruen had been a central figure in arranging the hero's welcome for William Prynne in Chester on his way to imprisonment in north Wales in 1637.[71]

In London meanwhile, Sir William Brereton organised a printed anti-episcopalian petition in the name of the county, but it was probably never seen in Cheshire. Brereton's failure to circulate his petition is curious, as he was supposed to have been elected to the Long Parliament on a 'popular ticket'. It claimed 12,000 subscribers – a crude doubling of the number of the previous petition.[72] Among the Aston Lodge Manuscripts is Aston's own copy of Brereton's petition with the beginnings of his notes and references in the margins, providing authorities to refute the claims made for the parity of ministers.[73]

According to Morrill, given the weak position of puritan interests in Cheshire, Aston over-reacted to Brereton's challenge, producing yet another petition in the name of the county, denouncing his former parliamentary colleague's petition as a fraud and demanding that the Lords issue warrants for the arrests of those responsible.[74] Aston also addressed the content of Brereton's petition. He was indignant at the charges it made against the institution of episcopacy: 'most schandalously reviling the whole order of Bishops as the profest enemies of the ghospell, That they are only of Ethnicall or Diabolicall Institution'. Aston further charged Brereton with saying that the bishops had exceeded the Roman emperors in 'shedding the blood of gods deere saynts' and that bishops had never – presumably in the entire history of the Christian church – taught a doctrine that accorded with God's word. Sir Thomas went on to accuse the Brereton group of misrepresenting the county in the vote on episcopacy in the Lords: 'Alledging (and traducing your honors) that your Lordships have already unanimously voted that the Bishops have corrupted the purity of the ghospell wee now professe with Romish Errors.'[75]

accused Aston personally of malpractice, alleging that he had obtained signatures by saying it was a petition calling for the reform of the ministry rather than its preservation. He added that some of the names obtained 'were of people dead or at sea; others madmen, children or papists'. Fletcher, *Outbreak*, p. 289. See above, pp. 95–8.

71 R. C. Richardson, *Puritanism in North-west England: a regional study of the diocese of Chester to 1642* (Manchester, 1972), p. 182.

72 *CSPD*, 1640–41, p. 529. This was done extremely crudely by Brereton: the petition in support of episcopacy claimed among its subscribers, e.g., 4 noblemen, 70 divines, and 6,000 freeholders. Brereton's petition, on the other hand, claimed 8 noblemen, 140 divines, 12,000 freemen. Aston himself noted: 'in every particular doubling the number of the former petition'. BL, Add. MS 36913, fol. 62.

73 Aston Lodge, MS JM/59 'To the High and Honourable Court of Parliament . . . In Answer to a Petition delivered in to the Lords Spirituall and Temporall, by Sir Thomas Aston, Baronet, from the County Palatine of Chester, concerning Episcopacy'.

74 Morrill, *Cheshire*, p. 51; BL, Add. MS 36913, fol. 62.

75 BL, Add. MS 36913, fol. 62. The exact timing is unclear, but presumably it followed the

At this point Sir Thomas committed a major miscalculation: in his haste to combat his nemesis Brereton, he failed to circulate this petition among the county establishment. The baronet nevertheless claimed to be speaking on 'behalfe of the Nobility, gentry & Inhabitants of the County palatine of Chester'.[76] Forty-eight gentlemen reprimanded the baronet for his presumption in an 'Attestation'. Aston had affronted them by speaking in their names without consultation: 'Wee whoe in respect of our Interests hold our selves to bee a Considerable part of this shire, doe utterly dislike that any one man should take so much power upon himselfe without publique trust & appointment to use the name of the county.'[77] The issue at stake to the signatories of the 'Attestation' was not the future of the church, but a question of proper procedure. Indeed not only, as Morrill has noted, did they 'specifically dissociate themselves from the Puritan petition', but they acknowledged the fraudulent nature of Brereton's petition as well.[78] 'And alsoe hee [Aston] takes notice of a late printed Libell in answeare to his former petition, wee disclayme as never approved or seene in this County till the presse made it common.'[79] Aston drafted an 'Answer to the Attestation' addressed to those who had put their names to the 'Attestation'. He adopted the stance of a wounded innocent, claiming:

Truly for any man to assume the name of the County to advance any private busines of his owne, or to set on foote any publique busines for the County without warrant from the County were a iust cause of dislike. But I conceiv'd it the duty of every man, that is a member of a County, to vindicate his Countrey from Scandall; Nor did I ever heare it charg'd as a reproach, but oft recorded with honor of the nation.[80]

Aston later received an open letter of support from forty-three Cheshire gentlemen in which they acknowledged his 'good service . . . for your Countrey'.[81] This same group also produced a letter to the earl of Bath,

vote in the Lords on the exclusion of the bishops which took place on 24 May 1641. Fletcher, *Outbreak*, p. 101.

[76] BL, Add. MS 36913, fol. 62.

[77] BL, Add. MS 36913, fol. 63v.

[78] Morrill, *Cheshire*, p. 46. Richard Cust, ed., *The Papers of Sir Richard Grosvenor, 1st Bart. (1585–1645)*, LCRS, 134 (1996), pp. xxi–xxii. I am grateful to Steve Hindle for this reference.

[79] BL, Add. MS 36913, fol. 63v.

[80] BL, Add. MS 36913, fol. 63v. Aston wrote a draft of his 'Answer' in the margins of his copy of the 'Attestation'.

[81] BL, Add. MS 36914, fols. 222–222v. Aston printed this letter with the names of its subscribers at the beginning of his *A Remonstrance Against Presbytery* (n.p., 1641). Comparing the signatories of the 'Attestation' and the letter of support for Aston reveal divisions among the county community similar to those which existed in the 1640 elections. Ideological and religious issues were not at stake, so much as 'the struggle for local pre-eminence'. Attempts were made by John Werden, however, to include the Booth-Wilbraham group in the production of the pro-church petitions. Morrill, *Cheshire*, pp. 46–7.

outlining their support to Aston's activities.[82] It would appear that the chief agent of the campaign to express solidarity for Aston's activities in Westminster was Lord Cholmondeley. He wrote to the baronet:

I have received your packetts & doe wonder much that people are so . . . audatious to put to print soe notorious lyes. I shall by the next post, reform the peticon signed you have sent or els a tru writt to you, & sygnd by most of the best, in thankes for your great care & industry to vindicate the Countrey & putting some of those people in hold which caused soe foule an imposter. . . upon the Countrye.[83]

It is clear that Aston was not fighting a solitary campaign, but represented a considerable body of opinion among the political elites in the county.[84]

Such a public show of support was necessitated by the storms of controversy surrounding Aston in Westminster. His second petition (the one which sparked the 'Attestation') apparently included a list of names of those responsible for the 'late printed Libell'. Aston had insisted that the Lords issue warrants for those responsible.[85] In fact, in early April 1641, the upper house did send for them, but they also sent for the baronet, displeased as they were by the strong language in his second petition.[86] Aston was called before the bar, 'and being called in he explained himself; upon which the Lords were pleased to pass the offence'.[87]

By now, Aston's position with the court was repaired. A new petition was produced in support of the Book of Common Prayer and was circulated in the county with a letter of support from the king.[88] The king's letter and the petition were met by a sympathetic response, at least according to Werden's account. The petition, with over 9,000 subscribers, was eventually presented to the Lords on 20 December 1641.[89]

This petition was one of the most strongly worded of all the conformist

---

[82] BL, Add. MS 36914, fols. 224–224v. This letter may be one survivor of a series of letters directed to a group of peers.

[83] BL, Add. MS 36914, fol. 212, dated 10 or 20 April 1641.

[84] The opinions of those of lower social standing who supported the petitioning campaign with signatures and marks will be explored in depth in chapter 5. How their signatures and marks were acquired is discussed below in this chapter. See below, pp. 151–6.

[85] BL, Add. MS 36913, fol. 62. Unfortunately, the list of malefactors is missing.

[86] *LJ*, iv, p. 205 (2 April 1641).

[87] The Lords discussed whether Sir Thomas ought to be required to kneel before the bar before he explained his actions. It was resolved that he should be called in but not required to kneel. *LJ*, iv, p. 205 (2 April 1641).

[88] I have not been able to locate a copy of the king's letter of support, which Werden referred to in a letter to Aston. BL, Add. MS 36914, fols. 216–217v. Morrill states that Aston was approached by the court to produce a new petition but it is unclear where the evidence lies for placing the initiative at the centre. He also describes this as a second petition on behalf of the bishops. However, the petition is primarily concerned with defending the Prayer Book against liturgical innovation. Cf. Morrill, *Cheshire*, p. 48.

[89] HLRO, Main Papers, HL, 20 December 1641. Copies of the text: BL, Add. MS 36913, fol. 55; Nalson, *Impartial Collection*, ii, pp. 758–9; Aston, *Collection*, pp. 34–6.

petitions on the subject of the Prayer Book.[90] The Book of Common Prayer, they argued, had been approved by all segments of society that matter; it owed its authorship to martyr-bishops and its establishment to the 'prudent Sages of [the] State'. It was also approved by foreign divines and had won the general consent of the clergy and people:

Our pious Laudable and Ancient Form of Divine Service, composed by the Holy Martyrs, and worthy Instruments of Reformation; Established by the prudent Sages of State, your religious Predecessors; honored by the approbation of many learned Foreign Divines; subscribed by the Ministry of the whole Kingdom; and with such general Content, received by all the Laity.

The petition continued with a bold and striking claim for the availability and therefore possible use and influence of Common Prayer for private individuals and family worship, as well as the public services of the church:

[There is] scarce any Family or Person that can read, but are furnished with the Books of Common Prayer; in the conscionable Use whereof, many Christian Hearts have found unspeakable joy and Comfort; wherein the famous Church of England our dear Mother hath just Cause to Glory: and may she long flourish in the Practice of so blessed a liturgy.[91]

Claims such as these should not be accepted uncritically. Effusive praise of the Book of Common Prayer must be laid alongside of views like those of one Mr Jones, curate at Tarporley in Cheshire, who was reported as saying about this time that the Book of Common Prayer was 'composed by the imps in hell' and 'did stinke in the nostrails of God'.[92] The views of those who supported the Prayer Book petition, however, deserve as much attention as those represented by the curate Jones.

'Getting hands'

In contrast to most of the petitions in support of the church, the two from Cheshire survive with their schedules of subscribers. There were roughly 6,000 hands for episcopacy in early 1641 and 9,000 for the Prayer Book at the end of the year. How were subscriptions obtained? The 'view from

---

[90] See above, pp. 113–24.

[91] Nalson, *Impartial Collection*, ii, p. 758. Richard Baxter's father always read family prayers from the Book of Common Prayer or other approved books. Richard Baxter, *Reliquiae Baxterianae: or Mr Richard Baxter's Narrative of the most Memorable Passages of his Life and Times* (London, 1676), p. 3. One Marjory Price of Chester, giving evidence in a case against a petty canon of the cathedral after he had spoken in favour of the petition to uphold the Prayer Book in 1641, reported, 'That Puritans were about to take away the booke of Common prayer whereby Ignorant people found Comfort as well in Church as at home.' Bodl., Dep. C., MS 165, fol. 68. See below, pp. 153–4.

[92] BL, Add. MS 36913, fols. 137–137v; Earwaker, *East Cheshire*, ii, p. 57.

above' – the network of gentlemen who co-ordinated their activities with Aston's efforts in Westminster – has already been discussed. But how, at the local level, were signatures and marks of thousands of men – gentle, clerical, yeomen, and day labourers – acquired?[93]

The evidence is partial and sometimes impressionistic but it would appear that copies of the petitions' texts were first circulated amongst the more substantial members of the community, often with a supporting letter such as the one Lord Cholmondeley produced.[94] Another example is Aston's letter to a Cheshire gentleman called William Moreton, written shortly after the production of 'the Attestation'. Aston was attempting to gain support for his actions, and this included seeking support from beyond his personal acquaintances. It is clear from his letter that he and Moreton had been brought into contact by the pro-church cause. 'Though I have not had the good fortune to bee earlier known to you', Aston wrote, 'yet finding your heart stood with us in the Christian desire & affection [that] was express[ed] by many of us to preserve the afflicted church from subversion' the baronet was certain of his support.[95] In the desire to gain wide support, written communications were backed up by personal visits. John Werden certainly took these responsibilities seriously. In May 1641 he related to Sir Thomas how he had approached numerous individuals directly, armed with the king's letter of support: 'I will hope it may prove a Reconcyler, and Gayne myrades of more hands unto it.'[96]

The main method for gaining hands varied according to the constituency. Assizes and quarter sessions, besides private meetings, provided the obvious opportunities to canvas support from the county elites. Also, the important role of the clergy in gaining hands which Anthony Fletcher has observed in places as far flung as Derbyshire, Essex, and Middlesex, seems to have been the case in Cheshire as well.[97] The clergy, as well as the gentry, felt themselves to be local leaders and those who did subscribe usually put their names near the top of the schedule of subscribers, next to the names of their gentle counterparts.[98]

Given the subject matter of the petitions and the involvement of the clergy, it is hardly surprising that divine service at parish churches provided the logical time and place to seek the subscriptions of ordinary adult male

---

[93] For a discussion of this issue in other counties, see above, pp. 95–98.
[94] BL, Add. MS 36914, fol. 205.   [95] BL, Add. MS 33936, fol. 232.
[96] BL, Add. MS 36914, fol. 220v.
[97] David Underdown, *Revel, Riot and Rebellion: popular politics and culture in England 1603–1660* (Oxford, 1985), p. 140; Fletcher, *Outbreak*, p. 194; 'Petitioning and the outbreak of the Civil War in Derbyshire', *Derbyshire Archaeological Journal* 93 (1973), pp. 35–6.
[98] HLRO, Main Papers, HL, [27] February 1640/1; HLRO, Main Papers, HL, 20 December 1641. Fletcher, *Outbreak*, pp. 195–6, 209.

parishioners.[99] Direct evidence for this is provided by a separate petition to the House of Commons from West Kirby in The Wirral. It is worth quoting almost in its entirety:

That your petitioners being assembled together immediately after the time of divine service and sermon upon the second day of this present May in our parish Church and having then and there showed unto us a Lyst of our particular names, pretended to have beene affixed unto a certaine writing without our privitie or consent, presented from divers Gentlemen and Inhabitants of this County to the Lords, for the maintenance of the present Government of our Church as it is nowe established by Lawe, without Innovation or alteration of Government; Doe hereby humbly certify that many of us did hereunto subscribe the same, and the rest of us gave allowance, and consented thereunto; And further wee doe hereby the second time avowe that wee doe approve thereof, and not revoke our act.

This petition was accompanied by 133 names, including many marks.[100]

The mother church of the diocese, as well as obscure Wirral parishes, was also a place to gather subscriptions. One Monday at Morning Prayer, cathedral prebend William Bispham, arranged for a petty canon, William Clarke, to lead divine service. Leaving only the blessing to be given, Clarke addressed the congregation concerning the petition to preserve the Prayer Book. According to the account of one witness, a shoemaker, Clarke began by attacking the whole notion of change: 'The said Clarke made a speech to the Congregation saying that Adam in paradise could not bee Content with the estate that God had sett him in but needs bee changing though for the worst. And ever since the nature of man did affect Noveltyes [and] Alterations.' It was clear to Clarke which parties were responsible for the current upheaval in the church: 'And ever since that time the Church hath bin invaded by two grand Enemyes, Papists and Puritans, the one hath sought the overthrow of [the] discipline of the Church and the other of the Litturgie.' Clarke gave the congregation his own interpretation of the Hampton Court Conference in which James I had challenged the puritans to produce a better liturgy than the one the church already had: a task they did not perform. The petty canon put the pro-Prayer Book petition in a context of a long struggle to defend the church against the twin evils of Romanism and puritanism:

And he further said that Herod and Pilat were utter enemyes yet agreed in the Crucifying of Christ. The Jews were not content onely to thrust the speare into Christ's side, but likewise to see his blood Run: to prevent which Danger, the Nobilitye [and] Gentrye of this county, have drawne a Petition to Certify to the houses of Parliament in the name of the wholle Countye that they are all content

---

[99] BL, Add. MS 39614, fol. 211.
[100] BL, Add. MS 36913, fols. 131–132v. Other Wirral parishes and townships endorsed this petition: Thurstaston (34 hands), Thornton in Neston parish (38 hands), Neston parish (58 hands). BL, Add. MS 36913, fols. 132v–135.

with [the] Litturgie and wish that it may continue. And for theire better satisfaction they should heare the Petition read, and desired every one that had received any benefitt by that booke, that after the Peace of God was ended [that is, the blessing said] they would repaire to the Communion Table and subscribe to the Petition.

In the evidence gathered by the mayor and alderman about Clarke, the witnesses disagreed as to how effective his arguments were. The shoemaker, John Jenison had, he claimed, only a partial recollection of events:

So he [Clarke] promised the peace of God which ended, the people going out. Mr Prebend Bispham asked the people what they meant to goe out for. Mr Maior, the Aldermen, and most of the best of the Cittye had subscribed to it . . . And further [Jenison] saith that some went upp to the Communion Table but how many or who they were he doth not well remember and further saith not.

Jenison's convenient amnesia, however, was not shared by another witness, Robert Hawkeshawe, yeoman. Not only did Hawkeshawe certify that the petition was well subscribed that morning, but in his enthusiasm he put down two more names besides his own: 'after the blessing [was given] . . . many people did resort, and he the said Hawkeshawe did not onely subscribe his owne name to but two more names'.[101]

Needless to say, the prominent role of both clergy and gentry raises the question of whose 'voice' we are hearing in these petitions. David Underdown has argued that, although such petitions represent the 'aspirations of clerical and gentry authors', Fletcher's analysis is correct:

as Mr Fletcher has shown in his comprehensive survey of the 1641–2 petitions, they can less easily be dismissed as artificially contrived 'parrot' petitions than some historians have supposed. Self-interested claims about their numerical support can be discounted, yet it is clear that many of them did express the consensus of a wide spectrum of local society.[102]

The fact that the schedules of subscribers survive for both pro-church Cheshire petitions, and additional individual petitions such as those from several Wirral parishes,[103] strongly suggests that these petitions, as much as those against the established church, fit Underdown's description of expressing 'the consensus of a wide spectrum of local society'.

It has already been mentioned that the pro-church campaign was accused of gaining hands in fraudulent ways. Werden even admitted:

that a Man of my Lord Cholmondeley & a Man of mr Bunburyes did put to all or

---

[101] Bodl., Dep. C, MS 165, fols. 66–67, 70. These depositions and a copy of Clarke's speech were taken on behalf of the mayor and aldermen of Chester to present to the House of Commons, dated 27 November 1641. For Clarke's own copy of his speech, see fols. 71–72. William Bispham was ejected from his living of Eccleston before July 1644. Of William Clarke, we know nothing more except that he was a petty canon of the cathedral. *Walker Revised*, pp. 3, 88.

[102] Underdown, *Revel*, pp. 138–9.   [103] BL, Add. MS 36913, fols. 131–135.

most of the whole inhabitants & tenants of Stavneyes [Stanneyes?] names without their pryvity to the petition. Which was done upon an assumption & presumption of mr Bunburyes Man that he would [?] that might speake to them all & get their consents.

Ever honest, Werden added: 'I was sory to understand this.'[104] Werden contacted Lord Cholmondeley about the accusation and the peer promised to investigate. What is most striking is Werden's sensitivity to charges of fraud and his desire to safeguard the integrity of the petition. Werden's concern contrasts sharply with Brereton's petition against episcopacy which was probably never circulated in the county and simply doubled the number of signatories obtained for the pro-episcopacy petition.[105]

Despite the numerous letters surviving from Werden in the Aston Papers, this Cheshire gentleman's obscurity is almost heartbreaking. A lawyer from a family of Chester merchants who had acquired land at Burton near Tarporley, Werden appears to have acted as an agent for a number of substantial Cheshire families.[106] His commitment to the cause of the preservation of the established church is clear. Werden's expectations of the ordained ministry, at least as far as the conduct of corporate worship is concerned, is revealed by his indignation at reports of non-conformity:

One Borden, a Notoryous infamous Adulterer beinge the Curate there [Wybunbury?] would not reade the absolution, nor the Letany, he did not nor ever dothe read either proper lessons or psalmes for the day & the psalmes he did reade he would not reade them out of the service booke but the bible.[107]

Werden's views, as well as his knowledge about the lawful conduct of Prayer Book worship, conforms well to the discussion of those issues in Chapter 2. But his piety had an interior life as well. He was not only concerned with the public acts of the church; a letter written to Aston on Good Friday 1641 concerning Calvin Bruen's petition, provides insight into his private spirituality: 'My Lady Cholmondeley sent me last night when I was in bed (disingaged from all earthly thoughts to receyve the blessed Sacrament the passion day) the letter to her and the copie of Calvyn Brynes petition and his assocyates.'[108] He seems to have had a spirituality that was

---

[104] BL, Add. MS 36914, fol. 210v.   [105] See above, p. 148.

[106] Dore, *Letter Books*, vol. I, p. 168n. Werden is listed as one of the royalist Commissioners for the City of Chester at its surrender to Parliamentary forces. Dore, *Letter Books*, vol. II, p. 528. Werden's letters: BL, Add. MS 36914, fols. 197–198v, 206–206v, 210–211v, 214–215v, 216–217v, 220–221v.

[107] BL, Add. MS 36914, fols. 214v–215. In other words, he did not read from Coverdale's translation of the Psalms or follow the lectionary in the Prayer Book.

[108] BL, Add. MS 36914, fol. 214. Werden's act of preparation before receiving Communion is hardly unique to 'Anglicanism'; nevertheless it is directed by the Book of Common Prayer. *1559 BCP*, pp. 256–9. It is interesting to note a glimpse of female activity in the pro-church cause. Women were generally not considered appropriate persons to subscribe to petitions.

both committed and pragmatic. Lord Cholmondeley's appellation of 'honest mr Werden', though biased, is consistent with his disapproval of the misconduct of his own side in gaining subscribers in underhanded ways already mentioned. It is obvious that Werden's activities in the county were as crucial to the petitioners' cause as Aston's presence at Westminster. This double focus was hardly unique to Cheshire, as Fletcher has commented from a national perspective: 'The close link between an MP' – or in Aston's case, an ex-MP based at Westminster – 'and an energetic friend in the shire was often crucial to getting a petition off the ground.'[109]

AN APOLOGIST FOR THE CHURCH OF ENGLAND

A lay apologist for episcopacy

During this time, Aston produced his most substantial published work, *A Remonstrance against Presbytery*, which appeared in May 1641.[110] The title of this 200 page tract is misleading, for it was as much a positive defence of what was *right* about episcopal government as it was an attack on what was *wrong* with presbyterian discipline. The *Remonstrance* reveals a man who had far more than a passing interest in theology and ecclesiology. The range of Aston's reading gathered together to make his case is impressive: besides the Old and New Testaments, he cited a range of patristic sources, Erasmus, and many continental reformers, including Calvin, Beza, Bullinger, and Bucer. English authorities were used too: Bede, Jewel, Foxe, and Aston's contemporary, the moderate Calvinist Bishop Joseph Hall.[111]

In his dedication to the king, Sir Thomas chose to deal immediately with a subject that he obviously felt to be an awkward one: why have not the bishops themselves been more forthcoming in their own defence?[112] Aston chose to be charitable about their silence; as a member of the laity, he maintained that he was free from any accusation of self-interest when he defended the episcopal order and was, therefore, a more persuasive advocate: 'The Bishops are suspect as parties, all that is writ by them as partiall; To all but the preiudicate, sure I stand unsuspect, being as free

---

[109] Fletcher, *Outbreak*, p. 193.

[110] According to the Thomason Tracts list. Cf. November 1641 in Morrill, *Cheshire*, p. 49.

[111] Hall was first bishop of Exeter (1627) and then, as part of Charles' belated fence mending exercise with non-Laudian senior churchmen, transferred to the more prestigious see of Norwich in 1641. *DNB*. For an introduction to Hall's writings on episcopacy, see A. J. Mason, *The Church of England and Episcopacy* (Cambridge, 1914), pp. 111–18, though Mason's interpretations should be used with caution.

[112] This same question was put in 'poetic form' by one of Aston's undergraduate admirers. See below, pp. 175–6.

borne, as independent as any man, I have no interest, but the love of truth and libertie.'[113] Aston's charitable gloss on episcopal inaction was, no doubt, admirable but the moderate, non-Laudian bishops proved to be bruised reeds indeed. Under the leadership of John Williams, the sub-committee entrusted with making positive proposals for ecclesiastical reforms to counterbalance the growing strength of the presbyterian party, failed even to shift their ideas out of committee and into concrete legislative proposals. Their poor follow-through earned the bishops little credit with MPs.[114] Their failure prefigures the widespread failure of the bishops in the years 1645–60 to provide much at all in the way of leadership or direction to the men and women who sought to be faithful, sometimes in the face of persecution, to the 'church of Elizabeth and James'.[115]

Aston made sophisticated use of evidence from the early church; for he did not consider the evidence of the New Testament and the Fathers in isolation from each other. He examined not only the role of bishops in the patristic era, but what the Fathers (being closer in time to the events of the New Testament era) had to say concerning the structures of the apostolic church.[116] Thus marshalling both biblical and patristic evidence, he concluded that not only were there bishops in the 'golden age' of the church's first few centuries, but that the Apostles themselves, according to both the evidence of the New Testament and of the Fathers *on* the apostolic church, *were* bishops. Paul, for example, ordained Timothy as a bishop: 'Paul, unto Timotheus ordained the first Bishop of the Church of the *Ephesians*.' But he added: 'Novellists except at that, and will not allow it to be Authenticke because, they say, [it] is not in some old Manuscript they have seen.' Aston had no time for the dubious and selective textual criticism of the presbyterians, but added smugly that Saint John Chrysostom supports his position: Timothy was bishop of the Asians and his see was at Ephesus. For good measure Sir Thomas added that Jerome said Titus was bishop of Crete, that Ambrose said all the Apostles were bishops, and he

---

[113] 'The Epistle Dedicatory' in Aston, *Remonstrance*. The *Remonstrance* is unpaginated but after introductory material it divides into two main parts, 'A Survey of Presbytery' and 'A Briefe Review of Episcopacy'. These two main parts are subdivided into short numbered sections. Different editions have the main parts in different order. To avoid confusion, therefore, references are made to the numbered section and whether it is in the 'Presbytery' or 'Episcopacy' half of the *Remonstrance*.

[114] Abbott, 'Issue of episcopacy', pp. 134–8.

[115] Morrill, 'The church in England', pp. 98–100. Another committed lay episcopalian John Evelyn commented on this when he attended an ordination conducted by the bishop of Galloway in Paris in 1651: '[there are] so few Bishops remaining, amongst the English Cleargy, as durst publiqly owne this Important Service, by which the people were depriv'd of their Lawfull Pastors'. *The Diary of John Evelyn*, ed. E. S. de Beer (6 vols., Oxford, 1955), iii, p. 633.

[116] Bishop Hall made this point as well. Mason, *Church of England*, p. 113.

concluded by saying that such reformers as Calvin, Beza, and Bullinger agreed with this view:

Calvin (u) writing of the State of the Ancient church sayes, That *the Presbyters ever chose one out of their number in every City, to whom specially they gave the Title of a Bishop, that there should not arise discord out of equalitie.* Beza (w) (no friend to the Bishops yet) acknowledges . . . *that* Timothy *was at that time* Antistes [sic], *the* Prelate *or* President *in the Presbyterie* at Ephesus.[117]

Aston maintained that only heretical groups in the early church such as the Arians insisted on the equality of ministers, motivated in part by frustrated ambition: 'Saint *Austin* observes, that being discontent [because] he [Arius] mist [missed?] of a Bishopricke, Arius fell into this Heresie; *Presbyterum ab Episcopo nulla differentia discerni.*'[118] Aston charged that presbyterians, like Arius, were really motivated by the desire to have the power of oversight. Arius is, of course, more often remembered for the subordinationism of his Christology, than for his position on the parity of ministers. Linking one's opponents to the fourth century heretic was a form of attack.[119]

Aston made extensive use of the writings of sixteenth-century continental reformers. The baronet cited Calvin perhaps with the greatest frequency, but almost always to note the ambivalence in Calvin's own position on the three-fold order.[120] It was with palpable pleasure that Aston provided evidence that Calvin's views on the episcopal office were not abstract absolutes but changed to reflect actual circumstances. The argument as filtered by Aston went: if many of the occupiers of the office were on the side of reform, by all means use the strength of the existing church system in the struggle with Rome:

Did Calvin onely confesse the name [or title of bishop], and nothing of the use of Bishops? In his Epistle to the King of Poland (b) hee commends the patterne of the Primitive times, *and advises the King to place Bishops in every Province, and over*

---

[117] Sec. 1, 'Episcopacy' in Aston, *Remonstrance.* Aston lists his sources as: '(u) *Calvin, de Statu vetieria Ecclesiae* Tom 7. fol. 218. *Illi ex suo numero in singulis civitatibus unum eligebant, cui Titulum Episcopi, &c.* (w) *Notandum in hoc loco Timotheum in Ephesio presbyterio tum suisse Antistitem.* Beza *annotat.* in I Tim. 5'.

[118] Sec. 12, 'Episcopacy' in Aston, *Remonstrance.*

[119] Rowan Williams, *Arius: Heresy and Tradition* (London, 1987), pp. 41–7.

[120] Such a reading of Calvin is less spurious than might be thought. Wolfgang Klausnitzer, 'Episcopacy', in *The Oxford Encyclopedia of the Reformation*, ed. Hans Hillerbrand (4 vols., Oxford, 1996), ii, pp. 52–3. Other contemporaries of Aston's also made cautionary remarks about fundamentalist Calvinism as well. Lucius Carey, Viscount Falkland remarked in a speech in the House of Commons: 'I am confident that we shall not thinke it fit to abolish upon a few dayes debate an order, which has lasted (as appeares by story) in most Churches these sixteene hundred yeares, and in all from Christ to Calvin, or in an instant change the whole face of the Church, like the scene in a Maske.' Viscount Falkland, *A Speech Made to the House of Commons Concerning Episcopacy* (London, 1641), p. 12.

them an Arch-bishop. And would hee advise the placing of them in the Church, if hee were of the minde of our men?

Aston concluded that the abolition of the office in many continental churches was more a matter of particular circumstances than theological principle. Theodore Beza, as glossed by Sir Thomas, pushed for parity of ministers in his own domain, yet disliked those who resisted episcopal authority where it promoted the interests of reform. Martin Bucer, however, 'who was a great reformer' (in contrast perhaps, in Sir Thomas' mind, to Calvin and Beza?) he cited as stating that all episcopal government should be restored and maintained and that from the Apostles' times there have always been 'chief ministers', that is, imparity among the ordained.[121] Philipp Melanchthon, in many ways the acceptable face of Lutheranism to Elizabethan and early Stuart protestants, was also a 'great reformer' for holding similar views, and Aston claimed that he too saw episcopacy as a defence against tyranny and abuse of power – a point the baronet also made in his introduction to the *Remonstrance*.[122] Sir Thomas' approval of Melanchthon – he described him as 'that most excellent German' – suggests that the divine's influence spread beyond simply the Laudian party in the pre-civil war period, as argued elsewhere, and influenced moderate episcopalian thought as well.[123] In fact, it could be argued that the Laudian

[121] For Bucer and the episcopate see the following articles all in *Martin Bucer: reforming Church and Community*, ed. D. F. Wright (Cambridge, 1994): Peter Matheson, 'Martin Bucer and the old church', p. 6; Peter Stephens, 'The church in Bucer's commentaries on the Epistle to the Ephesians', pp. 56, 59; Irena Backus, 'Church, communion and community in Bucer's commentary on the Gospel of John', p. 71; Cornelis Augustijn, 'Bucer's ecclesiology in the colloquies with the Catholics, 1540–41', pp. 114, 118. For Bucer's on again/off again relationship with Thomas Cranmer see Diarmaid MacCulloch, *Thomas Cranmer: a life* (New Haven, 1996), *passim*.

[122] Secs. 1, 11, 12, 'Episcopacy' in Aston, *Remonstrance*.

[123] Dewey D. Wallace, Jr, 'The Anglican appeal to Lutheran sources: Philipp Melanchthon's reputation in seventeenth-century England', *Historical Magazine of the Protestant Episcopal Church* 52 (1983), pp. 358–62, 366–7. Aston's title of 'most excellent German' was quite restrained. Other Stuart writers, such as Peter Heylyn, used phrases like 'the Phoenix of Germany', p. 362. For Melanchthon's influence beyond the Laudian circle in the pre-civil war period, see Trevor-Roper, *Catholics, Anglicans and Puritans*, pp. 47, 190. It has been argued that Luther's standing among English protestants was greater in the mid-sixteenth century and again under James I when the defence of the authenticity of the Church of England as a 'church' emphasized historical and international arguments. Luther, Ronald Fritze argues, was less use under Charles, when conformists largely preferred to stress the national characteristics of their church and its apostolicity. Ronald Fritze, 'Root or Link? Luther's position in the historical debate over the legitimacy of the Church of England, 1558–1625', *JEH* 37:2 (1986). Luther's own lack of interest in ecclesiology as it related to the formal structures of ordained ministry and church polity meant he would be of little use to Aston. H. H. Kramm, 'The "Pastor Pastorum" in Luther and early Lutheranism', in *And Other Pastors of thy Flock': a German tribute to the Bishop of Chichester*, ed. Franz Hildebrandt (Cambridge, 1942), pp. 124–34; William Clesbsch, 'The Elizabethans on Luther', in *Interpreters of Luther: essays in honor of Wilhelm Pauk*, ed. Jaroslav Pelikan (Philadelphia, 1968).

assessment of a figure like Melanchthon was far more equivocal and opportunistic.[124]

Aston's version of history, therefore, in no way allowed continental protestantism to be hijacked by English presbyterians against the English settlement. He was also aware that he had a difficult task on his hands to dislodge such a deeply embedded misconception: 'Yet many of us swallow this suggestion, that all Reformed Churches are so govern'd.' He listed many churches in protestant Europe that had retained some form of episcopacy, that is some form of ministerial imparity, including the countries of Scandinavia, parts of Germany, and numerous central European states.[125] Sir Thomas stood within a considerable tradition of Church of England thought which valued episcopacy but accepted the ministry and sacramental life of Lutheran and Reformed churches. At no point does he 'unchurch' the European ecclesial communities which had abandoned the three-fold order of ordained ministry. For all their disagreements, Aston shared his archbishop's aim of debunking the claim that a rejection of episcopacy in favour of presbyterianism enjoyed pan-protestant support.[126]

In such a war of words, it is worth asking what was meant by 'a bishop'. The crux of the matter, and here episcopalians and presbyterians would agree, is the superiority of one minister over another. Aston defended the imparity of ministers – of bishops over presbyters – from the New Testament and the Fathers. He cited Saint Jerome as saying that, in many ways, bishops and presbyters share the same ministry, but in order to avoid schism, they elected one to be authority over the rest.[127] Aston's ecclesiology stands in a considerable tradition by emphasizing the primary and

---

[124] Milton, *Catholic and Reformed*, pp. 242, 444. One William Beale produced an almanac in which the names of a number of protestant and proto-protestant 'saints' had been entered including Melanchthon. It was attacked by the Laudian pamphleteer John Pocklington. Milton, *Catholic and Reformed*, p. 314.

[125] Sec. 12, 'Episcopacy' in Aston, *Remonstrance*. In this he contrasts sharply with Laud. See Gareth Bennett, *To the Church of England* (Worthing, 1988), pp. 43–5. However Bennett also called into question the view that non-episcopal orders were widely accepted in the Church of England before the Restoration Settlement. The matter is surely less clear than he suggested. Bennett, *To the Church*, p. 42. For a far more thought provoking discussion of the modern implications of Anglican self-reflection on episcopacy and ecumenism, see Stephen Sykes, *The Integrity of Anglicanism* (London, 1978), pp. 83–6, 98–100. For the view that many early modern 'Anglicans' accepted the validity of the orders of non-episcopally ordained ministers on the continent, see Norman Sykes, *Old Priest and New Presbyter* (Cambridge, 1956), pp. 142–6 and Diarmaid MacCulloch, 'The myth of the English Reformation', *JBS* 30 (1991), pp. 15–16. However, cf. Mason, *Church of England*, p. 23, but see also p. 507.

[126] William Tighe, 'William Laud and the reunion of the churches: some evidence from 1637 and 1639', *HJ* 30:3 (1987), p. 720.

[127] Bucer argued for the equality of all *bishops* – an argument, of course, aimed at the claims of the See of Rome. Backus, 'Church', p. 71.

peculiar role of bishops, not only as foci of unity, but enforcers of unity by the exercise of discipline. In other words, the bishop's primary task was to keep the disparate elements within the church together; and he was aided in this task by the *im*parity between his office and the presbyters of his diocese. One is tempted to argue that the willingness of the Laudians to sacrifice unity for an unprecedented level of uniformity represented their profoundest departure from 'the church of Elizabeth and James' rather than any particular innovation. As for the word itself, Aston asked why one should prefer a bad Latin word, superintendent or supervisor, to a perfectly good Greek one.[128]

As a Christian, it was obviously important to Aston to establish his case from the New Testament and the Fathers. Nevertheless, it was satisfying to him as well to note that bishops were not only biblical and primitive, but were also *English*. He quickly established that from Bede, and stressed the crucial role bishops played in England's conversion to Christianity. In this way Aston argued from history as well as from theology. He drew on the familiarity of the stories enshrined in Foxe's *Book of Martyrs* of the Edwardian bishops who brought reformed religion to England and died martyrs' deaths under Mary I.[129] The examples of men like Cranmer, Latimer, and Ridley were 'proof' to Aston that episcopacy and godliness were not mutually exclusive.

Aston's first line of defence on the home front – that bishops had brought and preserved the gospel in England with their own blood – was used not only in the *Remonstrance* and in the Cheshire petitions, but also in many of the nearly thirty petitions produced in other counties in support of the

---

[128] Until the last decade of scholarship it would have been much more difficult to locate Aston's understanding of episcopacy near the centre of English ecclesiology – he would have been seen more as an 'evolutionary fluke' than a 'missing link'. It is not within the brief of this chapter or this book to embark on an examination of the larger theological climate concerning church polity. Fortunately, that task has been undertaken recently and it is therefore worth reflecting on how Aston fits in with recent scholarship. In the light of Lake's work, Sir Thomas' theology of ministry might best be described as 'Whitgiftian in the maximum mode'. The baronet went beyond simply claiming that episcopacy best suited monarchy (although he did maintain that) as Archbishop Whitgift did in his 'mininum mode'. In many ways, Aston represents an 'old-fashioned' conformist view of episcopacy – old fashioned at least compared to the Laudians. I have already indicated points where he diverged from the *iure divino* claims of the 'Laudians' like Cosin or Heylyn. However, even Whitgift, so anxious not to offend the queen and her ministers, did maintain that episcopacy was apostolic. Aston maintained that stance as well but like Whitgift he shied away from out-and-out claims of *iure divino* status for the order. Peter Lake, *Anglicans and Puritans? Presbyterian and English conformist thought from Whitgift to Hooker* (London, 1988), pp. 88–97; 'Presbyterianism, the idea of a national church and the argument from divine right', in *Protestantism and the National Church in Sixteenth Century England*, ed. Peter Lake and Maria Dowling (London, 1987), esp. pp. 214–17.

[129] Secs. 1, 2, 3, 6, 10, 12, 13, 'Episcopacy' in Aston, *Remonstrance*.

Church of England.[130] In the Long Parliament as well, the same argument was made. In a speech in the lower house Lord Falkland said that: 'the main conducers to the resurrection of Christianity (at least) here in the reformation (and we owe the light of the Gospell we now enjoy to the fire they then endured for it) were all Bishops'.[131] Statements of this sort from a variety of sources, reflect the long-term and pervasive influence of *The Book of Martyrs* on the English imagination – whether that imagination was 'godly' or not.

Calling to mind the deaths of the Marian martyrs, however, was a point of contrast as well as comparison; for it brought into sharp focus the differences between individuals like Cranmer, Latimer, and Ridley and some current occupiers of the episcopal bench. The saintliness of the Oxford Martyrs did not protect the followers of Laud from the baronet's fury. He had, to quote Morrill, 'nothing but contempt for Laudians'.[132] Aston argued passionately for the restoration of the dignity of episcopal ministry and at the same time for the punishment of those who have brought the office into disrepute:

Is it onely our present Arch-bishop hath op'd the gap of Calumny? . . . I would draw all the world to my opinion; that is to reverence their Calling, preserve their Order, yet with as free a resolution, and as respectlesse of their persons, submit to the exemplar punishment of such as staine the honour of their Coat; entrench upon our Liberties, negligently starve the flock, covetously engrosse the means of faithfull Labourers, or with their Novelties distract the Church, as any man that lives.[133]

Comparing the experience of moderate protestants like himself with those of a more radical persuasion, Aston said 'wee have had our swarme of flies to destroy our fruits; wee have felt the storme of a distempered fate, as well as they'.[134] Nevertheless, he went on to argue, as indeed did many others, that what was needed was a change in personnel, not a rejection of an entire system of church government.

The description 'Laudian', however, can be vague and unhelpful, and obscure more than clarify. Although the archbishop is explicitly mentioned in the passage cited above, the baronet was usually reticent about naming names in print or in public. His private papers and their marginalia, however, reveal more candidly who occupied the categories of 'good' and 'bad' bishops in the layman's mind. 'Good' bishops, by Aston's reckoning, fell into a number of sub-divisions. Martyrs, always a popular choice, included men like Cranmer, Latimer, Ridley, and Hooper. Another way to exercise a godly episcopate was to engage in polemics 'against [the]

---

[130] See above, pp. 115–16. [131] Falkland, *Speech*, p. 9.
[132] Morrill, *Provinces*, p. 49. [133] Secs. 3, 18, 'Presbytery' in Aston, *Remonstrance*.
[134] Cited in Morrill, *Provinces*, p. 49. Cf. G. W. Bernard, 'The Church of England c.1529–c.1642', *History* 75 (1990), pp. 199–200.

common enemy of Rome'. Such bishops included some of Sir Thomas' own contemporaries and near-contemporaries: Jewel of Salisbury, Andrewes of Winchester, White of Ely, Usher of Armagh, Morton of Durham, Davenant of Salisbury, and Hall of Norwich. If the baronet's list of episcopal martyrs contains no surprises, his list of approved anti-Roman bishops does. Andrewes died in 1626, which spared him from too much association with Laudianism, however strongly some may see the connection now. The presence of Francis White is harder to account for. White was firmly associated with the Durham House group and the policies of Thorough. Like Laud, White had engaged in anti-papal polemic in his *A Reply to Jesuit Fisher's Answer* (1624). Unlike Laud, however, White was no longer alive in 1641 (d. 1638) and therefore to Aston he may have seemed a safer authority to which to appeal.[135] In notes made about the parliament of 1628, perhaps in preparation for his book, Aston revealed very clearly what he identified as corruptions in the religious settlement and who he held responsible.[136] It is not a very surprising list of names: Montague, Laud, Cosin, Manwaring, Sibthorpe, Neile, and one 'Dr Alablaster [*sic*]'.[137] Their offences were described largely in ideological and doctrinal terms. This is to be expected in the 1620s, as the push in liturgical innovation came mostly in the next decade during the period of the Personal Rule. This portion of the manuscript is worth citing in full:

Violations of Religion. Parl. 1628.

His majesties' name used to stopp proceedings against Papists since the Parliament began. fol. 9. Sir Francis Seymour. contrary to his many Proclamations & many Instructions to the Iudges.

Montagues Appeale to Caesar for which hee had A Bishopricke. fol. 10.

The Bishop of London Dr Laud did entertaine for his Domestique chap[lain?] one that did dispute the Arminian points, & sayd what Arminians hold & wrote this I will maintaine & justify. folio 29.

Pardons graunted to Mountaque, Cozens, Manwaring & Sibthorpes.

The greatest Ennemies to church & state that ever was under the

---

[135] From Aston's marginal notes on his printed copy of the Cheshire petition for episcopacy. Aston Lodge, MS JM/27 'A petition Delivered in the House of Lords Spirituall and Temporal, by Sir Thomas Aston'. *DNB*; More and Cross, *Anglicanism*.

[136] The making of such lists was common amongst MPs and lawyers in the seventeenth century. I am grateful to Maija Janssen for advice on this manuscript.

[137] William Alabaster (1557–1640) was a poet and chaplain to James I, who converted to Roman Catholicism in 1596. Some years later he reconverted and enjoyed preferment in the Church of England and was known for his Arminian views. *DNB*; Christopher Hill, *God's Englishman: Oliver Cromwell and the English Revolution* (London, 1970), pp. 43–4; Frank Salmon, '*Praedatrix Praeda Fit Ipsa Suae*: Mary Magdalene, Frederico Borromeo and Henry Constable's Spirituall Sonnettes', *Recusant History* 18:3 (1987), p. 234.

Judgement of Parliament. they are pardoned betweene Parliaments. Sir Robert Phillips. fol. 30.

Mr Heath of Grayes Inne affirm'd that Dr Cozens in a publique meeting sayd, the king had noething to do to bee Head of the Church, & that hee had noe more power to Excommunicate than his Servant that rubbed his horse heels. Sir Robert Phillipps, pag. 31, 32.

The Bishop of Winchester prohibitts Dr Moore for preaching against Popery. Sir Dudley North. fol. 33, 45.

The Bishop of London Dr Laud restrained the Printing of books written against Popery & Arminianisme but allowed of the Contrary. Divers have beene Pursuivanted for printing of Orthodox Bookes. Fol. 39.

Dr Beard affirmed that Dr Allablaster preached flat Popery at Pauls crosse, & the Bishop of winchester Dr Neale commanded Beard as hee was his diocesan that hee should preach nothing to the contrary & Dr Marshall affirmes the BB sayed as much to him as hee sayed to Dr Moore. fol. 40.

Violations of Religion. Dr Cozens frequenting the Printing House caused the Booke of Common Prayer to bee new printed & hath changed the word minister into Priest & hath put out in annother place the word Elect. mr Kirton. pag. 41.

the Queenes masse there are 2 masses daily in the Queenes Court there come 500 at a time from masse. fol. 45.

There can be little doubt who this layman identified as the chief assets and the chief liabilities on the episcopal bench.[138]

Aston was not alone as a defender of episcopacy in admitting that recent years had seen corrupt men exercising sacred office. The offences of the Laudians were legion, and Lord Falkland put it even more forcibly than Aston:[139]

Master Speaker, a little search will serve to find them to have beene the destruction of unity under the pretence of uniformity, to have brought in superstition, and scandall, under the titles of reverence, and decency: to have defil'd our Church, by adorning our Churches; to have slackened the strictnesse of that union which was formerly betweene us, and those of our religion beyond the sea, an action as unpoliticke, as ungodly . . . wee shall finde them to have tith'd Mint and Anice, and have left undone the weightier workes of the law [Matthew 23.23], to have beene less eager upon those who damn our Church than upon those who upon weake conscience, and perhaps as weake reasons (the dislike of some commanded garment or some uncommanded posture) onely abstained from it . . . conformity to ceremonies hath beene more exacted than the conformity to Christianity.[140]

---

[138] Aston Lodge, MS JM/55 'Violations of Religion. Parl. 1628'; Wallace Notestein, ed., *Commons Debates for 1629* (Minneapolis, 1921), pp. 59, 139.

[139] See above, pp. 99–100, 106–13.

[140] Falkland, *Speech*, pp. 1–2.

Neither was Aston isolated in his appreciation that even in the current dark days there were still some godly bishops. John Williams of Lincoln, and later of York (1641), enjoyed considerable popularity in the early days of the Long Parliament, as has already been noted.[141] Lord Falkland too made this point:

and that even now in the greatest perversion of that order, there are yet some who have conduc'd in nothing to our late innovations, but in their silence, some who in an unexpected and mighty place and power have expressed an equal moderation and humility, being neither ambitious before, nor proud after, either of the Crosiers staffe or white staff [of secular office]: some who have beene learn'd opposers of Popery, and zealous opposers of Arminianisme, between whom and their inferiour clergy in frequency of preaching hath beene no distinction, whose lives are untouched, not onely by guilt, but by malice; scarce to be equalled by those of any condition, or bee excell'd by those in any Calendar [that is, the calendar of saints days]. I doubt not, I say, but if wee consider this, this consideration will bring forth this conclusion, that Bishops may bee good men, and let us give but good men good rules, wee shall have both good governours and good times.[142]

Falkland too called for a clear distinction between an office and the person holding the office:

that wee shall make no little complement to those, and no little apologie for those to whom this charge belongs, if we shall lay the faults of the men upon the order of the Bishops, upon the Episcopacy. I wish we may distinguish betweene those, who have been carried away with the streame, and those who have beene the streame that carry'd them; betweene those, whose proper and naturall motion was towards our ruine and destruction, and those who have beene whirl'd about to it contrary to their naturall motion by the force and swinge of superior *Orbes*; and as I wish, wee may distinguish betweene the more and lesse guilty; so I yet more wish, wee may distinguish betweene the guilty and the innocent.[143]

Neither Falkland or Aston provided an uncritical admiration of the hierarchy: a rebuke is to be found under Falkland's rather complicated, though commonplace, platonic metaphor of the spheres. Even the 'good' bishops had let themselves be swept away (albeit against their better 'natures') by the plotting Laudians – a serious charge against those on whom the gospel lays the responsibility 'to fede my shepe'.[144] Aston largely left such criticism unsaid in his *Remonstrance*, preferring to put a charitable gloss on the silence and inaction of certain bishops. By 1641, the parameters of the debate over church polity were clear: the Laudians, though

[141] Abbott, 'Issue of episcopacy', pp. 128–33; see above, pp. 144–5.
[142] Falkland, *Speech*, pp. 9–10.   [143] Ibid., pp. 8–9.
[144] The gospel reading for the consecration of bishops was either to be Christ's charge to Peter to 'fede my shepe' (John 21.15–17) or John 10.1–16. F. E. Brightman, *The English Rite: being a synopsis of the sources and revisions of the Book of Common Prayer* (London, 2 vols., 1921), ii, pp. 973–5, 1002–3.

useful in presbyterian polemic, had few friends among episcopalian apologists.

'9324 potential Popes'

The insistence on reform, not revolution, is a constant theme throughout the *Remonstrance*. The design of the presbyterian party, Aston claimed, was not reformation but total innovation and because of that, in the end, their designs were as wicked as those of the Laudians.[145] Predictably, Sir Thomas accused the presbyterians of distorting their evidence from the bible, the Fathers, and continental divines. But perhaps of greater concern to him was the disorder and chaos both in church and state that would follow the abolition of episcopacy. Presbyterianism, Aston claimed in a striking and significant phrase, would 'pull down 26 Bishops and set up 9324 potential Popes'. It was the logical outcome, he added, 'when in effect the Pastor of every parish church must be such'. The thought of every vicar operating in unchecked papal style over his parishioners was obviously more than this member of the laity could stomach. He continued pragmatically, observing that it was a safer and surer affair for civil government to deal directly with twenty-six bishops, whose powers were limited by statute and custom, than individually with thousands of presbyterian ministers.[146] As a lay Christian, Aston was perhaps more sensitive to the clericalism as much inherent in presbyterianism as in episcopalian polity than many of the former's ministerial advocates. He was certainly unmoved by the argument that lay elders would check the tyranny of these presbyterial popes:

Are we not taught, these Elders must bee chosen by the voyce of the people: and are not these people taught by the pastors, subordinate to them, the Elders being but temporary, for halfe a yeare or a yeare, is it probable they shall have that dependence upon one another? they shall have that interest in the parish, as hee that is *perpetuus Dictator*, Chancellour, Arbiter for life in his petty popedome.

Furthermore, if the thought of parliament dealing with 9,324 parochial popes was like a bad dream; how much more nightmarish was the thought of trying to keep to the rule of law 100,000 lay elders.[147] Besides, Aston insisted that the prospect of lay elderships was held out merely to seduce the vulgar. He reminded his readers that it was the presbyterian party which claimed its polity was *iure divino*, not moderate episcopalians. The claim of *iure divino* status put the parish pastor above *any* check from crown, parliament, magistrates, custom, or the rule of law, let alone from

---

[145] Sec. 1, 'Presbytery' in Aston, *Remonstrance*.   [146] Secs. 5, 8 in ibid.
[147] Sec. 16 in ibid.

his parishioners. The flock could not depose their shepherd once elected or appeal to any higher authority, as in an episcopal system, to check his abuses:[148]

Now let us well weigh what man lives so upright in all his wayes, that is not, or may not be a Delinquent at the mercy of these dreadfull Iudges, whose least chastisement is banishment (suspension from the food of Life, the blessed Word and Sacraments) whose easiest prison is Hell, and whose punishment . . . [is] eternall destruction?

He continued:

Where is then the promised libertie of this so much desired change when from the legall penalties of positive and regulated Lawes which awe our persons, and might (perhaps) pinch our purses, whereof we know how to avoyd the breach, or satisfie the penaltie, we shall become meere Tenants at will of our soules.[149]

The failure of the presbyterians to impose their discipline on a national basis after the abolition of the Church of England later in the decade may indicate that Aston's unease concerning the balance of power between clergy and laity was widespread.

The threat from presbyterial rule affected more than just parochial concerns – it struck at the crown itself. In fact, Aston suggested that the present attack on episcopacy was simply a smoke screen for a far more dangerous subversion of monarchy, the civil magistrate, and statute and common law.[150] Sir Thomas somewhat coyly declined from judging whether monarchy was *iure divino* or not,[151] but this circumspection came after a long list of authorities supporting such a view including the New Testament, the Fathers, continental divines, but principally the Old Testament. In the Hebrew scriptures it was quite clear, according to Aston, that God alone makes and unmakes kings: 'I conceived God himselfe had an high hand in the institution of Kings and Princes, when hee leaves this

---

[148] That parishioners did see their bishop or archdeacon as an authority to which to appeal over the head of their parson is well illustrated by cases from the ecclesiastical courts. See Chapter 2, *passim*. For the stress on an apostolic defence of episcopacy rather than a *iure divino* tack, see above, pp. 100–4.

[149] Sec. 14, 'Presbytery' in Aston, *Remonstrance*.

[150] Secs. 9–12, 'Presbytery' in Aston, *Remonstrance*.

[151] 'Now whether these Crownes and Scepters shall be held *Jure Divino* or not, I take not on me to determine: but I may be bold to deliver *Du-Moulins* owne words (x) *whosoever buildeth the authority of Kings upon mens institutions, and not upon the Ordinance of God, cutteth off three parts of their authoritie, and bereaveth them of that which assureth their Lives and their Crownes more than guards of their bodies, or puissant [sic] arme, which put terrour into subjects hearts, instead of framing them to obedience: Then the fidelity of the subjects will be firme and sure, when it shall be incorporated into piety, and esteemed to be a part of Religion, and of the service which men owe to God.'* Aston cites his source as: 'x Moulins Buckler of Faith, fol. 560'. Sec. 9, 'Presbytery' in Aston, *Remonstrance*.

principle in the Mosaick Law.'[152] The claims of the presbyterian party were quite incompatible with this view of monarchy. Potentially most dangerous of all to Aston's frame of mind was their claim that the prince is subject to the church or clergy. Aston cited Cartwright, Rogers, and Travers:

who tell us, *That Princes (m) must be made subject unto the Church, and submit their Scepters, and throw downe their Crownes before the Church, and lick up the dust of the feet of the Church*; all which is applyed to their Presbyterie, ascribing to every Presbyter what the Pope onely assumes to himselfe: *That all Kings ought to kisse his feet.*[153]

Such sentiments were as unacceptable to Aston as John Cosin's notorious remarks in the 1620s that the king had no more authority in church affairs than the man who rubbed his horses heels – that is, as any lay person.[154] Sir Thomas was quite clear that the temporal (as opposed to sacramental) and rightful power of the bishops, warranted in scripture and tradition, was mediated through the crown and subject to the rule of law and parliament. As Aston pointed out in his argument against lay elders: 'wee are sure in danger never to recover a free *Parliament* againe and instead of 26 Bishops, whose deputation is upon the King as supreame [governor], whose temporall power is wholly derived from, [and] limited by the Lawes'.[155] However, although '*Aaron* the high priest called *Moses* the chief prince, Lord'[156] and was subject to him, Moses did not take upon himself the priestly functions of his brother.[157] Understood in this way, the subjection

---

[152] Sec. 9, 'Presbytery' in Aston, *Remonstrance.*

[153] Aston cites his sources as follows: 'm T.C. Reply, p. 144. Rogers Preface . . . Travers, de Disciplina Ecclesiae, fol. 142. Baron, Annals, 1076'. Sec. 9, 'Presbytery' in Aston, *Remonstrance.*

[154] '[Cosin] instanced oft these words that in a public meeting he shold affirme the King was not supreme head of the church: that in Excummunicacions the King had noe more authority then his man that rubbed his horses heeles.' *Commons Debates 1629*, ed. W. Notestein and F. H. Relf (Minneapolis, 1921), p. 174. See also *CD 1629*, pp. 43–4, 130–1, 133, 174–7. So notorious were Cosin's remarks, that they were still a topic of discussion over ten years later in the Short Parliament of 1640. *The Short Parliament (1640) Diary of Sir Thomas Aston*, pp. 25–6.

[155] Sec. 16, 'Presbytery' in Aston, *Remonstrance.*   [156] Sec. 9 in ibid.

[157] The Elizabethan bishop John Aylmer in 1559 used the example of Moses and Aaron to justify how the Church of England could not only have a lay head, but a female one as well:

For in one (as policy) she hath a function; that is she must be a doer: in the other she hath the oversight but not the function and practices as we see in the commonwealth of the Jews, first betwixt Aaron and Moses. Moses controlled Aaron, but yet he executed not Aaron's office; he offered no incense nor sacrifice ordinarily; he meddled not with the ark, nor any such thing as belonged to the priesthood; he wore not the garments; he ministered not the sacraments, and yet had he authority to redress his [Aaron's] faults, as it appeareth in the matter about the calf.

John Aylmer, *A Harborow for Faithful and True Subjects against the Late Blown Blast*

of bishops to the crown was consistent with Sir Thomas' other claims for the scriptural and apostolic foundation of the episcopate.[158]

A lay apologist for the Book of Common Prayer

Aston's chief purpose in *A Remonstrance Against Presbytery* was, as the title indicates, to defend the polity of the Church of England. Nevertheless, he did touch upon issues related to conformity to the lawful worship of the church. Not insignificantly, his observations on these concerns belong to the half of the *Remonstrance* which is a direct attack on presbyterianism. As in his positive defence of episcopacy, Aston first reminded his readers of the vigour and animosity of the attack on the Book of Common Prayer and its ceremonies, citing his sources:

> They say (l) *The Communion Booke is culled and picked out of that Popish Dung-hill, the Portuise [sic], and Masse book. (m) The Sacraments are wickedly mangled and prophaned. (n) They eate not the Lords Supper, but play a Pageant of their owne. The publike Baptisme (o) is full of Childish and superstitious toyes, the Ceremonies (p) are popish fooleries, Romish Reliques, and ragges of Antichrist.*

In the face of such home-grown critics, Aston turned his attention to the views of continental reformers and dryly remarked: 'Miserable indeed were the condition of this forlorne state, if other Reformed Churches spake not better of us, than wee of one another.'[159]

Once again Aston rallied the giants of international protestantism to the support of the Church of England as he conceived it. Martin Bucer 'a learned Reformer', was requested by Cranmer to give his opinion of the Prayer Book:[160] '(w) . . . I praise God, that gave you light to reduce these Ceremonies to such purity; for I finde nothing in them, which is not taken from the Word of God, or at least wise, (if clearly interpretated) not repugnant to it.' Benedictions from Beza were produced as well: '(x) . . . That in England true Doctrine flourishes purely and sincerely'. The trump card in any early seventeenth-century hand was, of course, John Calvin. He cited Calvin writing to the Lord Protector: '(u) The forme of prayer, and

---

Concerning the Government of the Women (Strasburg, 1559) cited in Claire Cross, *The Royal Supremacy in the Elizabethan Church* (London, 1969), p. 121.

[158] Aston can be shown to be standing within a considerable tradition of thought. J. P. Sommerville, *Politics and Ideology in England 1603–1640* (London, 1986), pp. 208–11.

[159] Sec. 3, 'Presbytery' in Aston, *Remonstrance*. Aston lists his sources as follows: '(l) First Admonition to the Parliament, pp. 17, 24, 26. Syon Plea, 29. (m) Second Admonition, pag. 42. (n) Gilby, pag. 2. (o) First Admonition, pag. 40. (p) Gilby, pag. 40'. Even Aston's rival and adversary, Sir William Brereton, remarked after a visit to the Netherlands that Dutch services lacked the '"decency and reverence" of the English service'. Cited in Dore, *Letter Books*, ii, p. 34.

[160] A selective reading by the Cheshire layman of Bucer's assessment of the English rite. MacCulloch, *Cranmer*, pp. 505–8, and *passim*.

*the Ceremonies of the Church I doe exceedingly approve of, as that from
which the Ministers ought not to depart.'* The baronet foresaw dire
consequences if 'separatists' were allowed to overturn what 'Queen, Parliament, State, Clergie' approved and indeed 'all the world admires [and]
approve[s]'.[161] Sir Thomas was not a lone voice in asserting that the lawful
liturgy of the English church was 'approved by the best of Foreign
Divines'.[162]

The fabric of a Christian society

Aston, like many of his contemporaries, perceived a clear connection
between order in religious matters and the maintenance of the fabric of
society as a whole.[163] Critics of the established church, under 'the pretext
of pietie', injected 'popular poysons' into the body of the commonwealth.
Using the organic imagery that was commonplace among political theorists
at the time, Aston added that those poisons 'corrupt or dissolve the Nerves
& Ligaments of Government (conformity to Lawes) if not early prevented
by those precious Antidotes against Confusion, Loyalty and Constancy'.[164]
Sir Thomas' concern for order, both in and out of divine service, must be
placed in the context of violent disruptions in the churches. This was a
national problem and Cheshire experienced its share of incidents. In April

---

[161] Sec. 4, 'Presbytery' in Aston, *Remonstrance*. Aston lists his sources as follows: '(w) Martin
Bucer, Scrip. Anglican, pag. 456 . . . (x) *Beza superintendens Geneva* . . . (u) *Calvin* in his
Epistle to the L. Protector'. Basil Hall, 'Martin Bucer in England', in *Martin Bucer:
reforming church and community*, ed. D. F. Wright (Cambridge, 1994), pp. 158–9; E. C.
Whitaker, *Martin Bucer and the Book of Common Prayer*, Alcuin Club Collections, lv
(1974).

[162] *LJ*, iv, p. 677. See above, pp. 116–17 for a more extensive discussion. Not only was Aston
not alone in 1641 in his invocation of foreign protestant divines on behalf of the Book of
Common Prayer, Elizabethan apologists had done it before him. Hall, 'Martin Bucer in
England', p. 159n.

[163] Such a view was not limited to those who remained steadfast to the 'old church'. Sir
William Waller, MP for Andover and future parliamentary commander and presbyterian
leader remarked:

I see some are moved with a number of hands against the Bishops, which I confess, rather
inclines me to their defence: for I look upon Episcopacy as a Counterscarp, or outwork,
which, if it be taken by this assult of the people; and withall, this mystery once revealed,
That we must deny them nothing, when they ask it thus in troops, we may in the next
place, have as hard a task to defend our property, as we have lately had to recover it from
the Prerogative. If by multiplying hands, the Petitions they prevail for an equality in things
ecclesiastical, the next demand, perhaps, may be *lex agraria*, the like equality in things
temporal.

John Webb, *Memorials of the Civil War between King Charles I and the Parliament of
England as it Affected Herefordshire and the Adjacent Counties*, ed. T. W. Webb (2 vols.,
London, 1879), i, p. 46.

[164] Sec. 4, 'Presbytery' in Aston, *Remonstrance*.

1641 it was reported in the Lords: 'That some Disorders have lately happened in several Churches, within the County Palatine and City of *Chester*, whereby Divine Service has been disturbed, or otherwise neglected and disquieted.'[165] No doubt it was with incidents in mind like those described in the *Lords Journal*, that the Cheshire Prayer Book petitioners wrote:

> Yet it [the Prayer Book] is now not only depraved by many of those who should teach Conformity to Established Laws, but, in Contempt thereof, in many Places wholly neglected. All those dayly practised with Confidence, without Punishment, to the great infultation and rejoycing in some Separatists, as they do not only seem to portend, but menace some great Alteration; and not containing themselves within the Bounds of Civil Government, do commit many tumultuous, if not Sacrilegious Violences both Day and Night, upon divers churches.[166]

Although Fletcher's observation is certainly a correct one, that the Cheshire petitions are the most strongly worded of all the conformist petitions in equating the attack on church order with an attack on the social order, nevertheless many of the petitions expressed similar concern over violent disruptions of divine service.[167] Violent acts in church were objected to not only because they might spread to other areas of human society, but also because of what they were in themselves: 'tumultuous, if not Sacrilegious Violences'. The word 'sacrilege' was used by a number of like-minded petitions and not only theology but anthropology as well, would suggest that it is a word charged with significance. The fact that these disputes erupted in God's house, during God's service, was in itself offensive and repugnant to some contemporaries. The concept of 'sacred space' survived the Reformation as much among the so-called elite as among the so-called vulgar.[168]

It would be a grave mistake, therefore, to describe Aston's religious sensibilities as co-terminus with his desire for an ordered, hierarchical, and patriarchal society. After all, it was a desire he shared with the vast majority of Stuart male gentry of whatever religious leanings. There *was* something deeper in Aston's concern for the decent and orderly worship of God as set forth in the Book of Common Prayer than simply paranoia over the preservation of the social order. Standing within what we might call a Cranmerian tradition, Aston defended the right of the church to '*decree Rites and Ceremonies*'[169] and produced continental supporters of the view, such as Luther's chief interpreter, Philipp Melanchthon. But Sir Thomas went farther than Cranmer and maintained that ceremonies, rather than

---

[165] *LJ*, iv, p. 225. See also Morrill, *Cheshire*, pp. 34–8, 44–5, 51.
[166] Nalson, *Impartial Collection*, ii, p. 758.   [167] Fletcher, *Outbreak*, pp. 287, 360.
[168] See above, pp. 117–24 for a fuller discussion of the issue.
[169] Article 20 of the 39 Articles.

simply being 'indifferent', could, if rightly understood and practised, be aids to piety and devotion. Liturgy exists, he argued:

to enjoyne a decent forme of outward reverence, to accompany the inward devotion of the heart; in humbling the body as well as the soule at the reception of the pledge of our salvation [that is, kneeling to receive Communion]; in standing up in the profession of our Faith in the Creed, or in celebrating the obsequies of such as dye in the Lord, with thanks for their deliverance, and with prayers for the surviving faithfull, with the like.[170]

There are some striking resonances between the above passage of the *Remonstrance* and another conforming layman, Sir Thomas Browne:

I am, I confesse, naturally inclined to that, which misguided zeale termes super-stition; my common conversation I do acknowledge austere, my behaviour full of rigour, sometimes not without morosity; yet at my devotion I love to use the civility of my knee, my hat, and hands, with all those outward and sensible motions which may express or promote my invisible [that is, inward] devotion.[171]

Religio Medici, composed in 1636, was published without the author's knowledge in 1642, a year later than the *Remonstrance*. However, it circulated widely in manuscript before that, so that it became 'common unto many'.[172] Although it is purely speculative to say so, it is tempting to think that the Cheshire baronet may have been familiar with, and perhaps influenced by, the most famous work of the Norwich doctor.

It is interesting to compare the religious sensibilities of Aston with those of the Gloucestershire gentleman, John Smyth of Nibley, as described in David Rollison's imaginative article. Both were tireless economic 'improvers'. Both were undeniable protestants who nevertheless disliked what smacked of religious fanaticism against harmless rural pastimes, such as church-ales, maypoles, and feast day celebrations. An anonymous satirical poem among the manuscripts in Aston Lodge pokes fun at those persons holding attitudes Smyth described as 'severe and rigid coates . . . wayward disposi-tions, and men of too stern a judgement'.[173] The poet asked ironically:

> How canst thou choose, but seeing it,[174] complaine
> That Baall is worship'd in the grove again.

[170] Sec. 7, 'Presbytery' in Aston, *Remonstrance*.
[171] Sir Thomas Browne, *Selected Writings*, ed. Sir Geoffrey Keynes (Chicago, 1968), p. 8.
[172] Browne, 'Introduction' (unpaginated) in ibid.
[173] David Rollison, 'The bourgeois soul of John Smyth of Nibley', *Social History* 12:3 (1987), p. 310. For maypoles, see Christopher Haigh, 'The Church of England, the Catholics and the people', in *The Reign of Elizabeth I* (London, 1984), pp. 215, 217. Haigh provides the example of John Danvers who, it was claimed by Sir Francis Knollys, led a defence of church-ales and maypoles and 'leaned passionately to the strict observance of the ceremonies of the *Book of Common Prayer*'. 'Church of England', p. 217. However, Collinson describes Danvers as a 'suspected church papist'. Collinson, *Religion of Protestants*, p. 145.
[174] A maypole.

He or she contrasted the essentially harmless activities involved with the maypole with the hypocrisy of the 'regenerate' who,

> . . . have thought it good
> To challenge liberty and recreation
> Lett it be done in holy contemplation.
> Brother and sister in field may walke
> Beginninge of the holly word to talke
> Of David, and Uriahs lovely wife
> Of Tamar and her lustfull brothers strife
> Then underneath the hedge that wooes them next
> They may sit downe, and there act out the text.

The biblical stories chosen could hardly be described as 'improving' (see II Samuel 11, 13). The poet posits, with a stong measure of mockery, that it was because the regenerate were declining in number (it was ever thus), that they opposed dancing and games, as such activities kept young people from procreating, rather than encouraging sexual activity:

> Few are the righteous nor doe I know
> how wee this Idoll here shall overthrow
>
>   . . .
>
> The numbers of the righteous is decreas'd
> But wee doe hope these tymes[175]
>   will on and
>   breed
> A faction mighty for us, for indeede
> wee labour all and every sister wynes
> To have regenerate babes spring from her loynes
> Beside what many carefully have done
> To gett th'unrighteous man a righteous son
> Then stoutly on[,] lett not thy flock range[?] leawdly.
> One thing I pray thee doe not soe much thirst
> After Idolatry's last fall, but first
> Follow thy suite more close, lett it not goe
> Till it be thine as thou would'st hav't or soe
>   Thy successours uppon the same entayle
>   Hereafter may take up the Whitson ale.[176]

Far better for young people to engage in harmless pastimes than to fall into the hands of misguided zealots. Smyth and Aston differ sharply, however, over the matter of 'inward' and 'outward' religion. Whereas Rollison describes Smyth as almost indifferent to the established church and to the conventional outward expressions of orthodoxy, Aston was, as I hope I

---

[175] 'These times' meaning the putting down maypoles and attacks on popular pastimes.

[176] Aston Lodge, MS JM/31 'To Mr Hamon Parson of Beaudley for the beatinge downe of the May=pole'. However, other contemporaries claimed that maypoles and may games accounted for a great deal of fornication among the young. Collinson, *Religion of Protestants*, pp. 225–6.

have shown, passionately committed to them.[177] For Aston, the 'outward' was integrated with the 'inward'; it was its partner in the spiritual life, not its foe. It was the church's duty to her people to 'enjoyne a decent forme of outward reverence, to accompany the inward devotion of the heart; in humbling the body as well as the soul'.[178]

That Sir Thomas himself was concerned about decent behaviour in church, there can be little doubt, or indeed, little surprise. But his views were not unique. John Werden complained to Aston:

I was toulde yesterday by one that loves Sir William Brereton well, but yet (as I doe) loves decency, order and good discipline better, That his Lady very latedly in the Church of Neston [Weston?] where she lives did send to the Mynister or parson of the Church to take downe some painted ancyent Imagery which was in the Glasse wyndowes. But the man beinge sober said he knew none that tooke offence at them; Nether would the Churchwardens as he receyved give any way unto it. But as she said, she Came presently and brought a Man with her whoe with a Staffe most zealous broake all the wyndowes to splinters. I dare not give you this otherwise than I have it.[179]

Similar views to Werden's indignation at the attack on 'sacred space' were expressed by Aston's sister Mary Parsons. Her disquiet is palpable; in a poignant letter she wrote either to Thomas or John shortly after Easter 1642:

god send us once settled in peace againe to his glorie & our comforts that wee may have Religion once more in its puritie for now soe manie folks soe manie minds it would greive any Christian hart to heare & see in some places this blessed time of Easter noe sacrament at all administered & where there is, god knows tis not without much confusion some sitting & some kneeling & and so manie rude cariages that all can not continue long thus; good god that wee should live to see the blessed seale of our salvation thus abused we had need to pray & pray hartilie soe that god would gide & direct the king & parlament that all goe not to ruine as tis like without gods speedie help which that hee may worke to his glorie & our comforts letts all pray & say Amen Amen.[180]

Obsession with the role of the church as a bulwark of social order must be juxtaposed with sensibilities like these – feelings of the violation of the sacred – surely as valid and as important to the historian of religion as the complicated motives which drive iconoclasts. In the light of these concerns, it is reasonable to modify Fletcher's harsh description of Aston as 'obsessively preoccupied with the preservation of social order'.[181]

---

[177] Rollison, 'Bourgeois soul', pp. 326–7.
[178] Sec. 7, 'Presbytery' in Aston, *Remonstrance*.
[179] Written on Good Friday, 1641. BL, Add. MS 36914, fols. 215–215v. As John Morrill notes, Werden's handwriting is wretched and it is unclear whether the place is Neston in Cheshire or Weston in Staffordshire. Morrill, *Cheshire*, p. 36n.
[180] Aston Lodge, MS Letter of Mary Parsons, 17 May 1642.
[181] Fletcher, *Outbreak*, p. 107; see above, pp. 117–24.

FROM LOCAL CONCERNS TO A NATIONAL CAUSE

Aston's petitioning activities in Westminster and the publication of the *Remonstrance* earned him a national reputation as a defender of the lawful liturgy and episcopacy. Robert Heywood of Lancashire,[182] also a former Brasenose man, wrote to Aston from Westminster in October 1641, praising the *Remonstrance* and describing the wide approval it enjoyed.

> I have many Letters (if you were here) to show you of the Generall approbation and applause that in Oxford is given to your booke and its Author, and my Chamber fellow has now in his hands the Thankfull approbations under their hands of the most Considerable part of the whole universitie with the free offers of divers of our private friends (to assist in anythinge wherein you shall have neede in your endevors to advance the common cause) who wod take it as a great satisfaction to themselves if under your colours they might be admitted to contest and foile the insulting adversaries of Episcopacie.

Heywood urged the reprinting of the *Remonstrance*, offering to have it done in Oxford 'where besides the supervisall of your friends it shall not be in danger of being seisd on for a non-Licett booke, the hazard it lately rane'.[183]

Apart from Robert Heywood's specific offers of assistance, there is further evidence for the sympathetic reception of the *Remonstrance* in certain quarters. In late March 1642, a Fellow of Queen's College, Oxford, Thomas Barlow (a Calvinist episcopalian and future bishop of Lincoln in 1675) wrote to Heywood enclosing verse in English, Latin, and Greek 'brought to me by some . . . young poets (by way of exercise) in commendation of his [Aston's] learned book'.[184] One undergraduate particularly contrasted the inactivity of the bishops to defend their own office with Aston's labours in that cause.[185]

> When many zealous tapers were
> to light Religion to her Sepulcher,
> & carry Learning captive, then your Soule

[182] *DNB*.
[183] Aston Lodge, MS Letter of Robert Heywood to Sir Thomas Aston [date uncertain but perhaps 15 October 1641]. Among the manuscripts of the Gloucester gentlemen Richard Berkeley and his son Sir Maurice Berkeley is a printed copy of 'A Petition Delivered to the Lords Spirituall and Temporall by Sir Thomas Aston, Baronet, from the County Palatine of Chester Concerning Episcopacie . . . 1641'. Possession of the Cheshire petition by gentry in another county provides further evidence of Aston's reputation outside his own shire. GRO, D2700/K Shelf 1/504/M1431#21. I am grateful to Sears McGee for this reference.
[184] *DNB*; Aston Lodge, MS Letter of Thomas Barlow to Robert Heywood, 28 March 1642. This was a subject which Barlow himself was keenly interested in, as his undated letter on the offices of bishop and presbyter shows. Queen's College, Oxford, MS 340.
[185] See above, pp. 156–7. Barlow's own talent for bad verse can be seen in his 'A Simple Parson and a Woman a Little Lettered', Queen's College, Oxford, MS 284.

> wheel'd in an higher orbe, could I enrolle
> its worth in Marble; may it ever live,
> or only, till our Bishops dare not give
> their bones for Sacrifice, till they deinye
> to triumph at the Stake, or fear to dye:
> till then Religious Aston shine as bright
> as any starr, or as the midday light.[186]

Another young admirer expressed his praise in this poetic fashion:

> I pray dare speake in plaine English now?
> Aston, thou ventur'st faire, that dost not greet
> That Church, as others, with a winding sheet:
> That cryest not Downe with order, nor wilt say
> The miter's Aaron's calfe, the vestments gay
> Are the whores robe, The Liturgie is naught
> With magicke, and Amens (god blesse us) fraught;
> That dost not sacrifice unto the humour
> of the mad rabble, and increase their tumour:
> Lastly, that durst speake truth; who'le not proclaime
> Thy valour, and eternise Aston's name?[187]

If Heywood, who himself enjoyed an established reputation as a poet,[188] approved of the poems, Barlow suggested that he should pass them along to Sir Thomas: 'if you think fitt you may lett him see what our poets think . . . you may judge by these what Thousands more thinke, and [in] convenient time will not be afraid to speak and print'.[189] In addition to the outpourings of the undergraduate muse, Barlow also related the information to Heywood that elements within the university were sending copies of their petitions in support of the Church of England to Aston. This letter indicates the extent of Aston's reputation outside Cheshire.[190] It also throws light on how he was able to compile and publish in the summer of 1642 *A Collection of Sundry Petitions*. The *Collection* contains the texts of nearly twenty petitions, principally from various counties but also in-

---

[186] Aston Lodge, MS Poem by T. Tarne of Queen's College. *AO*; *Walker Revised*, p. 32.

[187] Aston Lodge, MS Poem by Thomas Tullit. Presumably Thomas Tully of Queen's College, Oxford. *AO*; Wood, *Athenae Oxonienses*, iii, pp. 1055–9. Notes of Tully and Tarne's theological exercises in the 1640s and 1650s are in the Barlow Papers. Queen's College, Oxford, MS 248, fols. 185, 197, 207, 225, 283, 401, 447.

[188] See Robert Heywood, *Observations and Instructions, Divine and Morall*, ed. James Crossley, Chetham Society, lxxvi (1869). For an account in verse of a visit to Heywood's Lancashire home, see Richard James, *Iter Lancastrense: a Poem*, ed. Thomas Corser, Chetham Society, vii (1845).

[189] Aston Lodge, MS Letter of Thomas Barlow to Robert Heywood, 28 March 1642. I am especially grateful to Howard Talbot for bringing these letters to my attention.

[190] Even the beleaguered Archbishop Laud sought contact with Aston. His account book records a meeting with 'Sir Thomas Aston's man with a book' in the week of 25 June 1641. Laud was impeached in December. I owe this reference to Ken Fincham. PRO, E101/547/5, fol. 154; Russell, *Fall*, pp. 182–3.

cluding the universities, written in defence of episcopacy and the Book of Common Prayer.[191] Both printed and manuscript copies of a number of the petitions included in the *Collection* survive among the Aston Lodge manuscripts. Aston's national standing which followed his petitioning activities in Cheshire and Westminster, his significant social status, and the publication of his *Remonstrance*, made him the obvious person to receive and prepare for publication like-minded petitions from other parts of the country. The project also enjoyed the support of the king and the tract bore a royal order for its publication. Aston was, if only briefly, the central figure in transforming parochial anxieties into a national movement.

Aston's preface to the *Collection* contrasts sharply with the more reasoned tone of the *Remonstrance*, although the conviction that innovation was as undesirable as the plague remained a strong theme. Gone was any attempt or even pretence at balanced, sophisticated, tempered argument; the baronet's polemical skills were fully deployed:

Reader: Let mee put thee in mind (as these times doe mee) of a special Law in (that singular Patterne of a well composed State), *Sparta*. So sensible were they of the ill effects of Innovation in Government, that who ever proposed a new Law, presented himselfe with a Halter about his neck, his Head paid the trespasse of a new invented Prejudice. But oh *Quantum mutantur Tempora, quantum nos*.

The whole structure of society was seen to be in danger of collapse as the governed attempted to usurp the role of the governors in church and state:

So rare a gift have the illuminated fancies of this all-knowing age, That old women without Spectacles can discover Popish plots, young men and prentizes assume to regulate the Rebellion in *Ireland*. Sea-men and Marriners Reforme the House of Peers; Poore men, Porters, and Labourers spy out a malignant party, and discipline them; The countrey clouted shoe renew the decayed Trade of the Citie. The Cobler patch up Religion and all these petition for a translation, both of Church and State, with so little feare of the Halter, that they would thinke themselves neglected, if they had not thankes for their care of the Re-publick; only he that desires the ratification of an old Law, or of a long setled Ecclesasticke Government, lookes as if the Halter was his share.

But such invective against the populace, not so different from that of the parliamentarian Sir William Waller cited above,[192] was only the warm-up for Aston's attack on those who mislead the 'credulous people':

That a few Innovators shall be able to summon to Blackheath, Southwarke, and Saint George his fields of thousands of credulous people, with implicite faiths, to goe along with Petitions, shall be shewed them when they come there, for the alteration of Lawes, and Government.

---

[191] Barlow owned a copy himself of Aston's *Collection* which he signed and in which he also identified the 'anonymous' tract as by Sir Thomas. Bodl., C13.15 Linc.

[192] See above, p. 170n.

His chief purpose in producing the *Collection* was to end the sense of isolation felt by lovers of the Church of England in the face of a mounting attack:

[that] the Resolutions of an Assizes or Sessions of Iustices, published in all parishes, signed by all the Free-holders of a County, for the supportation of Lawes of Government, shall not produce one Patriot to present the unanimous desires of a County: yet it fals out often, so when single hearted men are en'counter'd by a faction, each man thinkes he stands alone unassur'd of a second; when ten of the other confederated make more noise than the 10,000 silent men . . . But each orthodox sonne of the Church thinkes himselfe in *Eliahs* case, that hee alone is left of all the Prophets, alas, what can doe? And perhaps my Reader art one of those, *Courage man*, the same God that taught him to know, hee had reserved seven thousand, that had never bowed their knees to *Baall*, when he open thy eyes, can shew thee not seven, but seventy times seven thousand true Protestants, that will lend their hands and hearts to uphold that Apostolicke order, this blessed forme of divine service.[193]

The change in Aston's tone, of course, reflects not only a different readership but also the rising temperature in the political environment from the appearance of *Remonstrance* in May 1641 and the *Collection*'s publication in May 1642. The intervening twelve months had been, to say the very least, eventful. For Sir Thomas, the coming of the war meant the putting down of his pen and the taking up of the sword; where he served with courage, if not success, and certainly at great personal cost.

WAR AND DEATH

Sir Thomas' reconciliation with the king in 1641, and his activities on behalf of the church, helped to secure a large portion of the Cheshire gentry to royalism. At the beginning of the war, Aston, who had attended Charles at York in June, was obviously one of the king's most trusted representatives in the shire. Nevertheless Charles was somewhat surprised by the warm welcome he received in Chester on 23 September 1642.[194] Aston later joined the king at Shrewsbury and fought at the Battle of Edgehill, distinguishing himself by mounting a successful rescue of Prince Charles'

---

[193] 'The Collector to the Reader' in Aston, *Collection*.

[194] Morrill, *Cheshire*, pp. 53–4. For example, BL, Add. MS 36913, fols. 88–94v, 101, 103, 108. See also letters to Aston from Prince Rupert, BL, Add. MS 36913, fols. 105, 107. It is not my purpose here to relate in detail the history of the civil war in Cheshire or Sir Thomas' part in it. Howard Talbot, the owner of the Aston Lodge Manuscripts, is planning a biography of the baronet. See R. N. Dore, *The Civil Wars in Cheshire* (Chester, 1966); Morrill, *Cheshire*, pp. 56, 64–5, 75n., 75–6; Ronald Hutton, *The Royalist War Effort 1642–1646* (London, 1982), pp. 7–8, 22–30, 39, 44–6, 97–8, 127, 192–3. John Phillips, *Memoirs of the Civil War in Wales and the Marches 1642–1649* (2 vols., London, 1874), ii, pp. 10–15.

tutor, Dr Brian Duppa, bishop of Salisbury. Ironically, the apologist who stressed the importance of the office over the individual failed to save the office in the end but did snatch from the enemy one particular bishop. Charles appointed Aston major-general in Cheshire, and thereafter he was largely occupied by military affairs in the county. In early 1643, Sir Thomas was involved in a series of minor battles, principally those of Nantwich (28 January) and Middlewich (13 March). Sir Thomas now faced his former parliamentary colleague and electoral rival, Sir William Brereton, in a different, and far more deadly, contest. Brereton again emerged victorious and Aston's reputation after his defeat at Middlewich was in tatters. Fearful for the safety of Chester, Orlando Bridgeman, son of the bishop and the civilian royalist leader of Cheshire, petitioned the king for expert advice. Charles appointed Sir Nicholas Byron colonel-general of Cheshire, thus undercutting Aston's authority.[195]

Any informed verdict on Aston's lack of success on the battlefield must take into account the articles produced against the most active of the Commissioners of Array for the county, Orlando Bridgeman. This document drawn up by 'divers Commissioners of Array and Gentry' of Cheshire tells a long tale of Bridgeman's incompetence. Bridgeman was obsessed by the defence of Chester, so much so that he failed to release men and supplies to Aston and other officers who appreciated the strategic importance of more centrally located towns like Nantwich and Middlewich.[196] Given the information related in these articles, Aston's 'apology' after the defeat at Middlewich was remarkably restrained:

It was the plain truth, the enemy haveing no diversion, butt att liberty with theire full power to fall on us from all parts, were much too hard for us in a place not defensible. And without some more exprerienced foot officers, I must freely say noe number will be found sufficient to withstand readie men.[197]

After Middlewich, Aston saw action outside the county and was part of an ill-fated force based in Wales and under the command of Sir William Vaughan created to harass the troops laying seige to Chester. Brereton dispatched a larger force to deal with them before they ever got to Chester and smashed Vaughan's force at Denbigh. Vaughan's troops, including Aston, were scattered over the Marches. Sir Thomas' party encountered the

---

[195] Peter Young, *Edgehill, 1642* (Kineton, 1976), pp. 54–5, 86, 88, 212, 213, 301–2; Hutton, *Royalist War Effort*, pp. 44–6; Dore, *Civil Wars*, pp. 25–56. For Brereton's account of the Nantwich engagement see Bodl., Tanner MS 62, fols. 537–8; Phillips, *Memoirs*, ii, pp. 49–51, is another account. BL, Add. MS 34253, fols. 23–23v is Brereton's account of the battle at Middlewich. It is printed in Phillips, *Memoirs*, ii, pp. 54–5. BL, Harl. MS 2135, fols. 102–5 is Aston's letter of apology for his defeat at Middlewich. It is printed in Phillips, *Memoirs*, ii, pp. 56–61.

[196] BL, Add. MS 36913, fols. 122–127v, 124–125v.

[197] Phillips, *Memoirs*, ii, p. 61.

enemy in a bloody skirmish near Bridgnorth in November 1645. A parliamentary observer noted that Aston often rallied his men 'with such as he could procure to stand, and engaged for the saftie of his men untill our troops slew above twentie of his men upon the place'. Aston was wounded and captured, along with a number of his officers and forty troopers. He died either there of his wounds, or later in parliamentary prison in Stafford in 1646.[198] Among the papers taken from him at Bridgnorth was a 'commission for a regiment in the west, and another commission to place a garrison at Kinnsbury or Nuneaton in Warwickshire'.[199] It is sadly ironic that at the time of his capture or death, Aston was obviously regaining his former place in the regard of his superiors.

Sir Thomas' body was returned to Aston and buried in the chapel he had done much to refurbish. His family was left with the comfort of 'An elegie upon the Death of Sir Thomas Aston':

> Thou hast at length, most happy shade, out gone
> The malice of the Long-jamb Breerton;
> And in that blessed place thou doest reside,
> Triumphant above his malice and his Pride:
> Soe that thy Death appeard to us to be
> Not a Submission, but a Victory.[200]

In the end, Sir Thomas could not prevent the English church, its liturgy and government, from 'suffering'. Aston did ensure, however, as his son's memorial to him erected in 1697 says, 'having distinguished himself both by his learning and his courage in the defence of church and state', that at the very least, his vision of the Church of England did not 'suffer silently'.[201]

---

[198] HMC, 13th Report, Portland Manuscripts 1, p. 306; Dore, *Letter Books*, ii, pp. 226–7, 241–2, 246–7. It is unclear whether Sir Thomas died directly after the skirmish, or whether he died later of his wounds in prison, or indeed, of fresh wounds received while trying to escape. See HMC, 13th Report, Portland Manuscripts 1, p. 306; BL, Thomason Tracts E.309(24); Hutton, *Royalist War Effort*, pp. 192–3; *DNB*.

[199] HMC, 13th Report, Portland Manuscripts 1, p. 306.

[200] Aston Lodge, MS Poem 'An Elegie upon the death of Sir Thomas Aston' by Edward Williams. 'Long-jamb' probably means 'long-legged'. See *OED*.

[201] Ormerod, *Cheshire*, i, p. 727. 'Episcopacy and Lyturgie are both legally planted, [and] at this time both violently assaulted: The question is, whether the battery, or the defence, be stronger: the one side charges furiously, the other suffers silently.' 'Preface' in Aston, *Collection*.

5

Parishioners, petitions and the Prayer Book in the 1640s

Particulars ever awake and touch more than generalls.[1]

ISSUES AND SOURCES

It is now appropriate to return to one of the most difficult questions concerning support for the lawful liturgy and polity of the Church of England. What can be said, if anything, about the different sections of society from which the established church attracted commitment and even, perhaps, affection? Did the Church of England enjoy support predominantly from those at the higher end of the social structure, who combined their support for the church with their anxieties over the preservation of the social order? Or, as opponents maintained, were subscribers to the pro-church petitions most often drawn from 'gullible' labourers: 'hedgers at the hedg, plowmen at the plow, threshers in the barns'?[2] It was a commonplace in Tudor–Stuart polemics to accuse one's opponents of drawing support chiefly from socially inferior groups. This charge was made against the Lollards in the early sixteenth century and against dissenters in the seventeenth. The episcopalian Sir Thomas Aston accused the Root and Branch petitioners of the early 1640s of precisely the same 'fault'. The occasional and impressionistic evidence of the social spread of committed conformity provided by the ecclesiastical courts has been discussed in Chapter 2. It was demonstrated there that persons from a variety of backgrounds, from gentlemen and yeomen to husbandmen and day labourers, women and men, those who could sign their names and those

---

[1] George Herbert, 'The Parson Preaching', in *A Priest to the Temple or the Country Parson*, Everyman edn (1908), p. 226.
[2] 'W. Howell to Thos. Wise, Knt for the Co. of Devon at his lodgings at Savoy' (20 February 1641) in *Buller Papers*, Buller Family (n.p., printed privately, 1895), pp. 33–4; see above, pp. 95–7 and Chapter 3, *passim* for a discussion of these petitions. I am particularly grateful to Marjorie McIntosh who commented extensively on an earlier draft of this chapter.

181

who could only make their marks, could and did organize themselves to present clergy who were failing to perform their ministerial duties faithfully according to the Book of Common Prayer. A similar social spread, in contrast with their early modern image, has been found among the later Lollards. The court material discussed above suggests that support for the church defined by the Elizabethan Settlement came from a cross section of English society. It was not 'determined' by social or economic standing.[3]

This chapter marks the return to these questions concerning social class and religious feeling. It attempts to move from the general to the particular, from the nation, to the county, to the parish – a process of increasing the magnification on support for the lawful liturgy and polity of the Church of England made possible by the heightened tensions of 1640–42. Chapter 3 explored these questions in terms of a widespread movement, national in scale, by examining the various strands of theology and ideology found in the rhetoric of petitions for upholding the church. In Chapter 4, the struggle in one county, Cheshire, to organize on behalf of the established church was examined in detail, as well as the theology, politics, and spirituality of the leading lay protagonist. Chapter 5 continues to increase the magnification by establishing – as far as can be – a religious and socio-economic profile of the subscribers for the Cheshire petition for the Book of Common Prayer and the communities which provided the context of their production. This vexing question of what sort of people supported petitions for the lawful liturgy will be addressed by a detailed look at the elusive world of five particular Cheshire communities.

Cheshire, as related in Chapter 4, produced two petitions to parliament for the established church: one in support of episcopacy presented in February 1641 and a second in support of the lawful liturgy presented in December 1641.[4] The subscribers to the petition for the Prayer Book and their communities will be examined in detail as it relates more directly to the larger concerns of this study.

Identifying localities

It was necessary before any analysis of the subscribers to the Prayer Book petition could begin, to identify as many parishes and townships as possible

---

[3] Derek Plumb, 'John Foxe and the later Lollards of the Thames Valley' (University of Cambridge Ph.D., 1987), pp. 325–8; William Stevenson, 'The economic and social status of protestant sectaries in Huntingdonshire, Cambridgeshire, and Bedfordshire 1650–1725' (University of Cambridge Ph.D., 1989), pp. 285–93. See above, pp. 80–1, 151–6.

[4] HLRO, Main Papers, HL, [27] February, 1640/1; HLRO, Main Papers, HL, 20 December 1641. It should be noted that although the pages of subscribers are bound together, the manuscripts are unfoliated. This makes it impossible to refer to specific folios in the documents.

among the 9,000 subscribers. The places listed in Appendix 2 do not represent all the subscribing parishes. Rather they are the localities that it has been possible to identify with reasonable certainty. There are, among the many folios appended to the petition, schedules of subscribers which clearly state their place of origin. Oddly, the majority of schedules are not clearly marked in this way making the task of identification arduous and sometimes unsuccessful. In the end, it has been possible to identify perhaps as many as 63 out of a possible 78 subscribing parishes, independent chapelries, and extra-parochial jurisdictions, from a total number of 104 in the county.[5] The inclusion of many of the localities in Appendix 2 required more roundabout methods of identification. Usually, near the top of the page on most schedules, particular individuals indicated after their signatures their status as gentlemen or clerics. Identifying the place through these self-styled gentlemen was possible through a combination of the subsidy returns for Cheshire for 1640–41 and the information supplied by M. D. G. Wanklyn's study of the Cheshire gentry.[6] The clerical subsidy of 1639 was even more productive in matching individuals to localities.[7] Such a heavy reliance on the clerical subsidy in the process of identification, however, may create a lopsided effect and give the impression that if a parish or township subscribed for the Prayer Book, it was very likely that their local priest headed the list.

Such technical, one might even say tedious, concerns are a necessary prelude before asking far more interesting questions about what kind of individuals and communities subscribed for the Prayer Book in 1641. But in order to do that it was necessary to find other types of social and economic documentation to illuminate the localities and people. Sadly, an obvious first recourse like rentals or poor rate lists are not extant for

[5] Total number of parishes is based on Dorothy Sylvester and Geoffrey Nulty, *The Historical Atlas of Cheshire* (Chester, 1958), pp. 36–8. These are rough estimates, due to the problems of identification, especially in the case of the estimate of the total number of subscribing parishes and chapelries (78). It is often difficult to tell where one list of subscribers begins and another ends. In addition, there are a number of cases where schedules of subscribers for the same locality are scattered through the manuscript. The work of Sylvester and Nulty has recently been improved and corrected but no errors were found in their descriptions of the five localities under examination here. See F. I. Dunn, *The Ancient Parishes, Townships and Chapelries of Cheshire* (Chester, 1987).

[6] PRO, E179/85/131; PRO, E179/85/134; PRO, E179/85/135; PRO, E179/85/136; M. D. G. Wanklyn, 'Landed society and allegiance in Cheshire and Shropshire in the first Civil War' (University of Manchester Ph.D. thesis, 1976), pp. 152–62, Appendix II. For another description of the methodological problems, see Margaret Spufford, *Contrasting Communities: English villagers in the sixteenth and seventeenth centuries* (Cambridge, 1974), pp. 233–4.

[7] 'Loans, contributions, subsidies, and ship money, paid by the clergy of the diocese of Chester in the years 1620, 1622, 1624, 1634, 1635, 1636, and 1639', ed. G. T. O. Bridgeman, *Miscellanies relating to Lancashire and Cheshire*, LCRS, xii (1885).

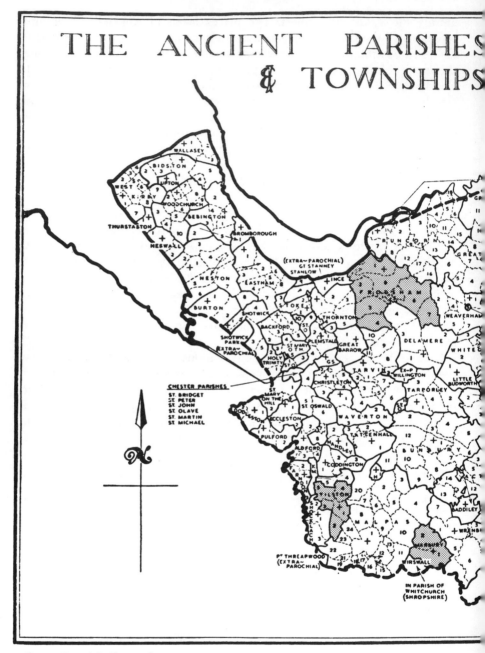

Figure 5.1　Five Cheshire communities. (D. Sylvester and G. Nulty, *The Historical Atlas of Cheshire*, Chester, 1958)

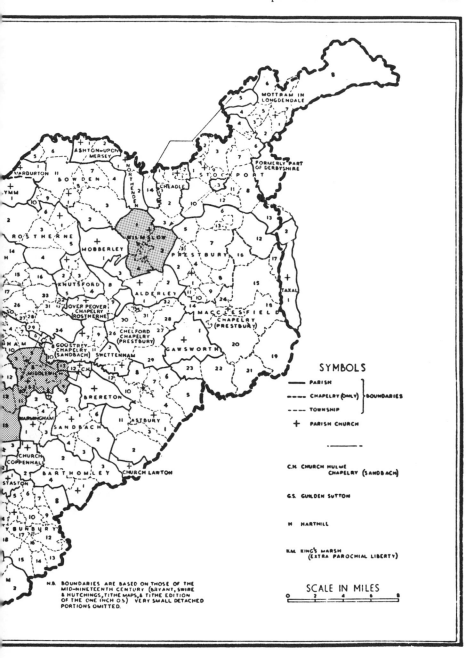

SYMBOLS

———— PARISH
- - - - CHAPELRY (ONLY) } BOUNDARIES
- - - - TOWNSHIP
+ PARISH CHURCH

————— -

C.H. CHURCH HULME
CHAPELRY (SANDBACH)

G.S. GUILDEN SUTTON

H HARTHILL

K.M. KING'S MARSH
(EXTRA PAROCHIAL LIBERTY)

SCALE IN MILES

0   2   4   6   8

N.B. BOUNDARIES ARE BASED ON THOSE OF THE
MID-NINETEENTH CENTURY (BRYANT, SWIRE
& HUTCHINGS, TITHE MAPS, & TITHE EDITION
OF THE ONE INCH OS) VERY SMALL DETACHED
PORTIONS OMITTED.

Cheshire for the years around 1641. Neither, alas, do subscription schedules for Cheshire's Root and Branch petition against the established
church – an obvious point of contrast between subscribers in the same
places – survive. However, by matching extant records of church rates, or
leys as they were sometimes called, with identified places, it has proved
possible to give the subscribers to the Prayer Book petition an economic
and social context in five Cheshire communities.[8]

The resulting yield of four parishes and one chapelry under examination,
therefore, was determined by the survival of complementary documentation. Happily, however, the five communities represent a reasonable
geographic spread across the county. Our locations for analysis are: Tilston
(Broxton Hundred), Frodsham (Eddisbury Hundred), Wilmslow (Macclesfield Hundred), Marbury (Nantwich Hundred), and Middlewich (Northwich Hundred) (see fig. 5.1). The parishes and chapelry share some similar
agrarian characteristics. The Cheshire plain was predominantly a cattle
farming area, with corn grown only for immediate use. Cattle rearing and
fattening was the preferred practice in the north while dairy farming was
preferred in the south and west. Cheshire was already nationally famous
for its cheese. Minor variations in this pattern apply to Frodsham and
Wilmslow. Frodsham was still a small port until the eighteenth century as
well as part of a rich grassland area in which sheep (rare in the rest of the
shire) were raised along with cattle. Wilmslow, in Cheshire's uplands, was
situated near the woollen areas of Prestbury and Macclesfield. As can be
seen in Figure 5.1 parishes in the west of the county were smaller; farmers
needed less land to make ends meet. The large parishes of central and
eastern Cheshire superimposed on a soil map reveal them as areas of
difficult cultivation. Although the population growth of Cheshire at this
time was small by southern standards, the western part of the county was
more densely populated. There is agreement that Cheshire was relatively
prosperous in 1640 and later hearth tax returns under Charles II reveal that
although there were fewer of the very rich, there were fewer of the very
poor in corn growing areas. Not only yeomen, but many tenant farmers as
well, enjoyed reasonable security of tenure. It was usual for farms to be
leased for long periods, often for three lives, and for successive holders to
be in the same family. Such a system of agricultural tenure gave tenant
farmers reasonable autonomy and security, even if the landowning gentleman was resident in the locality, as the tenants had the right to sell their

---

[8] Church rates were a locally assessed tax imposed to meet the running expenses of the parish
church. See below, pp. 188–92. I was greatly aided in the task of finding appropriate
documentation for the subscribers by Alan Thacker and the late Brian Harrison of VCH
Chester. See below, Appendix 2. The city of Chester has been excluded from consideration,
as the identification of urban parishes in the schedule of subscribers is very uncertain.

leases, sublet or add 'lives' as they wished. Further, such general stability promoted the cause of long-term agricultural improvement of land. Although generalizations should not be pushed too far, the security provided by the agricultural profile suggests that men and women in Cheshire may have been freer from the 'social control' of their social superiors than in other parts of the country and therefore at greater liberty to follow their consciences over subscription or non-subscription to the Cheshire petitions for the established church.[9]

Population estimates

An obvious question to ask is what proportion the subscribers to the Common Prayer petition formed out of the overall adult male population in each locality? Estimates have been provided in the detailed discussion of each of the five communities.[10] Set out below is a description of the method for obtaining these population estimates.

Taking the country as a whole, the population of England was remarkably stable from the 1640s to the 1660s.[11] If such a 'global' pattern occurred in Cheshire, then population figures derived from hearth tax sources in the 1660s would provide a reliable, if rough, estimate of the local population into which to place subscribing inhabitants.

The method for estimating population based on hearth tax returns was developed by Peter Laslett.[12] He suggests a multiplier of 4.75 for the number of households listed in the hearth tax, to give a rough population total for a parish. Wrigley and Schofield calculate that 65 per cent of the population was over sixteen in 1603.[13] Half of that 65 per cent should provide us with a very rough estimate of the total number of adult males.[14] Again, it cannot be emphasized enough that these are very rough estimates.

---

[9] Joan Thirsk, ed., *The Agrarian History of England and Wales IV 1500–1640* (Cambridge, 1967), pp. 80–4; *The Agrarian History of England and Wales 1640–1750, vol. i: regional farming systems* (Cambridge, 1984), pp. 131, 149, 153–4; Joan Beck, *Tudor Cheshire* (Chester, 1969), pp. 38–44, 52.

[10] See below, pp. 199, 204, 210–11, 217, 220.

[11] R. M. Smith, 'Population and its geography in England 1500–1730', in *An Historical Geography of England and Wales*, ed. R. A. Dodgshon and R. A. Butlin (London, 1978), p. 207; E. A. Wrigley and R. S. Schofield, *The Population History of England 1541–1871: a reconstruction* (London, 1981), p. 207.

[12] Peter Laslett, 'Mean household size in England since the sixteenth century', in *Household and Family in Past Times*, ed. Peter Laslett and Richard Wall (Cambridge, 1972), p. 126. The hearth tax concerned must include the exempt in order to be suitable for use in estimating population.

[13] Wrigley and Schofield, *Population History*, p. 569. Sixteen appears to have been the most common age for admittance to Holy Communion.

[14] In fact the bias slightly favours adult women.

Table 5.1 *Estimated percentage of adult males subscribing to the Prayer Book petition, 1641*

Place	% of subscribing adult males in parish
Tilston	27
Frodsham	27
Wilmslow	69
Marbury	29
Middlewich	41

Note: based on hearth tax returns for Cheshire in 1664. PRO, E179/86/145.

Two of the five communities under examination here, Frodsham and Wilmslow, have had their populations aggregated by the Cambridge Group for the History of Population and Social Structure. The Cambridge Group estimates are based on the baptisms and burials recorded in the parish registers. A comparison of the results of the two methods looks like this: for Frodsham, a population of 1,877 is estimated based on the registers as compared to 2,100 based on the hearth tax returns. For Wilmslow, the registers yield an estimate of 1,340 compared to 1,406 inhabitants using the hearth tax method. Besides offering some reassurance in a period where reliable statistics are hard to come by, the Cambridge Group figures indicate that the percentage of adult male subscribers in each place may be underestimated.[15] It should be emphasized that even in the places with the lowest rates of subscription, a quarter of the possible adult males did subscribe. At Wilmslow, over two-thirds of the eligible inhabitants put their hands or made their marks on the petition for upholding the Prayer Book. This is an impressive testimonial either to the depth of personal conviction, or the degree of parochial organization involved, or perhaps both.[16]

Church rates

Church leys, or rates, must not be confused with tithes which provided the income and maintenance of the incumbent minister and formed part of his freehold.[17] The levying of a rate on parishioners raised the funds needed,

[15] Taking the Cambridge Group population estimates, we achieve a subscription rate of adult males of 30 per cent for Frodsham and 72 per cent for Wilmslow.

[16] I am grateful to Roger Schofield for his guidance in arriving at these figures.

[17] Rates must also be distinguished from Easter Books. The latter was an annual fixed fee on communicants which was usually intended to supplement the priest's income, especially in

not only for repairs to the fabric of the nave (the chancel was generally regarded as part of the incumbent's freehold and therefore his responsibility), but also for the assorted 'utensils' needed to conduct the worship of God in conformity with the Prayer Book and canons of the Church of England. These included items that can commonly be found in churchwardens' accounts, such as mending the surplice and service books and purchasing bread and wine for Holy Communion. Although such leys were well established by the fourteenth century, it would appear that they remained voluntary until after the Reformation. Under Elizabeth, however, a compulsory church rating system was introduced (1562–63) and remained in effect until 1868. The enforcement of rates was a matter for the ecclesiastical courts, although provision was made in the 1562–63 act for the bishop to refer anyone in arrears to a civil magistrate.[18]

Rates were set by the churchwardens, theoretically with the consent of the major part of the parish, at a meeting sometimes called 'a vestry'. Humphrey Prideaux, DD, writing directions for churchwardens in the archdeaconry of Suffolk in the late seventeenth century, stated that proper warning of a vestry meeting must be given at divine service the Sunday before and a warning bell should be tolled prior to the meeting itself. The archdeacon's safeguards suggest that occasional skulduggery at vestry meetings was a concern.[19] Parish meetings could be lively gatherings – subject to pressure 'from below' as well as 'from above'. They were occasions of open discussion, acknowledging the collective responsibilities of the parishioners. They could also be forums for calling irresponsible churchwardens to account for their actions.[20] It had to be established, prior

---

urban parishes where the income from tithes could be quite small. Sue Wright, 'Easter Books and Parish Rate Books: a new source for the urban historian', *Urban History Yearbook* (1985), pp. 30–1, 33–4. I am grateful to Susan Wright for discussing some of these issues with me.

[18] 'Utensils' is the term used by Archdeacon Prideaux. Humphrey Prideaux, *Directions to Churchwardens for the Faithful Discharge of their Office for the Use of the Archdeaconry of Suffolk* (2nd edn, Norwich, 1704), p. 20; Edwin Cannan, *The History of Local Rates in England* (London, 1912), pp. 14–16; W. E. Tate, *The Parish Chest* (Cambridge, 1969), pp. 26–7; J. Charles Cox, *Churchwardens' Accounts* (London, 1913), pp. 2, 11–12, 26–7, 93–4; Richard Burn, *Ecclesiastical Law* (4 vols., London, 1767), i, p. 354; Sidney Webb and Beatrice Webb, *The Parish and the County* (London, 1906, repr. 1963), pp. 24–5.

[19] St Michael's in Stuart Chester provides an example of the sort of behaviour which concerned Archdeacon Prideaux. One William Parnell, 'conspired with the churchwarden James Lingley to procure the minister or curate to read divine service sooner than the accustomed time upon purpose to procure a sudden and secret dispatch of business when a few might be present'. Cited in Nick Alldridge, 'Loyalty and identity in Chester parishes 1540–1640', in *Parish, Church and People: local studies in lay religion 1350–1750*, ed. Susan Wright (London, 1988), p. 109.

[20] Examples of both can be found for two Chester parishes, St Oswald's and St Peter's. Alldridge, 'Loyalty', pp. 109–10, 111.

to setting a rate, which parishioners were entitled to vote. Prideaux, however, appears to have skirted over the issue of 'select vestries' to some extent – a problem that will be discussed below. In the unlikely event that no parishioners appeared at the public meeting, the wardens were allowed in ecclesiastical law to proceed and set a rate, as the law also held them liable for defects in the fabric and ornaments of the church.[21]

An important question remains: on what *basis* were parishioners assessed for the church rate – a crucial question when we come to compare the economic spread of assessed subscribers to the Prayer Book petition to non-subscribers in five selected Cheshire communities.

First of all, who was a 'parishioner'? The answer to that question is obvious in most circumstances, but not in all. A 1589 case in King's Bench which is often cited, established that any individual who held land in one parish but actually dwelt in another, was still liable for the ley, as he (or she, if a widow)[22] was entitled to attend the parish meeting. However, the court made it clear that if the owner was not the actual *occupier* of the land, but the *lessor*, it was the occupier or tenant who was liable for the rate. As Edwin Cannan emphasized in his pioneering history of local rates, we must not think in terms of *what* was rateable, but in terms of *who* was rateable.[23] According to Nick Alldridge's work on Chester, parish rates used a system of graduated contributions, and took into account that there were inhabitants below a certain economic level from whom nothing should be extracted. One contemporary source states that annual assessments were made on 'all men of ability . . . and according to everyman's estate'.[24] The weight of opinion appears to be, therefore, that inhabitants

---

[21] Prideaux, *Directions*, pp. 17–18; Burn, *Ecclesiastical Law*, i, pp. 346–7; Webb, *The Parish*, p. 39. Prideaux relates that, in strict law, there ought to be two rates: one on lands and houses for the fabric and another on 'personal estates' of the inhabitants for the repair of 'utensils' and all other incidental expenses. The rate for the fabric is not on the lands or houses themselves, but on those who occupy them. The charge is therefore 'personal', according to Prideaux, and cannot reach further than those persons of immediate possession. For the 'utensils' of the church, which included the clerk's or sexton's wages, costs incurred in visitations and in going on perambulation – these cannot in the 'Rule of Law', again according to the archdeacon, be charged to an inhabitant's lands or houses. Such incidentals, as Prideaux calls them, must be charged to 'the personal estates of the inhabitants'. Strictly speaking, therefore, there ought to be two rates. It must be said, however, that I have never seen any evidence of such a double rating system – certainly there is no trace of it in the Cheshire churchwarden's accounts surviving from before the civil war. Prideaux repeatedly used the phrase 'in strict law' or its equivalent, which may well indicate that things were not widely different in Suffolk than in Cheshire. Prideaux, *Directions*, p. 20.

[22] Although widows appear in lists and accounts as contributors to the parish rate, I am unaware of any evidence to suggest they had a vote at the parish meeting which set the rate.

[23] Cannan, *Local Rates*, pp. 22, 24–6, 79–80; Burn, *Ecclesiastical Law*, i, pp. 347, 351, 352.

[24] Cited in Alldridge, 'Loyalty', p. 91.

Table 5.2 *Total subscribers to rated subscribers*

Place	Total subscribers	Rated subscribers (No.)	(%)
Tilston	100	49	(49)
Frodsham	184	34	(18)
Wilmslow	313	124	(40)
Marbury	55	23	(42)
Middlewich	265	85	(32)

Note: See Appendix 3.

were assessed according to their ability to pay.[25] Prideaux noted, for example, that as the poor are exempt from the poor rate, so are they exempt from the ley.[26] This general precept can be further refined by taking note of the percentage of subscribers for the Prayer Book assessed in the ley, to the total number of signatories in the five localities.[27]

Taken together, it seems reasonable to assume that not only were church rates assessed on ability to pay, and are therefore good indicators of the relative wealth of the subscribers, but that only heads of households were liable for rates. The 82 per cent to 51 per cent of adult male parishioners who subscribed, but were not assessed, one assumes were composed of sons over sixteen but still at home, and male servants, as well as the poor.[28]

On balance, the evidence favours the view that church rates were assessed on heads of households on the 'old principle': ability to pay, not property occupied. Equally important too, is that they were imposed by the laity on the laity; by local people on local people to meet almost entirely

[25] Burn, *Ecclesiastical Law*, i, pp. 352–3; J. S. Purvis, *Dictionary of Ecclesiastical Terms* (London, 1962), pp. 46–7; Alldridge, 'Loyalty', pp. 91, 93–4; Susan Amussen, *An Ordered Society: gender and class in early modern England* (Oxford, 1988), pp. 16–17. I am grateful to Jeremy Boulton and Roger Schofield for discussing this problem with me.

[26] Prideaux adds that therefore the poor have no voice in the selection of parish officers. Prideaux, *Directions*, pp. 18–19.

[27] Women assessed in the leys have been excluded from all figures, as they were apparently considered inappropriate signatories for the petitions. Almost all the women who were assessed were identified as widows. I am grateful to Anthony Fletcher for answering my queries concerning suitable signers of petitions in the pre-civil war period.

[28] I am particularly grateful to Marjorie McIntosh for pointing this out to me. Concerning a pew dispute later in the century, Richard Gough of Myddle in Shropshire observed: 'It was held a thing unseemly and undecent that a company of young boys, *and of persons that paid no leawans [i.e. church-rates]*, should sitt (in those peiws which had been the passage) above those of the best of the parish.' My italics. Cited in David Hey, *An English Rural community: Myddle under the Tudors and Stuarts* (Leicester, 1974), p. 219. For an example of the spread of rates across one Norfolk community, see Amussen, *Ordered Society*, p. 17.

local needs.[29] This means church rates are helpful guides in comparing the economic standing of rated subscribers to rated non-subscribers, as well as what proportion of adult male parishioners did subscribe, but were not assessed for the ley.

Subsidies of 1640–1641

The 1640 and 1641 subsidies were forms of taxation imposed on localities by central government throughout the period of the Personal Rule. The subsidies were even more elitist than ship money, affecting only the most substantial members of the gentry. According to Graham Kerby, gentlemen were assessed both on lands (*in terris*) and on goods (*in bonis*) and paid on whatever was of greater value. Members of the Cheshire gentry appear to have developed a rota system for spreading out the burden of payment, at least in the 1620s.[30] The custom is described by the Yorkshireman Henry Best in 1641: 'Likewise, some subsidymen they will make only bearers and other men who had only been bearers they will make subsidymen, as they find them in ability or changed in estate.'[31] Such a rota system helps to explain why most of the self-styled gentlemen among the Prayer Book subscribers fail to appear in the 1640–41 subsidies. As the reader will see by looking at Tables A3.1, A3.4, A3.10, A3.13, A3.16, these subsidies throw light on a handful of subscribers and non-subscribers of the most economically substantial part of their localities.[32]

Parish officers and 'leading parishioners'

In the analysis of the strength of support for the lawful liturgy in five Cheshire communities which follows, considerable attention has been paid to the subscribing patterns of parish officers and to a group of men labelled

[29] Cannan, *Local Rates*, pp. 79–80; Alldridge, 'Loyalty', pp. 93–4. Alldridge rightly reminds us as well that although rates were set often by the more substantial members of the parish, they were the same persons on whom the heaviest financial burden fell.

[30] Graham Kerby, 'Inequality in a pre-industrial society: a study of wealth, status, office and taxation in Tudor and Stuart England with particular reference to Cheshire' (University of Cambridge Ph.D., 1983), pp. 117–19, Chapter 6, *passim*.

[31] Henry Best, *Rural Economy in Yorkshire in 1641*, Surtees Society, xxxiii (1857), p. 87.

[32] See below Appendix 3. Tilston, Broxton Hundred: PRO, E179/85/135 (1640); PRO, E179/ 85/131 (1641). Frodsham, Edisbury Hundred: subsidies are not usable. PRO, E179/85/134 (1640) simply lists townships and total contribution; PRO, E179/85/138 (1641) is virtually illegible. Wilmslow, Macclesfield Hundred: PRO, E179/85/136 (1640). Marbury, North-wich Hundred: PRO, E179/85/135 (1640). Middlewich, Northwich Hundred: no subsidy of 1640 or 1641 survives for this hundred. See below, Appendix 3. See also, Spufford, *Contrasting Communities*, pp. 233–4.

'leading parishioners'.[33] Out of the five sets of accounts considered, only Tiltson's lists other officers besides the wardens, the swornmen, overseers of the poor,[34] and of the highways. The office of churchwarden is an ancient one and, as with church rates, it is difficult to generalize either about its origins or its exact practices.[35] According to the Canons of 1604 (no. 89), two wardens were to be selected each year by the incumbent and the parishioners. If they failed to agree, one was appointed by the minister (the 'vicar's warden') and the other by the parishioners (the 'people's warden').[36] In practice, however, the number of wardens was by no means universal: Wilmslow and Middlewich, perhaps because of their size, each had four wardens a year during the period under discussion.

Wardens were selected at parish meetings, sometimes called vestries, the same meeting which set the church rate. Again, theoretically, these 'vestries' were meetings of all the rateable parishioners but during Elizabeth's reign a system of small oligarchies emerged in many places. Originally, these 'vestries' were probably elected by their neighbours at a meeting, but, after the original election, they worked by a system of co-option, not election, and so became self-perpetuating.[37] Thus 'select vestries', as they came to be known, is a precise term and should be used only when one is confident of the local custom. What have been termed here instead 'leading parishioners',[38] are the men who, along with the wardens and the minister, signed the memorandum in the accounts authorizing the ley for that year. These were obviously laypeople who took an active role in local church affairs, and therefore their willingness or refusal to put their hands to the petition

---

[33] See the following tables in Appendix 3: Tilston, Tables A3.2, A3.3; Frodsham, Tables A3.5, A3.6, A3.7, A3.8, A3.9; Wilmslow, Tables A3.11, A3.12; Marbury, Tables A3.14, A3.15; Middlewich, Tables A3.17, A3.18.

[34] An office formally recognized in an act of 1572. Tate, *Parish Chest*, p. 30. D. M. Palliser, 'Introduction: the parish in perspective', in *Parish, Church and People: Studies in lay religion 1350–1750*, ed. Susan Wright (London, 1988), pp. 14–15.

[35] As Eric Carlson has colourfully put it: 'When the first beings who resembled churchwardens emerged from the ecclesiastical primordial slime can never be known with precision.' Eric Carlson, 'The origins, function, and status of the office of churchwarden, with particular reference to the diocese of Ely', in *The World of Rural Dissenters 1520–1700*, ed. Margaret Spufford (Cambridge, 1995), p. 169. Carlson's article provides an excellent overview and assessment of the secondary literature concerning the social backgrounds of churchwardens as well as the function of the office. See also J. S. Craig, 'Co-operation and initiatives: Elizabethan churchwardens and parish accounts of Mildenhall', *Social History* 18:3 (1993); Beat Kumin, *The Shaping of a Community: the rise and reformation of the English parish, c.1400–1560* (Aldershot, 1996) examines the impact of the Reformation on the office of churchwarden.

[36] Purvis, *Dictionary*, pp. 47–8; *ODCC*; Webb, *The Parish*, pp. 21–3, 29–32, 39–40; Carlson, 'Office of churchwarden', pp. 180–91.

[37] Cox, *Churchwardens' Accounts*, pp. 13–14; Burn, *Ecclesiastical Law*, iv, pp. 6–8; Webb, *The Parish*, pp. 43–51, 173–93; Spufford, *Contrasting Communities*, p. 269, n.127.

[38] I am grateful to Dorothy Owen, for making this point to me and suggesting this term.

provides insight into the nature of local lay leadership in the campaign to uphold the lawful liturgy of the established church.

Modern studies have emphasized the social superiority of the men[39] who held parish office in the early modern period. Generally, offices tended to be filled from the groups below the gentry, yeomen and prosperous tradesmen. In some places, office holding was restricted to a small group of individuals – a sort of 'parochial freemasonry' – many of whom would hold office several times over a period of years.[40] Gradations appear as well between types of office and social standing: the more prestigious office of warden was held by yeomen and the less prestigious offices of overseer, constable and sidesman, exercised by husbandmen and craftsmen. Age too could be a factor; the minor offices being held by younger men, while churchwardenships were held by their elders, if not always their betters.[41]

This spread of social grades over the variety of local offices has led some historians to conclude that, rather than stratifying a community, such individuals could be bridges across social groups in a parish, militating against social division and friction. As Susan Amussen has put it 'the "Governors" were not too distant – or different – from those they governed'.[42] Gaining office could also be a *means* of achieving greater social standing, especially for newcomers to a locality, as well as a *sign* of existing social standing. In the parish, public service could be a way 'to rise'.[43]

Important aspects of the duties of churchwardens have already been discussed, namely, both the repair of the fabric of the church and the provision of assorted ornaments needed to conduct lawful worship. Wardens had clear obligations under the law, not only for the upkeep of the church, but also for the exercise of ecclesiastical discipline, usually in co-operation with the minister, but at times in spite of him, or even against him. In Chapter 2, specific examples were given of their role as instruments

---

[39] There is occasional evidence of women holding parish office, including as churchwardens, in our period, but none appear in the Cheshire parishes under discussion here. D. M. Palliser, 'Introduction: the parish in perspective', p. 23, in *The Age of Elizabeth: England under the later Tudors 1547–1603* (London, 1983), p. 64.

[40] Keith Wrightson and David Levine, *Poverty and Piety in an English Village: Terling 1525–1700* (New York, 1979), pp. 104–5, 106; Alldridge, 'Loyalty', pp. 106–7; Susan Amussen, 'Governors and governed: class and gender relations in English villages, 1590–1725' (Brown University Ph.D., 1983), pp. 66–9; Amussen, *Ordered Society*, pp. 27, 32, 135. I am grateful to Susan Amussen for her comments on this point.

[41] Wrightson and Levine, *Poverty and Piety*, pp. 104–5; Alldridge, 'Loyalty', pp. 107–8; Carlson, 'Office of Churchwarden', pp. 193–200; Craig, 'Co-operation', pp. 362–6.

[42] Amussen, *Ordered Society*, p. 135; see also Alldridge, 'Loyalty', p. 112.

[43] Alldridge is particularly interesting on this point. Alldridge, 'Loyalty', p. 108.

of church discipline in Cheshire and the diocese of Lincoln.[44] J. J. Scarisbrick has argued that the Reformation, with its destruction of guilds and lay fraternities, brought about a major shift of power out of the hands of lay Christians and into the hands of the clergy; although he admits that select wealthy laymen gained influence in the church through acquisition of ecclesiastical lands. Scarisbrick maintains that the majority of layfolk, who exercised influence through guilds and fraternities, lost considerable power by their destruction.[45] On the other hand, others have stressed the emerging strength of churchwardens and other minor parish officials after the Reformation as agents of 'social control' or the 'Reformation of Manners', especially, or perhaps only, because they were of a 'godly' persuasion.[46] But it has also been argued, by providing examples of similar behaviour by village 'elites' in the middle ages and the Counter-Reformation, that 'the Reformation' was not the watershed often imagined in terms of lay imposition of moral and religious standards by a 'godly' minority on their neighbours.[47] Certainly, the late fifteenth-century churchwardens of Havering, Essex, were made of stern stuff as they appointed their own priest without any regard to the patron of the living, New College.[48] Although arguments for continuity are strong, there is little doubt that in the early modern period, the parish developed new roles in the local government of both church and state, with a corresponding increase in the duties and obligations of its lay officers.[49] We should remember as well that churchwardens were, in a very real sense, as much a representative of the bishop's authority as the incumbent. The laity 'lost' some power *vis-à-vis* the clergy

[44] Until the creation of parochial church councils (PCCs) in 1921, wardens were the 'sole official representatives of the laity in each parish'. *ODCC*. For a brief summary of the duties of churchwardens, see Webb, *The Parish*, pp. 20–6.

[45] J. J. Scarisbrick, *The Reformation and the English People* (Oxford, 1984), pp. 39, 162–70; see above, Chapter 2, *passim*.

[46] E.g., Keith Wrightson, *English Society 1580–1680* (London, 1982), pp. 32, 180–2, 225–7; 'Two concepts of order: justices, constables and jurymen in seventeenth century England', in *An Ungovernable People: the English and their law in the seventeenth and eighteenth centuries*, ed. John Brewer and John Styles (London, 1980), pp. 21–46 *passim*; Wrightson and Levine, *Poverty and Piety*, pp. 115–16, 134–41; Amussen, *Ordered Society*, pp. 25, 175–6.

[47] Margaret Spufford, 'Puritanism and social control?', *Order and Disorder in Early Modern England*, ed. Anthony Fletcher and John Stevenson (Cambridge, 1985), pp. 41–57 *passim*. Cf. Amussen, *Ordered Society*, p. 23, n. 36. Cf. also Keith Wrightson's thoughtful response in 'Postscript: Terling revisited' in Wrightson and Levine, *Poverty and Piety* (1995 edn), pp. 197–211.

[48] Marjorie McIntosh, *Autonomy and Community: the Royal Manor of Havering 1200–1500* (Cambridge, 1986), pp. 235–8; see also Clive Burgess, '"A fond thing vainly invented": an essay on purgatory and pious motive in late medieval England', in *Parish, Church and People: local studies in lay religion 1350–1750*, ed. Susan Wright (London, 1988), pp. 76–8.

[49] Palliser, 'Introduction: the parish in perspective', p. 14; Anthony Fletcher, *Reform in the Provinces: the government of Stuart England* (New Haven, 1986), pp. 55, 127; Alldridge, 'Loyalty', pp. 104–5.

by the destruction of religious guilds and fraternities. Yet they 'gained' clout by the new powers and responsibilities developing for parish officers from Elizabeth's reign onwards. We are overattached, perhaps, to a 'conflict model' of clergy/lay relations in our period as well as the notion that the Reformation is entirely about discontinuity rather than continuity in the life of the church.

The wardens, minor officers, and leading parishioners of the five Cheshire communities under discussion here both challenge and confirm these views. Where the social status of the officers can be determined, it must be said that a majority of them were assessed for 2s or more around the time of the Prayer Book petition.[50] Such men occupied, by and large, the prestigious two central ranks of pews (of six) in Frodsham parish church.[51] That said, exceptions abound. In all five localities, there were parish officers and lay leaders in the years around 1641 who were either assessed for 1s or less in the ley or fell below the rate threshold, and not assessed at all. One swornman of Tilston actually received poor relief in 1641–42, calling into question the value of such generalizations.[52] Despite obvious unease with slippage in society's pyramid, the Elizabethan clergyman William Harrison noted that day labourers, poor husbandmen, copyholders, and 'artificers' (skilled workmen), due to the default of yeoman were 'in villages . . . commonly made churchwardens, sidesmen [and] aleconners'.[53]

Also of interest are questions surrounding definitions of 'social control' and 'godliness' in the parish context. It has already been argued by the use of church court evidence, that 'godliness', or a committed protestant stance, was not limited at the grass-roots to the 'hotter sort of protestant'. Churchwardens and ordinary parishioners, women as well as men, could and did use the church courts to enforce conformity to the lawful worship of the Church of England.[54] Nevertheless, the question must be put whether the estimated 27 per cent of adult males who subscribed for the Common Prayer in Tilston and Frodsham, or the 69 per cent in Wilmslow, can be dismissed as victims of campaigns of coercion by their social betters.[55] The individual circumstances of each locality will be discussed in detail below, including the role of the clergy and gentry, but two points are worth raising now. Although the Prayer Book petition in parishes like

---

[50] See below: Appendix 3, Tilston, Table A3.3, Frodsham, Table A3.9, Wilmslow, Table A3.12, Marbury, Table A3.15, Middlewich, Table A3.18.

[51] See below, Appendix 3, Frodsham, Table A3.5.

[52] See below, Appendix 3, Tilston, Table A3.3.

[53] Aleconners were inspectors of the ale. William Harrison, *The Description of England*, ed. George Edelen (New York, 1968, repr. 1994), p. 118; Carlson, 'Office of churchwarden', pp. 193–200; Craig, 'Co-operation', pp. 362–6.

[54] See above, Chapter 2, *passim*.   [55] See above, Table 5.1, p. 188.

Middlewich (41 per cent), Tilston (27 per cent), and Wilmslow (69 per cent) had strong support from its officers, the lay leadership did not present a solid front in Frodsham (27 per cent) and Marbury (29 per cent).[56] Without the survival of supporting documentation such as rentals, which would allow us to identify tenants and landlords, our conclusions must be speculative. Due caution expressed, we may still assert that a window onto the free expression of religious commitment is provided by comparing the proportion of subscribers and non-subscribers. It must be said though, that the number of subscribers *for* the Prayer Book is firmer evidence than the number who did not subscribe, as it is impossible to distinguish among non-subscribers between those who favoured the reform or abolition of the lawful liturgy and the religiously indifferent.

Pews

An eighteenth-century pew list including the allocation of seats in 1637 is extant for Frodsham parish church and it has been possible to match some subscribers to the Prayer Book petition to particular seats among the six ranks of pews. The basis on which seats were allotted in church, as with church rates and structures of parish meetings, appears to have been anything but systematic in the national church. Modern Christians are now largely unsympathetic to the custom of assigned pews, but the practice may have its origins in the admirable desire to provide seating for the elderly and infirm during Mass. After the Reformation, however, the system appears to have become more formalized and directly associated with reflecting the social hierarchy of the parish; although it is maintained that the practice of assigning pews pre-dates the Reformation.[57] But there appears to have been no consistent custom regarding pews over the country as a whole. The practice of paying pew rents, which in some parishes was a crucial source of income for parochial expenses, was absent in many others.[58]

The grounds on which people were placed in certain pews is diverse. Technically the ordinary had power over allotment, yet the evidence suggests that the often thankless task of allocation belonged to the churchwardens, or at times, to a parish meeting. In Richard Gough's *Myddle* in Shropshire, for example, the right to occupy a certain seat was

---

[56] See below: Appendix 3, Tilston, Table A3.2, Frodsham, Table A3.8, Wilmslow, Table A3.11, Marbury, Table A3.14, Middlewich, Table A3.17.

[57] Cox, *Churchwardens' accounts*, pp. 186–7.

[58] Ibid., pp. 67–9, 188; Christopher Hill, *Economic Problems of the Church: from Archbishop Whitgift to the Long Parliament* (Oxford, 1956), pp. 169, 175–6; Amussen, *Ordered Society*, p. 142.

attached to occupation of a particular house or property. As the right to occupy certain seats descended in families with the possession of a particular farm or house, so a change in a property's occupier meant, in theory, a change in the occupier of the pew. Although it would be mistaken to assume that economic distinctions were always paramount, Myddle with its gentry at the front, husbandmen behind, and cottagers relegated to the south-west corner, no doubt reflects wide-spread practice. In urban areas too, the seats closest to the altar were considered the most prestigious.[59] It is clear, however, that other factors could influence a person's place in church, especially in urban parishes. Concepts of 'honour' played a part, such as social rank, office holding, rateable value, and even age. The practice of separating the sexes was perhaps more the exception than the rule, as it meant ownership of two pews rather than one and therefore could only be indulged in by the most substantial members of the parish, if at all.[60]

The custom of attaching the right to sit in a pew to a particular property presupposed more social stability than was characteristic of early Stuart England. Too rigid adherence to the custom was seen as undermining the primary function of assigned seating: that is, that the centre of a parish, its church, should reflect the social order and hierarchy of its community. Villagers, as well as townspeople, were therefore reluctant to fix seating too rigidly. As the nuanced structures of parish life altered, so did the seating in church.[61] What *is* most important to note for our purposes is that, although the exact basis on which pews were assigned is neither clear nor consistent, contemporaries perceived it as a mirror of their community. Furthermore, not only was a person's place in church significant, the assignment of seats was an operation carried out by members of the community directly concerned. Anyone who has consulted material from the ecclesiastical

---

[59] Hey, *Myddle*, pp. 2, 18, 165, 219; G. W. O. Addleshaw and F. Etchells, *The Architectural Setting of Anglican Worship* (London, 1948), pp. 94–5; Burn, *Ecclesiastical Law*, i, pp. 329, 331; Alldridge, 'Loyalty', p. 94.

[60] I first heard these ideas put forward by Nick Alldridge in a paper given at the workshop 'The parish, the church and the common man 1450–1750' hosted by the Department of Local History, University of Leicester on 17 May 1986. I am grateful to him for discussing pew ownership with me at that time. His paper has since appeared as already cited, Alldridge, 'Loyalty', pp. 94–7. See Plate 4.2 for the plan of Aston Chapel where only Sir Thomas Aston's household was separated on the basis of gender.

[61] Amussen, *Ordered Society*, pp. 142–3. Amussen argues that pew conflicts were 'far less likely in arable areas, where parish elites tended to be more sharply differentiated'. In pastoral villages and towns, the 'social distance' between minor gentry and yeomen was far less. Therefore she concludes that stability itself could bring about conflict over seats: 'the conflict over control of seats was most likely to occur in a community with a broad elite and relatively stable social structure. If the community was not changing significantly, the best way to enhance status was to control a seat in the church, preferably as close to the chancel as possible', see pp. 141–2.

courts in our period is aware both of the frequency of pew disputes and, at times, the breathtaking ferocity of the participants.[62] Exchanges of verbal abuse and physical blows – sometimes during divine service – were not unknown between antagonists. The verbal and physical violence reflects the significance attached to seating by contemporaries themselves: well ordered seating in church was seen to reflect the social harmony of the parish as a whole. Bishop Goodman boasted that his Berkshire parish was so full of concord and goodwill that there was no need to assign pews, the parishioners, 'being free from pride and bred up in humility they did place themselves, still preferring the eldest or those who paid the greatest rent and rates in the parish'.[63] The creation by wardens of pew plans, such as the one for Frodsham church, which will be discussed below, shows the seriousness of the business. It was not a matter to be left to chance.[64] Susan Amussen has summed up the issue well: 'conflicts over church seats affirmed the social order; while details were called into question, the order itself was not'.[65]

TILSTON

Tilston: 'character' of the parish

The parish of Tilston comprised five townships in the hundred of Broxton, covering over 3,500 acres in the south-western part of the county. In the 1664 hearth tax, the parish contained 131 households. Roughly 27 per cent of the adult male population, including the rector and curate, subscribed to the Prayer Book petition in 1641. Sixty-two men signed for episcopacy in February 1641 and one hundred signed for the lawful liturgy later in the year. Of the sixty-two subscribing to the upholding of the three-fold ministry, 61 per cent (38) also subscribed to the maintenance of the Common Prayer Book.[66]

Tilston's churchwardens' accounts are particularly illuminating about the economic background of the subscribing parishioners. Of the seventy-five male heads of households assessed in the parish's ley and Easter roll of

---

[62] For examples of local disputes over pews see: Susan Amussen, 'Gender, family and the social order', in *Order and disorder*, ed. Fletcher and Stevenson pp. 212–14 and *Ordered Society*, pp. 139–42 (for Norfolk); Hey, *Myddle*, pp. 219–20 (for Shropshire); Palliser, *Age of Elizabeth*, pp. 81, 84 (for Oxford and Yorkshire); Alldridge, 'Loyalty', pp. 113–14 (for the city of Chester).

[63] Cited in Hill, *Economic Problems*, p. 177.

[64] Alldridge, 'Loyalty', p. 94.   [65] Amussen, 'Gender', p. 214.

[66] Tilston, Horton Green, Grafton, Carden, Stretton. Sylvester and Nulty, *Historical Atlas of Cheshire*, p. 38; *Parliamentary Gazetteer* (1845). See below, Appendix 3, Tilston, Table A3.1. For how these figures were obtained, see above, pp. 187–8.

1641, 65 per cent (49) subscribed to the Prayer Book petition.[67] Twenty-one male parishioners who were economically significant enough to be assessed for the ley and roll did not subscribe to either petition; 29 per cent (6) of those twenty-one were assessed for over 1s. Only 24 per cent (12) of the forty-nine parishioners who both signed for the Prayer Book and were assessed for the ley and roll, were assessed for over 1s (see Appendix 3, Tilston, Table A3.1, Figures, A3.1, A3.2).[68]

Unfortunately, lists of those receiving poor relief in the early 1640s are extant for only two of the five communities under examination, Tilston and Wilmslow. Of the twenty-two Tilston men who received alms in 1641, 68 per cent (15) subscribed to the Common Prayer petition. Yet 27 per cent (6) did not subscribe at all and one poor man subscribed only for episcopacy earlier in the year. The high percentage of men in Tilston who both received poor relief and subscribed for the Prayer Book might suggest a campaign of coercion by their 'betters' on the most vulnerable members of any community, the poor. If this were the case, however, a substantial minority was able to resist it. The smallness of the group alone should warn against speedy conclusions. The implications of the poor relief material will be discussed more fully in the conclusion to this chapter.[69]

The expenses listed in the churchwardens' accounts of Tilston for the 1620s and 1630s reflect the outgoings of a conforming parish. Regular annual expenditures are recorded for washing the 'church clothes' – the holy table linen and the surplice (usually around 6d). New copies of the required books were purchased: a Bible was bought in London for 38s (1620), the Homilies and Bishop Jewel's *Apology* for 29s 2d (1626) and a Communion book for nine 9s (1629?). The service book appears to have been used, as 6d was spent on mending it in 1631. More controversially in 1635, the Communion table was railed (22s 6d) and in 1639 a new table was purchased (19s).[70] The parishioners at Tilston, however, seem also to have prized their pulpit, reflecting the emphasis in the Prayer Book on 'Word *and* Sacrament'. In 1626, 6d was spent on a new pulpit cloth and in 1631, 13d was spent in making a seat for the pulpit. The same entry concerning the railing of the holy table (1635) records: 'for Rayling in the Communion table & mending the same, for a doore and Cover for the pulpit & for worke about the same. 22s 6d'.[71] It has already been mentioned that an expensive Bible was purchased in 1620, and in 1631

---

[67] Many of those who subscribed for the Prayer Book also subscribed for episcopacy earlier in the year. Only four men signed only the petition for episcopacy.

[68] Because the document is torn in places, the amount assessed is unknown for two of the male parishioners. In a number of cases it is impossible to tell the *exact* amount, only that the sum is under 1s, because of the damaged condition of the manuscript.

[69] See below, pp. 224–7.   [70] CRO, P/18/3608, pp. 18, 21, 34, 38, 51, 77.

[71] CRO, P18/3608, pp. 22, 51.

tables with the Lord's Prayer and Creed, and the Ten Commandments were made and set up for 2s 6d and 4s respectively. Furthermore, in the same year, they set up the King's arms '& writing in two corners over the Rood loft 2 sentences of scripture' which cost 10s.[72] We do not know, unfortunately, which texts were chosen. No rivalry appears to have been felt at Tilston between the lawful liturgy of the church and the preaching ministry. This lack of perceived conflict is nicely illustrated by this entry from 1631: 'Item paid for all the beginning of the booke of Common praier to the end of the Litanie, paid to Mr Catherall for putting the same for the Clarkes use . . . xiid. Item. paid for an houre glasse xd.'[73] Essex Clarke, the rector, appears either to have been resident, or if not, he took pains that the sacramental life of the church was not neglected. In the 1620s and 1630s, Holy Communion appears to have been celebrated from three to seven times a year.[74] In 1635, his parishioners bought him an academic hood, that he might perform his duties in a more seemly manner.[75] The overall impression from the Tilston accounts is of a parish which conformed with some enthusiasm and beyond the bare letter of the law.

Tilston: the gentry

Eight of the one hundred petitioners for the Prayer Book styled themselves as 'gentlemen' when they subscribed. In the Tilston subsidy returns for 1641, nine men were assessed: six subscribed, but three members of this economically significant group did not subscribe to either petition.[76] Among subscribing gentry, there was a wide range of prosperity. Edward Wright, John Catherall, and John Ley or Lea, all self-styled gentlemen, were assessed at 40s (*in terris*), 20s (*in terris*), and £3 (*in bonis*) respectively. Roger Becket, John Dod, and John Evanson, all Common Prayer subscribers but modestly unstyled as 'gentlemen', were all assessed at £3 in goods. Of the non-subscribers, John Leech[77] and Francis Fitton were assessed at 40s *in terris*, John Havson (or Homson?) at £3 *in bonis*. Most of the leading landowning families in the locality, as identified by the two chief nineteenth-century antiquarians of Cheshire, gave their support to the Prayer Book petition.[78]

---

[72] CRO, P18/3608, pp. 41–2.
[73] CRO, P18/3608, p. 41. I discuss this point about the *lack* of conflict between liturgical worship and the preaching ministry more generally elsewhere. For example, see above, pp. 64–8, 141–2.
[74] CRO, P18/3608, *passim.*   [75] CRO, P18/3608, p. 51.
[76] PRO, E179/85/135; PRO, E179/85/131.
[77] Could this be the same John Leech who was assessed for the rate at less than a shilling?
[78] The major landowning families in the parish identified by Ormerod and Lysons are listed as: Fitton, Dod, Leche (Carden); Stanley of Alderley (Grafton); Catheral (Horton); Wright

Tilston: the clergy

Both petitions for the Church of England received the support of local clergy. The rector Essex Clarke signed, as did an elusive 'cleric' Richard Gregory, who was presumably Clarke's curate, but nothing more can be said of him.[79] Considerably more can be said of the rector, however, as is often the case. Clarke was obviously a local cleric of consequence, although the sources are confused as to the details of his career. The *Alumni Oxonienses* claims he graduated from Saint Edmund's Hall in 1630, became a canon of Chester in 1634, and rector of Pulford in 1648, but does not make any reference to Tilston. Ormerod reports that he was presented to the living of Tilston in 1631 by the crown, acting during the minority of the patron, Lord Brereton. However, Clarke is recorded as rector of Tilston as early as 1624 in a clerical subsidy of that year. Along with Thomas Bridge, the rector of Malpas Superior, he was responsible for the collection of the 1635 ship money assessment of the Cheshire clergy in Malpas deanery, the year Sir Thomas Aston was ship money sheriff. In the 1639 clerical contributions for the Scottish war he appears as a prebend of Chester Cathedral as well as rector of Tilston.[80]

Clarke was obviously in tune with the conformist sympathies of many of his parishioners, but he was not one of Walker's 'sufferers'. According to the churchwardens' accounts, he was still the incumbent there at least until 1650.[81] Ormerod relates that Clarke continued in his living until his death in early 1654, at which point his successor George Bonniman was 'intruded' by the Lord Protector because of the delinquencies of the patrons, Lord Brereton and Lord Cholmondeley. However, even in the 1650s, there are grounds for assuming that the traditionalist preferences of the parishioners asserted themselves. Bonniman had received episcopal ordination to the diaconate and priesthood in 1648 by the bishop of Ardfert. He is listed by Calamy as a non-conformist at the Restoration, but

---

of Bickley (Stretton). Most of the major landowning families, therefore, as identified by the two nineteenth-century sources, subscribed for the Prayer Book. The Fitton and Stanley families were noteworthy exceptions. Due to a certain vagueness by both authors about dates, it is not always clear whether all these families held manors in 1641. G. Ormerod, *History of Cheshire*, rev. G. Helsby (3 vols., London, 1882), ii, pp. 700, 704–5, 708–9, 710; Daniel Lysons and Samuel Lysons, *Magna Britannia: Cheshire* (2 vols. London, 1810), ii, pp. 805–6.

[79] Tilston possessed a curate called Smyth in 1635. 'Loans, contributions, subsidies, and ship money, paid by the clergy of the diocese of Chester in the years 1620, 1622, 1624, 1634, 1635, 1636, and 1639', *Miscellanies relating to Lancashire and Cheshire*, ed. G. T. O. Bridgeman, *LCRS*, xii (1885), p. 101.

[80] *AO*; Ormerod, *Cheshire*, ii, p. 697; 'Loans 1620–1639', pp. 79, 99, 119, 121. Judging from Clarke's contributions on these various occasions, Tilston appears to have had an average value among Cheshire livings.

[81] CRO, P18/3608, p. 91.

according to Alan Thacker, he definitely did conform, subscribing in 1662. He continued exercising his ministry at Tilston until his death in 1668.[82] Given the fact that he sought episcopal ordination after the abolition of the Church of England in 1645 and continued shepherding the sheep at Tilston on both sides of the Restoration divide, Thacker is certainly right to set Calamy aside. Clarke's survival in his living until his death in 1654, and the succession of a man like Bonniman, also suggests that the 'sheep' at Tilston, like their pre-Reformation counterparts at Havering in Essex, knew both how to protect, and select, their 'shepherd'.[83]

Tilston: the parish officers

The evidence suggests that the local leadership for upholding the church was predominantly lay and vested in the parish officers. These were the men who protected Clarke and no doubt influenced the choice of Bonniman. (For what follows, see Appendix 3, Tilston, Table A3.2). Of the eight men who held the offices of churchwarden, swornmen, overseers of the poor, and overseers of the highways from Eastertide 1640 to Eastertide 1641 only one was a non-subscriber. Furthermore, of the eight 'leading parishioners' who, with Essex Clarke, signed the memorandum recording the election of officers in April 1641, six were subscribers. Of the eight parishioners fulfilling a year's term of office from Easter 1641, six signed both petitions, including both churchwardens and both overseers of the highways. Henry Heskye, a swornman, and Thomas (or Joshua?) Taylor, an overseer of the poor, did not sign. It is striking that one of the officers responsible for poor relief did not subscribe, strengthening the view that the poor of Tilston were free to follow their consciences.[84] The evidence from Tilston also throws strong doubt on whether such officers were always from 'the better sort'. (For what follows, see Appendix 3, Tilston, Table A3.3.) Certainly some of Tilston's officers in 1640–42 fit this description. However, neither Thomas Ball who signed the 1641 memorandum, nor John Conway, an overseer of the highways in 1641 were assessed for the rate, though they supported the Book of Common Prayer. One Randle Tanna who was an overseer of the highways in 1640 and of the poor in 1641 was assessed for only 6d. John Hanover and Bartholomew Evanson, swornmen in 1640 and 1641 respectively, paid less than 1s each

---

[82] Ormerod, *Cheshire*, ii, p. 697. The information on Bonniman comes chiefly from a list of Cheshire clergy at the Restoration compiled by Alan Thacker of the Victoria County History. I am very grateful to him for lending me his list.

[83] McIntosh, *Autonomy*, pp. 235–8. John Morrill, 'The Church of England, 1642–9', in *Reactions to the English Civil War 1642–1649*, ed. John Morrill (London, 1982), pp. 103, 108–12.

[84] CRO, P18/3608, pp. 75, 81.

for the ley and roll. Of the subscribers who held office, perhaps the most interesting in this regard were Thomas Christow, a churchwarden in 1640 and a 'leading parishioner' in 1641 who paid only 3d in the ley and roll, and William Povey, churchwarden in 1641 who failed to qualify for assessment. Of the non-subscribing officers, Henry Heskye was not only a swornman in 1641, but he received 1s in poor relief that same year. Thomas or Joshua Taylor, an overseer of the highways in 1640, paid less than 1s. We must not forget either that six of the males receiving poor relief – in other words, the very people most vulnerable to any pressure that may or may not have come from the officers – did not subscribe to either petition for the established church. As I have shown, not even all those on poor relief, never mind the middling sort, signed. Social and economic pressure alone is not sufficient explanation to account for the actions of individuals.

FRODSHAM

Frodsham: the 'character' of the parish

The parish of Frodsham on the edge of the Mersey in the hundred of Eddisbury consisted of 11 townships in the seventeenth century, covering just over 14,000 acres. In 1664 it contained 442 households according to the hearth tax. Based on rough population estimates from the hearth tax of 1664, 27 per cent of the adult males of the parish subscribed to the petition to uphold the Prayer Book. This included the signatures of the vicar, curate, and parish clerk.[85] Early in 1641, 165 individuals put their hands to the bishops petition,[86] while later in the year 184 men signed for the Prayer Book. (For what follows, see Appendix 3, Frodsham Table A3.4, Figures A3.3, A3.4.) The proportion of parishioners who signed both petitions, however, is much lower than that for Tilston: only 41 per cent (76) of those who signed for the bishops also signed for the lawful liturgy.

Frodsham's churchwardens' accounts are not as helpful for our purposes as those for Tilston. Although the records of a rate for 1641 survive, they show all the signs of lazy or inept record keeping, containing a great many entries which are simply the lump sums of the collector, or collections, for

---

[85] The townships were: Frodsham, Alvanley, Bradley, Helsby, Kingsley, Manley, Netherton, Newton, Norton, Overton, and Woodhouses. (Bradley, Netherton, Overton, and Woodhouses are considered by some as hamlets within the Lordship of Frodsham.) Lysons and Lysons, *Cheshire*, ii, p. 658; *Parliamentary Gazetteer* (1848). See below, Appendix 3, Frodsham, Table A3.4. See above, pp. 187–8 for description of how the hearth tax is used to make population estimates.

[86] Among the names of Frodsham's inhabitants who subscribed to the pro-episcopacy petition, there was one woman: Margery Hinson, widow.

particular townships. Neither is there any list of the deserving poor of the parish. As a result of the slipshod bookkeeping of Frodsham's officers, only 18 per cent (34) of the 184 individuals who put their hands to the Prayer Book petition appear as individually assessed in the rate. That contrasts poorly with the 49 assessed subscribers out of 100 for Tilston (see Appendix 3, Tilston, Table A3.1). It would be unwise, therefore, to place the same weight of interpretation on the Frodsham ley as on the Tilston ley. Despite all these shortcomings, however, no less than 95 individually assessed males can be identified.[87] Of those 95 assessed, 36 per cent (34) subscribed to the Prayer Book petition. Further only 6 per cent (6) of those 95 subscribed *only* to the petition supporting episcopacy. The actual amounts for which individuals were assessed in the Frodsham rate break down in a similar way to those for Tilston (See Appendix 3, Tilston, Table A3.1, Figures A3.1, A3.2 and Frodsham, Table A3.4, Figures A3.3, A3.4). Fifteen – that is nearly half – of Frodsham's inhabitants who both subscribed and were individually assessed, were assessed for 1s or less.

On a mundane, but perhaps more telling level, the accounts contain expenditures which demonstrate not only the possession of required objects, but, more importantly, evidence of their use for lawful worship. For example, regular outlays were made in the early seventeenth century for washing the surplice and 'church clothes'. Quite often this was done by the clerk's wife for 6d. In 1638, a new surplice was made: the materials cost £2 2s 1d, including the penny spent on a yard of lace, and 4s on labour. The parish possessed a Communion book and new ones were purchased in 1624 (2s 1d) and 1629 (9s). These service books received enough wear and tear to require 1s 6d to be spent in 1638 for rebinding. Neither was the Bible neglected. In 1610 it was rebound (including a fee for fetching it) for 8s, and in 1626 a new one was bought, but no sum given. Frodsham appears to have had an organ as well, as 7s 4d went to an organ maker in 1613. The 1630s saw considerable refurbishment of the church, and a good deal of money was spent. As in Tilston, sentences of scripture were put up on the church walls. One John Fromwell was paid £1 5s for painting on sentences and an additional 17s for decorating them with borders in 1633. Intriguingly, a Robert Rabone was paid 1s 'for reading to him portions of Scripture'. The Frodsham accounts provide local examples of the impact of national policy concerning the vexed issue of the holy table. In 1634, it was noted that a man came from Chester to 'view the table' and to see about having rails made for it. Later, in 1639, an additional 1s 6d was spent on

---

[87] CRO, P8/13/2, fols. 73–75v. Other difficulties with the ley are of a more technical nature and are described in the notes to Frodsham Table A3.4 in Appendix 3.

the altar, but it is unclear just what work this entailed. Other sums were also spent on moving the pulpit, reading desk, and the wardens' seats in 1635. Significantly, however, at the first available opportunity, 6d was paid to one John Boates for taking down the rails. From 1609 to 1627, Holy Communion was celebrated between three and five times a year. In the period following (1628 to 1641), however, there was a dramatic leap to near monthly Communions. The vicar Rowland Heywood, had already been at Frodsham from at least 1624, so the marked increase does not reflect a change of incumbent.[88]

The general impression of stability and harmony provided by the churchwardens' accounts may be more apparent than real. Other signs indicate that it may have been a community much more divided over religion than Tilston. For what it is worth, Frodsham was one of four areas described in Archbishop Neale's 1633 visitation as 'full of puritans and disorderly people'.[89] Exercises were held there before 1640 but conclusions should not be hastily drawn, as the record of their costs are carefully recorded by the churchwardens along with rebinding the Book of Common Prayer and washing the surplice.[90] In other words, the exercises had the official support of the Prayer Book subscribing vicar Rowland Heywood and members of the lay leadership. This same priest was later driven from his living with such bitterness that years later when he could return to his former cure, he chose to go elsewhere.[91] However, this is not to accept Archbishop Neale's appellation of 'puritan parish' for Frodsham.[92] It may even be suggested that many of those who subscribed for the Prayer Book approved of the removal of the altar rails. Rather, given the fact that roughly 27 per cent of adult males put their hands to a petition in support of the Book of Common Prayer, it was a community with deep divisions – not between the 'godly and ungodly' – but *within* the religiously committed population.

---

[88] This paragraph is based on CRO, P8/13/1; CRO, P8/13/2.

[89] The other areas listed were Chester, Nantwich and Bunbury. *VCH Chester*, iii, p. 33.

[90] R. C. Richardson, *Puritanism in North-west England: a regional study of the diocese of Chester to 1642* (Manchester, 1972), p. 68; CRO, P8/13/1; CRO, P8/13/2. Exercises, and even the rather dramatically named 'prophesyings', need not be a sign of religious radicalism but could be activities contained within the mainstream of the Church of England. Patrick Collinson, *The Religion of Protestants: the church in English society 1559–1625* (Oxford, 1982), pp. 129–31; 'Lectures by combination: structures and characteristics of church life in 17th-century England' (first published in 1975) in Patrick Collinson, *Godly People: essays on English protestantism and puritanism* (London, 1982), pp. 473–4.

[91] See below, pp. 208–9.

[92] In fact, an inventory of church goods made in 1637, lists all the various paraphernalia needed for lawful worship. The list includes two Communion books, two surplices (a new one and an old one) and, possibly unusually, a cope. CRO, P8/13/2.

Frodsham: pew list

The defects of the Frodsham ley are somewhat ameliorated by the survival of eighteenth-century lists of pew owners which include the 1637 owners alongside the owners in 1747. Presumably these lists were made by eighteenth-century churchwardens with antiquarian interests, copying from an older list which no longer survives.[93] I have constructed a pew plan for Frodsham, based on these pew lists (see Appendix 3, Frodsham, Table A3.5). Frodsham church contained three aisles with six ranks of pews.[94] Although it must be remembered that pew plans are necessarily biased economically and socially upwards (sub-tenants, since they do not own the property that goes with a particular seat, do not appear as owners), there appears to be a fairly even spread of subscribers over the range of pews.[95] Taken overall, 34 per cent of male pew owners subscribed to the Prayer Book petition. This rough figure is arrived at by pairing the pews with less prestige value, the north side pair (36 per cent) and the south side pair (33 per cent). In the case of the pair of middle rank pews, the highest places of honour, there is an overall average of 35 per cent (see Appendix 3, Frodsham, Table A3.6).[96] It appears that both those who signed for the Prayer Book and those who did not, were fairly well spread throughout the seating in the parish church. Even making allowances for the defects and gaps in the manuscript due to damage, and the space of four years between the pew list and the petition, the consistency is striking.

Frodsham: the gentry

It is not possible to use the subsidy return of 1640 for Frodsham as we did with Tilston. Two returns for Eddisbury Hundred survive, but one simply lists townships and total contributions and the other is illegible.[97] This means there is little that can be said about the major landowners with any degree of certainty. (For what follows, see Appendix 3, Frodsham, Tables A3.5, A3.6, A3.7.)

John, Viscount Savage, appears from the pew list of 1637 to have been the largest local landowner (he owned four pews). Savage did not subscribe

---

[93] There are two copies of the pew list: CRO, P8/4/3 and CRO, P8/4/2. I have used CRO, P8/4/3. 'A seat Role made for the Parish Church of Frodsham by John Brownent and Thomas Whitley, Church-wardens, Sep: 15, 1747'. CRO, P8/4/2.

[94] See Raymond Richards, *Old Cheshire Churches* (London, 1947; rev. edn, Manchester, 1973), illus. 146–50. Note: the pews have been replaced by chairs.

[95] For a general discussion of pew plans, see above, pp. 197–9.

[96] There is a discrepancy between the north middle rank (21 per cent) and the south middle rank (48 per cent).

[97] PRO, E179/85/134; PRO, E179/85/138.

to either petition, but his steward (or agent), Richard Janion (both senior and junior) did.[98] One Edward Savage appears both on the pew plan (SM20) and the Common Prayer petition; and a John Savage signed for episcopacy. The combination of an unusable 1640 subsidy return and the antiquarian Lysons' vagueness about the dates of the landowners he describes, makes it very difficult to say much more about the important families who could have exercised their 'social control' over the humbler sort.[99] Sir Gilbert Gerrard was obviously an important local figure. He was assessed for 10s in the rate, he owned two pews (one in the prestigious middle ranks), and he signed the 1640 memorandum as a leading parishioner. But he did not sign either petition for the church.[100] Wanklyn identifies Gerrard as a committed parliamentarian after the outbreak of the war. The Trafford family is also mentioned by Lysons as a major landowner in the parish. But at what date they become part owners of Helsby Manor is not given. However, a John (FSS8) and Hugh (FSS8, NS20) Trafford both owned pews in 1637 but did not subscribe in 1641. An ancient family, according to Lysons, were the Halls of Norley township, John (NS17), Peter (NM16), Randle (FSS9), Thomas (NM8, FNS25), and William (NM16) Hall were all pew owners but only Thomas subscribed to the Prayer Book petition. The Rutters were important landowners in Kingsley township. Mr Hugh Rutter owned a prestigious pew in the south middle rank. He signed both petitions, styling himself 'gent'. Rutter paid a large assessment of 3s 4d and signed the 1640 Memorandum. Wanklyn identifies him as a committed Royalist in the civil war. He was a subscriber of obvious local importance and contrasts well with Sir Gilbert Gerrard – a *non*-subscribing gentleman, also of obvious local importance.[101]

Frodsham: the clergy

The vicar and curate, as well as the parish clerk, subscribed to both pro-church petitions. Rowland Heywood had been vicar of Frodsham from at least 1624. Christ Church, Oxford held the right of presentation to the living. According to Matthews, Heywood was an M.A. of Oxford but the only Rowland 'haywood' in the *Alumni Oxonienses* matriculated at Broad-

[98] Neither does Savage appear among the subscribing Cheshire dignitaries who are listed at the beginning of the Prayer Book petition. HLRO, Main Papers, HL, 20 December 1641. It seems reasonable to assume that Janion was some sort of agent or representative for the Savage family as he was entered in the 1641 ley as making the payment for 'my lord Rivers'. CRO, P8/13/2, fol. 74. The Janion family owned two pews in their own right as well. CRO, P8/4/3.
[99] Lysons and Lysons, *Cheshire*, ii, pp. 654–62.
[100] CRO, P8/13/1 (accounts); CRO, P8/13/2 (accounts); CRO, P8/4/3 (pew list).
[101] Wanklyn, 'Landed society', pp. 374–80.

gates Hall in 1582, aged nineteen. That would make him seventy-eight in 1641 which, though possible, seems unlikely. Its likelihood is further reduced by the fact that he was still living at the Restoration. Walker describes Heywood as 'D.D.', and perhaps that honour came to him after the Restoration, for he does not appear as such in either of the clerical subsidies, and is not so styled in the petitions. Whatever difficulties there are in establishing a precise biography, Walker claims that during the civil war Heywood was 'harrassed and Persecuted, and thereby driven from this living'. He was succeeded first by a presbyterian, Samuel Boden, in 1645 and next by an 'anabaptist', James Cockayne. Cockayne was ejected in 1661, 'leaving most of the Parish either of his own Perswasion, or [of] the Quakers'. The assertion that Heywood had been 'harrassed and Persecuted, and thereby driven from this living' is strengthened by the fact that he formally resigned the parish in 1661 and a Theophilus Cooke was presented by Christ Church in his place, while he took the parish of Bishop's Aston in Worcestershire. Heywood appears to have had no desire to return to his flock at Frodsham.[102]

The minister, Richard Banner, who described himself as the curate on the schedule of subscribers, is presumably the same Banner who was also a B.A. (1632) and M.A. (1635) of Brasenose, Oxford, as well as curate of Stoke (1641–8), curate of Burton (1662), and vicar of Eastham from 1661 to his death in 1666. Whether he was able to exercise any kind of formal ministry in the 1650s remains a mystery. William Urwick, the nineteenth-century historian of Cheshire non-conformity, described Banner as a 'puritan'. If so, he was a 'puritan' who supported, judging from his signature on both petitions, the Book of Common Prayer and episcopal polity. He may, of course, have been a man who moved with the times.[103] Banner, however, did take pains to see that his name was affixed to the episcopacy petition early in 1641. Next to his name is an entry: 'this gent gave his consent and desired that Mr Vicar have his hand . . . [that] he woulde condescend & bid us subscribe if he were not present'.[104] Thomas Modsley signed both petitions and described himself as the 'clerke of Frodsham'. Nothing more is known of him, except that he appears to have owned no less than three pews. Yet it is worth noting that the leading laity remained divided.[105]

---

[102] He appears in a subsidy of 1624, assessed for £4 4s. 'Loans 1620–1639', p. 78, see also pp. 92, 100, 115, 120; this paragraph is based on pp. 78, 92, 100, 115, 120; *Walker Revised*, p. 91; Ormerod, *Cheshire*, ii, p. 58; *AO*; John Walker, *The Sufferings of Clergy* (London, 1714 edn), p. 261.

[103] William Urwick, *Historical Sketches of Non-conformity in the Co. Palatine of Chester* (London, 1864), p. 71. This paragraph is based largely on a list of Cheshire clergy at the Restoration compiled by Alan Thacker of VCH Chester; *AO*. Banner's will survives.

[104] HLRO, Main Papers, HL, 27 February 1640/1.   [105] CRO, P8/4/3.

Frodsham: the parish officers

The Frodsham accounts relate only the names of two churchwardens for each year – none of the other offices, swornmen, overseers of the poor, and of the highways are mentioned. However, the accounts do provide a memorandum of 1640, authorizing the ley of that year. Seven laymen signed the memorandum and could be described as among the active or 'leading parishioners'.[106]

The unified stance provided by the vicar and the curate over the Prayer Book petition contrasts sharply with the divisions among the leading laymen of the parish. (For what follows, see Appendix 3, Frodsham, Table A3.8.) The two churchwardens sent out a conflicting set of signals to the rank and file. In the year of the petition itself, one warden, William Witter, subscribed and the other, Thomas Norman, did not; although the wardens for 1642 were both subscribers. The same sort of split can be seen among the 'leading parishioners' as defined by the 1640 memorandum: four subscribed for the Prayer Book, three did not. There appears to have been considerable independence of mind among leading laity, despite the fact that the vicar and the curate both supported the Prayer Book petition.

Because of the deficiencies of the Frodsham ley already discussed,[107] far less can be said about the economic standing of the men holding parish office. (For what follows, see Appendix 3, Frodsham, Tables A3.7, A3.9.) Where we have an assessment, both subscribing and non-subscribing officers appear to have been more prosperous than their counterparts at Tilston. A little more light is shed by looking at pew ownership. Wardens appear to have been generally drawn from men owning pews in the more prestigious two centre ranks of pews – although no obvious distinction between subscribers and non-subscribers is apparent (see Appendix 3, Frodsham, Tables A3.5, A3.7). The leading members of the community were by no means united in their support for the Book of Common Prayer.

WILMSLOW

Wilmslow: the 'character' of the parish

Wilmslow, in the hundred of Macclesfield, consisted in our period of four townships, covering just over 7,000 acres. There were 296 households in the parish in the early 1660s, according to the hearth tax returns of 1664. A total of 313 men signed their names or made their marks to the Prayer

---

[106] See above, pp. 192–7, for a definition of 'leading parishioners'.
[107] See above, pp. 204–5.

Book petition: an impressive (estimated) 69 per cent of the adult male population, and by far the highest proportion of any community that can be examined in depth. It is fortunate that we also know the number of those receiving poor relief in the parish.[108]

Of the 313 subscribers – the largest sample of the five localities under examination – 40 per cent (124) were rated in the 1641 church rate. (For what follows, see Appendix 3, Wilmslow, Table A3.10, Figures A3.5, A3.6.) Of the 191 male heads of households assessed for the parish rate and poor relief, 65 per cent put their hands to the Common Prayer petition. Of those receiving poor relief, non-subscribers slightly outnumber subscribers. But such an even spread of rated subscribers and non-subscribers is not repeated until examining the most substantial locals – those who were assessed in the 1641 subsidy. Among the 'middling sort', the bias among the assessed favours the subscribers, particularly in the 2s 1d to 4s group. In the category of 1s and under, however, the spread looks more even again, with thirty-nine assessed subscribers to twenty-seven assessed non-subscribers. That is, 59 per cent of men rated for 1s or less also subscribed for upholding the lawful liturgy. Two striking points are revealed by these figures. The first is that the local 'elites' as identified by the subsidy were almost evenly divided in their support for the Prayer Book. Secondly, the members of society most vulnerable to coercion, the poor or those rated for 1s or less, were also roughly evenly divided between subscribers and non-subscribers. These figures, then, do not suggest a campaign of pressure on the 'humble' by their 'betters'.[109]

The churchwardens' accounts record regular outlays in the late sixteenth and early seventeenth centuries on the items needed for the conduct of lawful worship: making a new surplice (1633, 2s 6d), a new carpet for the Communion table (1633, £1), a new book of Homilies (1633, 3s), a new Great Bible and two Communion books (1637, £3 18s). The church was whitewashed in 1633 (1s 2d). As with Tilston and Frodsham, the accounts also show that these items were used. There were annual outlays on washing the surplice, tuning the organ, and sweeping the church. Throughout the 1630s, the Holy Communion was celebrated at Wilmslow at least three times a year, but never more than five times a year. The railing

---

[108] Pownall Fee, Bollin Fee, Fulshaw, and Chorley: according to Sylvester and Nulty, *Historical Atlas of Cheshire*, p. 38 and Ormerod, *Cheshire*, iii, p. 586. However, Lysons lists six. Lysons and Lysons, *Cheshire*, ii, p. 819. See below, Appendix 3, Wilmslow, Table A3.10. I have been unable to identify this particular parish among the 6,000 who subscribed for episcopacy earlier in the year. For how this estimate calculated, see above, pp. 187–8.

[109] Poor relief for the year 1640 extended from a loaf of bread every sabbath to up to 6d from several bequests administered on the feast of St Thomas the Apostle. CRO, P123/3466/9/2, fols. 70v–71; PRO, E179/85/136; PRO, E179/85/134.

of the Communion table in 1634 is also recorded (£2 2s). There is no mention of steps or whether the altar was moved permanently back to the east end. This entry in the accounts for 1634, as well as entries referring to 'severall meetings about seatinge the formes' (4s) reflect the impact of Bishop Bridgeman's reluctant and half-hearted attempt to enforce new Laudian reforms on his diocese, brow-beaten as he was by Archbishop Neile, Archbishop Laud, and the king.[110]

Wilmslow: the gentry

Only 2 of the 313 Wilmslow subscribers style themselves as gentlemen: Francis Hanmer and William Newton; and only Newton was assessed in the 1641 subsidy at £10 *in terris*.[111] He was obviously a man of very substantial wealth to be assessed at that sum in lands as opposed to goods. (For what follows, see Appendix 3, Wilmslow, Table A3.10.) Thirteen men were of sufficient economic significance to be assessed in the 1641 subsidy and the ratio of subscribers to non-subscribers is almost even (seven to six). Four subscribers were valued at £3 *in bonis*: Edward Alcock, Jr, Roger Boulton, George Dickens, and possibly one Thomas Pendditor. Two further supporters of the lawful liturgy were valued at £4 *in bonis*: Richard Farknor and Thomas Powell. Among the subscribers, only William Newton was assessed on the basis of his holdings in land. Strikingly, all six of the non-subscribing subsidy men were assessed *in terris*. Two are described in the subsidy as 'gentlemen': John Hobson (26s) and Edward Latham (16s). The remaining four were all valued at 20s *in terris*: Edmund Curbishley, Edmund Hotham, Coherd (*sic*) de Pownall, and Robert Royley.[112] These six wealthy non-subscribers do not seem to have had much influence, given the high proportion of the adult male population that subscribed. It is arguable, therefore, that the high subscription rate in Wilmslow was not simply the result of pressure from subscribing gentry but represents the convictions of those who signed or made their marks.

[110] CRO, P123/3466/9/1 and CRO, P123/3466/9/2. See B. W. Quintrell, 'Lancashire ills, the king's will and the troubling of Bishop Bridgeman', *THSLC*, 132 (1983), pp. 67–102; and above, pp. 137–41.

[111] The following subsidy figures are based on PRO, E179/85/136 and PRO, E179/85/137.

[112] The major landowning families of the parish in 1641 as can be best determined from Lysons and Ormerod were: Trafford, Booth, Ryle, Curbishley, Fitton, Latham, Newton and Hobson. Only one of these, Newton, is in both the subsidy and a subscriber. Whereas Curbishley, Hobson and Latham were assessed in the subsidy only. Lysons and Lysons, *Cheshire*, ii, pp. 819–21; Ormerod, *Cheshire*, iii, pp. 586, 590–3, 601–3.

Wilmslow: the clergy

Thomas Wright the rector and the curate Edward Green, identified themselves as clergymen in the schedule of subscribers. Little more can be said of Green, except that he paid 5s as curate of 'Wilmesley' in the first ship money subsidy of Cheshire clergy in 1635. It is just possible that he is the same Edward Greene of Cheshire who matriculated as a plebeian at Brasenose (a popular college for north-westerners) in 1583, aged twenty-six. However, that would make him eighty-four years old in 1641. As is usual in the case of rectors, as opposed to curates, a great deal more can be said of Thomas Wright. The rector of Wilmslow may well be the same Thomas Wright who proceeded to the B.A. degree in 1603 and the M.A. in 1606 at Christ Church. Upon the death of the previous incumbent, William Massie, B.D., Wright was presented to the living in 1610 by the patron, who was possibly also his father, Lawrence Wright, gentleman. Thomas came of prominent local stock, being the son of Lawrence Wright of Nantwich who married the sister of William Newton of Pownell Hall. Wilmslow provided a good living – one source estimated its value in excess of £200 per year. In the various clerical contributions and subsidies of Charles' reign, Wright usually paid over £5, a substantial assessment.[113]

During the three decades of his incumbency before the civil war, Wright appears to have been a responsible and resident pastor. One contemporary, a Dr Newton, stated 'Mr Wright was a very pious and good man.'[114] Even allowing for the bias of Dr Newton, who was one of Walker's sources for his conformist *Sufferings of the Clergy*, Wright seems to have enjoyed local regard. Indeed, when Sir William Brereton sequestered the living of Wilmslow in March 1644/5(?) none of the usual charges of scandalous living were made against Wright. Rather it was the rector's royalism that caused concern: it was reported that Wright absented 'himself from his said church . . . betaking himself to the forces raised against the parliament'.[115] The parson did not lay down his cure quietly, however. Later in the year parliamentary troopers laid siege to the rectory:

Captaine Duckenfield, a commander of the Rebels in Cheshire, came to Mr Wright's house, Parson of Wemslow . . . a man of fourscore yeares of age, of a very honest

[113] 'Loans 1620–1639', p. 103; AO; Ormerod, *Cheshire*, iii, p. 595; J. P. Earwaker, *East Cheshire* (2 vols., London, 1877), i, p. 91, ii, p. 91n; 'Loans 1620–1639', pp. 80, 93, 103, 122.
[114] Bodl., Walker Manuscripts, vol. iii, fol. 825 cited in Earwaker, *East Cheshire*, ii, p. 91n.
[115] *Minutes of the Committee for the relief of Plundered Ministers and Trustees for the Maintenance of Ministers; relating to Lancashire and Cheshire 1643–1660*, LCRS, xxviii (1893), pp. 146–7.

life and conversation, and eminent for his hospitality amongst his neighbours. The Captain and his followers entered the house by violence, killed two of his maid servants, wounded others, and in all probability had murthered Mr Wright himself, had not his neighbours that loved him well, rescued him out of their hands.[116]

If Wright was eighty years old in 1645, he was over ninety-five when restored to his living in 1660. The air of Wilmslow was obviously conducive to clerical longevity!

Sir William Brereton 'intruded' one John Brereton into the living in 1642 or 1643. Although Sir William left books of divinity to the minister in his will, it is unclear what their exact relationship was.[117] John Brereton appears to have followed a predictable course of iconoclasm in the parish church: the organ, so carefully tuned each year in the 1630s, was removed and sold, and the font was replaced with a pewter basin. He also 'displaced and degraded the altar by making it a common table, around which the congregation sat down in the middle of the chancel to eat and drink in commemoration of the Lord's Supper'.[118] It is unclear, however, how often the parishioners were invited by their pastor to 'eat and drink', in commemoration or otherwise. The accounts record no expenditure on bread and wine for the Eucharist from 1645 to 1650, though they do record the 2s 8d spent on the pewter basin, presumably for Baptism. Indeed, the noted non-conformist Adam Martindale, records a meeting of ministers at Wilmslow in 1653 in which it was resolved 'that suspension [of Holy Communion] would keep the Lord's Supper from pollution as well as excommunication [of particular individuals]'. Martindale's own moderate nature favoured the use of individual excommunication as means of discipline, rather than blanket suspension – a sort of protestant interdict – in order to keep the sacrament safe from the 'pollution' of 'unworthy' communicants.[119] However, judging from the evident lack of celebrations

---

[116] *Mercurius Rusticus* (1648), p. 114 cited in Earwaker, *East Cheshire*, ii, p. 91. Another account reports the death of a maid servant. Bodl., Walker Manuscripts, vol. iii, fol. 825 cited in Earwaker, ibid., ii, p. 91n. See also Urwick, *Historical Sketches*, p. 267.

[117] John was baptized at Stockport in Cheshire but received his M.A. degree from Edinburgh in 1637. *Calamy Revised*; Urwick, *Historical Sketches*, pp. 260–9. The noted non-conformist Henry Newcome had some dealings with Brereton.

[118] Based on Finney's manuscript survey of Wilmslow in *Lancashire and Cheshire Historical Collector*, p. 6 cited in Earwaker, *East Cheshire*, ii, p. 92. Finney wrote c. 1730 and relied on oral traditions in the village. Finney's account is substantiated from the churchwarden's accounts. CRO, P123/3466/9/2. Extracts of the accounts are printed in Earwaker, ibid., ii, p. 92. For other examples of outlays on organs in parish churches, see Nicholas Temperley, *The Music of the English Parish Church* (2 vols., Cambridge, 1979), i, pp. 51–2. Temperley's analysis of the religious divisions under Elizabeth and the early Stuarts, however, relies heavily on the 'puritan vs. Anglican' model.

[119] CRO, P123/3466/9/2; *Life of Adam Martindale written by Himself*, ed. Richard Parkinson, Chetham Society, iv (1845), p. 113.

of the Eucharist, Brereton may well have preferred the same solution to the problem of considering most of one's congregation unregenerate, as Ralph Josselyn: suspending the Holy Communion altogether.[120] This contrasts sharply with Wright's practice of celebrating the Eucharist three to five times a year, and no doubt caused considerable resentment among inhabitants who were used not only to more frequent celebrations of Communion, but also to being allowed to take the sacrament on those occasions. Such resentment may have been particularly strong in a parish with such a high proportion of subscriptions for the Prayer Book petition.

Brereton appears not to have been responsive to the needs of some of his parishioners. The Plundered Ministers' Accounts record that Wright's wife Anne had to petition twice, once in July 1646 and again in April 1647, to the Committee in order to force Brereton to pay the fifth of the income of the tithes, rents, glebe lands, and Easter books due to the dependent family of a sequestered priest. The Committee had to threaten Brereton with sequestration before he would finally pay. The Wrights apparently remained in the area, as Thomas, who was perhaps then ninety years old, appears on the Major-Generals' List of Suspected Persons in 1655. He was, by all accounts, a formidable individual.[121]

Wright was restored to his living in July 1660, but died shortly thereafter, as so many freshly restored clergymen seem to have done.[122] Sir Cecil Trafford presented Peter Ledsham. Ledsham had been curate of Didsbury from 1651 following the dismissal of the previous curate for refusing to attend the Manchester classis. However, he too had been a 'thorn in the side of Presbyterian authorities' and refused also to attend the classis. The fact that he had already been ordained a priest in 1626, and his trouble-free presentation to the living, suggested that his difficulties with the classis were due perhaps to his 'Anglicanism' rather than to any leanings towards

---

[120] See above, pp. 51–2. See also, Margaret Spufford, 'Can we count the "godly" and the "conformable" in the seventeenth century?', *JEH* 36:3 (1985), pp. 432–3; Eamon Duffy, 'The godly and the multitude in Stuart England', *The Seventeenth Century* 1:1 (1986), pp. 37–8.

[121] *Plundered Ministers*, pp. 157, 179; Earwaker, *East Cheshire*, ii, p. 91. Wright was listed as of Bollin Fee. *Walker Revised*, p. 94.

[122] His will and inventory survive. The dedicatory clause of this committed conformist is low key, though he did express the value he placed on lawful rites of passage: 'First I commend and committ my soule into the hands of Almighty God, my Creatour truly and faithfully beleeveinge to bee saved by the death and passion of my Saviour Jesus Christ, and my Bodie to Christian Buriall.' He had few books to leave in 1660, as his inventory states: 'Item. Some few Latine bookes, bookes of devinitie . . . and other smale Bookes, [the] best bookes being plundered and some lost.' CRO, Will and Inventory of Thomas Wright, W.S. 1661.

independency. Ledsham ministered in Wilmslow until resigning the living in 1673. He died a few years later in 1678, aged seventy-four, and was buried in the chancel of the church.[123]

Wilmslow: the parish officers

The evidence from Wilmslow provides no strong correlation between assessed wealth for parish rates and the expression of conformist conviction through subscriptions to the Prayer Book petition (see Appendix 3, Wilmslow, Table A3.10, Figures A3.5, A3.6). However, a strong connection between subscribers and parish officers does appear to exist (see Appendix 3, Wilmslow, Table A3.11). Yet even here individual choices were made, as nearly a fifth of those holding parochial office between 1639 and 1648 did not subscribe to the petition. The parish had four churchwardens per year, and in the year of the petition's production (1641), all four wardens subscribed. The bias also favours subscribers quite heavily among the men who held parish office in the few years before and after 1641. Significantly, after the abolition of the Church of England in 1645, the Prayer Book subscribers managed to retain control of this lowly but significant level in church government despite the fact that Sir William Brereton placed the presbyterian John Brereton in the living. This may help explain the unease apparent between the minister and his own parishioners, manifesting itself in Brereton's withholding of Anne Wright's rightful fifth and his failure to administer the sacrament regularly to the people committed to his care. Wilmslow also appears to have drawn its wardens from the parochial 'elite', judging from their rated sums (see Appendix 3, Wilmslow, Table A3.12). All three of the wardens in the period 1639–48 who were non-subscribers failed to be rated in the 1641 rate. It would appear that Thomas Wright was the most significant figure in achieving a high rate of subscription in Wilmslow; the gentry were not. Striking too is the fact that, despite such strong support for the petition, more than half of those receiving poor relief did not sign. This strengthens the case for regarding the subscribers as acting independently of pressure from above.

---

[123] Earwaker, *East Cheshire*, ii, pp. 92–3; Ormerod, *Cheshire*, iii, p. 595; *VCH Chester*, iii, p. 40; *A History of the Ancient Chapels of Didsbury and Chorlton*, Chetham Society, xlii (1857), p. 60; Alan Thacker's (of the VCH) unpublished list of Cheshire clergy at the Restoration.

MARBURY

Marbury: the 'character' of the chapelry

Marbury, in the Hundred of Nantwich, was a parochial chapelry within the parish of Whitchurch, Shropshire. It contained two dependent townships: Marbury-cum-Quoisley and Norbury. It was a small parish in north-western terms, covering just over 3,000 acres and in the 1664 hearth tax returns, containing only 122 households. In late 1641, fifty-five individuals subscribed to the Prayer Book petition: roughly 29 per cent of the adult male population.[124]

The Marbury Common Prayer subscribers would appear to be of a more humble economic background than the other communities examined so far (for what follows, see Appendix 3, Marbury, Table A3.13, Figures A3.7, A3.8). Of the fifty-five total subscribers, 42 per cent (23) were assessed in the 1640 ley. The breakdown of the rated subscribers is as follows: 65 per cent (15) paid 1s or less and 22 per cent (5) paid between 1s 1d and 2s. Only one subscriber paid between 2s 1d and 4s, while none paid over 4s. Among the rated non-subscribers, no man was assessed for over 4s either. Taking into account the 1664 hearth tax figures as well (see Appendix 3, Marbury, Table A3.13), this argues for a rather impoverished community. Unfortunately, the Marbury churchwardens' accounts do not contain any record of poor relief for the chapelry.

The 'character' of the chapelry is very hard to determine. The churchwardens' accounts suggest a conforming community, with an average of three celebrations of Holy Communion per year in the 1620s and 1630s, and regular expenditure on service books, church furniture, and the washing of the surplice. Communion continued to be celebrated twice a year throughout the 1640s. The only overt sign of 'puritanism' in Marbury in the early seventeenth century is a single visitation presentation in 1625 of four laymen for failing to kneel and bow at the appointed places in the service. In 1633 a new Communion table was purchased for 8s and in 1634, 2s 8d was paid to a joyner (plus 3s 4d for hinges and latches) for railing the table; 8d was also spent for lowering pews. The accounts simply refer to the rail 'in the chancel'; it is not at all clear whether the holy table was moved to the more controversial east end or not. Again, one sees the effects of Bishop Bridgeman's reluctant campaign to enforce Laudian

---

[124] Lysons and Lysons, *Cheshire*, ii, p. 685; *Parliamentary Gazetteer* (1848); see below, Appendix 3, Marbury, Table A3.13; HLRO, Main Papers, HL, 20 December 1641. Population estimates based on the 1664 hearth-tax returns. See above, pp. 187–8. I have been unable to identify Marbury among the subscribers to the petition in favour of episcopacy.

innovations on parish churches, strong-armed as he was by Archbishop Neile. Also in the year 1634, there is an entry for the delivery of a certificate to Bridgeman, certifying the 'uniformity of the seates in the church and chancel' (20d). Perhaps these innovations over the holy table and pews were what prompted roughly 29 per cent of the male population of Marbury to subscribe to the Cheshire petition against innovations in the traditional worship of the Common Prayer Book.[125]

Marbury: the gentry

Of the nine members of the community who were substantial enough to be assessed in the 1641 subsidy, only three were subscribers.[126] Among these were George Bickerton, gentleman, valued at 20s *in terris*, Robert Nevett, valued at £4 *in bonis*, and Thomas Wicksted, who with his wife Elizabeth is listed as 'recusant' in his payment of 2s 8d. All three are listed as landowning families by the antiquarian Lysons.[127] Amongst the six non-subscribers, two, Thomas Heath and Thomas Poole (both valued at 20s *in terris*) possessed family names identified as landowners by Lysons. The others were valued in goods, or were backward in payment. I have omitted Lord Cholmondeley, who was assessed in the 1641 subsidy for Marbury, from consideration altogether, as his signature does not appear with the Marbury petitioners, but among the county establishment figures, whose names come at the front of the shire's subscribers.

Marbury: the clergy

As already stated, Marbury was a parochial chapelry within the parish of Whitchurch. The curate was provided by the rector of Whitchurch but nevertheless Marbury's exact ecclesiastical status at the time we are concerned with remains somewhat obscure.[128] The curate, Thomas Orpe, did not subscribe to the Common Prayer petition and his failure might be considered surprising in the light of what little we can piece together about his career in the priesthood. Orpe matriculated at Saint Mary's Hall, Oxford in 1632, aged twenty-one. Walker suggests that he was a school-master at Tarporley, until 'driven out' for refusing to sign the Covenant in 1643, and settled at Whitchurch as schoolmaster and curate to the rector, one T. Fowler. In 1646 both curate and rector were ejected from Whit-

[125] R. C. Richardson, 'Puritanism in the diocese of Chester to 1642' (University of Manchester Ph.D., 1969), p. 41; CRO, P39/8/1; for Bishop Bridgeman, see above, pp. 137–41.
[126] PRO, E179/85/135.
[127] Lysons and Lysons, *Cheshire*, ii, pp. 685–6.
[128] Ormerod, *Cheshire*, iii, p. 462; cf. Richards, *Old Cheshire Churches*, p. 226.

church; Fowler was specifically accused of visiting the royalist garrison at Shrewsbury.[129] No mention is made of Orpe's curacy at Marbury in any of the biographical sources, but presumably he knew Fowler from his time at Marbury and sought aid from him when he was 'driven from' Tarporley.[130] He appears later in the Interregnum as vicar of Stanton in Shropshire and an Inquisition of 1655 relates that, although he is a preaching minister, he was also 'one whose life we cannot approve of'.[131] The exact nature of the Committee's disapproval was not stated, but Orpe was ejected again, and later officiated at Battlefield and Preston Gubbals. He died in 1677. Taken together, the few facts that can be pieced together about Orpe suggest a cleric who might well have been inclined to subscribe to the Prayer Book petition. Yet his failure to do so remains.

Marbury: the parish officers

In contrast to the parishes considered so far, the majority of those holding parish office in the years before and after 1641 did not put their hands to the Common Prayer petition (for what follows, see Appendix 3, Marbury, Tables A3.14, A3.15). From 1633 to 1648 there were twenty-five church-wardens at Marbury; only nine subscribed in 1641, while sixteen did not. Again, among the 'leading parishioners' (excluding the wardens and curate) who authorized the church ley in 1640, three subscribed and five did not. Only one of the nine officer/subscribers was rated at less than 1s and two men were not assessed at all. In contrast, six of the sixteen officer/non-subscribers were assessed at 1s or less (five of the sixteen were not assessed). This bias in favour of non-subscribers amongst the men who held church office is particularly striking when it is remembered that Marbury's subscribers formed roughly 29 per cent of the adult male population. Marbury's figure of 29 per cent is comparable to the figures for Tilston and Frodsham – both at 27 per cent – two parishes where, in contrast, the Common Prayer petition enjoyed greater support from parochial officials. The critical importance of gentry, clerical, and local elite leadership in 'getting hands', is therefore called into question.

---

[129] *AO; Walker Revised*, pp. 305, 306. The rector and curate of Tarporley at this time were zealous puritans. See above, p. 73.

[130] Nevertheless, we are sure of his presence there, as his signature appears in the churchwardens' accounts in 1640. CRO, P39/8/1. According to Richards, Marbury was served by: John (?) Fowler (1635), William Heywood (1635), Charles Jonas (d.1647), William Bruce (1647), William Anderson (1666). Richards, *Old Cheshire Churches*, p. 227. Jonas was buried in the church. Urwick, *Historical Sketches*, p. 150.

[131] H. E. Evens, ed., 'An Inquisition in Salop, 1655', *Transactions of the Shropshire Archaeological Society*, 47 (1933–4), p. 7; *Walker Revised*, p. 306.

MIDDLEWICH

Middlewich: the 'character' of the parish

The parish of Middlewich, 'a considerable market town' in the Hundred of Northwich was composed of fifteen townships and covered just over 13,300 acres.[132] According to the 1664 hearth tax returns the parish contained 422 households. Towards the end of 1641, 265 men signed the petition for upholding the lawful liturgy of the established church: roughly 41 per cent of the adult male population of the parish.[133]

Of the 265 total subscribers to the Prayer Book petition, 32 per cent (85) were assessed in the 1640 church rate (for what follows, see Appendix 3, Middlewich, Table A3.16, Figures A3.9, A.3.10). Examining rated subscribers more closely, we see 33 per cent (28) were assessed for 1s or less and 18 per cent (15) paid between 1s 1d and 2s. In common with Wilmslow, the more prosperous category of 2s 1d to 4s is well represented among the subscribers at 28 per cent (24).[134] However, the significantly high proportion of petitioning parishioners rated at between 4s 1d and 8s is unmatched by any of the other communities under examination, at 18 per cent (15). No parish or chapelry considered so far comes anywhere near that figure – the closest was Wilmslow again with 5 per cent (6). Strikingly, the breakdown of the rated non-subscribing males is quite similar to that of the subscribers – the sharpest contrast coming at the lower end of the economic scale: those rated at 1s or less (50 per cent = 74). Unfortunately the Middlewich accounts contain no record of poor relief for the parish.

The estimated high proportion (41 per cent) of the adult male population of Middlewich which subscribed to the Prayer Book petition is all the more striking in the light of the 'strong puritan element' in the parish, as described by R. C. Richardson. Near the beginning of the century (1605) eight laypeople were presented in the visitation for their refusal to kneel at Communion and an emerging 'vocal puritan element' consisting of fourteen individuals were also presented for keeping a private fast on Christmas

---

[132] Middlewich, Byley-cum-Yatehouse, Clive, Croxton, Kinderton-cum-Hulme, Minshull-Vernon, Moresbarrow-cum-Parne, Newton, Occleston, Ravencroft, Sproston, Stublach, Sutton, Weaver, and Wimboldsely-cum-Lea Hall. Lysons and Lysons, *Cheshire*, ii, pp. 687–8; *Parliamentary Gazetteer* (1848). See also Sylvester and Nulty, *Historical Atlas of Cheshire*, pp. 36, 38.

[133] See below, Appendix 3, Middlewich, Table A3.16. Population estimates are based on the 1664 hearth tax returns. See above, pp. 187–8. The returns for the Hundred of Northwich are available in print in *Northwich Hundred Poll Tax, 1660 and Hearth Tax, 1664*, ed. G. O. Lawton, LCRS, cxix (1979). I have been unable to identify Middlewich among the schedules of subscribers for the petition for episcopacy presented earlier in the year.

[134] Compare with Wilmslow at 31 per cent (39).

day.[135] In 1622, both the lecturer Thomas Langley and the vicar Robert Halliley were presented for unlawful liturgical practices. Langley had not worn the surplice at divine service and Halliley had not only admitted 'strangers' to Communion, but had administered the sacrament to people who remained sitting. The churchwardens, meanwhile, were presented for letting the church fall into decay.[136] In the metropolitan visitation of 1630, the vicar was presented for (among other items) failure to wear the surplice and administering Communion – yet again – to non-parishioners. At the same visitation, the lecturer Langley was presented for not showing his licence to preach and the wardens were enjoined: 'not to suffer him to preach untill the Lord Archbishop of Yorke his pleasure be first knowne, or until he shew sufficient Certificate of his conformity'.[137] Langley was for a time forbidden to preach by Bishop Bridgeman, his diocesan succumbing to pressure from Archbishop Neile to act firmly. The noted non-conformist, Oliver Heywood, later remarked:

Old Mr Langley of Middlewich in Cheshire may also be mentioned, who was a minister there before the wars; and though *he was seven years together silenced*, yet when he was restored to his liberty he returned to them, when he had but a very pitiful maintenance, and continued there to the day of his death.[138]

So, despite the non-conformity of both its lecturer and vicar, and activity of an anti-establishment kind amongst some laity earlier in the century, Middlewich was nevertheless able to produce a significant proportion of men who supported the liturgy of the established church. In part, this simply illustrates the point made elsewhere that a few presentments for liturgical aberrations do not a 'puritan stronghold' make.[139] Perhaps more importantly, however, it illustrates that even with a distinguished and respected preacher such as Thomas Langley in their midst, the laity were still perfectly capable of disagreeing with him and holding sincere and differing religious views themselves. As Ian Green has rightly observed, the fact that we know about the non-conformity of individuals is because their neighbours chose to inform the ecclesiastical authorities about them.[140]

It is hard to say how frequently Holy Communion was celebrated at

---

[135] Many of those presented were the same individuals. Richardson, *Puritanism*, pp. 77, 86–7; Richardson, 'Puritanism', pp. 23–5.

[136] CRO, EDV 1/24, fol. 84.

[137] Borthwick Institute of Historical Research, University of York, York v.1629 and 1630/CB, fols. 195–195v; Richardson, 'Puritanism', pp. 24–5. I am grateful to Bill Sheils for the first reference.

[138] Cited in Urwick, *Historical Sketches*, p. 166. See also pp. xii, 7, 165–6; Richardson, *Puritanism*, p. 137.

[139] See above, Chapter 2, *passim*.

[140] Ian Green, 'Career prospects and clerical conformity in the early Stuart Church', *P&P* 90 (1981), p. 112. This point is discussed at greater length in Chapters 1, 2.

Middlewich, between 1635 and 1640, as the accounts simply give the total amount spent that year on wine for the Eucharist.[141] However, *frequency* of Communion, is not a good test of conformity in a parish, as Mattins followed by Ante-communion were perfectly permissible forms of service in the Prayer Book. Perhaps significantly, a rail was not erected until 1639 at the cost of £2.[142] This late date may reveal a reluctance to conform with the policy of Thorough on the part of the supporters of the Prayer Book, as well as its detractors.

Middlewich: the gentry

Another example of ill-fortune in the historical record, is that no subsidy of 1641 survives for Northwich Hundred. This renders it impossible to discuss the local gentry in the same depth as with the other parishes. The Astons appear to have owned land in Minshull Vernon, purchased in the reign of Elizabeth I. However, the most prominent local family is that of Peter Venables, Baron Kinderton, Sir Thomas Aston's successful partner in the elections for the Long Parliament in the autumn of 1640. Venables' bias for 'Anglicanism' continued after the civil war and can be seen in his opposition to leading local puritan clergy like Adam Martindale.[143]

Middlewich: the clergy

Due to its size, both in area and population, Middlewich had two clergymen to serve it. Thomas Langley, the venerable non-conformist, ministered in the parish as its lecturer from 1609 until his death in 1657. A considerable amount is known about him, and the great esteem and affection in which he was held by such prominent non-conformists as Oliver Heywood, Henry Newcome, and John Bruen.[144] In contrast, little is known of the vicar, Thomas or Robert Halliley. He served the parish from 1616 until his death in 1641. He is listed as 'poor and in debt' in the clerical contribution of 1634–36.[145] Perhaps Halliley died before the production of

[141] 5s 11d (1635); 5s (1636); £1 8s 10d (1639); 4s 7d (1640). CRO, P13/22/1.

[142] CRO, P13/22/1.

[143] Lysons, although providing information about the major landowners in each township, is usually quite unhelpful about the exact point in time a family held a particular manor. However, this does not satisfactorily account for why the subscriptions of the townships of Minshull Vernon appear separately from the rest of the parish, and under a separate heading. HLRO, Main Papers, HL, 20 December 1641. See above, pp. 135–7.

[144] *Plundered Ministers*, pp. 173–4, 199; Urwick, *Historical Sketches*, pp. 7, 62, 164–7, 201, 213–14; 'Loans 1620–1639', p. 63.

[145] Urwick, *Historical Sketches*, p. 164; Ormerod, *Cheshire*, iii, p. 185; 'Loans 1620–1639', pp. 51, 60, 79, 93, 102, 117, 122. A Robert Hallely took his B.A. in 1608 and M.A. in 1611 at Christ's, and was vicar of Calkwell, Lincolnshire from 1614 to 1615. It seems just possible that this is the same man. AC.

the petition, for one James Rowlandson identified himself as a clerk in holy orders by putting 'M' by his signature.[146] Nothing further at all is known about Rowlandson. At some point before January 1647, a Matthew Clayton was appointed to Middlewich, and he, with Langley, received a £50 increase in his maintenance from the Committee for Plundered Ministers. In July 1658, one Richard Bowker, clerk, was admitted to the parish, under the seal of the Lord Protector. Bowker toiled for only a few years in this particular vineyard, however. He was ejected at the Restoration and replaced by Laurence Griffith who ministered there until 1680.[147]

Middlewich: the parish officers

Ordinarily, Middlewich appears to have had four churchwardens: two appointed by the barons of Kinderton, one by the vicar and one by the parishioners.[148] The churchwardens of Middlewich appear to have been a more economically prosperous group than those in the other parishes described so far, although even so, there were exceptions (for what follows, see Appendix 3, Middlewich, Table A3.18). The wardens of 1640 and 1641 were assessed for: 3d, 2s, 6s, 7s. Only two wardens from 1635 to 1641 were assessed for 1s or less – one was a subscriber and one not. Only one warden, during that period (1635), a non-subscriber, was not assessed at all in 1640. The trend among the officers is towards supporting the Prayer Book petition – although in 1639, the proportion of subscribers to non-subscribers is even (for what follows, see Appendix 3, Middlewich, Table A3.17). The same four men occupied the wardenships in both 1640 and 1641. We know this despite the fact that the extant accounts jump from 1640 to 1648, because they identified themselves as the wardens in the petition itself, signing together as a group at the top of the page.[149] Given the fact that the parish lecturer was a noted non-conformist and that the vicar may have been dead at the time subscriptions were sought, the initiative in Middlewich on behalf of the lawful liturgy must have come from the laity. Their achievement of 41 per cent is striking in the face of clerical opposition.

---

[146] This is one of the standard ways in which clerics identified themselves as such in the petition.
[147] 'Loans 1620–1639', pp. 173–4, 199, 233, 234, 243. This may be the same Richard Bowker of Manchester who was admitted to the B.A. degree at St John's, Cambridge in 1651, and afterwards held a fellowship there. AC; Urwick, *Historical Sketches*, p. 151; Ormerod, *Cheshire*, iii, p. 185; Richards, *Old Cheshire Churches*, p. 237. Bowker does not appear, however, in *Calamy Revised*.
[148] Richards, *Old Cheshire Churches*, p. 235.
[149] HLRO, Main Papers, HL, 20 December 1641.

CONFORMITY AND ITS CHARACTERISTICS

In 1981 Margaret Spufford lamented that: 'At no period is it possible to distinguish the conforming believer from the apathetic church-goer, who merely wished to stay out of trouble.'[150] It is suggested here that despite all the defects and pitfalls of the documentary evidence – not least the smallness of the sample – the above analysis of five Cheshire communities provides an opportunity both to distinguish between the convinced con-formist and the apathetic and, with due caution, to 'count' them.[151] It is important to note that this is made possible by a series of happy accidents in the survival of the schedules of subscribers for the Cheshire petitions in support of the church with records of parish rates for 1640 or 1641. Equally important to note is the altered context from the period before the Long Parliament. Anxiety over the future of the Church of England necessitated open expressions of loyalty and support. The Short and Long Parliaments were in part – along with the policies of Archbishop Laud – responsible for raising these anxieties while also providing forums for the airing of grievances. This is why discussions of conformity using church court evidence before 1640 is more impressionistic than conclusions drawn from the study of petitions. When faced with the loss of a religious settlement that conformists respected and perhaps even loved they had reason to ensure their voice was heard. Furthermore, it could be suggested that the attack on the Church of England created a sense of 'group identity' among conformists that had been lacking before.[152]

Due caution about the defects of the statistics provided in this chapter noted, the other chief concern is how 'genuine' are the expressed signs of support expressed in the petitions? The 'signs' under examination here are the signatures or marks put on the petition for upholding the Book of Common Prayer. To put it bluntly, were signatories simply caving in to 'pressure from above' when they subscribed for the Prayer Book? I would like to argue that, based on the evidence provided by four parishes and one chapelry, the subscriptions for the Prayer Book represent a 'free-will offering'.

Take, first, the male groups of those presumably most susceptible to social control: those receiving poor relief, those too economically insignif-icant even to be rated, and men rated for 1s or less. Among the two parishes

---

[150] Margaret Spufford, *Small Books and Pleasant Histories: popular fiction and its readership in seventeenth century England* (London, 1981), p. 194.

[151] Spufford later drew attention to this possibility, 'Can we count', pp. 428–38.

[152] See above, Chapter 3. A future project that could be undertaken is to trace the careers of all the clergy who subscribed for the Book of Common Prayer through the Commonwealth and Restoration.

with poor relief records extant, in Tilston the poor slightly favoured subscription, whereas in Wilmslow they were fairly evenly divided. In all cases, non-rated subscribers outnumber rated subscribers (see above Table 5.2). Among men assessed for 1s or less, there are no clear trends. In Tilston, subscribers are favoured slightly but otherwise non-subscribers are favoured, or the difference is so small given the size of the numbers involved, as to be insignificant. This is true also of the 'middling sort', the sort of men who by and large filled parish offices. Again, amongst the substantial men paying the subsidy, those of Tilston gave strong support (6:3) to the petition. In Marbury, however, the reverse was true and only three out of nine subsidy men supported the petition. In Wilmslow, the men paying the subsidy were divided.

Out of a group of five communities it is hard to generalize about the clergy. In parishes with clerical support for the petition, Frodsham (27 per cent), Tilston (27 per cent), and Wilmslow (69 per cent) there are no clear patterns. Frodsham's incumbent was ejected with great bitterness, whereas Tilston's Essex Clarke continued to minister in his living until his death in 1654. Thomas Wright of Wilmslow, although ejected for his royalism, obviously enjoyed considerable local regard and support, but even he did not control absolutely the opinions of his churchwardens, or even those receiving poor relief. In Marbury, 29 per cent subscribed – similar to Tilston and Frodsham – without any lead from their minister. And perhaps most striking of all, in Middlewich with its noted non-conformist lecturer, an estimated 41 per cent of adult males subscribed.

It is by examining the allegiances of parish officers that a pattern can be suggested. In Tilston, Wilmslow, and Middlewich, there was strong support among officers and leading parishioners for the Prayer Book petition. In Frodsham they were fairly evenly divided. Only in Marbury was there a clear majority of officers and leading parishioners who did not subscribe. Marbury, with its subscription rate of 29 per cent is the strongest case of all for viewing the petition as an expression of individual consciences given the absence there of strong support from the gentry, clergy, or church officers. In Tilston, one of the few parish officers who did not subscribe was an overseer of the poor, which adds weight on the side of the view that the poor subscribed as they desired, as there would have been contradictory signals from those who had the greatest immediate influence over them. One critic of petitioning activity for the lawful liturgy and episcopacy was right when he observed that 'hedgers at the hedge, plowmen at the plow, threshers in the barnes' were among the supporters of pro-church petitions.[153] He was

---

[153] 'W. Howell to Thos. Wise, Knt for the Co. of Devon at his lodgings at Savoy' (20 February 1641) in *Buller Papers* (n.p., privately printed, 1895), pp. 33–4.

mistaken, however, in assuming that petitions for the Prayer Book and episcopacy enjoyed support from only one segment of society. Support for the lawful liturgy, as expressed by signatures and marks on a petition, cut across the social spectrum of all five local communities. But several other questions need now to be considered.

First of all, how is one to interpret *non*-subscription for the Prayer Book? Given that it is not clear whether the Cheshire Root and Branch petition was ever actually circulated in the county before being presented at Westminster – in sharp contrast to the petitions for episcopacy and liturgy – it is hardly surprising that no schedules of subscribers are extant which would have allowed the comparison of places and individuals.[154] Furthermore, we are left with the interpretative problem that more usually dogs studies of conformity: is *failure* to subscribe an indication of opposition, or of apathy, to the established church? We can, however, be more sure of the positive nature of those who did subscribe as a legitimate expression of committed conformity.

Second, the historiographical questions concerning social control are put in a new light.[155] Bearing in mind that it has only been possible to analyze 5 communities (although the 5 localities include 917 individuals), nevertheless there is a tendency for the Prayer Book petition to receive support from the lay officers of the parish. But this support does not appear to have had a direct effect on the rate of subscriptions. These are just the sort of men who are often presented as the agents of the 'reformation of manners' and 'preciser protestantism'. This chapter suggests, however, that such men could equally be agents for committed conformity, supporting the established church not simply passively, but actively. The men who held parish office, who signed the memoranda authorizing rates, were individuals who provided local lay leadership and influence. That leadership, however, could be just as much for the maintenance of the religious settlement as for its reconstruction or transformation. For example, over a third of the parish officers in nine Cambridgeshire parishes put their weight behind a petition against Bishop Wren in particular and episcopal government in general in 1640–41.[156] Men (and sometimes women) who filled parish offices were, perhaps more than the clergy, the 'natural' local church leaders. And their expressions of religious commitment could be as often on behalf of the established church as against it. Nevertheless, as this chapter shows, ordinary parishioners, even the poor, were capable of what

[154] See above, p. 148.
[155] Spufford, 'Social control?', *passim*. For the social control argument, see for example, William Hunt, *The Puritan Moment: the coming of revolution in an English county* (Cambridge, Mass., 1983), pp. 143–5.
[156] Spufford, *Contrasting Communities*, pp. 232–3, 267–71, *passim*; 'Can we count', p. 434.

appears to be a free expression of their own religious commitment. Even with strong lay leadership generally a minority of adult males subscribed for the Church of England. It reinforces the evidence from church court records that conformity was a real and active strand in parish religion. Spufford's earlier verdict of conformist petitions as only allowing us to count the '"conformable", [but] not the "godly"' may be over cautious. Committed conformists may not have been 'godly' in the way the word is usually used by contemporaries and they were usually a minority in the strict sense, but their expressions of religious belief were as legitimate as puritanism, 'godliness', open dissent, recusancy, church papistry, or folk religion in early modern England.[157]

[157] Spufford, 'Can we count', p. 437 n. 20.

6

Conclusion: laity, clergy, and conformity in post-Reformation England

Yes, my too self-confident juvenile friend, I do believe in those mysteries which are so common in your mouth; I do believe in the unadulterated word which you hold there in your hand; but you must pardon me if, in some things I doubt your interpretation. The Bible is good, the Prayer-book is good, nay you yourself would be acceptable, if you would read to me some portion of those time-honoured discourses which our great divines have elaborated in the full maturity of their powers . . . We are not forced into church! No: but we desire more than that. We desire not to be forced to stay away. We desire, nay, we are resolute, to enjoy the comfort of public worship; but we desire also that we may do so without an amount of tedium which ordinary human nature cannot endure with patience; that we may be able to leave the house of God, without that anxious longing for escape, which is the common consequence of common sermons.[1]

'But after all', I said one day, 'the great practical objection still remains unanswered – the clergy? Are we to throw ourselves into their hands after all? Are we, who have been declaiming all our lives against priestcraft, voluntarily to forge again the chains of our slavery to a class whom we neither trust nor honour?' She smiled. 'If you will examine the Prayer Book, you will not find, as far as I am aware, anything which binds a man to become the slave of the priesthood, voluntarily or otherwise. Whether the people become priest ridden or not, hereafter, will depend, as it always has done, utterly on themselves.'[2]

Though a Clergie man has noe faults of his owne yett ye faults of ye whole Tribe shall be layd upon him soe he shall be sure not to lacke.[3]

CONFORMITY AND 'ANTI-CLERICALISM'

The way in which the two arguably major constituencies of the Christian church, clergy and laity, relate is a far more complex matter than simple

[1] Anthony Trollope, *Barchester Towers* (Harmondsworth 1987; 1st edn 1857), pp. 46–7.
[2] Charles Kingsley, *Alton Locke*, ed. Elizabeth Cripps (Oxford, 1983; 1st edn 1850), p. 377.
[3] John Selden, *Table Talk of John Selden*, ed. Frederick Pollock (London, 1927), p. 30.

models of 'clericalism' or 'anti-clericalism' will allow.[4] Even in a pre-industrial society, the way clergy and laypeople related was a nuanced and intricate affair: as much about co-operation as competition; independence as dependence; hierarchy as accountability; unearned respect as unwarranted contempt; priestcraft as priesthood.[5] A set liturgy, in this case the Book of Common Prayer, need not be seen only as something imposed 'from above' – as the Cornish rebels had grounds to see it in 1549.[6] Given time, the Prayer Book gained lay supporters who knew perfectly well that a set liturgy actually limited the freedom of a clergyman to fashion the worship of the whole community according to his own particular prejudices or predilections.[7] As this study has demonstrated, members of the laity would use the church courts as a last resort in order to bring their minister into conformity, and to bring about forms of worship which met with their approval.[8]

One final example will have to serve to illustrate this particular point. Ralph Kirk, the Manchester curate whose relationship with his flock was less than ideal, attempted to stop lay people from making the congregational responses in divine service set out in the Book of Common Prayer, by invoking Article 38 of the 1559 Royal Injunctions. It was a misuse of the Injunction which says that: 'no man, woman or child shall be otherwise occupied in the time of service than in quiet attendance to hear, mark and understand that [which] is read, preached, and none other'.[9] The parishioners who drafted the articles against Kirk in 1604 saw this was a spurious

---

[4] It is worth saying 'arguably' here, as it could be reasonably suggested that men and women form the two major constituencies in the church.

[5] In many respects, one of the most thoughtful treatments of the complex relationship between parish clergy and laity that I know remains the unpublished thesis of Jane Freeman. Freeman, 'The parish ministry in the diocese of Durham, c. 1570–1640' (University of Durham Ph.D., 1979).

[6] The Cornish rebels, objecting to the first English Prayer Book, singularly failed to see it as a 'monument of English prose' and strongly resented its imposition:

Item we wil not recyve the newe servye because itt is but lyke a Christmas game, but we wyll have oure olde service of Mattens, masse, Evensong and procession in Latten not in English, as it was before. And so we the Cornyshe men (whereof certen of us understande no Englysh) utterly refuse thys newe Englysh.

'The Demands of the Western Rebels 1549' in Anthony Fletcher, *Tudor Rebellions* (London, 1968; 2nd edn 1973), p. 135. For the 'Reformation from above or below', see Christopher Haigh, 'The recent historiography of the English Reformation', in *The English Reformation Revised*, ed. C. Haigh (Cambridge, 1987). See also above, pp. 1–19.

[7] There is some evidence that the 'vigorous idiom' of the new English Prayer Book influenced the theological content and expression in the preambles of wills as early as Mary's reign. Margaret Cook, 'Eye (Suffolk) in the years of uncertainty, 1520–1570' (University of Keele Ph.D., 1982), pp. 141, 174–5.

[8] See Chapter 2, *passim*.

[9] 1559 Royal Injunctions in W. H. Frere and William Kennedy, eds., *Visitation Articles and Injunctions of the Period of the Reformation*, Alcuin Club 3 vols. (1910), iii, p. 21.

and deliberate misapplication of the Injunctions: 'thereby pretending [they said] . . . to defende his own disordered course in this behalfe'.[10] There is a sense here that the laity too had a responsibility for church discipline and not all priests found that a threatening proposition – at least in theory. George Herbert, the Wiltshire rector, endorsed this view of the responsibility of the laity and the necessity of communication and co-operation between churchwardens and the clergy:

> The countrey parson doth often, both publically and privately, instruct his churchwardens what a great charge lies upon them, and that, indeed, the whole order and discipline of the parish is put into their hands. If . . . [the parson] reform anything, it is out of the overflowing of his conscience; whereas . . . [the churchwardens] are to do so by command and oath . . . Now the canons being the churchwardens' rule, the parson adviseth them to read or hear them read often, as also the visitation articles, which are grounded upon the canons, that so they may know their duty and keep their oath the better.[11]

It was not always the case that members of the clergy and laity lived in enmity, or held divergent and hostile views on such matters. This does not reflect 'clericalism' or 'anti-clericalism', but rather the existence of a 'working relationship' between parish priests and the people, diocesan authorities and the larger flock. Most of the cases cited in this study involve parishioners presenting their parish clergy for various offences, but it was not my intention to present these cases as examples of 'anti-clericalism', or necessarily even as examples of 'anti-puritanism', as it is usually impossible to tell whether the minister's failure to perform lawful ceremonies was the result of negligence or conviction on his part.[12] It is argued here, however, that those who desired the orderly and decent observance of the national Christian religion as laid down in the Book of Common Prayer, including members of the ordinary laity, were sometimes as capable of seeing themselves as part of the church as those 'hotter sort of protestants' whom Patrick Collinson has described as 'not alien to the properly "Anglican" character of the English Church but as equivalent to the most vigorous and successful of religious tendencies within it'.[13]

Further, the hierarchy explicit in an episcopal church polity need not work against lay interests, as has been demonstrated. One can see the attraction of parity for presbyters, if one was a presbyter, but to many members of the laity presbyterianism only promised more clerical control.

---

[10] CRO, EDC.5/1604 (misc.) (Manchester). Kirk and his parishioners are discussed above in Chapter 2.

[11] George Herbert, *The Temple and A Priest to the Temple* (Everyman edn, London, 1908), pp. 269–70.

[12] See above, pp. 70–6.

[13] Patrick Collinson, 'A comment: concerning the name puritan', *JEH* 31:4 (1980), pp. 484, 488 and see above, pp. 8–10.

Bishops, exercising *episkopé* (that is, oversight), could, and were appealed to by lay men and women, in order to bring their parish priest into conformity with the lawful liturgy.[14] Sir Thomas Aston put it vividly when he warned that parity of ministers would only increase the imparity between clergy and laity. The Church of England would gain '9324 potential popes', each ruling without check in the parish, his own 'petty popedom'.[15] Another layman, the author of the widely read *Divine Fancies*, Francis Quarles (1592–1644), put this lay view in poetic form. This member of the laity placed non-conformist clergy under the judgement of Christ, the Great Shepherd, by using the dramatic setting of the Great Assize in the Gospel of Saint Matthew (25.31–end).

> O When our Clergie, at the dreadfull *Day*
> Shal make their Audit; when the *Judge* shal say
> Give your acompts: What, have my Lambs bin fed?
> Say, doe they all stand sound? Is there none dead
> By your defaults? come shephards, bring them forth
> That I may crowne your labours in their worth.

The puritan clergy, who have been deprived because of their scruples over such Prayer Book ceremonies as the surplice and the sign of the cross in the baptismal service, attempt to place the blame on the bishops.

> O what an answer will be given by some,
> We have bin silenc'd: Canons struck us dumbe;
> The Great ones[16] would not let us feed thy flock,
> Unles we plai'd the fooles, and wore a Frock:
> We were forbid unles wee'd yeeld to signe
> And crosse their browes, They say, *a mark of thine.*
> To say the truth, great Iudg, they were not fed,
> Lord, here they be; but Lord, they be all dead.

Quarles' Great Shepherd, however, who endured the ignominy of torture and public crucifixion for the sake of the human race, is not impressed by the tender consciences of non-conformist ministers who cannot bring themselves to wear a surplice for the sake of the people committed to their care.

> Ah cruel Shepheards! Could your conscience serve
> Not to be fooles, and yet to let them sterve?
> What if your Fiery spirits had bin bound
> To Antick Habits; or your heads bin crown'd
> With *Peacock's* Plumes; had yee bin forc'd to feed

---

[14] See above, Chapter 2, *passim*. The order of bishops is one model of *episkopé* in the church, but hardly the only one. For a modern discussion of 'oversight' in the Christian church, see *Baptism, Eucharist and Ministry*, Faith and Order Paper no. 111, World Council of Churches (Geneva, 1982), p. 25.
[15] See above, pp. 166–7.   [16] That is, the bishops.

> Your Saviour's dear-bought Flock in a fool's weed;
> He that was scorn'd, revil'd; endur'd the *Curse*
> Of a base death, in your behalfs; nay worse,
> Swallow'd the cup of wrath charg'd up to th' *brim*,
> Durst yee not stoope to play the fooles for him?[17]

Quarles' poem vividly illustrates one strand of lay thought in post-Reformation England. As we have seen in church court presentations and the petitioning activities for Common Prayer and episcopacy on the eve of the civil war, this is not 'anti-clericalism' but the desire by some laity to have the ministry exercised conscientiously and in conformity with the lawful liturgy.[18]

CONFORMITY AND THE 'GODLY'

We also need to be more critical concerning the 'godly's' assessment of the quality of the religious lives of their conforming neighbours. Non-conformist innovations, as well as conformity to the Book of Common Prayer, could drive people out of the parish church. Petitioners from Manchester in 1604 complained of the curate Ralph Kirk's innovations, 'whereby he hath driven a great number from the service of god'.[19] The 'godly', it must be said, were not always consistent about the 'multitude'. Richard Baxter's description in his autobiographical writings of a religiously and morally lazy Church of England in the 1620–30s should be weighed against another of his descriptions of the religious activities of the people during the Commonwealth.

The profane, ungodly, presumptuous multitude . . . are as zealous for Crosses, and Surplices, Processions and Perambulations, reading of a Gospel at a cross way, the observation of Holidays, and Fasting days, the repeating of the Letany, or the like forms in the Common Prayer, the bowing at the naming of the word Jesus (while they reject his Worship) the receiving of the Sacrament when they have no right to it, and that upon their knees, as if they were more reverent and devout then the true laborious servants of Christ; with a multitude of these things which are onely the tradition of their Fathers; I say, they are as zealous for these, as if eternal life consisted in them.[20]

---

[17] Quarles was for some years secretary to the moderate Archbishop Usher of Armagh. He was certainly no 'Laudian'. Francis Quarles, *The Complete Works in Prose and Verse of Francis Quarles*, ed. Alexander Grosart (3 vols., New York, 1967, repr. of 1880 edn), ii, p. 205. See *DNB*; 'Memorial-Introduction' in ibid., i, pp. ix–xxiv.

[18] See above Chapters 2 and 3.   [19] CRO, EDC.5/1604 misc. (Manchester).

[20] Richard Baxter, *The Saints Everlasting Rest* (1650), pp. 342, 344–334v; *Reliquiae Baxterianae or Mr Richard Baxter's Narrative of the most Memorable Passages of his Life and Times* (London, 1695), pp. 1–3. Baxter's presentation in his autobiography of the Church of England before the civil war is a retrospective and highly polemical work, written after the restoration of the Church of England in the 1660s and concerned to justify his dissent from it. I am grateful to Eamon Duffy for making this point to me.

Near the beginning of this book, I stated that it was my intention to treat religious conformity with the same seriousness that is usually accorded puritanism and non-conformity.[21] I hope that has been achieved if nothing else. Even critics of the Church of England sometimes acknowledged the existence of enthusiasm for its worship and corporate liturgical life, however misguided they felt it to be. The time has come for historians of the Tudor–Stuart church to acknowledge it as well. Whether the enthusiasm of conformists was misplaced or not is a question, I would suggest, which deserves far greater even-handedness than it has largely received heretofore. Familiarity does not always breed contempt: it may nurture devotion.

A RESTORATION POSTSCRIPT: CONFORMITY AND 'ANGLICANISM'

In 1681, at a time of intense political and religious crisis, Sir Thomas Aston's 1642 tract *A Collection of Sundry Petitions* was republished. Its robust defence of the Prayer Book and episcopacy, presented as a 'middle way' between the excesses of Laudianism and presbyterian puritanism, was co-opted into a context nearly forty years later in which elements within the Church of England felt themselves again to be in a two-front war – this time between popery and dissent. Once again, as in the period of the Personal Rule and the early days of the Long Parliament, royal policy itself was undermining what many felt should be a natural affinity between the Church of England and the crown. In reality, however, after the first Stuart, James I, one might say conformists did not have another Stuart monarch deserving their loyalty until the last one, Queen Anne. Nearly four decades after the outbreak of the civil war, the threat was perceived not in attempts to redefine the practices and the doctrines of the church as under Charles I, but in Charles II's manoeuvres to lighten penalties on his Nonconformist and Roman Catholic subjects, his pressure on the established church for greater comprehension, and his resistance to the exclusion from the succession of his brother the duke of York, a Roman Catholic suspected of absolutist preferences. As John Spurr has noted: 'for all the talk of Moses and Aaron, ministry and magistracy, alliance of altar and sword, the Church of England did not enjoy the committed support of the governors of England in the 1660s'.[22] The 1670s had seen a rise of anxiety about Romanism unparalleled since the early 1640s. Attempts by some Anglicans of latitudinarian leanings to woo protestant dissenters back into the fold in

---

[21] Above, p. 2.
[22] John Spurr, *The Restoration Church of England, 1646–1689* (New Haven, 1991), p. 59.

order to strengthen the established church's hand against popery alarmed some Tory Anglicans.[23] In their minds, such moves would have the opposite result and weaken the Church of England in its struggle with Rome by undermining the two most distinctive and defining features of the Anglican Church, the Prayer Book and episcopacy.[24] They knew, of necessity, that liturgy and polity had to be at the top of any agenda for greater ecclesial comprehension.[25] The conformist rhetoric compiled by Sir Thomas, the man long since buried in Aston Chapel after his death in a parliamentary prison, was useful again in the cause of the established church. Those responsible for the republication made this clear by adding to the title page of the 1681 edition that it was 'Printed and Published by the Kings Special Command in the year 1642 and now again published to precaution the ill-meaning Zealots of this Age.'[26] Once again, the Church of England was perceived as 'in danger' not only from outside, but from elements within which did not properly value its defining characteristics: a reformed episcopate and the Book of Common Prayer.[27]

In 1662 the experiment with privatization and free market Christianity (excluding 'popery or prelacy') was ended and the Church of England was restored, if not to its former powers, at least to its national monopoly on the Christian faith.[28] It was not to last and not only because of the resolve

---

[23] Ibid., pp. 63–7. Spurr's book is one of the most important new interpretations on the origins and development of Anglicanism to be written in a long time.

[24] Neither, of course, like the monarchy itself, was the church 'restored' exactly in the pre-civil war form. Ronald Hutton, *The Restoration: a political and religious history of England and Wales 1658–1667* (Oxford, 1985), p. 155. It worth noting that not only members of the established church perceived a danger. Some dissenters were troubled by the Declaration of Indulgence because it granted rights to Roman Catholics as well. Oliver Heywood admitted that the Declaration was a 'cause of grief that papists and atheists [should] enjoy so much liberty'. For some members of the Free Churches, it was simply too high a price to pay. Cited in Spurr, *Restoration Church*, p. 62.

[25] See for example, Timothy J. Fawcett, *The Liturgy of Comprehension, 1689: an abortive attempt to revise the Book of Common Prayer*, Alcuin Club Collections, 54 (1973).

[26] Sir Thomas Aston, *A Collection of Sundry Petitions* (London, 1681 edn).

[27] The debate within the Church of England over the degree of compromise which might bring dissenters back in the established church continued into the eighteenth century. See the excellent essay 'Introduction: the church and Anglicanism in the "long" eighteenth century' by John Walsh and Stephen Taylor in *The Church of England c. 1689–1833*, ed. John Walsh, *et al.* (Cambridge, 1993).

[28] See 'The Instrument of Government 1653' in S. R. Gardiner, ed., *The Constitutional Documents of the Puritan Revolution 1625–1660* (3rd edn, Oxford, 1906), p. 416. The coercive powers of the 'restored' church were reduced, as was its ability to act semi-independently of parliament. The controversy over the legality of the 1640 Canons, which had been passed by convocation but not parliament, was in a sense finally resolved in the Restoration Settlement. The Church of England lost its right to make canons without parliamentary approval. Although modified by subsequent acts of parliament, most significantly the Enabling Act of 1919, this remains the situation to this day. J. P. Kenyon, *The Stuart Constitution: documents and commentary* (Cambridge, 1966), pp. 361–86; E. R. Norman, *Church and Society in England 1770–1970* (Oxford, 1976), pp. 272–5.

and commitment of Christian dissenters. Committed members of the 'restored' Church of England had been changed forever by their experiences of persecution, marginalization and the tactical quietism necessitated by the civil war and Commonwealth.[29] There was no going back to the Jacobean consensus.[30]

There were ironies as well, for although the restored church was not a posthumous victory for Archbishop Laud, members of the established church began to define themselves less broadly. In short, they became 'Anglicans'. The series of penal laws enacted against dissenters in the 1660s and 1670s, reveal more of a desire for retribution by the Tory Anglican squirearchy and clergy for the sufferings of the Commonwealth, than any real hope of creating a truly national church by the successful suppression of dissent. Ivan Roots' analysis of the the political side of the Settlement is apposite for its religious aspects as well: 'there was only a smear of blood at the Restoration, but a whole streak of meanness'.[31] Archbishop Laud may have narrowed the bands of conformity but he brooked no opt-out clause; under Archbishop Sheldon, nonconformists could opt-out at a price, thus giving post-1662 Anglicans the room to define themselves *less* broadly than conformists could do under Elizabeth and James. The will to return to a Hookerian ideal of a national church in which Christian allegiance was no more a matter of choice for individuals than their citizenship was gone for good, destroyed forever by the experiences of 1642–60. The Toleration Act sealed this process. In 1689 a *national* church was finally replaced by the more pragmatic idea of an *established* church: one tradition of Christianity enjoying special privileges, while dissenters, though not banned, paid the price for their opting out and for their political radicalism in the 1640s and 1650s, by living under a series of laws which circumscribed (for men chiefly, of course) their participation in the political and educational life of their country. By the end of the next century, the people of England could choose from an extraordinary range of Christian and other religious expressions which, despite establishment, made the society more akin to America than much of the rest of Europe.[32]

For a twentieth-century example (1928–29) of parliament rejecting an attempt by the established church to change its liturgy see Andrian Hastings, *A History of English Christianity 1920–1985* (London, 1986), pp. 204–9.

[29] The experience of 'Anglicans' during this period of marginalization and persecution is worthy of a major study. John Spurr, however, makes important connections between the 1646–60 period and the shape the restored Church of England took.

[30] Interesting to note, however, that even after 1662 the rhetoric of appealing to the 'church of Elizabeth and James' was still being used. See above, pp. 126–7 and Spurr, *Restoration Church*, pp. 19, 37.

[31] Ivan Roots, *The Great Rebellion 1642–1660* (London, 1966), p. 261. I am grateful to Sam Thomas for his assistance with this citation.

[32] 'For a while the established churches in Britain [i.e. the Church of England and the Church

Readers may have noticed that the word 'Anglican' has been used more in the past few pages than in all of the previous chapters.[33] At this point I may venture to use the word with more confidence and with less resort to quotation marks. For Anglicanism, in any sense which we might understand it now, owes more to the Restoration than the Reformation.[34] Ironically, Richard Hooker's standing as a sort of Thomas Aquinas of Anglicanism owes much to the use to which he was put in post-1660 period, as Tory Anglicans sought to define their religious tradition in ways distinct from protestant dissent. The choice of the layman, Izaak Walton, to write the *Lives* of Hooker, Donne, Sanderson, Herbert, and Wootton has done more than Richard Hooker's *Lawes* to define the Anglican identity before the civil war by writing out of the story the puritan voices which were as much a part of the *Ecclesia Anglicana* as Prayer Book conformity.[35] Defining boundaries is a way of excluding as well as including: one might almost say that the period from the Restoration to 1689 was Anglicanism's Council of Trent. Once the Church of England could no longer claim to

---

of Scotland] were comparable to those in Europe; there was also, as in America, an array of competing independent denominations.' James Obelkevich, 'Religion', in *The Cambridge Social History of Britain 1750–1950*, ed. F. M. L. Thompson (Cambridge, 1990), p. 311 and *passim*.

[33] See above, Chapter 1 for a fuller discussion of the reasons and the historiography.

[34] See Spurr, *Restoration Church*, pp. 1–28. Or, as Spurr would have it, the critical transition begins in the experience of abolition and persecution in the period 1646–60.

[35] Jessica Martin has produced a fascinating and important study of Izaak Walton as a fashioner of Anglican identity. It is noteworthy that Walton's *Life* of Hooker was commissioned after the Restoration, intended partly to discredit the notion of Hooker's authorship of the controversial later books of the *Lawes*. See her 'Izaak Walton and his precursors: a literary study of the emergence of the ecclesiastical *Life*' (University of Cambridge Ph.D., 1993), especially her comments on Walton and Hooker, pp. 303–9 and ch. 6, *passim*.

   To illustrate this point further, contrast the collections of primary sources both published by the Anglican publishing house SPCK, the recent *The Anglican Tradition* and the older collection *Anglicanism*. The elderly More and Cross, *Anglicanism*, compiled before the explosion of scholarship on the early Stuart church presents a much fuller picture of the pluralism of the Church of England in the seventeenth century, by including authors like Richard Baxter and other 'puritans'. Published only in 1991, Evans and Wright's *The Anglican Tradition* chose a narrower and more uniform range of authors, in which Hooker is by far their most popular choice, thus defining 'Anglicanism' in a way that would have not been recognized by many contemporaries of the Elizabethan and early Stuart period. *The Anglican Tradition: a handbook of sources*, ed. G. R. Evans and J. Robert Wright (London, 1991), esp. ch. 5; *Anglicanism: the thought and practice of the Church of England, illustrated from the religious literature of the seventeenth century*, ed. P. E. More and F. L. Cross (London, 1935, repr. 1951). It is telling that in some recent semi-official Anglican attempts to define the tradition, Prayer Book conformity has simply been absorbed into Laudianism – the Laudians becoming the defence against aggressive puritanism, rather than a probable cause of the Church of England's undoing in the middle of the seventeenth century. See William P. Haugaard, 'From the Reformation to the eighteenth century', in *The Study of Anglicanism*, ed. Stephen Sykes and John Booty (London, 1988), pp. 19–20.

have the allegiance of every man and woman in the kingdom, it was free to define itself more clearly, in so far as clarity has ever been an Anglican virtue.

Further, colonial expansion necessitated greater self-definition as transplanted Anglicanism left establishment and monarchy behind. The transition of colonial Anglicanism into the Episcopal Church in the United States, with a modified Prayer Book, demonstrates that the crown and establishment are not Anglicanism's most distinctive features.[36] At the end of the twentieth century, the vast majority of practising Anglicans live not only outside England, but outside the United Kingdom. A recent study has revealed that the 'typical' communicant Anglican is African, female, and does not speak English as a first language.[37] Without a doubt, the Anglican bishop of the greatest stature this century has not occupied the see of Canterbury, but that of Cape Town. In common with every other religious tradition, Anglicanism has not remained static, but has changed and developed. Like Methodism, one might suggest that it has been more successful as an export for overseas than at home. In England it struggles to come to terms with the end of its monopoly and most of its privileges, yet burdened by an establishment and an ambiguous and double-edged set of public expectations unknown anywhere else in the Anglican Communion. The religious traditionalists at the heart of this book, Prayer Book conformists before the civil war, changed by the persecutions of the Commonwealth, helped to shape the course of Anglicanism after the Restoration. They provide the strand of continuity back before 1642 – but before 1642 they did not comprise the whole of the *Ecclesia Anglicana*. Those who now find the degree of pluralism in the Church of England too great, should note that it was once even greater.

[36] J. F. Wolverton, *Colonial Anglicanism in North America* (Detroit, 1984); Frederick V. Mills, *Bishops By Ballot: an eighteenth-century ecclesiastical revolution* (New York, 1978); Peter Doll, 'The idea of the primitive church in High Church ecclesiology from Samuel Johnson and J. H. Horbart', *Anglican and Episcopal* 65:1 (1996).

[37] Based on figures gathered by the Anglican Communion Office, Partnership House, London. I am grateful to Donald Anderson of the Anglican Communion Office for supplying this information.

Appendix 1: Petitions for the Book of Common Prayer and episcopacy, 1640–1642[1]

1640

Hertfordshire[2]
Date: 18 April 1640.
Text: BL, Harl. MS 4931, fols. 42–42v; Esther Cope, ed., *Proceedings of the Short Parliament of 1640*, Camden Fourth Series, xix (1977), pp. 277–8.
Content: for the Book of Common Prayer.
Addressed: to the Commons.
Diocese/bishop: London/William Juxon cons. October 1633 – trans. Canterbury, September 1660.

1641

Bedfordshire
Date: January 1641.
Text: PRO, SP16 476.[3]
Content: episcopacy and the Book of Common Prayer.
Subscriptions claimed: unknown.
Addressed: to parliament.
Diocese/bishop:[4] Lincoln/John Williams cons. November 1621 – trans.

---

[1] I am preparing for publication the complete texts of these petitions for a forthcoming miscellany of the Church of England Record Society.

[2] It is ironic to note that Sir Thomas Aston's diary of the Short Parliament, by far the longest and most detailed, and despite the baronet's central role in organizing and collating petitions for bishops and the liturgy in the Long Parliament, fails to mention this petition. Judith Maltby, ed., *The Short Parliament (1640) Diary of Sir Thomas Aston*, Camden Fourth Series, xxxv (1988).

[3] An abstract of the manuscript is in *CSPD 1640–41*, pp. 445–6.

[4] Dates for episcopates come from F. D. Powicke and E. B. Fryde, *Handbook of British Chronology* (London, 1961). Counties have been placed in the diocese in which most of the county is located.

York December 1641; Thomas Winniffe cons. February 1642 – d. September 1654.

Cheshire (1)
Date: presented to parliament in late February 1641.
Text: HLRO, Main Papers, HL, [27] February 1640/1; Aston, *Collection*, pp. 1–4; BL, Thomason Tracts 669f.4(8); PRO, SP16/479 (*CSPD*, 1640–41, p. 458); Nalson, *Impartial Collection*, ii, pp. 759–61. There are two printed copies of the petition with Aston's marginal notes in the Aston Lodge Manuscripts.
Content: for episcopacy.
Subscriptions claimed: 4 noblemen; 80 knights, baronets, and esquires; 70 divines; and 6,000 freeholders.
Addressed: to parliament.
Diocese/bishop: Chester/John Bridgeman cons. May 1619 – d. 1652.

London and Westminster
Date: uncertain, but published with Cheshire's first pro-church petition which is dated 27 February 1641.
Text: CUL, Syn. 7.59.30(10).[5]
Content: for episcopacy.
Subscriptions claimed: 'Which is the humble suit of Ten thousand thousand.'
Addressed: to the Commons.
Diocese/bishop: London/William Juxon cons. October 1633 – trans. Canterbury, September 1660.

Devon[6]
Date: late winter/early 1641.
Text: Aston, *Collection*, pp. 40–1.
Content: for episcopacy.
Subscribers claimed: 8,000.
Addressed: to the Lords.
Diocese/bishop: Exeter/Joseph Hall cons. December 1627 – trans. Norwich, December 1641; Ralph Brownrigg cons. May 1642 – d. 1659.

Oxfordshire
Date: drafted probably after May 1641.
Text: Aston, *Collection*, pp. 62–4.

[5] A printed copy of the petition published with Cheshire's episcopacy petition. This is the only copy of the petition I have found.
[6] These petitioners also describe themselves as persons 'within the Diocesse of Exeter'.

Content: for episcopacy and the Book of Common Prayer.
Subscriptions claimed: unknown.
Addressed: to the Commons.
Diocese/bishop: Oxford/John Bancroft cons. October 1632 – d. February 1641; Robert Skinner trans. Bristol, December 1641 – trans. Worcester, November 1663.

Essex
Date: uncertain, but produced after the Protestation Oath (May 1641).[7]
Text: Leicestershire RO, Acc. No. DE221/13/2/26.[8]
Content: for the Book of Common Prayer.
Subscriptions claimed: unknown.
Addressed: to the king.
Diocese/bishop: London/William Juxon cons. October 1633 – trans. Canterbury, September 1660.

Rutland
Date: 18 November 1641.
Text: Nalson, *Impartial Collection*, ii, pp. 656–60; Aston, *Collection*, pp. 24–33.
Content: for episcopacy.
Subscriptions claimed: 800 knights, justices, gentry, and free-holders; 40 clergy.[9]
Addressed: to parliament.
Diocese/bishop: Peterborough/Francis Dee cons. May 1634 – d. October 1638; John Towers cons. January 1639 – d. January 1649.

Worcestershire
Date: November–December 1641.
Text: Henry Townshend, *Diary of Henry Townshend of Elmley Lovett 1640–1663*, ed. J. W. Willis Bund, Worcestershire Historical Society (part ii, 1916), pp. 44–6.
Content: for episcopacy and the Book of Common Prayer.
Subscriptions claimed: 835 names from 16 parishes.[10]

---

[7] Although the Protestation was not printed and dispersed around the country until January 1642, it was circulated in manuscript and subscribed in many places prior to parliament's formal order. David Cressy, *Literacy and the Social Order; Reading and Writing in Tudor and Stuart England* (Cambridge, 1980), pp. 66–7.

[8] There are two versions of the petition, one of which appears to be a rough draft for the other. I am grateful to John Walter for this reference.

[9] Nalson gives these figures as estimates. John Nalson, *An Impartial Collection of the Great Affairs of State* (2 vols., London, 1682), ii, p. 660.

[10] Willis Bund lists the parishes and numbers of subscribers for each. See Henry Townshend,

Addressed: to the king and parliament.
Diocese/bishop: Worcester/John Thornborough trans. Bristol, February 1617 – d. July 1641; John Prideaux cons. December 1641 – d. July 1650.

Shropshire[11]
Date: after 10 December 1641.
Text: Nottingham University Library PW2/HY/173.
Content: for episcopacy and the Book of Common Prayer.
Subscriptions claimed: unknown.
Addressed: to king and parliament.
Diocese/bishop: Hereford/George Coke trans. Bristol, July 1636 – d. December 1646. Worcester/John Thornborough trans. Bristol, January 1617 – d. July 1641; John Prideaux cons. December 1641 – d. July 1650.

Dorset
Date: drafted November–December 1641.
Text: BL, Add. MS 29975, fol. 130.
Content: episcopacy and the Book of Common Prayer.
Subscribers claimed: unknown.
Addressed: to parliament.
Diocese/bishop: Bristol/Robert Skinner cons. January 1637 – trans. Oxford, December 1641; Thomas Westfield cons. April 1642 – d. June 1644.

Huntingdonshire
Date: delivered to the Lords 8 December 1641.
Text: HLRO, Parchment Coll., HL, 8 Dec. 1641; Nalson, *Impartial Collection*, ii, pp. 720–2; Aston, *Collection*, pp. 15–20.
Content: for episcopacy and the Book of Common Prayer.
Subscriptions claimed: roughly 2,000 hands in manuscript.
Addressed: to the Lords and Commons.[12]
Diocese/bishop: Lincoln/John Williams cons. November 1621 – trans. York, December 1641; Thomas Winniffe cons. February 1642 – d. September 1654.

Diary of Henry Townshend of Elmley Lovett 1640–1663, ed., J. W. Willis Bund (3 vols., Worcestershire Historical Society, 1916, 1917, 1920), ii, p. 46.

[11] The petition refers to the king's proclamation on religion of 10 December 1641, so it must have been produced after that date. No number of subscribers is given, but it must have had enough support to spark an anti-episcopacy petition from the county. BL, Loan MS 29/123/ Misc. 37. The petition is similar in places to Worcestershire's petition for the church and the Cheshire petition for the Book of Common Prayer. I am grateful to Paul Gladwish for the manuscript references.

[12] 'Presented to the House of Peeres by the Lord Privy Seale the 8 of December, 1641.' Thomas Aston, *A Collection of Sundry Petitions Presented to the Kings Most Excellent Majestie* (n.p., 1642), p. 15.

Somerset
Date: presented to parliament 10 December 1641.
Text: HLRO, Parchment Coll., HL, 10 December 1641; Nalson, *Impartial Collection*, ii, pp. 726–27; Aston, *Collection*, pp. 21–23.
Content: for episcopacy and the Book of Common Prayer.
Subscriptions claimed: 200 knights; 221 divines; 14,350 in all.[13]
Addressed: to parliament.[14]
Diocese/bishop: Bath and Wells/William Piers trans. Peterborough, December 1632 – d. April 1670.

Nottinghamshire
Date: presented to parliament 15 December 1641.
Text: Aston, *Collection*, p. 13–14.[15]
Content: for episcopacy and the Book of Common Prayer.
Subscriptions claimed: 1 viscount, 5 knights, 'above a hundred Gentlemen of quality, all the clergy of the County, and above six thousand commoners, being all of them communicants'.
Addressed: to the Commons.
Diocese/bishop: York/Richard Neile trans. Winchester March 1632 – d. October 1640; John Williams trans. Lincoln, December 1641 – d. March 1650.

Cheshire (2)
Date: presented to parliament 20 December 1641.
Text: HLRO, Main Papers, HL, 20 Dec. 1641; BL, Add. MS 36913, fol. 55; Nalson, *Impartial Collection*, ii, pp. 758–9; Aston, *Collection*, pp. 34–6; BL, Thomason Tracts E.669f.4(74).
Content: for the Book of Common Prayer.
Subscriptions claimed: 94 by lords, knights, JPs and Esquires; 440 by gentlemen of quality; 86 by divines; 8,936 by free-holders and others.
Addressed: to the king, Lords and Commons.
Diocese/bishop: Chester/John Bridgeman cons. May 1619 – d. 1652.

Gloucestershire
Date: drafted December 1641.

---

[13] '*Knights, Esquires, Divines, Gentlemen, Free-holders, Inhabitants of the County of* Somerset, *none of them Papists; but all Protestants of the Church of* England, *and his Majesties Loyal Subjects*'. Nalson, *Impartial Collection*, ii, p. 727.
[14] 'Delivered to the *House of Peers*, by the Lord Marquesse Hartford, the 10 of December, 1641.' Nalson, *Impartial Collection*, ii, p. 726.
[15] The manuscript is in the Nottingham Free Library; Sir Simonds D'Ewes, *The Journal of Sir Simonds D'Ewes*, ed. W. H. Coates (New Haven, 1942), p. 290.

Text: BL, Add. MS 11055, fols. 130v–131.[16]
Content: for episcopacy and the Book of Common Prayer.
Subscriptions claimed: 10 JPs.[17]
Addressed: to parliament.
Diocese/bishop: Gloucester/Godfrey Goodman cons. March 1625 – depr. 1640 (d. January 1656).[18]

1642

Herefordshire
Date: drafted January 1642.
Text: Aston, *Collection*, pp. 69–70; John Webb, *Memorials of the Civil War* (2 vols., London, 1879), ii, pp. 337–8.[19]
Content: for episcopacy and the Book of Common Prayer.
Subscriptions claimed: 68 knights, esquires, and 'Gentlemen of Quality'; 8 doctors; 150 'Ministers of good repute'; 3,600 freeholders and inhabitants of the county, a total of 3,826.[20]
Addressed: to Lords and Commons.
Diocese/bishop: Hereford/George Coke trans. Bristol, July 1636 – d. December 1646.

Staffordshire
Date: probably drafted shortly after the Herefordshire petition.[21]
Texts: Aston, *Collection*, pp. 42–3.
Content: for episcopacy and the Book of Common Prayer.
Subscriptions claimed: 3,000 'of the best quality of the County'.
Addressed: to the Lords and Commons.
Diocese/bishop: Lichfield/Robert Wright trans. Bristol, November 1632 – d. August 1643.

North Wales (Flint, Denbigh, Montgomery, Caernarvon, Anglesey, Merioneth)

[16] See also supporting letter, GRO, D2510/13.
[17] The names of the same ten JPs which appear on the petition, appear on the letter of support. GRO, D2510/13. No schedule of subscriptions appears to be extant.
[18] According to *The Handbook of British Chronology* no successor to Goodman was appointed until the Restoration.
[19] The Herefordshire petition was further supported by a *Declaration or Resolution of the Countie of Hereford*. See Webb, *Memorials of the Civil War*, ii, pp. 343–4.
[20] According to the *Muster Books of the Clergie of the Diocese of Hereford* taken in October 1608 among the Scudamore Manuscripts, there was a total of 147 clergy including the bishop and the cathedral clergy, but this did not include the Shropshire archdeaconry. John Webb, *Memorials of the Civil War* (2 vols., London, 1879), i, pp. 44–5.
[21] The Herefordshire and Staffordshire petitions are textually similar.

Date: claims it was presented to parliament 5 March 1642.
Text: Aston, *Collection*, pp. 47–50.
Content: for episcopacy and the Book of Common Prayer.
Subscriptions claimed: 30,000 hands.
Addressed: to the Commons.
Diocese(s)/bishop(s): Bangor/William Roberts cons. September 1637 – d. August 1665. St Asaph/John Owens cons. September 1629 – d. October 1651.

Kent

1. *Date:* possibly produced between September and November 1641.[22]
Text: Larking, *Proceedings in Kent*, pp. 60–4; BL, Stowe MS 744, fol. 13; BL, Add. MS 26785, fols. 49–50.
Content: for episcopacy and the Book of Common Prayer.
Subscriptions claimed: 168 subscribers (44 gentlemen, 6 clergy, 63 free-holders, 48 freemen of the Port of Dover, 7 subsidie-men).[23]
Addressed: to the Commons.
2. *Date:* major petition, late March 1642.
Text: HLRO, Main Papers, HL, 28 March 1642; *LJ*, iv, pp. 677–8; BL, Thomason Tracts E.142(10).
Content: for episcopacy and the Book of Common Prayer.[24]
Subscriptions claimed: unknown.
Addressed: to the Commons.
3. *Date:* before May 1642.
Text: Aston, *Collection*, pp. 44–6.[25]
Content: for episcopacy and the Book of Common Prayer.
Subscriptions claimed: 24 baronets and knights, 'above' 300 esquires and gentlemen 'of note'; 108 divines; 800 freeholders and subsidy men.[26]
Diocese/bishop: Canterbury/William Laud trans. London, September 1633 – d. January 1645. Rochester/John Warner cons. January 1638 – d. October 1666.

---

[22] See *Proceedings in Kent*, ed. L. B. Larking, Camden Series, lxxx (1862), p. 61.
[23] Ibid., pp. 62–4.
[24] Many other grievances are raised as well. *LJ*, iv, pp. 677–8.
[25] Of the three Kentish pro-church petitions I have identified, this one from the diocese of Canterbury is the most elusive in its genesis. Judith Maltby, 'Approaches to the study of religious conformity in late Elizabethan and Early Stuart England: with special reference to Cheshire and the diocese of Lincoln' (University of Cambridge Ph.D., 1991), p. 173.
[26] Over 1,232 subscribers claimed in total 'all within the Diocese of Canterbury'. Identification with an ecclesiastical, as opposed to a secular unit of government is unusual in these petitions for the Church of England. See also Devon and Herefordshire.

Cornwall
1. *Date:* 22 May 1642.
Text: Aston, *Collection,* pp. 55–6; BL, Thomason Tracts E.150(28).
Content: against the flood of seditious petitions and for a reconciliation of king and parliament.
Subscriptions claimed: unknown.[27]
Addressed: to the king.
2. *Date:* May–June 1642.
Text: Aston, *Collection,* pp. 65–8; BL, Thomason Tracts E. 669f.4(70), E. 150(28).
Content: for episcopacy and the Book of Common Prayer.
Subscriptions claimed: unknown.
Addressed: to parliament
3. *Date:* before June 1642.
Text: in Aston, *Collection* in BL, Thomason Tracts E. 150(28).
Content: for episcopacy and the Book of Common Prayer.
Subscriptions claimed: unknown.
Addressed: to the Commons.
Diocese/bishop: Exeter/Joseph Hall cons. December 1627 – trans. Norwich, December 1641; Ralph Brownrigg cons. May 1642 – d. 1659.

Surrey
Date: 12 June 1642.
Text: BL, Thomason Tracts E. 151(11).
Content: for episcopacy.
Subscribers claimed: unknown.
Addressed: to parliament.
Diocese/bishop: Winchester/Walter Curle trans. Bath and Wells, November 1632 – d. 1647.

Southwark ('Burrough of . . . and other places near adjacent')
Date: 12 June 1642.
Text: BL, Thomason Tracts E. 151(11).
Content: chiefly for the Book of Common Prayer.
Subscribers claimed: 428 subscribers.[28]
Addressed: to Lords and Commons.

---

[27] 'Wee the Petitioners to this Petition, doe constitute, and appoint Peter Courtney, Walter Langdon, Benatus Bellot, and Nevill Bligh, Esquires to deliver this Petition in the name of the county of Cornwall, to his sacred Majesty.'
[28] 'Subscribed by the Knights, Justices of the Peace, and Gentlemen, and Freeholders at the quarter Sessions, for the County of Surrey, and after by the chiefe Inhabitants of the Borough of Southwarke, and the parts adjacent, in which Boroughs, and adjacent parts,

Diocese/bishop: Winchester/Walter Curle trans. Bath and Wells, November 1632 – d. 1647.

PRODUCED BEFORE MAY 1642

Texts of petitions that are difficult to date but appear in Aston's *Collection*, so therefore were produced before May 1642

Lancashire
Date: after July 1641 but before May–June 1642.
Text: Aston, *Collection*, pp. 51–4.
Content: chiefly for the Book of Common Prayer.
Subscriptions claimed: unknown.[29]
Addressed: to the king.
Diocese/bishop: Chester/John Bridgeman cons. May 1619 – d. 1652.

The Universities, Colleges, and Halls
1. *University of Oxford*
Date: 22 June 1641
Text: Aston, *Collection*, pp. 5–8; Nalson, *Impartial Collection*, ii, pp. 305–7.
Content: for episcopacy.
Subscriptions claimed: unknown
Addressed: to parliament
Diocese/bishop: Oxford/John Bancroft cons. October 1632 – d. February 1641; Robert Skinner trans. Bristol, December 1641 – trans. Worcester, November 1663.
2. *University of Cambridge*[30]
Date: April 1641.
Text: Aston, *Collection*, pp. 9–12.
Content: in defence of cathedral foundations and learning.
Subscriptions claimed: unknown.
Addressed: to the Commons.
Diocese/bishop: Ely/Matthew Wren trans. Norwich, April 1638 – d. April 1667.

---

besides other parts of the whole County did Subscribe. Knights, 13. Esquires, 15. Divines, 18. Gentlemen, Freeholders, and other of good account, 382.'

[29] However, a 1642 edition of Aston's *Collection* which belonged to Thomas Barlow of Queen's College, Oxford has the following marginal note: 'Presented by the sheriff of the County Jun: 2d 1642. Attested by knights and Esq: – 64, Gentlemen – 740, Divines – 55, Freeholders – 7000', Bodl., C13, 15 Linc.

[30] With Latin preface.

3. 'Colledges and **Halls,** and others, well-wishers to Piety and Learning, throughout the Kingdome of England'
Date: before May 1642
Text: Aston, *Collection,* pp. 37–9.
Content: for episcopacy and the Book of Common Prayer.
Subscriptions claimed: unknown.[31]
Addressed: to king and parliament.

PETITIONS WITHOUT EXTANT TEXTS

Places for which no text is extant but where there is evidence of pro-church petitioning activity.

Suffolk
Date: activity in early autumn 1641.
Alleged content: for episcopacy.
Source: The Suffolk Committee for Scandalous Ministers 1644–1646, ed. Clive Holmes, Suffolk Record Society (1970); BL, Tanner MS 66, fol. 181.
Diocese/bishop: Norwich/Richard Montague trans. Chichester May 1638 – d. April 1641; Joseph Hall trans. Exeter, December 1641 – d. September 1656.

Lincolnshire
Date: no date but produced after the Root and Branch petition in May 1641.
Alleged content: for episcopacy.
Source: J. W. F. Hill, 'The Royalist Clergy of Lincolnshire', Lincolnshire Architectural and Archaeological Society, Reports and Papers, new ser. 2 (1940).
Diocese/bishop: Lincoln/John Williams cons. November 1621 – trans. York, December 1641; Thomas Winniffe cons. February 1642 – d. September 1654.

---

[31] But the petition for Colleges and Halls also claimed subscriptions *'generally by all the* Doctors, Masters, *and* Batchelors *of all Degrees and Faculties in the Universitie of* Oxford; *And by very many other Persons of Quality:* Baronets, Knights, Esquires, Ministers *and* Gentlemen, *within the Counties of* Oxford, Berks, Wilts, South-hampton, Dorset, Kent, Surrey, Westmerland [*sic*], Cumberland, *and other shires'.*

Appendix 2: Subscribing Cheshire parishes and townships, 1641

Appendix 2 lists the localities it has been possible to identify as subscribing to the Cheshire petition in support of the Book of Common Prayer. They are arranged alphabetically by hundred. Parishes or townships, which belong to more than one hundred have been consigned to the hundred containing the township with the parish church. (It should be noted that most Cheshire parishes were geographically large and covered many townships.) These parishes and townships are then compared to a series of other sources (as discussed in Chapter 5), including 'additional material' which may throw light on the social and economic status of some subscribers, for example, receipts of church rates or pew plans. The identification of some places is not always certain because of the nature of the documents.

A2.1 *Broxton Hundred*

Parish	BCP petition[1]	Episcopacy petition[2]	Additional material	Subsidy[3]
Alford	+	+	−	+
? St Mary, C.	+	−	+[4]	−
? St Oswald, C.	+	−	−	−
Christleton	+	+	−	+
Dodleston	+	−	−	+
Eccleston	−	−	+[5]	+
Farndon	+	Crewe-by-Farndon (Farndon Parish)	−	+
Guilden Sutton	+	−	−	+
Harthill (and/or Malpas)	+	−	−	+
Malpas (and/or Harthill)	+	+	−	+
Bickerton	+	−	−	+
? Plemstall	+	−	−	
Pulford	+	−	−	+
Shocklach	+	?+	−	+
Tilston	+	+	+[6]	+
Waverton (and Guilden Sutton)	+	−	−	+

Sources: 1. HLRO, Main Papers, HL, 20 December 1641.
2. HLRO, Main Papers, HL [27] February 1640/1.
3. PRO, E179/85/135; PRO, E179/85/131.
4. Receipts for pews. CRO, P20/3/1
5. Church rate, 1641. CRO, P20/3/1.
6. Churchwardens' accounts. CRO, P18/3608. These accounts include receipts for a church ley for 1641 as well as a list 'of the poore that Received money uppon Good Friday, 1641'.

Appendix 2

A2.2 *Bucklow Hundred*

Parish	BCP petition	Episcopacy petition	Additional material	Subsidy[1]
Gr. Budworth (principally in Bucklow Hundred)	+	−	−	+
? Knutsford (or Great Budworth?)	+	−	−	+
Lymm	−	−	+[2]	+
Mobberley	+	−	−	+
Runcorn	+		−	
Aston Grange	+	+	−	+
Aston-by-Sutton	+	+	−	+
? Halton	+	?−	−	+

Sources: 1. CRO, DLT/B11, pp. 35–41.
2. Mizebook, 1643. CRO, P119/2924/9/1.

A2.3 *City of Chester*

Parish	BCP petition	Episcopacy petition	Additional material	Subsidy
St Bridget	+	?−	−	−
St John the Baptist	+	?−	+[1]	−
St Michael	+	?−	+[2]	−
St Peter	−	?−	+[3]	−
Holy Trinity	+	?−	+[4]	−

Sources: 1. Easter Book, 1642, CCRO, CR65/39.
2. Assessment for payment of minister and clerk's wages, 1640–1, 1641–2. CRO, P65/8/1
3. Assessment, 1641. CRO, P63/7/1.
4. Assessment for the poor, 1641 and receipts for seats, 1641. CRO, P51/12/1.

A2.4 *Eddisbury Hundred*

Parish	BCP petition	Episcopacy petition	Additional material	Subsidy[1]
Frodsham	+	+	+[2]	−
? Little Budworth	+	−	−	−
Over	+	−	−	−
Weaverham	−	−	+[3]	−
Whitegate	+	−	−	−

Sources: 1. PRO, E179/85/134 simply lists places and total contributions. PRO, E179/85/138 is virtually illegible.
2. Church rate, 1640/1, CRO, P8/13/2; Pew list, 1637, CRO, P8/4/3.
3. Church rate, 1640. Churchwardens' accounts, Weaverham Parish Church, Cheshire.

A2.5 *Macclesfield Hundred*

Parish	BCP petition	Episcopacy petition	Additional material	Subsidy[1]
Alderley	+	−	−	+
Cheadle	+	?+	−	+
Gawsworth	+	−	−	+
Prestbury	+		+[2]	
Aldington	+			+
Poynton	+			+
Prestbury	+			+
Macclesfield Chap.	+	+	+	−
Hurdesfield	+			+
Macc. township	+	?+		+
Pott	+			?+
Rainow				?+
Shringley				
Sutton				
Chelford Chap.	+	−/+	−	
Siddington	+	−		+
Marton	−	−		?+
Taxall	+	−	−	+
Wilmslow	+	? Wilmsley	+[3]	+

Sources: 1. PRO E179/85/136.
2. Receipts of church rate, 1642. Churchwardens' accounts, Prestbury Parish Church, Cheshire.
3. Church rate, 1641. CRO, P123/3466/9/2.

A2.6 *Nantwich Hundred*

Parish	BCP petition	Episcopacy petition	Additional material	Subsidy[1]
Acton	+	−	+[2]	+
Audlem	+	+	−	+
Baddiley	−	−	+[3]	+
Church Coppenhall	+	+	−	+
Marbury	+	−	+[4]	+
Nantwich	+	+	+[5]	+
Wrenbury	−	−	+[6]	+

Sources: 1. PRO E179/85/135.
2. 'A plan of the seats in Acton Church, 1635'. This document is still held at the parish church. I am grateful to the Rev. D. A. Martin for making it available to me.
3. Church rate, 1641. CRO, P173/6/1.
4. [Church?] rate, 1640. CRO, P39/8/1.
5. Pew list, 1633. This list is still held at the parish church of St Mary, Nantwich. See J. Hall, *Nantwich* (1883, repr. 1971), pp. 131–4. I am grateful to Dr Nancy Ball of Nantwich for not only making the manuscript available and discussing it with me, but for the reference to Hall.
6. Allotment of pews, 1636. CRO, P172/6/4–6.

A2.7 *Northwich Hundred*

Parish	BCP petition	Episcopacy petition	Additional material	Subsidy[1]
Astbury	+	+	+[2]	
Brereton	+	−	−	
Davenham	+	+	−	
Gr. Budworth	+	−		
Nether Tabley	+			
Nether Peover	+			
Northwich	+	−	−	
Middlewich	+	−	+[3]	
Sandbach	+	+	−	
Churcholme Chap.	+			
Goostrey Chap.	+	−	+[4]	
Swettenham	+	+	−	
Warmingham	+	−	−	

Sources: 1. No subsidy of 1641 is extant for Northwich Hundred.
2. Astbury petition against alehouses. CRO, QSF1/76, 1646.
3. Church rate, 1640. CRO, P39/8/1
4. Disbursements for 1640, 1641, but no receipts. Church rate, 1645. CCRO, CR63/2/203.

A2.8 *The Wirral*

Parish	BCP petition	Episcopacy petition	Additional material	Subsidy
Bebington	+	−	−	−
Bromborough	+	−	−	−
Eastham	+	−	−	−
Neston	+	+	+[1]	−
Shotwick	+	−	−	−
? Capenhurst	+			
? Gr. Saughall	+			
Shotwick	+			
Woodbank	+			
Stoke	+	−	−	−
Thornton (in the parish of Neston)	−	−	+[2]	−
Thurstaston	−	−	+[3]	?+
W. Kirby	+	+	+[4]	−

Sources: 1. An individual petition from Neston in support of the established church. BL, Add. MS 36913, fols. 124–5.
2. An individual petition from Thornton in support of the established church. BL, Add. Ms 36913, fol. 133.
3. An individual petition from Thurstaston in support of the established church. BL, Add. MS 36913, fol. 132v.
4. A communicant list appended to the Prayer Book petition. HLRO, Main Papers, HL, 20 December 1641. An individual petition from West Kirby in support of the established church. BL, Add. MS 36913, fols. 131–132v. See also J. Brownbill, *West Kirby* (Liverpool, 1928), pp. 333–6.

Appendix 3: Five subscribing Cheshire communities for the Book of Common Prayer Petition in 1641

A3.1 *Tilston: subscribers/non-subscribers assessed in rate*

Assessed in churchwardens' accounts 1641 (men only)[a]	Total assessed in rate		Signatories for BCP petition (Dec. 1641)		Men not subscribing BCP petition, but assessed in rate		No. of men subscribing only to Bishops petition (Feb. 1641)	No. assessed in subsidy, 1641		Households assessed in 1664 hearth tax		
	No.	%	No.	%	No.	%		sub-scribing	non-sub-scribing	No.	%	
Liable for poor relief (1s–2s 6d)												
1s and under	22	29	15	31	6	28	1	0	0	47	36	Exempt
	28[b]	37	20	41	8	38	0	1	0	62	47	1 hearth
1s 1d–2s	8	11	7	14	0	0	1	1	1	8	6	2 hearths
2s 1d–4s	10	13	3	6	5	24	2	0	0	7	5	3 hearths
4s 1d–8s	3	4	1	2	1	5	1	1	0	0	0	4 hearths
8s 1d and over	1	1	1	2	0	0	0	1	0	7	5	5 or more hearths
Unknown	3	4	2	4	1	5	0	0	0			
Sub-total	75	99	49	100	21	100	5	4	1	131	99	
Total signatories not assessed for rates or receiving relief			51									
Assessed for subsidy but not rates							2	2	2			
Total	75	100	100		21		10	6	3	131		

a The spread of assessments for Tilston is not even, but as follows: 1s 3d–1s 6d; 2s 6d–3s 3d; 4s 5d–5s; 10s+ were also assessed for church rates; all for 1s or less. They have been counted in with those receiving relief and excluded from the total number of those assessed for the rate.

b Eight men who received poor relief in 1641 were also assessed for church rates; all for 1s or less. They have been counted in with those receiving relief and excluded from the total number of those assessed for the rate.

Appendix 3

A3.2 *Tilston: parish officers, subscribers/non-subscribers*[1]

Year and office	Subscribers to BCP petition	Non-subscribers to BCP petition
1640–1641		
Churchwardens	2	0
Swornmen	2	0
Overseers of the poor	2	0
Overseers of the highway	1	1
1641–1642		
Churchwardens	2	0
Swornmen	1	1
Overseers of the poor	1	1
Overseers of the highway	2	0
'Leading parishioners'[a]	6	2
Total[b]	15	4

a 'Leading parishioners' are defined as those individuals who signed with the rector Essex Clark, the memorandum recording the election of parish officers in April 1641. CRO P18/3608.

b It should be noted that during this period (1640–41), some individuals served more than once in the same or different offices. These totals, therefore, represent the total number of individuals involved.

Source: CRO, P18/3608; HLRO, Main Papers, HL, 20 December 1641.

A3.3 *Tilston: assessment of parish officers rate in 1641*[a]

Year and office	Subscribers to BCP petition	Non-subscribers to BCP petition
1640–1641		
Churchwardens	3d, 5s	–
Swornmen	1s or less, 1s 6d	–
Overseers of the poor	1s 3d, 2s 9d	–
Overseers of the highway	6d	1s or less
1641–1642		
Churchwardens	n.a., n.a.	–
Swornmen	1s or less	Received poor relief of 1s
Overseers of the poor	6d	n.a.
Overseers of the highway	n.a., 1s 5d	–
'Leading parishioners'[a]	n.a., n.a., 3d, 2s 9d, 3s 3d, 5s[b]	2n.a., 2s 6d
Total[c]	15	4

n.a. = Not assessed in rate

a 'Leading parishioners' are defined as those individuals who signed with the rector Essex Clarke, the memorandum recording the election of parish officers in April 1641. CRO, P18/3608.

b John Catherald was not assessed in the 1641 ley, but he was valued at 2s *in terris* in the 1641 subsidy, PRO, E179/85/135; PRO, E179/85/131.

c It should be noted that during this period (1640–41), some individuals served more than once in the same or different offices. These totals, therefore, represent the total number of individuals involved.

Source: CRO, P18/3608; HLRO, Main Papers, HL, 20 December 1641.

A3.4 *Frodsham: subscribers/non-subscribers assessed in rate*[a]

Assessment for church rates[b] (men only)	Totals		Signatories for BCP petition		Men assessed not subscribing to BCP petition[c]		No. of men subscribing only to Bps petition	1641 subsidy	Households assessed in 1664 hearth tax[d]		
	No.	%	No.	%	No.	%				No.	%
No poor relief	–	–	–	–	–	–	–	–	Exempt	99	22
1s and under	49	52	15	44	28	56	6	–	1 hearth	265	60
1s 1d–2s	20	21	11	32	7	14	2	–	2 hearths	57	13
2s 1d–4s	19	20	7	21	11	22	1	–	3 hearths	9	2
4s 1d–8s	3	3	0	0	2	4	1	–	4 hearths	4	1
8s 1d and over	4	4	1	3	2	4	1	–	5 hearths or more	8	2
Sub-total			34[c]	100	50		11	–		442	100
Total signatories not assessed	150		150				78				
Total	95	100	184	100	50		89	–		442	100

a The following guidelines have been used in compiling this table:
  A. Entries in the 1641 rate have been used. However, 1640 entries have been used for individuals with no 1641 entry.
  B. In cases of individuals with more than one entry in the 1641 rate; (1) debits have been added together; (2) but debits and credits have not been added together – the greater sum has been taken.

b These sums represent a minimum assessment. The spread of assessments is not even, but as follows: 1s and under; 1s 1d–2s; 2s 2d–3s 4d; 4s 1d–6s 10d; 10s and over.

c Only 18 percent of the 184 signatories for the Prayer Book petition appear individually assessed in the 1640–41 rate. Of those 18 per cent, just under half, were assessed for 1s or less, and just over 75 per cent for 2s or less.

d Based on PRO, E179/86/145. The dependent townships of Bradley, Woodhouses, and Netherton (3 out of 12) are not listed. It is quite possible that their inhabitants were assessed under one of the other townships.

A3.5 *Frodsham: pew ownership of parish officers 1638–1642, subscribers/*
non-subscribers in parish church[a]

Pew	North side			East End (front) South side		
	FNS	NS	NM	SM	SS	FSS
1						cw
2						
3						
4						lp
5						cw
6						
7			lp	*lp*		cw
8				*lp*		lp
9						
10						
11						
12						
13						
14		lp		*lp/cw*		
15		cw				
16						cw
17						
18						
19			cw			
20			cw			
21			lp			
22			*cw*			

West End
(back)

FNS = Far north side
NS = North side
NM = Middle rank on north side
SM = Middle rank on south side
SS = South side
FSS = Far south side
cw = churchwarden
lp = 'leading parishioner'
Subscribers to Prayer Book Petition in italics.
Among churchwardens and leading parishioners who do not appear on the pew list,
3 subscribed for the Prayer Book and 4 did not. Some held more than 1 pew. This
table should be used in conjunction with Table A3.7.
a These figures have been adjusted for owners of more than 1 pew as well as female
owners and pews assigned to farms and were based on a 1637 pew list for Frodsham
parish church. CRO, P8/4/3. See also below, Figure A3.3.

A3.6 Frodsham: ownership of pews in parish church

	North side			East End (front)	South side	
	FNS	NS	NM	SM	SS	FSS
Subscribing owners	3	11	8	13	7	12
Non-subscribing owners (adjusted)	6	17	30	14	17	21
% of subscribing owners in each rank	33	39	21	48	29	36
				West End (back)		

FNS = Far north side
NS = North side
NM = Middle rank on north side
SM = Middle rank on south side
SS = South side
FSS = Far south side

These figures have been adjusted for owners of more than 1 pew as well as female owners and pews assigned to farms, and were based on a 1637 pew list for Frodsham parish church.

Source: CRO, P8/4/3. See also Figure A3.3.

A3.7 *Frodsham: pew ownership of parish officers*

Year and office	Subscribers to BCP petition	Non-subscribers to BCP petition
1638 Churchwardens	n.l.	NM20
1639 Churchwardens	n.l.	NS15
1640 Churchwardens	–	n.l., NM19/FSS16
1640 'Leading parishioners'[a]	SM14, SSS4 SM7/SSS8, SM8	n.l., NM7/NS14, NM21, n.l.
1641 Churchwardens	FSS5	n.l.
1642 Churchwardens	n.l., SM14/SSS7, NM22/FSS1	NM20
Total[b]	9	8

FNS = Far north side
NS = North side
NM = Middle rank on north side
SM = Middle rank on south side
SS = South side
FSS = Far south side
n.l. = Not listed in pew list
The numbers indicate the particular pew, with 1 being nearest the front (east end) and higher numbers towards the back (west end). See above, Table A3.5.
a 'Leading parishoners' are defined as those laymen who signed the memorandum authorising the 1640 ley. CRO, P8/13/1.
b It should be noted that during this period (1638–42), some individuals served more than once in the same or different offices. These totals, therefore, represent the total number of individuals involved.
Sources: CRO, P8/13/1; CRO, P8/4/3; HLRO, Main Papers, HL, 20 December 1641.

A3.8 *Frodsham: parish officers, subscribers/non-subscribers*

Year and office	Subscribers to BCP petition	Non-subscribers to BCP petition
1638 Churchwardens	1	1
1639 Churchwardens	1	1
1640 Churchwardens[a]	0	2
1640 'Leading parishioners'[b]	4	3
1641 Churchwardens	1	1
1642 Churchwardens	2	0
Total[c]	9	8

a Neither churchwarden for 1640 put their hands to the Common Prayer petition. However, one John Barker did subscribe to the petition to uphold episcopacy.

b 'Leading parishoners' are defined as those laymen who signed the memorandum authorizing the 1640 ley. CRO, P8/13/1.

c It should be noted that during this period (1638–42), some individuals served more than once in the same or different offices. These totals, therefore, represent the total number of individuals involved.

Source: CRO, P8/13/1; HLRO, Main Papers, HL, 20 December 1641.

A3.9 *Frodsham: assessment of parish officers in 1640–1641, 1642 rates*

Year and office	Subscribers to BCP petition	Non-subscribers to BCP petition
1638 Churchwardens	n.a.	n.a.
1639 Churchwardens	n.a.	n.a.
1640 Churchwardens	–	n.a., 2s
1640 'Leading parishioners'[a]	n.a., 2s 2d unpaid, 3s 4d unpaid, 15s, n.a.	n.a., n.a., at least 5s, 6s 4d
1641 Churchwardens	n.a.	n.a.
1642 Churchwardens	1s 5d, 1s 8d	–
Total[b]	9	8

n.a. = Not assessed in rate

a 'Leading parishioners' are defined as those laymen who signed the memorandum authorizing the 1640 ley. CRO, P8/13/1.

b It should be noted that during this period (1638–42), some individuals served more than once in the same or different offices. These totals, therefore, represent the total number of individuals involved.

Sources: CRO, P8/13/1; HLRO, Main papers, HL, 20 December 1641.

A3.10 Wilmslow: subscribers/non-subscribers assessed in rate

Assessed in churchwardens' accounts (men only)	Total assessed in rate		Signatories for BCP petition (Dec. 1641)		Men not subscribing to BCP petition, but assessed		No. assessed in 1641 subsidy		Households assessed in 1664 hearth-tax		
	No.	%	No.	%	No.	%	sub-scribing	non-sub scribing	No.	%	
Liable for poor relief[a]	20	10	9	7	11	16	0	0	145	49	Exempt
1s and under	66	35	39	31	27	40	0	0	113	38	1 hearth
1s 1d – 2s	19	10	28	26	10	15	1	0	28	9	2 hearths
2s 1d – 4s	61	32	39	31	14	21	2	0	5	2	3 hearths
4s 1d – 8s	21	11	6	5	4	6	2	0	3	1	4 hearths
8s 1d and over	2	1	1	1	1	1	1	0	2	1	5 or more hearths
Unknown	2	1	2	2	0		1	0			
Sub-total	191	110	124	103[b]	67	99[b]	1	0	296	100	
Total signatories not assessed for rates or receiving relief			189								
Assessed for 1641 subsidy but not rated							1	6			
Total	191		313		67		7	6	296		

[a] Individuals who were both assessed for the rate and received poor relief, have been counted only among the poor.
[b] Percentages rounded to nearest whole number.

A3.11 *Wilmslow: parish officers' subscribers/non-subscribers*

Year and office	Subscribers to BCP petition	Non-subscribers to BCP petition
1639 Churchwardens	4	0
1640 Churchwardens	3	1
1641 Churchwardens	4	0
1642 Churchwardens	3	1
1644–48 Churchwardens	3	1
Total[a]	16	3

a It should be noted that during this period (1639–48), some individuals served more than once in the same or different offices. These totals, therefore, represent the total number of individuals involved.
Sources: CRO, P123/3466/9/2; HLRO, Main Papers, HL, 20 December 1641.

A3.12 *Wilmslow: assessment of parish officers in 1641 rate*

Year and office	Subscribers to BCP petition	Non-subscribers to BCP petition
1639 Churchwardens	n.a., $1\frac{1}{2}$d, 1s 8d, 3s 10d (or 3d?)	–
1640 Churchwardens	1s 9d, 2s 6d, 3s 4d, 4s 4d, 6s 3d	n.a.
1641 Churchwardens	2s 6d, 3s 4d, 4s 4d, 6s 3d	–
1642 Churchwardens	1s $7\frac{1}{2}$d, 1s 9d	n.a.
1644–1648 Churchwardens	n.a., n.a., 2s 4d	n.a.
Total[a]	16	3

n.a. = Not assessed in rate
a It should be noted that during this period (1639–48), some individuals served more than once in the same or different offices. These totals, therefore, represent the total number of individuals involved.
Sources: CRO, P123/3466/9/2; HLRO, Main Papers, HL, 20 December 1641.

A3.13 Marbury: subscribers/non-subscribers assessed in 1640 rate

Assessed in churchwardens' accounts 1640 (men only)[a]	Total assessed in rate		Signatories for BCP petition (Dec. 1641)		Men not subscribing to BCP petition, but assessed in 1640 rate		No. assessed in 1641 subsidy		Households assessed in 1664 hearth tax		
	No.	%	No.	%	No.	%	sub-scribing	non-sub scribing	No.	%	
Liable for poor relief[b]	–	–	–	–	–	–	–	–			
1s and under	60	79	15	65	45	85	0	1	36	30	Exempt
1s 1d–2s	8	11	5	22	3	6	2	1	63	52	1 hearth
2s 1d–4s	6	8	1	4	5	9	1	2	15	12	2 hearths
4s 1d–8s	0	0	0	0	0	0	0	0	4	3	3 hearths
8s 1d and over	0	0	0	0	0	0	0	0	3	2	4 hearths
Unknown	2	3	2	9	0	0	0	0	1	1	5 or more hearths
Sub-total	76	101	23	100	53	100	3	4	122	100	
Total signatories not assessed for rates			32								
Assessed for 1641 subsidy but not rated								2			
Total	76		55		53		3	6	122		

a CRO, P39/8/1. Based on the rate for 1640.
b The Marbury churchwardens' accounts contain no information on poor relief for the year 1640.

A3.14 *Marbury: parish officers, subscribers/non-subscribers*

Year and office	Subscribers to BCP petition	Non-subscribers to BCP petition
1633 Churchwardens	2	0
1634 Churchwardens	1	1
1635 Churchwardens	0	2
1636 Churchwardens	0	2
1637 Churchwardens	0	2
1638 Churchwardens	0	2
1639 Churchwardens	1	1
1640 Churchwardens	1	1
Curate	0	1
1640 'Leading parishioners'[a]	3	5
1642 Churchwardens	1	1
1644 Churchwardens	1	1
1647 Churchwardens	1	1
1648 Churchwardens	0	1
Total[b]	9	16

a These are the eight laymen, excluding the wardens, who along with the curate Thomas Orpe, signed the authorization for the 1640 ley. CRO, P39/8/1, fol. 80.
b It should be noted that during this period (1639–48), some individuals served more than once in the same or different offices. These totals, therefore, represent the total number of individuals involved.
Sources: CRO, P39/8/1; HLRO, Main Papers, HL, 20 December 1641.

A3.15 *Marbury: assessment of parish officers in 1640 rate*

Year and office	Subscribers to BCP petition	Non-subscribers to BCP petition
1633 Churchwardens	n.a., 1s 4d	–
1634 Churchwardens	2s 6d	8d
1635 Churchwardens	–	3d, 1s
1636 Churchwardens	–	n.a., 4d
1637 Churchwardens	–	n.a., n.a.
1638 Churchwardens	–	n.a., 1s 4d
1639 Churchwardens	1s 4d	8d
1640 Churchwardens	1s 4d	8d
1640 Curate	–	n.a.
1640 'Leading parishioners'[a]	n.a., 4d 1s 4d	4d, 6d 1s 4d, 2s 4d
1642 Churchwardens	1s 4d	n.a.
1644 Churchwardens	2s 6d	6d
1647 Churchwardens	1s 4d	n.a.
1648 Churchwardens	–	n.a., 2s 4d
Total[b]	9	16

a These are the eight laymen, excluding the wardens, who along with the curate Thomas Orpe, signed the authorisation for the 1640 ley. CRO, P39/8/1, fol. 80.
b It should be noted that during this period (1633–48), some individuals served more than once in the same or different offices. These totals, therefore, represent the total number of individuals involved.
Sources: CRO, P39/8/1; HLRO, Main Papers, HL, 20 December 1641.

A3.16 *Middlewich: subscribers/non-subscribers assessed in 1640 rate*

Assessed in church-wardens' accounts	Total assessed in rate		Signatories for BCP petition		Men not subscribing to BCP petition but assessed in rate		Households assessed in 1664 hearth tax		
	No.	%	No.	%	No.	%	No.	%	
Liable for poor relief	–	–	–	–	–	–	148	35	Exempt
1s and under	102	44	28	33	74	50	162	38	1 hearth
1s 1d–2s	42	18	15	18	27	18	60	14	2 hearths
2s 1d–4s	55	24	24	28	31	21	23	5	3 hearths
4s 1d–8s	28	12	15	18	13	9	11	3	4 hearths
8s 1d and over	4	2	2	2	2	1	18	4	5 or more hearths
Unknown	1	0	1	1	0	0	0		
Sub-total	232	100	85	100	147	99[a]	422	99[a]	
Total signatories not assessed for rates			180						
Total	232		265		147		422		

a Percentages rounded to nearest whole number.
Sources: CRO, P39/8/1; HLRO, Main Papers, HL, 20 December 1641.

A3.17 *Middlewich: parish officers' subscribers/non-subscribers*

Year and office	Subscribers to BCP petition	Non-subscribers to BCP petition
1635 Churchwardens	3	1
1636 Churchwardens	1	0
1637 Churchwardens	0	1
1639 Churchwardens	2	2
1640 Churchwardens	4	0
Total[a]	9	3

a It should be noted that during this period (1635–40), some individuals served more than once in the same or different offices. These totals, therefore, represent the total number of individuals involved.
Source: CRO, P13/22/1: HLRO, Main Papers, HL, 20 December 1641. Please note that the accounts jump from 1640 to 1648 with no record of the intervening years.

A3.18 *Middlewich: assessment of parish officers in 1640 rate*

Year and office	Subscribers to BCP petition	Non-subscribers to BCP petition
1635 Churchwardens	3s 3d, 4s 2d, 7s	n.a.
1636 Churchwardens	3s 4d	–
1637 Churchwardens	–	7d
1639 Churchwardens	3s 4d, 7s	7d, 3s 4d
1640 Churchwardens	3d, 2s, 6s, 7s	–
Total[a]	9	3

n.a. = Not assessed in rate.
a It should be noted that during this period (1635–40), some individuals served more than once in the same or different offices. These totals, therefore, represent the total number of individuals involved.
Source: CRO, P13/22/1: HLRO, Main Papers, HL, 20 December 1641. Please note that the accounts jump from 1640 to 1648 with no record of the intervening years.

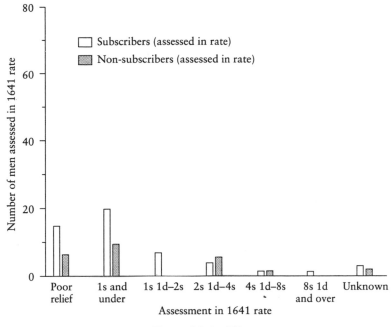

Figure A3.1   Tilston

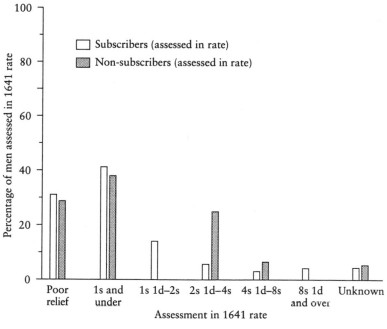

Figure A3.2   Tilston

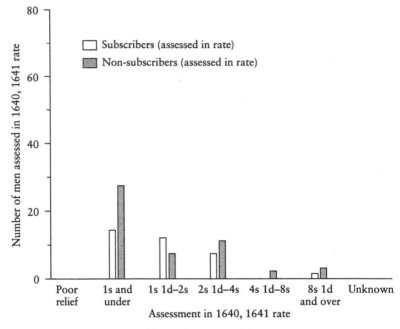

Figure A3.3   Frodsham

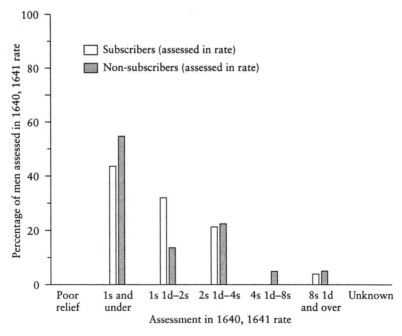

Figure A3.4   Frodsham

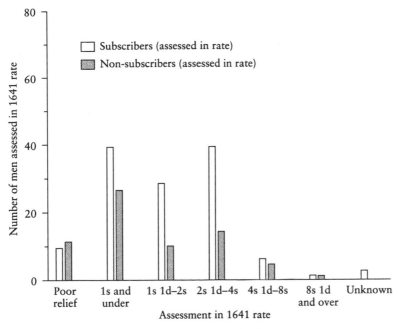

Figure A3.5   Wilmslow

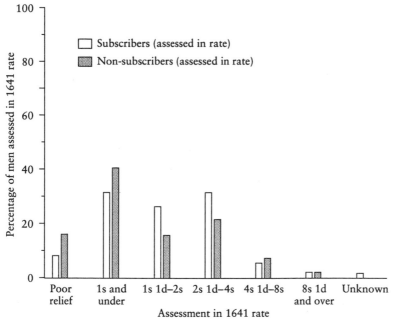

Figure A3.6   Wilmslow

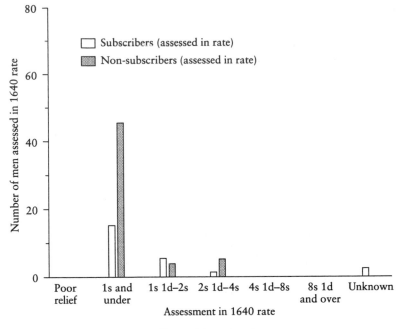

Figure A3.7   Marbury

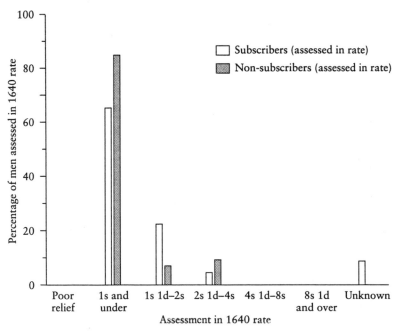

Figure A3.8   Marbury

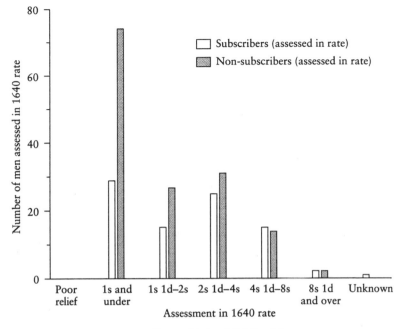

Figure A3.9   Middlewich

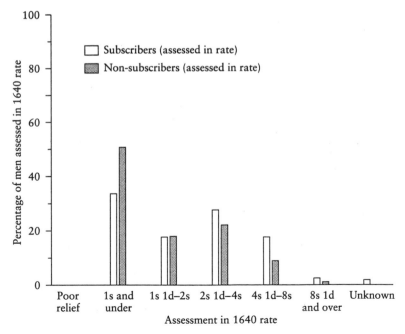

Figure A3.10   Middlewich

BIBLIOGRAPHY

MANUSCRIPT SOURCES

Aston Lodge Manuscripts, Aston, Cheshire

Unlisted manuscripts of the Aston Family held at Aston Lodge, Cheshire

Bedfordshire Record Office

ABC. 3; ABC. 5: Archdeaconry of Bedford court books

Bodleian Library, Oxford

Clarendon MS 29: Clarendon Papers
Dep. C. MS 165: Nalson Papers
Tanner MS 62: Letters and papers chiefly of 1643
Tanner MS 66: Letters and papers chiefly of 1644

Borthwick Institute of Historical Research, University of York

York v. 1629: Metropolitan visitation books
1630/CB: Consistory court books

British Library, London

Add. MS 11055: Letters of bishops, with miscellaneous theological and ecclesiastical papers
Add. MS 26785: Orginal petitions and papers relating to proceedings in the county of Kent in ecclesiastical matters
Add. MS 29975: Official and political papers
Add. MS 33936: Correspondence of the Moreton Family of Moreton, Cheshire
Add. MS 34253: Correspondence and papers relating to the Civil War, mainly letters to Edward Montagu, earl of Manchester, as Speaker of the House of Lords
Add. MS 36913; 36914; 36919: Aston Papers
Harl. MS 2135: Papers relating to the city of Chester, before, during, and after the civil war
Harl. MS 6424: Extracts from the Journal of the House of Lords
Stowe MS 744: Private correspondence, vol. ii

Cambridgeshire Record Office, Cambridge

Ely Archdeaconry Court, Will of John Downing, 1598

Cambridgeshire Record Office, Huntingdon

Archdeaconry 4: Archdeaconry of Huntingdon Court Book

Cheshire Record Office, Duke Street, Chester

EDC. 5: Diocesan consistory court books
EDV. 1: Diocesan visitation books
QJF; QJB: Quarter Sessions
P/8, 13, 18, 39, 123: Parish bundles
Will and Inventories

Chester City Record Office, City Hall, Chester

CR63/2/132: Manuscript copy of sermons by Nathaniel Lancaster

Gloucestershire Record Office, Gloucester

D2510: Letters of John Smyth of Nibley

House of Lords Record Office, Westminster, London

Main Papers, HL, [27] February 1640/1 and 20 December 1641. Two petitions for
    episcopacy and the Prayer Book (respectively) from Cheshire
HL, Main Papers, 28 March 1642: Kent petition
Parchment Coll., HL, 8 Dec. 1641: Somerset petition

Lincolnshire Archives Office, Lincoln

Ch. P/2, 6, 7, 10: Parish bundles 58/1, 58/2, 59/1, 62/2, 69/1, 69/2: Diocesan
    consistory court papers
LT&D.: Letters testimonial and dimissory

New College, Oxford

MS 9502: Diary of Robert Woodford

Nottingham University Library

PW2/HY/173: petition from Shropshire for episcopacy and the liturgy

Public Record Office, London

SP16: State Papers, Domestic Series
E179/85: Court of Exchequer, Hearth-tax returns, 1664
LC5: Lord Chamberlain's Department, Miscellanea

Queen's College, Oxford

Papers of Thomas Barlow

Staffordshire Record Office, Stafford

D1287/P/399: Correspondence of Bishop Bridgeman of Chester

UNPUBLISHED THESES

Abbott, William A., 'The issue of episcopacy in the Long Parliament: the reasons for abolition', University of Oxford D.Phil., 1981.

Amussen, Susan, 'Governors and governed: class and gender relations in English villages, 1590–1725', Brown University Ph.D., 1983.

Cook, Margaret, 'Eye (Suffolk) in the years of uncertainty, 1520–1570', University of Keele Ph.D., 1982.

Evans, Nesta, 'The community of South Elmham, Suffolk, 1550–1640', University of East Anglia M.Phil., 1978.

Freeman, Jane, 'The parish ministry in the diocese of Durham, c. 1570–1640', University of Durham Ph.D., 1979.

Hajzyk, Helena, 'The church in Lincolnshire, c. 1595–1640', University of Cambridge Ph.D., 1980.

Hart, James, 'The House of Lords and the reformation of justice, 1640–1643', University of Cambridge Ph.D. 1984.

Kerby, Graham, 'Inequality in a pre-industrial society: a study of wealth, status office and taxation in Tudor and Stuart England with particular reference to Cheshire', University of Cambridge Ph.D., 1983.

Maltby, Judith D., 'Approaches to the study of religious conformity in late Elizabethan and early Stuart England: with special reference to Cheshire and the diocese of Lincoln', University of Cambridge Ph.D., 1991.

Martin, Jessica, 'Izaak Walton and his precursors: a literary study of the emergence of the ecclesiastical *Life*', University of Cambridge Ph.D., 1993.

Perrott, Mark, 'Richard Hooker and the problem of authority in the context of Elizabethan church controversies', University of Cambridge Ph.D., 1997.

Pickles, J. T., 'Studies in royalism in the English Civil War 1642–1646, with special reference to Staffordshire', University of Manchester M.A., 1968.

Plumb, Derek, 'John Foxe and the later Lollards of the Thames Valley', University of Cambridge Ph.D., 1987.

Richardson, R. C., 'Puritanism in the diocese of Chester to 1642', University of Manchester Ph.D., 1969.

Stevenson, William, 'The economic and social status of protestant sectaries in Huntingdonshire, Cambridgeshire, and Bedfordshire 1650–1725', University of Cambridge Ph.D., 1989.

Wanklyn, M. D. G., 'Landed society and allegiance in Cheshire and Shropshire in the first Civil War', University of Manchester Ph.D., 1976.

Watt, Tessa, 'Cheap print and religion c. 1550 to 1640', University of Cambridge Ph.D., 1988.

PRINTED PRIMARY SOURCES

Anglicanism: the thought and practice of the Church of England illustrated from the religious literature of the seventeenth century. P. More and F. Cross, eds. London, 1962.

Aston, John, 'North counties diaries', Surtees Society, cxviii, 1910.

Aston, Sir Thomas, *A Brief Relation*, n.p., 1642.

A Collection of Sundry Petitions Presented to the King's Most Excellent Majestie, n.p., 1642.

A Petition Delivered in to the Lords Spirituall and Temporall by Sir Thomas Aston, Baronett, from the County Palatine of Chester concerning Episcopacy, n.p., n.d.

A Petition Delivered by Sir Thomas Aston, from the County Palatine of Chester concerning Episcopacy, n.p., n.d. Thomason Tracts: 669.f.4(8).

A Remonstrance against Presbytery, n.p., 1641.

Aubrey, John, *Brief Lives*. Harmondsworth, 1978.

Aylmer, John, *At Harborow for the Faithful and True Subjects Against the Late Blown Blast Concerning the Government of Women*. Strasburg, 1559.

Baddeley, Richard and John Naylor, *The Life of Dr Thomas Morton, Late Bishop of Duresme*. York, 1669.

Barrow, Henry, *A Briefe Discoverie of the False Church* in *The Writings of Henry Barrow 1587–90*, ed. Leland Carlson, London, 1962.

Baxter, Richard, *Reliquiae Baxterianea: or Mr. Richard Baxter's Narrative of the Most Memorable Passages of his Life and Times*. London, 1696.

The Saints Everlasting Rest. 1650.

Beer, B. L., 'The Commocyon in Norfolk, 1549', *Journal of Medieval and Renaissance Studies* 6 (1976).

Best, Henry, *Rural Economy in Yorkshire in 1641*, Surtees Society, xxxiii, 1957.

Bibliotheca Lindesiana: A Bibliography of Royal Proclamations of Tudor and Stuart Sovereigns 1485–1714. Oxford, 1910.

Book of Common Prayer 1559, ed. John Booty, Washington, DC, 1976.

Brightman, F. E., *The English Rite: being a synopsis of the sources and revisions of the Book of Common Prayer*. 2 vols., London, 1921.

British Library, Thomason Tracts

E. 84(37): *The Unfaithfulness of Cavaliers*. London, 1643.

E. 145(6): *Strange Newes from Kent*. April, 1642.

E. 150(28): *A Collection of Petitions Presented to the Kings Majestie*. June 1642.

E. 151(11): *To Parliament [Two petitions from the Inhabitants of Surrey and Southwark Respectively Praying for the Maintenance of the True Protestant Religion]*. June, 1642.

E. 160(4): *A Petition Presented to the Parliament from the Countie of Nottingham Complaining of the Ecclesiastical Government of Archbishops, Bishops, etc.* June 1641.

669, f.4(8): Sir Thomas Aston, *A Petition Delivered by Sir Thomas Aston, from the County Palatine of Chester Concerning Episcopacy*, n.p., n.d.

E. 1273: Chisenhale, Edward, *Catholike History*. London, 1652.

Browne, Sir Thomas, *Religio Medici* in *Selected Writings*, ed. Geoffrey Keynes, Chicago, 1968.

Buller Papers. Buller Family. n.p., 1895.

Calendar of State Papers Domestic, 1628–1629.

Calendar of State Papers Domestic, 1629–1631.

Calendar of State Papers Domestic, 1639–1640.

Calendar of State Papers Domestic, 1640–1641.

Calendar of State Papers Venetian, 1642–1643.

Cardwell, Edward, ed., *Documentary Annals of the Reformed Church of England.* 2 vols., Oxford, 1834.

Chisenhale, Edward, *Catholike History.* London, 1652. BL, Thomason Tracts E. 1273.

Colet, John, 'Convocation Sermon' in J. H. Lupton, *A Life of John Colet, D.D.* London, 1887.

Cope, Esther, ed., *Proceedings of the Short Parliament of 1640.* Camden Fourth Series, xxxv, 1977.

Cowley, Abraham, *The Civil War.* ed. Alan Pritchard, Toronto, 1973.

Cross, Claire, ed., *The Royal Supremacy in the Elizabethan Church.* London, 1969.

Cust, Richard, ed., *The Papers of Sir Richard Grosvenor, 1st Bart. (1585–1645).* Lancashire and Cheshire Record Society, cxxxiv, 1996.

Dering, Sir Edward, *Collection of Speeches.* London, 1642.

D'Ewes, Sir Simonds, *The Journal of Sir Simonds D'Ewes*, ed. W. H. Coates. New Haven, 1942.

Donne, John, *Sermons*, ed. Evelyn Simpson and George Potter. 10 vols., Berkeley, 1956.

Dore, R. N., ed., *The Letter Books of Sir William Brereton.* Lancashire and Cheshire Record Society, cxxiii, cxxviii, 1983–4, 1990.

Evans, G. R. and J. Robert Wright, eds., *The Anglican Tradition: a handbook of sources.* London, 1991.

Evelyn, John, *The Diary of John Evelyn*, ed. E. S. de Beer. 6 vols., Oxford, 1955.

Evens, H. E., ed., 'An Inquisition in Salop, 1655', *Transactions of the Shropshire Archaeological Society* 47, 1933–4.

Falkland, Viscount (Lucius Carey), *A Speech made to the House of Commons Concerning Episcopacy.* London, 1641.

Farington Papers, ed. S. M. Farington. Chetham Society, xxxix, 1856.

Fawcett, Timothy J., *The Liturgy of Comprehension: an abortive attempt to revise the Book of Common Prayer.* Alcuin Club Collections, liv, 1973.

Fincham, Kenneth, ed., *Visitation Articles and Injunctions of the Early Stuart Church*, vol. I. Church of England Record Society, i, 1994.

Foster, C. W., *The State of the Church in the Reigns of Elizabeth and James as Illustrated by Documents Relating to the Diocese of Lincoln*, Lincoln Record Society, xxiii, 1926.

Foxe, John, *The Acts and Monuments*, ed. G. Townsend and S. R. Cattley. 8 vols., London, 1837–41.

Frere, W. H. and William Kennedy, eds., *Visitation Articles and Injunctions of the Period of the Reformation.* 3 vols., Alcuin Club, 1910.

Gardiner, S. R., *The Constitutional Documents of the Puritan Revolution 1625–1660.* London, 1889, 1958.

Harrison, William, *Harrison's Description of England in Shakespeare's Youth*, ed. F. J. Furnivall. 2 vols., London, 1877.

The Description of England, ed. George Edelen. New York, 1968, 1994.

Harvey, Christopher, 'The Book of Common Prayer' in *The Complete Poems of Christopher Harvey*, ed. A. B. Grosart. n.p., 1874.

Herbert, George, *A Priest to the Temple, or the Countrey Parson his Character and Rule of Holy Life*. London, 1927.

Heywood, Robert, *Observations and Instructions, Divine and Morall*, ed. James Crossley. Chetham Society, lxxvi, 1869.

Hierurgia Anglicana, ed. Vernon Staley. 3 vols., London, 1902–4.

Historical Manuscripts Commission, 13th Report, Portland Mss.1.

History of the Ancient Chapels of Didsbury and Chorlton. Chetham Society, xlii, 1857.

Homilies Appointed to be Read in Churches in the time of Queen Elizabeth, ed. John Griffiths. London, 1938.

Hooker, Richard, *Of The Lawes of Ecclesiastical Polity*, ed. John Keble. 3 vols., Oxford, 1874.

   The Lawes of Ecclesiastical Polity Book V, ed. W. Speed Hill. Cambridge, Mass., 1977.

James, Richard, *Iter Lancastrense: a poem*, ed. Thomas Corser. Chetham Society, vii, 1845.

Josselin, Ralph, *The Diary of Ralph Josselin 1616–1683*, ed. Alan MacFarlane. London, 1976.

The Journals of the House of Commons. London, 1803.

The Journals of the House of Lords. London, 1846.

Kennedy, W. P. M., ed., *Elizabethan Episcopal Administration*. 3 vols., Alcuin Club, 1924.

Kenyon, J. P., *The Stuart Constitution*. Cambridge, 1966.

Kingsley, Charles, *Alton Locke*. Oxford, 1983.

'Loans, contributions, subsidies, and ship money, paid by the clergy of the diocese of Chester in the years 1620, 1622, 1624, 1634, 1635, 1636, and 1639', *Miscellanies relating to Lancashire and Cheshire*, ed. G. T. O. Bridgeman. Lancashire and Cheshire Record Society, xii, 1885.

Lovelace, Richard, 'To Lucasta, from Prison', *Ben Johnson and the Cavalier Poets*, ed. Hugh Maclean. New York, 1974.

Maltby, Judith D., ed., *The Short Parliament (1640) Diary of Sir Thomas Aston*. Camden Fourth Series, xxxv, 1988.

Martindale, Adam, *Life of Adam Martindale Written by Himself*, ed. Richard Parkinson. Chetham Society, iv, 1845.

Merbecke, John, *The Book of Common Prayer Noted*, n.p., 1550.

Minutes of the Committee for the relief of Plundered Ministers and Trustees for the Maintenance of Ministers: relating to Lancashire and Cheshire 1643–1660. Lancashire and Cheshire Record Society, xxviii, 1893.

Nalson, John, *An Impartial Collection of the Great Affairs of State*, 2 vols., London, 1682.

Northwich Hundred Poll Tax, 1660 and Hearth Tax, 1664, ed. G. O. Lawton. Lancashire and Cheshire Record Society, cxix, 1979.

Notestein, Wallace, ed., *Commons Debates for 1629*. Minneapolis, 1921.

Pepys, Samuel, *The Diary of Samuel Pepys*, ed. Robert Latham and William Matthews. 11 vols., London, 1974.

Phillips, John, *Memoirs of the Civil War in Wales and the Marches 1642–1649*. 2 vols., London, 1874.

Plume, Thomas, *An account of the Life and Death of the Right Reverend Father in God, John Hacket, late Lord Bishop of Lichfield and Coventry*, ed. Mackenzie E. C. Walcott. London, 1865.

Prideaux, Humphrey, *Directions to Churchwardens for the Faithful discharge of their Office for the use of the Archdeaconry of Suffolk.* 2nd edn, Norwich, 1704.
Proceedings in Kent, ed. L. B. Larking. Camden Society, lxxx, 1862.
Quarles, Francis, *The Complete Works in Prose and Verse of Francis Quarles*, ed. Alexander Grosart. 3 vols., New York, 1967, repr. of 1880 edn.
Raines, F. R., ed., *The Fellows of the Collegiate Church of Manchester.* Chetham Society, xxi, 1891.
   The Rectors of Manchester and Wardens of the Collegiate Church. Chetham Society, v, vi, 1885.
Rushworth, J., *Historical Collections.* 8 vols., London, 1657–1701.
Selden, John, *Table Talk*, ed. Frederick Pollock. London, 1927.
Stanley, James, seventh earl of Derby, *Private Devotions and Miscellanies*, ed. F. R. Raines. Chethem Society, lxxii, 1867.
Storey, Matthew, ed., *Two East Anglian Diaries, 1641–1729: Isaac Archer and William Coe.* Suffolk Records Society, xxxvi, 1994.
Thirty-nine Articles of Religion, 1571.
Townshend, Henry, *Diary of Henry Townshend of Elmley Lovett 1640–1663*, ed. J. W. Willis Bund. 3 vols., Worcestershire Historical Society, 1916, 1917, 1920.
Transactions of the Shropshire Archaeological Society, 47 (1933–4).
Trollope, Anthony, *Barchester Towers.* London, 1987.
Udall, Ephraim, *Communion Comlinesse.* London, 1641.
Unfaithfullness of Cavaliers, The. London, 1643, BL Thomason Tracts E. 84(37).
A View of Popish Abuses Yet Remaining in the Englishe Church, in *Puritan Manifestoes: a study of the origin of the puritan revolt with a reprint of the Admonition to Parliament and kindred documents, 1572*, eds. W. H. Frere and C. E. Douglas. London, 1954.
Visitation Articles of the dioceses of Chester and Lincoln:
   For Chester: 1604, 1605, 1617, 1634, 1637.
   For Lincoln: 1571, 1574, 1577, 1585, 1591, 1601, 1604, 1607, 1613 (metropolitan visitation), 1614, 1618, 1625, 1630–1, 1635, 1641.
Walker, John, *The Sufferings of the Clergy.* London, 1714.
Webb, John, *Memorials of the Civil War between King Charles I and the Parliament of England as it affected Herefordshire and the Adjacent Counties*, ed. T. W. Webb, 2 vols., London, 1879.
Whitaker, E. C. *Martin Bucer and the Book of Common Prayer.* Alcuin Club Collections, lv, 1974.
Williams, John, *The Holy Table, Name and Thing.* Diocese of Lincoln, 1635.
Wood, Anthony, *Athenae Oxonienses.* Revised by Philip Bliss. 5 vols., London, 1815.
Wright, J. Robert, ed., *Prayer Book Spirituality: a devotional companion to the Book of Common Prayer compiled from classical Anglican sources.* New York, 1989.

SECONDARY SOURCES

Addleshaw, G. W. O. and F. Etchells, *The Architectual Setting of Anglican Worship.* London, 1958.
Addy, John, *Sin and Society in the Seventeenth Century.* London, 1989.
Alldridge, Nick, 'Loyalty and identity in Chester parishes 1540–1640', in *Parish,*

Church and People: local studies in lay religion 1350–1750, ed. S. Wright. London, 1988.

The Alternative Service Book 1980. Oxford, 1980.

Alumni Cantabrigienses, ed. J. Venn and J. A. Venn. 4 vols., Cambridge, 1922–7.

Alumni Oxonienses, ed. J. Foster. 4 vols., Oxford, 1891–2.

Amussen, Susan, 'Gender, family and the social order', in *Order and Disorder in Early Modern England*, eds. Anthony Fletcher and John Stevenson. Cambridge, 1985.

An Ordered Society: gender and class in early modern England. Oxford, 1988.

Andriette, Eugene A., *Devon and Exeter in the Civil War*. Newton Abbot, Devon, 1971.

Aston, Margaret, 'Puritans and iconoclasm, 1560–1660', in *The Culture of English Puritanism, 1560–1700*, ed. Christopher Durston and Jacqueline Eales. London, 1996.

Augustijn, Cornelius, 'Bucer's ecclesiology in the colloquies with the Catholics, 1540–41', in *Martin Bucer: Reforming Church and Community*, ed. D. F. Wright. Cambridge, 1994.

Axon, William E. A., *Cheshire Gleanings*. Manchester, 1884.

Babbage, S. B., *Puritanism and Richard Bancroft*. London, 1962.

Backus, Irena, 'Church, communion and community in Bucer's commentary on the Gospel of John', in *Martin Bucer: Reforming Church and Community*, ed. D. F. Wright. Cambridge, 1994.

Baker, C. H. Collins, 'John Souch of Chester', *Connoisseur* 80 (1928).

Baptism, Eucharist and Ministry. World Council of Churches, Faith and Order Paper no. 111, Geneva, 1982.

Barnes, T. G., *Somerset 1625–1640: a county's government during the 'Personal Rule'*. London, 1961.

Bauckam, Richard, 'Richard Hooker and John Calvin: a comment', *Journal of Ecclesiastical History* 32:1 (1981).

Beaver, Dan, '"Sown in dishonour, raised in glory": death, ritual and social organization in northern Gloucestershire, 1590–1690', *Social History* 17:3 (1992).

Beck, Joan, *Tudor Cheshire*. Chester, 1969.

Belcher, Margaret, 'Pugin Writing', in *Pugin: A Gothic Passion*, eds. Paul Atterbury and Clive Wainwright. New Haven, 1994.

Bennett, Gareth, *To the Church of England*. Worthing, 1988.

Bernard, G. W., 'The Church of England, c. 1529–c.1642', *History* 75 (1990).

Blackwood, B. G., 'The Catholic and Protestant gentry of Lancashire during the Civil War period', *Transactions of the Historical Society of Lancashire and Cheshire* 126 (1976).

The Lancashire Gentry and the Great Rebellion 1640–1660. Manchester, 1978.

Booker, John, *A History of the Antient Chapels of Didsbury and Chorlton in Manchester Parish*. Chetham Society, xlii, 1857.

Booty, John, 'Anglicanism', in *Oxford Dictionary of the Reformation*, ed. Hans Hillerbrand. 4 vols., Oxford, 1996.

'Communion and commonweal: the Book of Common Prayer', in *The Godly Kingdom of Tudor England*, ed. John Booty. Wilton, Conn., 1981.

'Preparation for the Lord's Supper in Elizabethan England', *Anglican Theological Review* 49 (1967).

Three Anglican Divines on Prayer: Jewel, Andrewes, and Hooker. Cambridge, Mass., 1978.

Bossy, John, 'Christian life in the later middle ages: prayers', *Transactions of the Royal Historical Society*, 6th ser., London, 1991.

Christianity in the West 1400–1700. Oxford, 1985.

The English Catholic Community 1570–1850. London, 1975.

'The mass as a social institution, 1200–1700', *Past & Present* 100 (1983).

Bouch, C. M. L., *Prelates and People of the Lake Counties: a history of the Diocese of Carlisle 1133–1933*. Kendal, 1948.

Boulton, J. P., 'The limits of formal religion: the administration of Holy Communion in late Elizabethan and early Stuart London', *London Journal* 10:2 (1984).

Neighbourhood and Society: a London suburb in the seventeenth century. Cambridge, 1987.

Bowker, Margaret, *The Henrician Reformation: the Diocese of Lincoln under John Longland 1521–1547*. Cambridge, 1981.

Brigden, Susan, *London and the Reformation*. Oxford, 1989.

Burgess, Clive, '"A fond thing vainly invented": an essay on Purgatory and pious motive in late medieval England', in *Parish, Church and People: local studies in lay religion 1350–1750*, ed. Susan Wright. London, 1988.

Burke, Peter, 'Religion and secularization', in *The New Cambridge Modern History: Companion Volume XII*, ed. P. Burke. Cambridge, 1979.

Burn, Richard, *Ecclesiastical Law*. 2nd edn, 4 vols., London, 1767.

Calamy Revised, ed. A. G. Matthews. London, 1934.

Cannan, Edwin, *The History of Local Rates in England*. 2nd edn, London, 1912.

Carlson, Eric Josef, *Marriage and the English Reformation*. Oxford, 1994.

'The origins, function, and status of the office of churchwarden, with particular reference to the diocese of Ely', in *The World of Rural Dissenters*, ed. Margaret Spufford. Cambridge, 1995.

Chalklin, C. H., *Seventeenth-century Kent: A Social and Economic History*. London, 1965.

Christianson, Paul, 'Reformers and the Church of England under Elizabeth I and the Early Stuarts', *Journal of Ecclesiastical History* 31:4 (1980).

Clark, Peter, *English Provincial Society from the Reformation to the Revolution: religion, politics and society in Kent 1500–1640*. Hassocks, Sussex, 1977.

'The ownership of books in England, 1560–1640: the examples of some Kentish townsfolk', in *Schooling and Society*, ed. Lawrence Stone. Baltimore, 1976.

Clebsch, William, 'The Elizabethans on Luther', in *Interpreters of Luther: essays in Honor of Wilhelm Pauk*, ed. Jaroslav Pelikan. Philadelphia, 1968.

Collinson, Patrick, 'A comment: concerning the name puritan', *Journal of Ecclesiastical History* 31:3 (1980).

'Cranbrook and the Fletchers: popular and unpopular religion in the Kentish Weald', in *Reformation Principle and Practice*, ed. Peter Brooks. London, 1980.

The Elizabethan Puritan Movement. London, 1967.

'Lectures by combination: structures and characteristics of church life in 17th-century England', first published in 1975, republished in *Godly People: Essays on English Protestantism and Puritanism*. London, 1982.

The Puritan Character: polemic and polarities in early seventeenth-century English culture. Los Angeles, 1989.

The Religion of Protestants: the Church in English society 1559–1625. Oxford, 1982.

'Shepherds, sheepdogs, and hirelings: the pastoral ministry in post-Reformation England', in *The Ministry: Clerical and Lay*, eds. W. J. Sheils and Diana Woods. Studies in Church History, xxvi, 1989.

Cox, J. Charles, *Churchwardens' Accounts*. London, 1913.

Craig, J. S., 'Co-operation and initiatives: Elizabethan churchwardens and parish accounts of Mildenhall', *Social History* 18:3 (1993).

Cressy, David, *Bonfires and Bells: national memory and the protestant calendar in Elizabethan and Stuart England*. London, 1989.

Literacy and the Social Order: reading and writing in Tudor and Stuart England. Cambridge, 1980.

'Purification, thanksgiving and the churching of women in post-Reformation England', *Past and Present* 141 (1993).

Cross, Claire, *Church and People 1450–1660: the triumph of the laity in the English church*. Glasgow, 1976.

'Lay literacy and clerical misconduct in a York parish during the reign of Mary Tudor', *York Historian* 3 (1980).

Darlow, T. H. and H. F. Moule, *Historical Catalogues of Printed Editions of the English Bible 1525–1961*, revised and expanded by A. S. Herbert. London, 1968.

Davies, Horton, *The Worship of the English Puritans*. London, 1948.

Worship and Theology in England: from Andrewes to Baxter and Fox, 1603–1690. Princeton, 1975.

Davies, Natalie Zemon, 'Some tasks and themes in the study of popular religion', in *The Pursuit of Holiness in late Medieval and Renaissance Religion*, eds. C. Trinkaus and H. Oberman. Leiden, 1974.

Dawley, Powel Mills, *John Whitgift and the English Reformation*. New York, 1954.

Dickens, A. G., *The English Reformation*. 2nd edn, London, 1989.

Lollards and Protestants in the Diocese of York 1509–1558. Oxford, 1959.

Dictionary of National Biography.

Doll, Peter, 'The idea of the primitive church in High Church ecclesiology from Samuel Johnson to J. H. Hobart', *Anglican and Episcopal* 65:1 (1996).

Dore, R. N., *The Civil Wars in Cheshire*. Chester, 1966.

Duffy, Eamon, 'The godly and the multitude in Stuart England', *The Seventeenth Century* 1:1 (1986).

'The appropriation of the sacraments in the later middle ages', *New Blackfriars* 77 (January, 1996).

'Prejudice unmasked: the Reformation revisited', *The Tablet* (4 March 1995).

The Stripping of the Altars: traditional religion in England 1400–1580. New Haven, 1992.

Dunn, F. I., *The Ancient Parishes, Townships and Chapelries of Cheshire*. Chester, 1987.

Eales, Jacqueline, *Puritans and Roundheads: the Harleys of Brampton Bryan and the outbreak of the English Civil War*. Cambridge, 1990.

Earwaker, J. P., *East Cheshire*. 2 vols., London, 1877.

The History of the Ancient Parish of Sandbach including the two Chapelries of Holmes Chapel and Goostrey. Manchester, 1890, repub. 1972.

A History of the Ancient Chapels of Didsbury and Chorlton. Chetham Society, xlii, 1857.

Eliot, T. S., 'Religion and literature', in *Selected Prose*, ed. Frank Kermode. London, 1975.

Elton, G. R., *England Under the Tudors*. London, 1955, 1974.

Emmison, F. G., *Elizabethan Life: morals and the church courts*. Colchester, 1973.

Everitt, Alan, *The Community of Kent and the Great Rebellion 1640–60*. Leicester, 1966.
  Suffolk and the Great Rebellion 1640–1660. Suffolk Record Society, 1960.

Fenlon, Dermont, *Heresy and Obedience in Tridentine Italy: Cardinal Pole and the Counter Reformation*. Cambridge, 1972.

Fincham, Kenneth, 'Introduction', in *The Early Stuart Church, 1603–1642*, ed. Kenneth Fincham. London, 1993.
  Prelate as Pastor: the episcopate of James I. Oxford, 1990.

Fincham, Kenneth and Peter Lake, 'The ecclesiastical policy of James I', *Journal of British Studies* 24 (1985).

Fletcher, Anthony, *The outbreak of the English Civil War*. London, 1981.
  'Petitioning and the outbreak of the Civil War in Derbyshire', *The Derbyshire Archaeological Journal* 93 (1973).
  Reform in the Provinces: the government of Stuart England. New Haven. 1986.
  Tudor Rebellions. London, 1968, 2nd edn, 1973.

Foster, Andrew, 'Church policies of the 1630s', in *Conflict in Early Stuart England: studies in religion and politics 1603–1642*, eds. Richard Cust and Ann Hughes. London, 1989.

Fritze, Ronald H., 'Root or link? Luther's position in the historical debate over the legitimacy of the Church of England, 1558–1625', *Journal of Ecclesiastical History* 37:2 (1986).

Fuller, Reginald H., 'The classical High Church reaction to the Tractarians', in *Tradition Renewed: The Oxford Movement Conference Papers*, ed. Geoffrey Rowell. London, 1986.

George, C. H., 'Puritanism as history and historiography', *Past and Present* 41 (1968).

Gittings, Claire, *Death, Burial and the Individual in Early Modern England*. London, 1984.

Greaves, Richard, *Religion and Society in Elizabethan England*. Minneapolis, 1981.

Green, Ian, 'Career prospects and clerical conformity in the early Stuart Church', *Past and Present* 90 (1981).
  ' "For children in yeeres and children in understanding": the emergence of the English catechism under Elizabeth and the Early Stuarts', *Journal of Ecclesiastical History* 37:3 (1986).
  The Christian's ABC: cathechisms and catechizing in England c. 1530–1740. Oxford, 1996.
  The Re-Establishment of the Church of England 1660–1663. Oxford, 1978.

Greg, W. W., *A Companion to Arber: being a calendar of documents in Edward Arber's transcript of the Registers of the Company of Stationers of London 1554–1640 with text and calendar of supplementary documents*. Oxford, 1967.

Griffiths, D. N., 'The early translations of the Book of Common Prayer', *The Library*, 6th ser., 3:1 (1981).
  'Prayer Book translations in the nineteenth century', *The Library*, 6th ser., 6:1 (1984).

Gruenfelder, John, 'The election to the Short Parliament, 1640', in *Early Stuart Studies*, ed. Howard Reinmuth. Minneapolis, 1970.

Haigh, Christopher, 'The Church of England, the Catholics and the people', in *The Reign of Elizabeth I*, ed. C. Haigh. London, 1984.

English Reformations: religion, politics, and society under the Tudors. Oxford, 1993.

'Puritan evangelism in the reign of Elizabeth I', *English Historical Review* 92 (1977).

'The recent historiography of the English Reformation', in *The English Reformation Revised*, ed. C. Haigh. Cambridge, 1987.

Reformation and Resistance in Tudor Lancashire. Cambridge, 1975.

'Review: Claire Cross, *Church and People 1450–1660*', *Journal of Ecclesiastical History* 28:3 (1977).

'Some aspects of the recent historiography of the English Reformation', in *The Urban Classes, the Nobility and the Reformation*, eds. W. J. Mommsen, et al. Stuttgart, 1979.

Hall, Basil, 'Martin Bucer in England', in *Martin Bucer: Reforming Church and Community*, ed. D. F. Wright. Cambridge, 1994.

Hall, James, *A History of the Town and Parish of Nantwich.* Manchester, 1883.

Halley, Robert, *Lancashire: its puritanism and nonconformity.* 2 vols., Manchester, 1869.

Hamilton, A. H. A., *Quarter Sessions from Queen Elizabeth to Anne.* London, 1878.

Hart, A. Tindal, *The Country Clergy in Elizabethan and Stuart Times 1558–1660.* London, 1958.

The Country Priest in English History. London, 1959.

The Man in the Pew 1558–1660. London, 1966.

Hart, James S., *Justice Upon Petition: the House of Lords and Reformation of Justice 1621–1675.* London, 1991.

Hastings, Adrian, *A History of English Christianity 1920–1985.* London, 1986.

Hatchet, Marion J., *Sanctifying Life, Time and Space.* New York, 1976.

Haugaard, William P., 'From the Reformation to the eighteenth century', in *The Study of Anglicanism*, eds. Stephen Sykes and John Booty. London, 1988.

Heal, Felicity, 'The English Reformation Revisited', *Ecclesiastical Law Journal* 18:4 (1996).

Of Prelates and Princes: a study in the economic and social position of the Tudor episcopate. Cambridge, 1980.

Heales, Alfred, *The History and Law of Church Seats or Pews.* 2 vols., London, 1872.

Hey, David, *An English Rural Community: Myddle under the Tudors and Stuarts.* Leicester, 1974.

Hill, Christopher, *Economic Problems of the Church: from Archbishop Whitgift to the Long Parliament.* Oxford. 1956.

God's Englishman: Oliver Cromwell and the English Revolution. London, 1970.

Hill, J. W. F., 'Royalist clergy of Lincolnshire', Lincolnshire Architectural and Archaeological Society, Reports and Papers, 40, 1940.

Tudor and Stuart Lincoln. Cambridge, 1956.

Hirst, Derek, 'The defection of Sir Edward Dering 1640–1641', *Historical Journal* 15:2 (1972).

The Representative of the People? Cambridge, 1975.

Hodgett, Gerald, *Tudor Lincolnshire.* Lincoln, 1975.

Hoffman, John, 'The Arminian and the iconoclast: the dispute between John Cosin and Peter Smart', *Historical Magazine of the Protestant Episcopal Church* 48 (1979).

Holifield, E. Brooks, *The Covenant Sealed: the development of Puritan sacramental theology in Old and New England 1570–1720*. New Haven, 1974.

Holmes, Clive, *The Eastern Association in the English Civil War*. London, 1974.

Seventeenth Century Lincolnshire. Lincoln, 1980.

The Suffolk Committee for Scandalous Ministers 1644–1646. Suffolk Record Society, 1970.

Houlbrooke, Ralph, *Church Courts and the People during the English Reformation 1520–1570*. Oxford, 1979.

'Death, church, and family in England between the late fifteenth and the early eighteenth centuries', in *Death, Ritual and Bereavement*, ed. Ralph Houlbrooke. London, 1989.

The English Family 1450–1700. London, 1984.

English Family Life 1576–1716. Oxford, 1988.

Hunt, William, *The Puritan Moment: the coming of revolution in an English county*. Cambridge, Mass., 1983.

Hutton, Ronald, *The Restoration: a political and religious history of England and Wales 1658–1667*. Oxford, 1985.

The Rise and Fall of Merry England: the ritual year 1400–1700. Oxford, 1994.

The Royalist War Effort 1642–1646. London, 1982.

Ingram, Martin, *Church Courts, Sex and Marriage in England 1570–1640*. Cambridge, 1987.

Jessup, Frank W., *Sir Roger Twysden 1597–1672*. London, 1965.

Karant-Nunn, Susan C., 'Churching', in *The Oxford Encyclopedia of the Reformation*, ed. Hans Hillerbrand. 4 vols., Oxford, 1996.

Kendall, R. T., *Calvin and English Calvinism*. Oxford, 1979.

King, Peter, 'The reasons for the abolition of the Book of Common Prayer in 1645', *Journal of Ecclesiastical History* 21:4 (1970).

Klauser, Theodor, *A Short History of the Western Liturgy: an account and some reflections*. 2nd edn, Oxford, 1979.

Klausnitzer, Wolfgang, 'Episcopacy', in *The Oxford Encyclopedia of the Reformation*, ed. Hans Hillerbrand. 4 vols., Oxford, 1996.

Kramm, H. H., 'The "Pastor Pastorum" in Luther and early Lutheranism', in *'And Other Pastors of thy Flock': a German tribute to the Bishop of Chichester*, ed. Franz Hildebrandt. Cambridge, 1942.

Kumin, Beat, *The Shaping of a Community: the rise and Reformation of the English parish, c. 1400–1560*. Aldershot, Hants., 1996.

Lake, Peter, *Anglicans and Puritans? Presbyterian and English Conformist Thought from Whitgift to Hooker*. London, 1988.

'Anti-popery: the structure of a prejudice', *Conflict in Early Stuart England: Religion and Politics 1603–1625*, eds. Richard Cast and Ann Hughes. London, 1989.

'Calvinism and the English church 1570–1635', *Past and Present* 114 (1987).

'The collection of ship money in Cheshire during the sixteen-thirties: a case study of relations between central and local government', *Northern History* 17 (1981).

'The Laudian style: order, uniformity and the pursuit of the beauty of holiness', in *The Early Stuart Church 1603–1642*, ed. Kenneth Fincham. London, 1993.

'Presbyterianism, the idea of a national church and the argument from divine right', in *Protestantism and the National Church in Sixteenth Century England*, eds. Peter Lake and Maria Dowling. London, 1987.

The significance of the Elizabethan identification of the Pope as Anti-Christ', *Journal of Ecclesiastical History* 31 (1980).

Lamont, William, *Godly Rule*. London, 1969.

'The squire who changed sides', *History Today* 16 (May, 1966).

Laroque, Francois, *Shakespeare's Festive World: Elizabethan seasonal entertainment and the professional stage*. Cambridge, 1988, first English translation 1991.

Laslett, Peter, 'Mean household size in England since the sixteenth century', in *Household and Family in Past Times*, eds. Peter Laslett and Richard Wall. Cambridge, 1972.

Leedham-Green, E. S., *Books in Cambridge Inventories: book-lists from vice-chancellor's court probate inventories in the Tudor and Stuart periods*. 2 vols., Cambridge, 1986.

Lewalski, Barbera, *Protestant Poetics and the Seventeenth Century Religious Lyric*. Princeton, 1979.

Llewellyn, Nigel, *The Art of Death*. London, 1991.

Lysons, Daniel and Samuel Lysons, *Magna Britannia: Cheshire*. 2 vols., London, 1810.

Macaulay, Rose, *The Towers of Trebizond*. London, 1981.

MacCulloch, Diarmaid, *The Later Reformation in England 1547–1603*. London, 1990.

'The myth of the English Reformation', *Journal of British Studies* 30 (1991).

Suffolk and the Tudors: politics and religion in an English county 1500–1600. Oxford, 1986.

Thomas Cranmer: a life. New Haven, 1996.

'Was Methodism a mistake?', *The Epworth Review* 15:2 (1988).

Major, Kathleen, *A Handlist of the Records of the Bishop of Lincoln and the Archdeaconries of Lincoln and Stow*. London, 1953.

Maltby, Judith, '"By this Book": parishioners, the Prayer Book and the established church', in *The Early Stuart Church 1603–1642*, ed. Kenneth Fincham. London, 1993.

Marchant, Ronald, *The Church Under the Law: justice, administration and discipline in the Diocese of York 1560–1640*. Cambridge, 1969.

The Puritans and the Church Courts in the Diocese of York 1560–1642. London, 1960.

Marcotte, Elaine, 'Shrieval administration of ship money in Cheshire, 1637: limitations of early Stuart governance', *Bulletin of the John Rylands University Library of Manchester* 58 (1975).

Marshall, Peter, *The Catholic Priesthood and the English Reformation*. Oxford, 1994.

Martos, Joseph, *Doors to the Sacred*. London, 1981.

Mason, A. J., *The Church of England and Episcopacy*. Cambridge, 1914.

Matheson, 'Martin Bucer and the Old Church', in *Martin Bucer: Reforming Church and Community*, ed. D. F. Wright. Cambridge, 1994.

McGee, J. Sears, *The Godly Man in Stuart England: Anglicans, Puritans and the two tables 1620–1670*. New Haven, 1976.

'Puritanism in Jacobean London?: The case of Thomas Adams', unpublished paper read at the Pacific Coast Conference on British Studies, 23–24 March 1984.

McIntosh, Marjorie, *Autonomy and Community: the Royal Manor of Havering 1200–1500*. Cambridge, 1986.

Mendle, M. J., 'Politics and political thought 1640–42', in *The Origins of the English Civil War*, ed. Conrad Russell. London, 1973.

Mills, Frederick V., *Bishops by Ballot: an eighteenth century ecclesiastical revolution*. New York, 1978.

Milton, Anthony, *Catholic and Reformed: the Roman and Protestant churches in English Protestant thought 1600–1640*. Cambridge, 1995.

  'The Church of England, Rome and the True Church: The demise of Jacobean consensus', in *The Early Stuart Church, 1603–1642*, ed. Kenneth Fincham. London, 1993.

  'Review of Nicholas Tyacke, *Anti-Calvinists: the rise of English Arminianism c. 1590–1640*', *Journal of Ecclesiastical History* 39:4 (1988).

Morely, Janet, '"The faltering words of men": exclusive language in the liturgy', in *Feminine in the Church*, ed. Monica Furlong. London, 1984.

Morrill, John, 'The attack on the Church of England in the Long Parliament, 1640–42', in *History, Society and the Churches: essays in honour of Owen Chadwick*, eds. Derek Beales and Geoffrey Best. Cambridge, 1985.

  Cheshire 1630–1660: county government and society during the English Revolution. Oxford, 1974.

  'The church in England 1642–9', in *Reactions to the English Civil War 1642–1649*, ed. John Morrill. London, 1982.

  'The religious context of the English Civil War', *Transactions of the Royal Historical Society*, 5th ser., 34 (1984).

  The Revolt of the Provinces: conservatives and radicals in the English Civil War 1630–1650. London, 1976.

  'Sir William Brereton and England's Wars of Religion', *Journal of British Studies* 24:3 (1985).

Neil, Charles and J. M. Willoughby, *The Tutorial Prayer Book*. London, 1963.

New, J. H., *Anglican and Puritan: the basis of their opposition 1558–1640*. Stanford, 1964.

Norman, E. R., *Church and Society in England 1770-1970*. Oxford, 1970.

Nuttall, Geoffrey E., *Visible Saints: the Congregational Way 1640–1660*. Oxford, 1957.

O'Day, Rosemary, *The English Clergy: the emergence and consolidation of a profession*. Leicester, 1979.

Obelkevich, James, 'Religion', in *Cambridge Social History of Britain 1750–1950*, ed. F. M. L. Thompson. Cambridge, 1990.

Ormerod, G., *History of Cheshire*, revised by G. Helsby. 3 vols., London, 1882.

Owen, Dorothy M., *The Records of the Established Church of England*. British Records Association, 1970.

Oxford Dictionary of the Christian Church, ed. F. L. Cross and E. A. Livingstone. 2nd. edn, Oxford, 1974.

Painter, W. Borden, 'Anglican terminology in recent Tudor and Stuart historiography', *Anglican and Episcopal History* 56:3 (1987).

Palliser, D. M., *The Age of Elizabeth: England under the later Tudors 1547–1603*. London, 1983.

  'Introduction: the parish in perspective', in *Parish, Church and People: local studies in lay religion 1350–1750*, ed. Susan Wright. London. 1988.

Parker, Kenneth L., *The English Sabbath: a study of doctrine and discipline from the Reformation to the Civil War*. Cambridge, 1988.

Parliamentary Gazeteer. 1845.

Pettegree, Andrew, *Marian Protestantism: six studies*. Aldershot, 1996.

Pointer, Michael, *The Glory of Grantham*. Grantham, 1978.

Pollock, Linda, *Forgotten Children: parent–child relations from 1500 to 1900*. Cambridge, 1983.

Press, Volker, 'Constitutional development and political thought in the Holy Roman Empire', in *The New Cambridge Modern History: the Reformation 1520–1559*, ed. G. R. Elton. 2nd edn, Cambridge, 1990.

Purvis, J. S., *Dictionary of Ecclesiastical Terms*. London, 1962.

Questier, Michael C., *Conversion, Politics and Religion in England, 1580–1625*. Cambridge, 1996.

Quintrell, B. W., 'Lancashire ills, the king's will and the troubling of Bishop Bridgeman', *Transactions of the Historical Society of Lancashire and Cheshire* 132 (1983).

Reinburg, Virginia, 'Liturgy and the laity in late medieval and Reformation France', *Sixteenth Century Journal* 23:3 (1992).

'Response to John Bossy's, "Christian life in the later middle ages: prayers"', *Transactions of the Royal Historical Society*, 6th ser., 1 (1991).

Richards, Raymond, *Old Cheshire Churches*. London, 1947, revised and enlarged, Manchester, 1973.

Richardson, R. C., *Puritanism in North-west England: a regional study of the diocese of Chester to 1642*. Manchester, 1972.

Richmond, Colin, *John Hopton: a fifteenth century Suffok gentleman*. Cambridge, 1980.

Roberts, B. Dew, *Mitre and Musket: John Williams, Lord Keeper, Archbishop of York 1582–1650*. London, 1938.

Rogers, Malcolm, 'Acquisition in Focus: an English *Memento Mori*', *The Art Quarterly of the National Art Collections Fund* 11 (1992).

Rollison, David, 'The bourgeois soul of John Smyth of Nibley', *Social History* 12:3 (1987).

Russell, Conrad, *The Causes of the English Civil War*. Oxford, 1990.

The Crisis of Parliaments. New York, 1971.

The Fall of the British Monarchies 1637–1642. Oxford, 1991.

Salmon, Frank, '*Praedatrix Praeda Fit Ipsa Suae*: Mary Magdalene, Frederico Borromeo and Henry Constable's Spirituall Connettes', *Recusant History* 18:3 (1987).

Salt, S. P., 'The origins of Sir Edward Dering's attack on the ecclesiastical hierarchy, c. 1625–1640', *Historical Journal* 30:1 (1987).

Scarisbrick, J. J., *The Reformation and the English People*. Oxford, 1984.

Scribner, R. W., 'Incombustible Luther: the image of the reformer in early modern Germany', in R. W. Scribner, *Popular Culture and Popular Movements in Reformation Germany*. London, 1987.

'Politics and the institutionalisation of reform in Germany', in *The New Cambridge Modern History: the Reformation 1520–1559*, ed. G. R. Elton. 2nd edn, Cambridge, 1990.

'Ritual and Reformation', in Robert Scribner, *Popular Culture and Popular Movements in Reformation Germany*. London, 1987.

Seaver, Paul, *The Puritan Lectureships: the politics of religious dissent 1560–1662*. Stanford, 1970.

Sharpe, J. A., *Defamation and Sexual Slander in Early Modern England: the church courts at York*. Borthwick Papers no. 58, 1980.

Sharpe, Kevin, 'Archbishop Laud', *History Today* 33 (1983).
  The Personal Rule of Charles I. New Haven, 1992.
Shaw, William A., *A History of the English Church During the Civil Wars and under the Commonwealth 1640–1660.* 2 vols., London, 1900.
Sheils, W. J., *The Puritans in the Diocese of Peterborough 1558–1610.* Northamptonshire Record Society, 1979.
Smith, David L., *Constitutional Royalism and the Search for Settlement, c. 1640–1649.* Cambridge, 1994.
Smith, R. M., 'Population and its geography in England 1500–1730', in *An Historical Geography of England and Wales*, eds. R. A. Dodgshon and R. A. Butlin. London, 1978.
Sommerville, J. P., *Politics and Ideology in England 1603–1640.* London, 1986.
Spaeth, Donald, 'Common prayer? Popular observance of the Anglican liturgy in Restoration Wiltshire', in *Parish, Church and People: local studies in lay religion 1350–1750*, ed. Susan Wright. London, 1988.
Spufford, Margaret, 'Can we count the "godly" and the "conformable" in the seventeenth century?', *Journal of Ecclesiastical History* 36:3 (1985).
  Contrasting Communities: English villagers in the sixteenth and seventeenth centuries. Cambridge, 1974.
  'First steps in literacy: the reading and writing experiences of the humblest seventeenth-century spiritual autobiographers', *Social History* 4:3 (1979).
  'The importance of religion in the sixteenth and seventeenth centuries', in *The World of Rural Dissenters 1520–1725*, ed. Margaret Spufford. Cambridge, 1995.
  'Puritanism and social control?', in *Order and Disorder in Early Modern England*, eds. Anthony Fletcher and John Stevenson. Cambridge, 1985.
  Small Books and Pleasant Histories: popular fiction and its readership in seventeenth century England. London, 1981.
Spurr, John, *The Restoration Church of England 1646–1689.* New Haven, 1991.
Stannard, David E., *The Puritan Way of Death: a study in religion, culture, and social change.* New York, 1977.
Stephens, Peter, 'The church in Bucer's commentaries on the Epistle to the Ephesians', in *Martin Bucer: reforming church and community*, ed. D. F. Wright. Cambridge, 1994.
Stieg, Margaret, *Laud's Laboratory: the Diocese of Bath and Wells in the early seventeenth century.* London, 1982.
Stone, Lawrence, *The Family, Sex and Marriage in England 1500–1800.* London, 1977.
Sykes, Norman, *Old Priest and New Presbyter.* Cambridge, 1956.
Sykes, Stephen W., *The Integrity of Anglicanism.* London, 1978.
Sykes, Stephen and John Booty, eds., *The Study of Anglicanism.* London, 1988.
Sylvester, Dorothy and Geoffrey Nulty, *The Historical Atlas of Cheshire.* Chester, 1958.
Tate, W. E., *The Parish Chest.* Cambridge, 1969.
Temperley, Nicholas, *The Music of the English Parish Church.* 2 vols., Cambridge, 1979.
Thirsk, Joan, ed., *The Agrarian History of England and Wales 1500–1640.* Cambridge, 1967.
  The Agrarian History of England and Wales 1640–1750: regional farming systems. Cambridge, 1984.

Thomas, Keith, *Religion and the Decline of Magic*. New York, 1971.

Tighe, W. J., 'William Laud and the reunion of the churches: some evidence from 1637 and 1638', *Historical Journal* 30:3 (1987).

Trevor-Roper, Hugh, *Catholics, Anglicans and Puritans*. London, 1987.

Tyacke, Nicholas, *Anti-Calvinists: the rise of English Arminianism c. 1590–1640*. Oxford, 1987.

'Puritanism, Arminianism and counter-revolution', in *Origins of the English Civil War*, ed. Conrad Russell. London, 1973.

Tyacke, Nicholas and Peter White, 'Debate: the rise of Arminianism reconsidered', *Past and Present* 115 (1987).

Underdown, David, 'The chalk and the cheese: contrasts among the English clubmen', *Past and Present* 85 (1979).

Somerset in the Civil War and Interregnum. Newton Abbot, Devon, 1973.

Revel, Riot and Rebellion: popular politics and culture in England 1603–1660. Oxford, 1985.

Urwick, William, *Historical Sketches of Non-conformity in the County Palatine of Chester*. London, 1864.

Vatican Council II: the Conciliar and Post Conciliar Documents, ed. Austin Flannery. Leominster, Herefordshire, 1981 edn.

Victoria County History of Bedford.

Victoria County History of Chester.

Victoria County History of Gloucester.

Victoria County History of Hereford.

Victoria County History of Lancaster.

Victoria County History of Nottingham.

Victoria County History of Oxford.

Victoria County History of Somerset.

Victoria County History of Worcester.

Wabuda, Susan, 'Revising the Reformation', *JBS* 35:2 (1996).

Walker Revised, ed. A. G. Matthew. London, 1948.

Wallace, Jr, Dewey D., 'The Anglican appeal to Lutheran Sources: Philipp Melanchthon's reputation in seventeenth-century England', *Historical Magazine of the Protestant Episcopal Church* 52 (1983).

Walsh, John, Colin Haydon and Stephen Taylor, eds., *The Church of England c. 1689–1833*. Cambridge, 1993.

Walsham, Alexandra, *Church Papists: Catholicism, conformity and confessional polemic in early modern England*. Woodbridge, Suffolk, 1993.

Watson, G., ed., *The New Cambridge Bibliography of English Literature*. Cambridge, 1974.

Webb, Sidney and Beatrice, *The Parish and the County*. London, 1906.

Whitaker, E. C., *Martin Bucer and the Book of Common Prayer*. Alcuin Club Collections 55, 1974.

White, Peter, *Predestination, Policy and Polemic: conflict and consensus in the English church from the Reformation to the Civil War*. Cambridge, 1992.

'The rise of Arminianism reconsidered', *Past and Present* 101 (1983).

Williams, Rowan, *Arius: heresy and tradition*. London, 1987.

'Religious experience in the era of reform', in *The Companion Encyclopedia of Theology*, eds. Peter Byrne and Leslie Houlden. London, 1995.

Wolverton, J. F., *Colonial Anglicanism in North America*. Detroit, 1984.

Wood, Alfred C., *Nottinghamshire in the Civil War*. Oxford, 1937.

Woods, T. P. S., *Prelude to Civil War 1642: Mr. Justice Malet and the Kentish petitions*. Salisbury, 1980.

Wright, Susan, 'Catechism, confirmation and communion: the role of the young in the post-Reformation Church', in *Parish, Church and People: local studies in lay religion 1350–1750*, ed. Susan Wright. London, 1988.

'Easter Books and Parish Rate Books: a new source for the urban historian', *Urban History Yearbook* (1985).

Wrightson, Keith, *English Society 1580–1680*. London, 1982.

'Postscript: Terling revisited', in Keith Wrightson and David Levine, *Poverty and Piety in an English Village: Terling, 1525–1700*. Rev. edn, Oxford, 1995.

Wrightson, Keith and David Levine, *Poverty and Piety in an English Village: Terling 1525–1700*. New York, 1979.

'Two concepts of order: justices, constables and jurymen in seventeenth century England', in *An Ungovernable People: the English and their law in the seventeenth and eighteenth centuries*, eds. John Brewer and John Styles. London, 1980.

Wrigley, E. A. and R. S. Schofield, *The Population History of England 1541–1871: a reconstruction*. London, 1981.

Yates, Nigel, *Buildings, Faith and Worship: the liturgical arrangement of Anglican churches 1600–1900*. Oxford, 1991.

Young, Peter, *Edgehill, 1642*. Kineton, 1976.

INDEX

Page references in *italics* indicate illustrations and tables; those in **bold** type indicate maps.

Titles in the series

Godly Clergy in Early Stuart England: The Caroline Puritan Movement
c. 1620–1643
  TOM WEBSTER
Prayer Book and People in Elizabethan and early Stuart England
  JUDITH MALTBY
Sermons at Court, 1559–1629: Religion and Politics in Elizabethan and Jacobean
Preaching
  PETER E. MCCULLOUGH

* Also published as a paperback